A
Better
War

ALSO BY LEWIS SORLEY

Arms Transfers under Nixon: A Policy Analysis

Thunderbolt: General Creighton Abrams and the Army of His Times

Honorable Warrior: General Harold K. Johnson and the Ethics of Command

LEWIS SORLEY

A Better War

**THE UNEXAMINED VICTORIES
AND FINAL TRAGEDY OF
AMERICA'S LAST YEARS IN VIETNAM**

HARCOURT BRACE & COMPANY

New York   San Diego   London

Library of Congress Cataloging-in-Publication Data
Sorley, Lewis, 1934–
A better war: the unexamined victories and final tragedy of
America's last years in Vietnam/Lewis Sorley.
p.   cm.
Includes bibliographical references and index.
ISBN 0-15-100266-5
1. Vietnamese Conflict, 1961–1975—United States.   I. Title.
DS558.S65   1999
959.704'3373—dc21   99-10495

Designed by Linda Lockowitz
Text set in Bembo
Printed in the United States of America
First edition
F   E   D   C   B   A

For Judith

CONTENTS

MAPS

You know, it's too bad. Abrams is very good.
He deserves a better war.

—ROBERT SHAPLEN
New Yorker Correspondent
Saigon 1969

PROLOGUE

THE SOUTH VIETNAMESE government awarded campaign medals to Americans who served in the Vietnam War. Each decoration had affixed to the ribbon a metal scroll inscribed "1960–   ." The closing date was never filled in, perhaps prophetically, since for many Americans the war has never ended. That should not be surprising, for those years constituted one of the most complex and difficult periods the country, and its armed forces, has ever gone through—a limited war within the larger Cold War within a global cultural revolution, and ultimately a failed endeavor.

If, as the scroll suggests, American participation is dated from 1960, its early years were primarily advisory. Then, starting in the spring of 1965, American ground forces began deploying to take part in the war, with the supporting air and naval campaigns also expanding proportionately. At the peak, in the spring of 1969, some 543,400 Americans were serving in South Vietnam, with many thousands more operating from ships offshore and airfields in adjacent countries.

In early 1968 there occurred what may now be seen as the pivotal event of the war, at least from the American viewpoint, a series of battles that came to be known as the Tet Offensive. Beginning on the night of 30 January, and intensifying the following night, Communist forces launched a series of coordinated attacks against major population centers all across South Vietnam, violating a truce by timing them to coincide with the celebration of the lunar new year, known as Tet, traditionally a time of peace, brotherhood, and family reunion for all Vietnamese.

The attackers—North Vietnamese Army and Viet Cong forces—suffered grievous casualties, principally among the Viet Cong indigenous to the South, and the offensive was defeated quickly save in Saigon and Hue, where the fighting raged for a month. More important, however, the psychological effect of these unexpected and widespread assaults was devastating, especially in the United States, where hopes for an early end to the war had been raised by progress reported during the preceding year. General William C. Westmoreland, then commanding U.S. forces in Vietnam, had been particularly sanguine in his predictions, saying in the autumn that he had never been more encouraged in his four years in Vietnam and that we had reached a point where the end had begun to come into view. The contrast between those pronouncements and what now appeared to be happening on the battlefield precipitated a dramatic downturn in the American public's willingness to continue supporting the war.

Soon after Tet 1968 General Westmoreland was replaced as U.S. commander in Vietnam by General Creighton W. Abrams, renowned as a troop leader since World War II, when he commanded a battalion of tanks in the drive across Europe, en route breaking through to the 101st Airborne Division where it was encircled at Bastogne during the Battle of the Bulge, and winning two Distinguished Service Crosses and a battlefield promotion to colonel in the process.

Abrams joined Ambassador Ellsworth Bunker, a patrician Vermonter and international businessman-turned-diplomat, recently acclaimed for dextrous handling of a volatile situation during U.S. intervention in the Dominican Republic. Bunker had settled into the Saigon post the previous spring, thereby ending a long series of frequent ambassadorial changes.

Soon these men were joined by Ambassador William E. Colby, a career officer of the Central Intelligence Agency who had earlier been the Agency's Chief of Station, Saigon, then Chief of the Far East Division at CIA Headquarters. Building a brilliant intelligence career on World War II service with the Office of Strategic Services, service that saw him decorated for valor after parachuting behind enemy lines, Colby arrived to take over American support of the pacification program.

In the wake of Tet 1968, the tasks confronting the new leadership triumvirate were challenging indeed. America's long buildup of forces was at an end, soon to be supplanted by a progressive reduction in the forces deployed. Financial resources, previously abundant, were becoming severely constrained. Domestic support for the war, never robust, continued to decline, the downward spiral fueled in reinforcing parts by opponents of the war and others deploring inept prosecution of it. Lyndon Johnson had in effect been driven from office by these escalating forces, while Richard Nixon's tenure would of necessity constitute an extended attempt to moderate and adapt to them without losing all control.

Whatever the mood of the country, for those in Vietnam the war still had to be fought, and the new leadership went about doing that with energy and insight. Shaped by Abrams's understanding of the complex nature of the conflict, the tactical approach underwent immediate and radical revision when he took command. Previously fragmented approaches to combat operations, pacification, and mentoring the South Vietnamese armed forces now became "one war" with a single clear-cut objective—security for the people in South Vietnam's villages and hamlets. And under a program awkwardly titled "Vietnamization," responsibility for conduct of the war, largely taken over by the Americans in the earlier period, was progressively turned back to the South Vietnamese.

Most of the better-known treatments of the Vietnam War as a whole have given relatively little consideration to these later years. Stanley Karnow's *Vietnam: A History*, for example, does not get beyond Tet 1968 until page 567 out of 670, and indeed Karnow does not even list Abrams, who served in Vietnam for five years and commanded U.S. forces there for four, in his "Cast of Principal Characters."

George Herring's admirable academic treatment of the conflict, *America's Longest War*, is similarly weighted toward the early years, with 221 pages devoted to the period through Tet 1968 and 60 pages to the rest of the war. William J. Duiker's *Historical Dictionary of Vietnam* likewise emphasizes the early stages, with entries for Lodge, Taylor, and Westmoreland, but none for Bunker, Abrams, or Colby.

The most pronounced example of concentration on the earlier years is Neil Sheehan's Pulitzer Prize–winning book *A Bright Shining Lie*. Sheehan devotes 725 pages to events through Tet 1968 and only 65 pages to the rest of the war, even though John Paul Vann, the nominal subject of his book, lived and served in Vietnam for four years after the Tet Offensive. And of course the famous *Pentagon Papers*, first made public in June 1971, cover the war only through the end of Defense Secretary Robert Mc-Namara's tenure in 1968. William Colby once observed that, due to the prevalence of such truncated treatments of the Vietnam War, "the historical record given to most Americans is . . . similar to what we would know if histories of World War II stopped before Stalingrad, Operation Torch in North Africa and Guadalcanal in the Pacific."[1] To many people, therefore, the story of the early years seems to be the whole story of the war in Vietnam, a perception that is far from accurate.

Bunker, Abrams, and Colby, and the forces they led in the later years of American involvement in Vietnam, brought different values to their tasks, operated from a different understanding of the nature of the war, and applied different measures of merit and different tactics. They employed diminishing resources in manpower, matériel, money, and time as they raced to render the South Vietnamese capable of defending themselves before the last American forces were withdrawn. They went about that task with sincerity, intelligence, decency, and absolute professionalism, and in the process came very close to achieving the elusive goal of a viable nation and a lasting peace.

A
Better
War

1

Inheritance

WHEN, IN JANUARY 1964, General William C. Westmoreland was sent out to Vietnam as deputy to General Paul Harkins—and became, a few months later, his successor in command of U.S. forces there—he was chosen from a slate of four candidates presented to President Lyndon Johnson. The others proposed were General Harold K. Johnson, who instead became Army Chief of Staff; General Creighton Abrams, who was assigned as Vice Chief of Staff to Johnson; and General Bruce Palmer, Jr., who replaced Johnson as the Army's Deputy Chief of Staff for Military Operations. The choice of Westmoreland was a fateful one in terms of how the war would be fought. As later events demonstrated conclusively, the other three candidates were of one mind on that matter, all differing radically from Westmoreland's approach.[1]

Beginning in the spring of 1965, Westmoreland repeatedly requested additional troops, the better to prosecute his self-devised strategy of attrition warfare. Simply stated, his intention was to inflict on the enemy more casualties than they could tolerate, thereby forcing them to abandon efforts to subjugate South Vietnam. A key element of this approach was reaching the "crossover point," the point at which allied forces were causing more casualties than the enemy could replace, whether

through recruitment and impressment in South Vietnam or infiltration from North Vietnam. At a February 1966 conference
with President Lyndon Johnson in Honolulu, Westmoreland had
been given an explicit directive to achieve this goal, to demonstrate that he could make good on his chosen strategy of attrition. "Attrit by year's end, Viet Cong and North Vietnamese
forces at a rate as high as their capability to put men in the
field," he was told.[2] While Westmoreland eventually claimed to
have accomplished that mission, in fact—despite horrendous
losses—the enemy buildup continued throughout his tenure, as
did Westmoreland's requests for more and more troops to meet
what he once called his "relatively modest requirements."

Westmoreland often predicted that the enemy was going to
run out of men, but in the event it turned out to be the United
States that did so, or at least found it extremely difficult to deploy more forces in the face of reluctance to call up reserve
forces and pressures to reduce draft calls.[3] Resistance to calling
reserves was a constant during Lyndon Johnson's presidency, a
stance apparently dictated by unwillingness to have the war affect the lives of millions of ordinary citizens and families affili-
ated with the reserves. Ironically, that impact fell instead on those
who were drafted or volunteered for service. Meanwhile, failure
to call up reserve forces had an adverse impact on all the services,
and especially the Army, since all contingency plans for deployments of any magnitude had included at least partial reliance on
mobilized reserves.

Types of units found primarily in the reserve components
and needed in Vietnam now had to be created from scratch,
while the existing units and seasoned leaders in the reserves remained unavailable. Instead the expansion of forces consisted, as
Creighton Abrams once observed, "entirely of privates and second lieutenants," resulting in progressive decline of experience
and maturity of the force, particularly at junior levels of leadership. This in turn seems directly related to later problems of
indiscipline in the services.

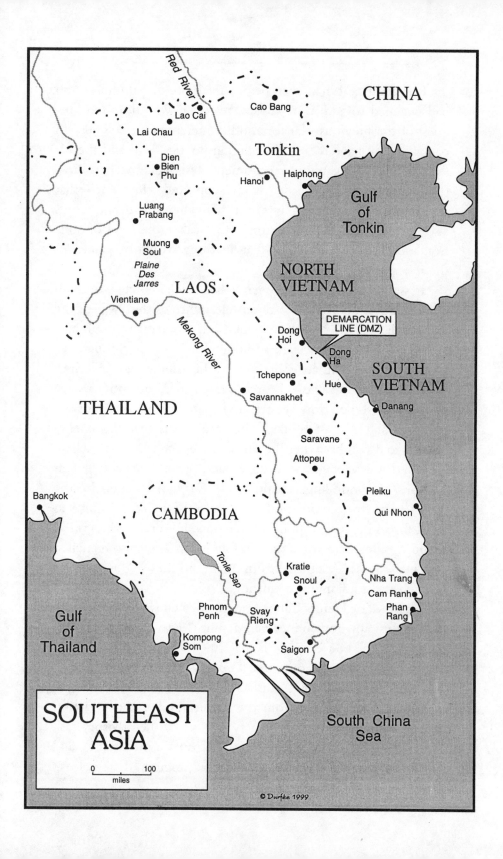

CHINA

Red River

Cao Bang

Lao Cai

Lai Chau

Dien
Bien
Phu

Tonkin

Hanoi

Haiphong

Gulf
of
Tonkin

Luang
Prabang

Muong
Soul

*Plaine
Des
Jarres*

LAOS

NORTH
VIETNAM

Vientiane

Mekong River

DEMARCATION
LINE (DMZ)

Dong
Hoi

Dong
Ha

Tchepone

Hue

SOUTH
VIETNAM

THAILAND

Savannakhet

Danang

Saravane

Attopeu

Bangkok

Pleiku

Qui Nhon

CAMBODIA

Tonle Sap

Kratie

Snoul

Nha Trang

Phnom
Penh

Svay
Rieng

Cam Ranh

Gulf
of
Thailand

Kompong
Som

Saigon

Phan
Rang

SOUTHEAST
ASIA

0   100
miles

South China
Sea

© Durfée 1999

It is significant that, even before Tet 1968, the administration had declined to add more troops, rejecting Westmoreland's request of the previous year for another increment of 200,000. In part this may have reflected declining political will and the effects of a growing antiwar sentiment, but widespread realization—even among those who supported the war—that Westmoreland's approach was not achieving significant results also spawned unwillingness simply to escalate the level of confrontation with no assurance that anything would be gained in the process.

Losses imposed on the enemy had been inflicted through concentration on what was often referred to as the "war of the big battalions," an operational approach emphasizing multibattalion, and sometimes even multidivision, sweeps through remote jungle areas in an effort to find the enemy and force him to stand and fight. These "search-and-destroy" operations were costly in terms of time, effort, and matériel, but often disappointing in terms of results. The reality was that the enemy could avoid combat when he chose; accept it when and where he found it advantageous to do so; and break contact at will as a means of controlling casualties. He was aided in this by the use of sanctuaries in adjacent Laos and Cambodia, off limits to allied forces because of political restraints. His principal logistical support route, nicknamed the Ho Chi Minh Trail, also branched out into South Vietnam from main arteries spiking down through those adjoining countries.

Ambassador Henry Cabot Lodge reflected some of the frustration this situation induced in a June 1966 cable to Lyndon Johnson. "The best estimate is that 20,000 men of the Army of North Vietnam have come into South Vietnam since January," he wrote, "and as far as I can learn, we can't find them."[4]

Other costs derived from the single-minded concentration on the Main Force war—notably neglect of the advisory task and of the need to improve South Vietnam's armed forces, and equally neglect of the crucial pacification program, thereby leaving largely undisturbed the enemy's shadow government, its infrastructure within the villages and hamlets of rural South Vietnam. "Westmoreland's interest always lay in the big-unit war," said his senior intelligence officer, Lieutenant General Phillip B. Davidson. "Pacification bored him."[5] And, in his enthusiasm for taking over the Main Force war, Westmoreland in effect pushed the South Vietnamese out of the way, thus also abdicating his assigned role as the senior advisor to those forces and essentially stunting their development for a crucial four years.

At the end of 1966, the *Pentagon Papers* authors later observed, "the mood was one of cautious optimism, buoyed by hopes that 1967 would prove to be the decisive year in Vietnam."[6] In an interview published in *Life* magazine, Westmoreland went further. "We're going to out-guerrilla the guerrilla and out-ambush the ambush," he asserted. "And we're going to learn better than he ever did because we're smarter, we have greater mobility and firepower, we have more endurance and more to fight for. . . . And we've got more guts."[7] This was ominous, for Westmoreland had by then been in Vietnam for nearly three years. Indeed, the previous year he had told the President that the war would be over by the summer of 1967.[8]

In February 1967 General Earle G. Wheeler, Chairman of the Joint Chiefs of Staff, made one of his periodic visits to South Vietnam, afterward reporting to the President that "the adverse military tide has been reversed, and General Westmoreland now has the initiative. The enemy can no longer hope to win the war in South Vietnam," he added. "We can win the war if we apply pressure upon the enemy relentlessly in the North and in the South."[9]

INSTEAD OF BEING the decisive year in the war, 1967 became the year in which criticism of Westmoreland's war built from many quarters. "From inside and outside the government," wrote historian George Herring, "numerous civilians joined [Secretary of

Defense Robert] McNamara in urging [President] Johnson to
check dissent at home by changing the ground strategy. [Nich-
olas] Katzenbach, [William] Bundy, McNamara's top civilian advisers in the Pentagon, a group of establishment figures meeting
under the auspices of the Carnegie Endowment, and the president's own 'Wise Men' agreed that Westmoreland's search-and-
destroy strategy must be abandoned."[10]

In Vietnam, reported William Conrad Gibbons, compiler of
an authoritative collection of documents on the war, Ambassador Henry Cabot Lodge "was so strongly opposed to attrition
strategy that he contemplated resigning in the spring of 1967
and making a public statement of opposition."[11] Nor was the
military leadership in full support. Lieutenant General Frederick
C. Weyand, commanding a U.S. corps, was convinced that "the
key to the war was in providing security to the villages and
towns of Vietnam."[12]

While he was Chief of Staff, General Johnson had sponsored
a study called "A Program for the Pacification and Long-Term
Development of Vietnam," known as PROVN for short, that
thoroughly repudiated Westmoreland's concept, strategy, and
tactics for fighting the war. "People—Vietnamese and American, individually and collectively—constitute both the strategic
determinants of today's conflict and 'the object . . . which lies
beyond' this war," the study maintained. Thus the imperative
was clear: "The United States . . . must redirect the Republic of
Vietnam–Free World military effort to achieve greater security."
Therefore, read the study's summary, "the critical actions are
those that occur at the village, the district and provincial levels.
This is where the war must be fought; this is where the war and
the object which lies beyond it must be won." The study also
made it clear that body count, the centerpiece of Westmoreland's
attrition warfare, was not the appropriate measure of merit for
such a conflict. What counted was security for the people, and
search-and-destroy operations were contributing little to that.

Abrams was Army Vice Chief of Staff when PROVN was

conducted, and the results were briefed for his approval. As would become clear when he took command in Vietnam, they subsequently formed the blueprint for his fundamental revision of how the war was fought.

While the PROVN study was in progress, General Johnson made one of his many trips to the war zone, meeting in the field with a group of colonels. "We just didn't think we could do the job the way we were doing it," recalled Edward C. Meyer, then one of those colonels and later Army Chief of Staff, and that's what they told Johnson. Another officer, who said he had pleaded with Westmoreland to "end the big unit war," told Johnson, "we're just not going to win it doing this."[13]

Even the American public sensed the effects of Westmoreland's having shouldered the South Vietnamese armed forces out of the way. "At a highest level meeting today," General Wheeler cabled Westmoreland in late October, "a major subject concerned the deteriorating public support in this country for the Vietnamese war. One of the problems cited by a number of persons is the fact many people believe that the ARVN [Army of the Republic of Vietnam] is not carrying its fair share of the combat effort."[14]

Richard H. Moorsteen, a White House staffer assigned to the pacification program, reported from Vietnam that "chasing after victory through attrition is a will-o'-the-wisp that costs us too much in dollars, draft calls and casualties, makes it too hard to stay the course."[15] Similar views were expressed in early December by a group of prominent Americans, including General Matthew Ridgway, meeting under the auspices of the Carnegie Endowment for International Peace. "The emphasis should not be on the military destruction of Communist forces in the South but on the protection of the people of South Vietnam and the stabilization of the situation at a politically tolerable level," their report held. "Tactically, this would involve a shift in emphasis from 'search-and-destroy' to 'clear-and-hold' operations."[16]

McNamara's Systems Analysis office in the Pentagon, run by

Dr. Alain Enthoven, concluded that "small patrols were much more effective and much less costly in casualties than big sweeps" and recommended "expanded use of small-unit operations, particularly patrols."[17] Enthoven also accurately characterized the task at hand. "I see this war," he wrote to McNamara in May 1967, "as a race between, on the one hand, the development of a viable South Vietnam and, on the other hand, a gradual loss in public support, or even tolerance, for the war. Hanoi is betting that we'll lose public support in the United States before we can build a nation in South Vietnam. We must do what we can to make sure that doesn't happen. . . . Our horse must cross the finish first."[18]

Even S. L. A. Marshall, a military columnist usually very supportive of the senior leadership, raised the key question: "Do the big sweeps such as the envelopment of the Iron Triangle or the attack on War Zone C really have a payoff justifying an elaborate massing of troops and mountains of supply? Many of the generals doubt it and the statistics of what is actually accomplished gives some substance to these doubts."[19] Surveyed after the war, Army generals who had commanded in Vietnam confirmed those doubts. Nearly a third stated that the search-and-destroy concept was "not sound," while another 26 percent thought it was "sound when first implemented—not later." As for the execution of search-and-destroy tactics, a majority of 51 percent thought it "left something to be desired," an answer ranking below "adequate" in the survey instrument.

"These replies," observed the study's author, Brigadier General Douglas Kinnard, "show a noticeable lack of enthusiasm, to put it mildly, by Westmoreland's generals for his tactics and by implication for his strategy in the war."[20] Meanwhile, neglect of other aspects of the war continued to be costly. Late in the year Ambassador Ellsworth Bunker reported "very little overall gain in population security."[21]

Finally even General William E. DePuy, Westmoreland's

closest tactical advisor as his Deputy Chief of Staff for Operations, conceded that their chosen methods had been flawed.
"Our operational approach was to increase the pressure on the
other side (size of force, intensity of operations, casualties) in the
belief that it had a breaking point," he wrote after the war. "But
the regime in Hanoi did not break; it did not submit to our
logic."[22]

At a "Tuesday Lunch" at the White House in early December 1967, Secretary of Defense McNamara told Lyndon Johnson
and their most senior colleagues of his conviction that "the war
cannot be won by killing North Vietnamese. It can only be won
by protecting the South Vietnamese."[23] In this same season William Bundy pressed the President to conduct a comprehensive
review of ground strategy for the war at the "highest military
and civilian levels," pointing out that "if the strategy was not
wise or effective, the work of the field commander 'must be
questioned.' "[24]

Despite this barrage of criticism, Westmoreland survived, for
he retained one very important patron, ultimately the only one
who mattered. "Aware as I am of the mistakes Generals have
made in the past," LBJ told Dean Rusk at that same Tuesday
Lunch, "I place great confidence in General Westmoreland."[25]
But even LBJ recognized the problem. "We've been on dead
center for the last year" in Vietnam, he told the Wise Men in
early November.[26]

DURING 1967, HOWEVER, very important augmentations of the
American leadership in Vietnam took place, beginning in March
with the appointment of Ellsworth Bunker as ambassador to the
Republic of Vietnam. Bunker was a consummate gentleman and
an unusual diplomat, having come to diplomacy professionally
after a long and successful business career. The Bunkers were
descendants of French Huguenots; the name, anglicized from
Boncoeur (good heart), fit him well. Bunker had the qualities

Creighton Abrams admired most—integrity, fortitude, loyalty, dedication, selflessness, and wit—and those would soon form the basis for an enduring friendship between the two men.

That same month Lieutenant General Bruce Palmer, Jr., had been ordered to Vietnam, where he soon became deputy commander of the Army component of the U.S. Military Assistance Command, Vietnam (MACV). Palmer, like Westmoreland and Abrams a 1936 West Point graduate, had gone initially into the horse cavalry and then, as had Abrams, migrated to the armored force when World War II was imminent. Known throughout the Army as a man of fine intellect and rock-solid integrity, Palmer led American forces deployed to the Dominican Republic in 1965 and there, while demonstrating sound judgment and a cool head in a confused and confusing situation, had come to know and respect Ambassador Bunker and in turn had earned the respect and liking of the older man.

In May, pursuant to Lyndon Johnson's public commitment to strengthen U.S. leadership in Vietnam and to deploy the first team, Robert Komer was dispatched to take charge of American support for pacification, newly brought under control of the military headquarters. Komer was a professional bureaucrat who had begun as an analyst at the Central Intelligence Agency, then moved to the White House staff during Lyndon Johnson's presidency. At the same time General Creighton Abrams was assigned as deputy to Westmoreland.

These new arrivals shared an outlook on conduct of the war, an outlook much different from Westmoreland's. Convinced that the key to winning the war lay not in the remote jungles, but rather in the hamlets and villages of South Vietnam, they set about trying to reorient the American effort.

WHEN ABRAMS FIRST arrived to be the deputy commander, Palmer took him aside. "I just poured out my soul about my feelings about Vietnam, the almost impossible task we had, given

the national policy, limited objectives, and so on," Palmer recalled. "I told him I really had basic disagreements with Westy
on how it was organized and how we were doing it." Abrams
listened carefully, then replied, "You know, I'm here to help
Westy and, although I privately agree with many things you are
saying, I've got to be loyal to him. I'm going to help him."[27]
(Abrams may also have had in mind that he was scheduled to
take command himself in a very short time, even though subsequently that did not happen as planned.) "This loyalty to
Westmoreland," said Palmer, "was typical of Abrams, who was
first and last a soldier."[28]

Komer, too, was extremely critical of the Westmoreland approach to conduct of the war. "I also happen to be one of those
who favored a much more small-unit war," he said later. "Americans should have operated much more in small units as a matter
of course, and with much less use of artillery and air strikes."
Subsequently Komer watched approvingly as Abrams changed
the war in that way. "We complained about H&I"—harassment
and interdiction—"fire, but really credit on this goes to Abrams.
He very discreetly started cutting down the ammo allocations
to conserve ammunition, which automatically meant cutting
down H&I fire."[29]

Abrams spent much of his year as Westmoreland's deputy
traveling the country from one end to the other, visiting South
Vietnamese forces at every level in an effort to improve their
leadership, equipment, and combat effectiveness. Along the way
he developed a particular interest in the Regional Forces (RF)
and Popular Forces (PF), the territorials who formed the first
line of defense in the hamlets and villages. It reached the point,
said Major General Walter "Dutch" Kerwin, where Abrams
came to be recognized "as the man who knew more about the
RF and PF than anybody else in MACV." Later, when some of
the bloodiest battles of the war took place, these territorial
forces proved formidable, repaying the interest Abrams had

taken in them and the priority he gave them for equipment and
training.

DURING 1967 General Westmoreland again asked for more
troops, in fact 200,000 more, which would have brought the
overall total of U.S. forces in Vietnam to more than 675,000.
He didn't get them. Washington's tolerance for further troop
increases had finally been exhausted. Only a token increase was
authorized as Tet 1968 approached.

The Tet Offensive was in many ways the watershed event
of the war. The fact that the Viet Cong and North Vietnamese
Army could mount a coordinated assault on most of the major
towns and military installations across South Vietnam gravely
undermined the optimistic assessments Westmoreland had been
retailing for many months. For the general public, the government's credibility was so damaged that forever after people were
skeptical about positive military news of the war. Within the
government, Westmoreland's credibility as the field commander
further declined—dramatized, someone observed, by many who
had habitually called him "Westy" now referring instead to
"Westmoreland"—and even the Commander in Chief's confidence seemed badly shaken. Later bitter commentators observed
that Tet had proved the domino theory, even though only one
domino—Lyndon Johnson—fell as the result of it.

A "general uprising" of the populace in support of the invaders had been predicted by North Vietnam but failed to materialize, and without this support the offensive was quickly
defeated except in two key cities, Saigon and Hue, where the
fighting continued for many days. Abrams was sent to the northern provinces to take command of the battle there, operating
from an ad hoc headquarters established for that purpose and
designated MACV Forward. After a month of hard fighting, the
last enemy troops were ejected from Hue, essentially ending the
Tet Offensive of 1968.

The costs to the enemy had been enormous, later estimated

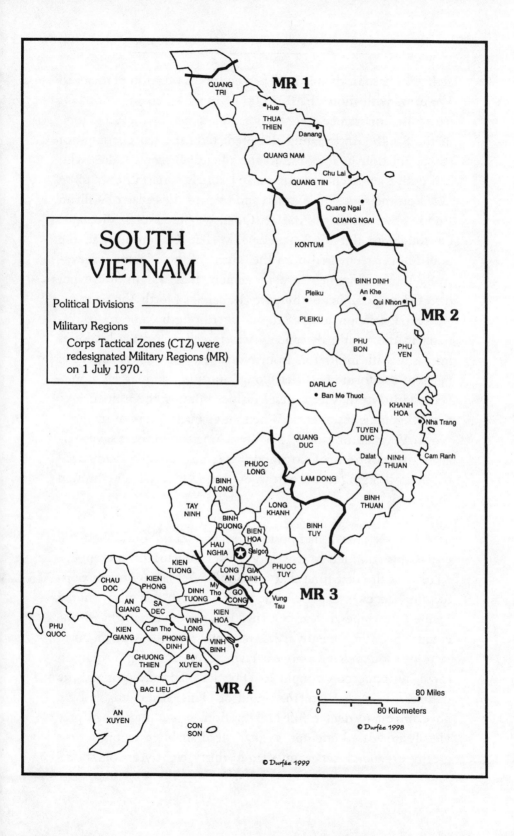

MR 1

QUANG TRI

Hue
THUA THIEN

Danang

QUANG NAM

Chu Lai
QUANG TIN

Quang Ngai
QUANG NGAI

KONTUM

BINH DINH

Pleiku
An Khe
Qui Nhon

PLEIKU

MR 2

PHU BON

PHU YEN

DARLAC
Ban Me Thuot

KHANH HOA
Nha Trang

TUYEN DUC

Dalat
NINH THUAN

Cam Ranh

QUANG DUC

LAM DONG

PHUOC LONG

BINH THUAN

BINH LONG

TAY NINH

LONG KHANH

BINH DUONG

BIEN HOA

BINH TUY

HAU NGHIA
Saigon

KIEN TUONG

LONG AN
GIA DINH

PHUOC TUY

CHAU DOC

KIEN PHONG

DINH TUONG

My Tho
GO CONG

Vung Tau

MR 3

AN GIANG

SA DEC

KIEN HOA

PHU QUOC

KIEN GIANG

Can Tho
VINH LONG

PHONG DINH

VINH BINH

CHUONG THIEN

BA XUYEN

BAC LIEU

MR 4

AN XUYEN

CON SON

SOUTH VIETNAM

Political Divisions ———————

Military Regions ▬▬▬▬▬▬

Corps Tactical Zones (CTZ) were redesignated Military Regions (MR) on 1 July 1970.

0   80 Miles

0   80 Kilometers

© Durfée 1998

© Durfée 1999

at 45,000 dead or disabled, 20 percent of his total forces in South
Vietnam, with more than 33,000 of those killed in action. Of
particular importance were the losses sustained by the Viet Cong
in the South. Anticipating the predicted "general uprising" of
the population in response to the offensive, many cadres who
had until then been operating clandestinely surfaced, only to be
killed on the spot or identified and tracked down later. William
Bundy observed that in the Tet Offensive "the North Vietnamese fought to the last Viet Cong."[30] The Communists in the
South never recovered from the effects of these losses, progressively losing influence in a movement that was in any event
directed and dominated by party leaders in North Vietnam.

As pacification progressed and recruiting became more difficult in the South, the enemy was forced to replace his losses
primarily with infiltrators from North Vietnam. Over time, the
ranks of the formerly "Viet Cong" units became largely populated with North Vietnamese, further diluting the influence of
the indigenous insurgents. When, after many years of struggle,
North Vietnam prevailed, the Viet Cong found themselves relegated to positions of no importance, an outcome dramatized
by their bringing up the rear of the victory parade through
Saigon.

THE TET OFFENSIVE had positive results within South Vietnam,
results not confined to the heavy losses inflicted on the enemy.
"This was the first time that our South Vietnamese urban population had ever experienced the hazards of real war," noted
Lieutenant General Ngo Quang Truong.[31] The firsthand encounter with the enemy's destructiveness and—as in his massacre of thousands of innocent civilians in Hue—his cruelty to
those he supposedly sought to "liberate" radically changed the
outlook of South Vietnam's populace. This change enabled the
government to decree full mobilization, something it had previously not dared attempt, so that the draftable categories were
greatly expanded (set at nineteen to thirty-eight years old, com-

pared with twenty-one to twenty-eight previously, and then eighteen to thirty-eight), and the armed forces were expanded from 600,000, eventually reaching 1,100,000. One of the great, if unremarked, ironies of the war was that the enemy's "General Offensive/General Uprising" provoked not the anticipated uprising of the population in support of the invaders, but just the opposite—general mobilization in support of the government. "The expansion took place primarily in territorial forces which were indigenous to the areas where they were assigned," explained the legendary John Paul Vann. "An enduring government presence in the countryside was thus established."[32]

The General Mobilization Law of June 1968 included an important provision favoring those territorial forces, the Regional Forces and the Popular Forces. Men thirty-one to thirty-eight years old could volunteer to serve in the RF or PF rather than be inducted in the regular armed forces. The incentive of remaining close to home motivated many to do so, allowing the greatly expanded RF and PF authorizations to be met.[33]

THE PLAN HAD BEEN that when Abrams went to Vietnam in May 1967 he would, within a few weeks, succeed to the top command in place of Westmoreland. As things played out, though, more than a year elapsed before Abrams formally took command. While the evidence is strong that an early succession was intended,[34] Secretary of Defense McNamara inadvertently precipitated a change of outlook on Lyndon Johnson's part. After a July 1967 visit to Saigon, he suggested in remarks to the press that, rather than asking for additional forces, General Westmoreland ought to make more effective use of the forces he already had. Westmoreland, who happened to be in the United States at the time, objected, after which LBJ called his commanding general in for consolation and reassurance, including public expressions of undiluted support. Johnson could scarcely then relieve him, lest he give credence to critics of Westmoreland, and of himself as the man who had chosen Westmoreland

and continued to back him despite increasingly widespread criticism.

   Westmoreland therefore remained in command until the Tet
Offensive erupted. LBJ temporized yet a while longer, probably
for the same reasons as before. Then, in late March, two months
after Tet began, it was revealed that Westmoreland would become Army Chief of Staff in June. On 10 April, General
Creighton Abrams was announced as the commander-designate
in Vietnam. There lay ahead a better war.

2

New Tactics

CREIGHTON ABRAMS formally assumed command of U.S. forces in Vietnam in early June, but the message traffic makes it clear that he was in de facto command much earlier. His stamp was on conduct of the fighting during "mini–Tet" in May, as it had been in the northern provinces when he commanded from MACV Forward during Tet 1968.

"The tactics changed within fifteen minutes of Abrams's taking command," affirmed General Fred Weyand, who was in a position to know. Under General Westmoreland, Weyand had commanded the 25th Infantry Division when it deployed to Vietnam from Hawaii, then moved up to command II Field Force, Vietnam, a corps-level headquarters. From that vantage point he observed the year Abrams spent as Westmoreland's deputy, then Abrams's ascension to the top post.

What Weyand saw was a dramatic shift in concept of the nature and conduct of the war, in the appropriate measures of merit, and in the tactics to be applied. Former Secretary of the Army Stephen Ailes, who had known Abrams well for a number of years, perceived that he understood—as General Harold K. Johnson used to say and as the PROVN Study emphasized— "the object beyond the war." That object was not destruction

but control, and in this case particularly control of the population.

Abrams also understood that the war was a complex of interrelated contests on several levels, and that dealing with the
enemy effectively meant meeting and countering him on each
of those levels. "The enemy's operational pattern is his understanding that this is just one, repeat one, war," stressed Abrams.
"He knows there's no such thing as a war of big battalions, a
war of pacification or a war of territorial security. Friendly forces
have got to recognize and understand the one war concept and
carry the battle to the enemy, simultaneously, in all areas of conflict."[1] This insight was also the answer to a false dichotomy
that has grown up in discussing the war, with contending view-
points arguing that it was a guerrilla war on one hand or a
conventional war on the other. The fact is that it was both, in
varying degrees and at different times and places. The "one war"
approach recognized and accommodated this pervasive though
shifting reality.

When Admiral John S. McCain, Jr.—the Commander in
Chief, Pacific (CINCPAC), based in Hawaii—came out to visit,
Abrams explained to him that "the one war concept puts equal
emphasis on military operations, improvement of RVNAF [Re-
public of Vietnam Armed Forces] and pacification—all of which
are interrelated so that the better we do in one, the more our
chance of progress in the others."[2] Lieutenant General Julian
Ewell, commanding the corps-level II Field Force, said of
Abrams's "one war" concept that "like most powerful ideas it
was very simple. Also, like most ideas in Vietnam it was rather
difficult in execution."[3]

Ellsworth Bunker was in complete agreement with Abrams,
and had demonstrated his understanding of the true nature of
the war in his very first interview with President Nguyen Van
Thieu. Presenting his credentials as the new U.S. ambassador
to the Republic of Vietnam, Bunker stated his view that "the

essence of success" in the war lay in providing security for the people in South Vietnam's hamlets and villages.[4]

Abrams and Bunker from the start formed a close relationship, one based on shared values and a shared objective: preparing the South Vietnamese to defend themselves before American forces were withdrawn. Abrams personally instructed key staff members on how to deal with the embassy. The first night Major General Charles Corcoran was in Vietnam, newly assigned as MACV J-3, Abrams emphasized to him that he never wanted to take any major action without prior consultation with Bunker. "I never want to withhold the bad news from the ambassador, nor the good news," Abrams said. "We will give it to him just like we have it. I do not want our ambassador ever to be surprised."[5] Other senior officers recalled being told by Abrams, "If you can't get along with the ambassador, there's no sense in your being here."

While the convoluted Washington policy apparatus sought to play off one faction against another, Bunker and Abrams stood apart from such machinations. South Vietnam's ambassador to the United States, Bui Diem, gained some insight into this from his discussions with Bunker, who told him that during peace negotiations there were some things that Washington didn't feel were appropriate to share with the military command. "But Ellsworth Bunker was of a different opinion," said Diem. "He had a high regard for Abrams and many times, he told me, he insisted on having Abrams briefed too on some of these political problems. And so it reflected a kind of confidence between the two men, walking together like that."[6]

Bunker was also fully supportive when Abrams set about implementing the approach to the war proposed by the PROVN study. One of the study's key contributors had been Lieutenant Colonel Don Marshall, who thereby came to Abrams's attention. Even before Abrams assumed command in Vietnam, he asked the Army Chief of Staff to reassign Marshall

to MACV "to put to use on the ground the considerable study
he has accomplished for you."[7] Soon, on orders to Vietnam,
Marshall received a letter from Abrams. "I look forward to your
arrival," he wrote. "You will need your 'notes.' " The cryptic
reference was to the results of PROVN and related studies on
which Marshall had worked.[8]

PROVN insisted that "at no time should . . . combat operations shift the American focus of support from the true point
of decision in Vietnam—the villages." The underlying objective
was, as General Johnson had made clear, "the restoration of stability with the minimum of destruction, so that society and law-
ful government may proceed in an atmosphere of justice and
order." Abrams fully agreed with those findings, as Lieutenant
General Phillip B. Davidson, who served as MACV Deputy
Chief of Staff for Intelligence for both Westmoreland and
Abrams, could attest. Westmoreland had rejected the study when
it was published, said Davidson, because "he could not embrace
the study's concept without admitting that he and his strategy
were wrong." But later, "under different circumstances and a
different commander, [PROVN] would gain support and credence."[9]

Instead of thrashing about in the deep jungle, seeking to
bring the enemy to battle at times and in places of his own
choosing—the typical maneuver of the earlier era—allied forces
now set up positions sited to protect populated areas from invading forces. This put friendly forces in more advantageous
situations and forced the enemy to come through them to gain
access to the population, the real objective of both sides in the
war. As early as August 1968, Abrams noted that the entire 1st
Cavalry Division was operating in company-size units, suggesting "that gives you a feel for the extent to which they're deployed and the extent to which they're covering the area." The
implication was that instead of a smaller number of operations
by large, and therefore somewhat unwieldy, units, current operations featured fuller area coverage by widely deployed and

more agile small units. Once enemy contact was established, larger and more powerful forces could be concentrated at the critical point.

"Where Westmoreland was a search-and-destroy and count-the-bodies man," wrote a perceptive journalist, "Abrams proved to be an interdict-and-weigh-the-rice man."[10] The reference was to Abrams's insistence on the value of discovering and seizing the enemy's prepositioned supplies, including the rice he needed to feed his troops. Abrams had discovered the enemy's reliance on a logistics "nose," the technique of pushing the wherewithal needed to fight a battle out in front of the troops rather than, as traditional armies would do it, supplying them from the rear by means of a logistical "tail." In this approach, necessitated by lack of transport and secure lines of communication, Abrams had identified a major enemy vulnerability.

This insight in turn dictated important changes in allied tactics. Because of the need for advance emplacement of the logistics nose, major enemy operations required substantial time for preparation of the battlefield, positioning supplies, constructing bunkers, moving in the forces, and so on. Armed with this knowledge of enemy vulnerabilities, Abrams set about preempting enemy offensives by seeking out and cutting off that logistics nose. The large-scale search-and-destroy operations that typified the Westmoreland years gave way to numerous smaller operations such as patrols and ambushes, both day and night, designed to find the enemy and his crucial caches of matériel, then seize the supplies and interdict troop movement toward the populated areas.

EVERY ASPECT OF the war seemed almost calculated to put a strain on professional integrity, from the lushness of the support establishment to the allocation of battlefield resources, but body count may have been the most corrupt—and corrupting—measure of progress in the whole mess. Certainly the consensus of senior Army leaders, the generals who commanded in

Vietnam, strongly indicates that it was. Sixty-one percent, when polled on the matter, said that the body count was "often in-flated." Typical comments by the respondents were that it was "a fake—totally worthless," that "the immensity of the false reporting is a blot on the honor of the Army," and that "they were grossly exaggerated by many units primarily because of the incredible interest shown by people like McNamara and Westmoreland."[11]

Westmoreland denied it. "I believe one of the great distortions of the war has been the allegation that casualties inflicted on the enemy are padded," he asserted. "I can categorically state that such is not the case."[12] A large majority of his generals did not agree.

The appropriate measure of merit in such a conflict was, Abrams thought, not "body count" but "population security"—security from coercion and terrorism for the people in South Vietnam's villages and hamlets. "There's a lot of evidence to go around of a developing disinterest in body count per se," Abrams told McCain during the next enemy offensive in August 1968. "*Weapons* are important." That word seemed to be getting out, since during the last quarter of 1968 operations initiated by friendly forces captured 6,961 enemy weapons while losing 49, a gratifying ratio of 142:1.[13]

Abrams moved to deemphasize the body count in two ways: he focused his own interest on other measures of merit and progress; and his shift in tactics to concentrate on population security made that, rather than killing the enemy per se, the most important determinant of success. And he very explicitly stated that body count was far less important than some other measures of how well things were going, a message he delivered in person, in cables, and in the campaign plans and planning documents issued by his headquarters. "I know body count has something about it," said Abrams in a typical comment on the matter, "but it's really a *long* way from what is involved in this war. Yeah, you have to do that, *I* know that, but the *mistake* is to think that's the central issue." Amplifying, he added, "I don't think it makes any difference how many losses he [the enemy] takes. I don't think *that* makes any *difference*."

ABRAMS'S MOST significant impact as the new MACV commander was in his conduct of the war—his concept of the nature of the war itself, the "one war" response to that perception, identification and exploitation of the enemy's dependence on a logistics nose, emphasis on security of the populace and the territorial force improvements that provided it, effective interdiction of enemy infiltration, and development of more capable armed forces for the South Vietnamese. But there were matters of style that were also very important, not least in the example they set for the South Vietnamese.

"Effective now," Abrams told senior commanders even before his official appointment, "the overall public affairs policy of this command will be to let results speak for themselves. We will not deal in propaganda exercises in any way, but will play all of our activities at a low key." And, he added, "achievements, not hopes, will be stressed."[14]

After receiving a complaint from Lieutenant General Robert Cushman, the Marine commander of III MAF, that Armed Forces Radio was broadcasting too much coverage of antiwar protests in America, Abrams looked into the programming, then replied. "I am satisfied they are presenting a balanced picture of what is now happening in the United States—good and bad—within their capabilities," he began. "We should never protect our men from the truth, because the very system of government for which they fight and sacrifice has its basic strength in its citizenry knowing the facts. I believe the Armed Forces Radio is presenting a balanced set of facts. It is our job to persevere in the atmosphere of the facts."[15]

Next Abrams stated his views on how bad news was to be handled. "If [an] investigation results in 'bad news,' no attempt will be made to dodge the issue," he specified. "If an error has

been made, it will be admitted . . . as soon as possible." These
expressions of style were also manifestations of values, particularly the classic soldierly virtues of integrity, selflessness, and
courage. Shared in full measure by Bunker and Colby, they constituted a consistent and admirable basis for conduct of the war.

THE ENEMY RENEWED offensive actions in May 1968, striking in
what came to be known as "mini-Tet" at multiple locations,
concentrating on the area around Saigon. This time the allies
had plenty of advance warning, and were able to take preemptive action. Thus, while a total of twenty-seven VC and NVA
battalions were scheduled to take part in the attack on Saigon,
for example, elements of only nine battalions were in fact able
to enter the city. Within a week the ground attacks were defeated, again at a horrendous cost to the attackers. One estimate
was that 12,500 enemy were killed during the first two weeks
of May alone. That did not, however, serve to deter further
such costly offensives, former NVA Colonel Bui Tin later recalled. "Nor did we learn from the military failures of the Tet
Offensive," he wrote. "Instead, although we had lost the element of surprise, we went on to mount further major attacks in
May and September 1968 and suffered even heavier losses."[16]

There followed, beginning on 19 May (Ho Chi Minh's
birthday), what Colonel Hoang Ngoc Lung called "the fiercest
rocket attacks the enemy had ever unleashed against Saigon." In
June rockets crashed into the city on twelve consecutive days,
and enemy propagandists threatened a hundred rockets a day for
a hundred days. Already more than a hundred civilians had been
killed and more than four hundred wounded.[17]

In his departure press conference Westmoreland had dispar-
aged the importance of protecting Saigon against rocket attacks.
It was a very difficult thing to stop such attacks, he said, "almost
an impossibility." And besides, he added, although "there are
civilians getting killed, some properties being damaged . . . this
is of really no military consequence."[18]

Abrams saw the situation much differently, believing not only that human lives were important but also that South Vietnam's senior leadership could not function effectively in the siege mentality produced by frequent and indiscriminate enemy rocket attacks on the capital city. He took personal charge of a purposeful campaign to end such attacks, saying publicly that "we are going to put a stop" to enemy rocketing of Saigon "because we have to stop them, and we have the means to stop them."[19] Ambassador Bunker noted that indiscriminate rocketing of the civilian population was "an easy, cheap, and profitable tactic for the enemy so long as he has no fear of retaliation."[20] Abrams set about arranging some retaliation.

To Weyand, then commanding U.S forces in the region that included Saigon and its environs, Abrams observed that "we all together have not succeeded in defending Saigon as it must be defended if we are to guarantee that the government will not fall or be pressured into a solution that is not satisfactory. I believe the enemy has made Saigon/Gia Dinh his number one effort at this time; I have made it mine."[21] Soon counterbattery radars were installed, saturation day and night patrols scheduled, rivers swept, a network of observation towers erected around the city perimeter, the sewer system interdicted, specially trained dogs brought in for detection of munitions and infiltrators, helicopter gunships put into continuous nighttime orbit over likely firing positions, infantry put to work conducting thousands of ambushes. "We took the Rome plows and cut a 1,000-meter swathe from the Michelin all the way to the Song Be River," reported General Weyand in mid-July. "Before long we're going to have a ring quite a ways out from Saigon."

The Vietnamese named Major General Nguyen Van Minh, an experienced division commander, to be Military Governor of Saigon. Abrams, in turn, established a Capital Military Assistance Command and put Major General John Hay in charge, also giving him operational control of all U.S. forces in the capital region. Together these two officers worked to carry out

Abrams's dictum that rocketing of the capital was to cease.[22] Pretty soon the coordinated operation began uncovering caches of rockets and other weaponry, thus preempting their use in attacks on Saigon. In late June a MACV briefer could report that "not even a token of [the enemy's] threatened hundred-rocket-a-day attacks ever materialized" while noting the seizure two days earlier of 146 122mm rocket rounds in Hau Nghia Province.

One evening Abrams invited Major General Julian Ewell, then commanding the 9th Infantry Division, and his assistant division commander, Brigadier General Ira Hunt, to dinner. The Na Be oil refinery was in their division's tactical area of interest. During the visit Abrams brought out a presento, the tail fin from an NVA rocket—mounted on a plaque inscribed "The Last Rocket to Hit Na Be on the Saigon River." The two generals got the message.

In an earlier day, people visiting Saigon from other parts of the country might be taken to dine at the rooftop restaurant of the Rex, a hotel taken over for use as an American BOQ (Bachelor Officers' Quarters). Many who had this experience came away from it almost disoriented, feeling as though they had visited some kind of surrealistic landscape. There they were, safe and dry and with a couple of drinks under their belts, having a good dinner high above the city. And off in the distance, but not that far off, they could see the star shells and tracers and flares of people fighting for their lives, sometimes even hear the detonations of artillery or mortar rounds. It was an eerie and unsettling experience, and many troopers just in from their own piece of the battlefield felt uncomfortable, even guilty, watching in ease and safety the fiery traces of others who were not.

"The first year I was there," recalled the MACV Inspector General, Colonel Robert M. Cook, "every night you had aircraft flying around, dropping flares, and you could hear artillery close in around Saigon. Then General Abrams took over and, all of a sudden, it was quiet. Within a period of weeks, he'd pushed the goddamn fighting back out towards the enemy, as opposed to this siege-type stuff. It was almost like somebody just turned the volume down." When, on 22 August, an enemy rocket attack struck Saigon, it was the first in two months, clear evidence of the success of the countermeasures campaign.

By autumn General Davidson could quote an agent nick-named "Superspook" on what a tough target Saigon had become. "ARVN forces are defending Saigon so tightly," he said, "it is hard to find a weak point to attack." Caches were being discovered and seized, and B-52s were keeping secret zones under constant attack. To compound these problems, troops from North Vietnam did not know their way around Saigon. Thus "the majority [of cadres] believe an attack is possible only if defensive forces can be lured from the capital area."[23]

In those days Abrams was going over to the Capital Military District every Sunday morning to review progress in buttressing Saigon's defenses. Later he recalled an occasion when he arrived in time to witness "a damn formal ceremony in which they decorated a *goose*. That's right! They put them in a pen outside the outpost. And there's no way to sneak up on a goose at night. They just start going, just creating a hell of a racket. They're better than a dog. And this goose had alerted the outpost, they'd made a successful defense, and the Vietnamese were decorating the goose. And by god nobody was laughing!"

A COMBAT ACCIDENT during mini-Tet underscored the problem of damage done to civilians during combat in populated areas. A U.S. helicopter gunship, supporting efforts to root out enemy forces holed up in some residential buildings in Saigon, fired a rocket that hit a nearby location where a group of rather senior Vietnamese officials were watching the action. Six were killed and two others wounded. The matter was complicated by the fact that all those injured were strong supporters of Vice President Nguyen Cao Ky, and charges were made that it had been a deliberate attack rather than an accident. Even putting aside the impossibility of the helicopter pilot's having known that those people were in that location, a joint U.S.–South Vietnamese investigation established that a malfunction could have been responsible, although it might also have been crew error in the midst of a heated battle.

Abrams, although not yet in formal command, reacted strongly. He had been furious with Weyand for what he thought was overuse of fire support in the fighting around Y Bridge, something he later learned had been prompted by orders from Westmoreland. Now he established a prohibition on action by artillery, bombing, or gunships within the city except with his personal authorization, then convened a task force to devise better tactics for dealing with enemy forces mixed in with the population.[24] Abrams also put Cook, the Inspector General, to work on the problem. Cook had aerial reconnaissance photographs taken of the affected areas of Saigon, then compared them with earlier photos to determine just what damage had been caused in what precincts. He correlated that with the units operating in those areas, and with the ammunition records, nailing down who had done what and where. Then Cook learned that, over a period of time, certain units had been abusing the rules of engagement—for example, getting clearance to fire a thousand meters to the front, then adding on to that as they moved forward without getting new clearances for the advanced areas. Cook reported all this to Abrams, who instructed him, "Cook, rewrite the rules of engagement." Cook did, and the new procedures remained in effect for the rest of the war.

Abrams also sought to tutor the South Vietnamese on the need for restraint, even in heavy contact. He took the occasion of an address to the first class of the National Defense College of Vietnam to speak to the issue. "I can assure you," he stressed, "that no matter how frustrating, no matter what our past experience, restraint will and must govern virtually all of our activities." Thus, he explained, "we cannot apply the full firepower capabilities of our military force throughout the countryside at will, for to do so would further endanger the lives and property and the governmental relationships with the very people we are all fighting to protect: your own citizens of Vietnam." Telling these experienced officers "we're here to win," Abrams then defined what that meant. "To win is to achieve our fundamental allied objective: an independent South Vietnam, free to determine your own future."[25]

Later Abrams, seeking to dramatize the need for restraint to his own staff, recalled an episode during mini-Tet. He had been out to see Lieutenant General Fred Weyand at II Field Force, and Weyand had briefed him on how successful they had been at countering the enemy offensive. Then, said Abrams, "as I rode back in my helicopter after hearing how well we were doing, smoke was billowing up in Saigon, flames shooting up in the air. I have estimated that we can successfully defend Saigon seven more times, and then we're going to be faced with the embarrassment that there's no *city* left. And I don't know *how* the hell we're going to explain these nine successful defenses of Saigon, but no goddamn city."

When, near the end of summer, the enemy mounted his third offensive of the year, Ambassador Bunker was able to comment in a cable to the President on the "great care in our use of air and artillery," which had "resulted in far fewer civilian casualties and property destruction than in May or during Tet."[26]

LATER, WHEN General William B. Rosson arrived to succeed Andrew Goodpaster as Abrams's deputy, it was very clear to him how things had changed since his last tour of duty in Vietnam. "Abrams (with Bunker) had made it 'clear and hold' instead of 'search and destroy,'" he observed succinctly. Said Bunker of "clear and hold" as the tactical approach, "it proved to be a better policy than the policy of attrition. The policy of attrition simply meant under those circumstances a very prolonged type of warfare, whereas if you can clear and hold and keep an area secure and keep the enemy out, psychologically as well as from a military point of view you have got a better situation. In effect, you shifted the initiative from the enemy to you."[27]

A subsequent analysis of these new tactics came from an unexpected source, a group led by Daniel Ellsberg that in late 1968 and early 1969 prepared a paper on the situation in Vietnam. The section "U.S. Military Efforts" reported that "in the last six months our military efforts against enemy main force units seem to be significantly improved," citing changed operational tactics under Abrams as the reason. "We are using more small patrols for intelligence and spoiling, and we are conducting fewer large-scale sweeps, and those sweeps that we are conducting are smaller in territorial scope. General Abrams has begun to concentrate much more on area control than on kills. He has been aided in this approach by his defense in depth, particularly around the major cities."[28] Saigon, the most major city of all, was a showcase for this new approach.

The impact of these changes on the Saigon government's outlook was just as Abrams had anticipated. "I am more optimistic now," confirmed newly appointed Premier Tran Van Huong. "It is working much better. Abrams . . . is a good man, shrewd, sincere, a fighter. No politics."[29]

Even General Vo Nguyen Giap, the venerable North Vietnamese commander, testified to the changes. "General Abrams was different and had different fighting tactics," said Giap. "He based his leadership on research; he studied his own and others' experiences to see what he could apply to the real situation here."[30]

In due course Abrams changed what he could—*everything* he could. He inherited an awkward chain of command, lack of unified operational control over South Vietnamese and other allied forces, an elaborate and wasteful base camp system, an exposed string of static border camps, severe geographical and procedural restrictions on conduct of the war, greatly diminished domestic support. These he had to live with. The rest he changed.

3

Third Offensive

ONCE HE WAS IN command, Abrams confronted urgent tasks in every one of the multiple dimensions of the job. There were years of neglect to be made up in the role of senior advisor to the South Vietnamese. Working closely with Bunker, he was responsive and patient in dealing with often uncoordinated and sometimes conflicting instructions from various superiors in Washington. And as field commander he was very clear on how the job must be done. "The one unforgivable sin will be to gloss over or ignore shortcomings which demand prompt remedy," he cabled his field commanders in an early message, one in which he also said that "the result I am looking for is a conscious, determined effort by all allied forces to seek battle with a will to win."[1] In the United States the leadership, the people, and the media might have given up on the war, but in Vietnam Abrams had a different outlook.

Abrams's forces were formidable indeed: 7 divisions, which included 112 maneuver battalions, 60 artillery battalions, and some 400 helicopters. With support forces, the total came to 543,400 troops at the high-water mark in early 1969.[2] Added to these American forces were Free World Military Assistance Forces (FWMAF) from South Korea, Thailand, Australia, New Zealand, and the Philippines, and indigenous South Vietnamese

forces that, in all components, would over succeeding years
grow to 1.1 million men. (Significantly, Defense Secretary
Melvin Laird was told by MACV on his first visit to Saigon in
March 1969 that the estimated level of RVNAF that could be
sustained over a period of years by Vietnam's manpower base
was 855,000.)[3]

Control over these forces was fragmented, both with respect
to U.S. elements and more generally. Abrams, for example, had
no authority over U.S. Navy forces offshore, nor over the
bombing campaign in North Vietnam, nor over South Vietnamese or other allied forces, except as he might be able to persuade
or influence their commanders to act. "Countrywide," said
Charlie Corcoran, "there was really nobody in command. I
don't think Westy ever really understood that he wasn't in command. Abe understood that from day one."

THE MAIN FORUM for discussion of tactics, intelligence, logistics,
and in fact the entire spectrum of concerns dealt with by the
top American military leadership in Vietnam was the Weekly
Intelligence Estimate Update (WIEU—pronounced woo—for
short). This session, typically held on Saturday mornings at
Headquarters MACV, brought together Abrams, his deputy, and
the staff principals—those responsible for operations, logistics,
and the like—for a crowded agenda of briefings and debate.
Once monthly, the slate of participants was expanded by bringing in the principal subordinate commanders from around the
country for what was called a Commanders WIEU. At those
sessions in particular, the J-2 (MACV Deputy Chief of Staff for
Intelligence) often presented estimates or evaluations on topics
specified by Abrams, followed by wide-ranging discussion of the
conclusions and their implications for allied actions.

Abrams, who had inherited the WIEUs from his predecessor,
began the first session after assuming command by saying that
they would continue these meetings much as in the past and
then, from time to time, he might introduce some changes. The

second briefer up began by saying, "General, I've got some good news." Abrams put his hand up, stopping the man right there. "Gentlemen," he said, "we'll have the first change in the procedures of these meetings. From now on, we'll take up the bad news first, then if there is any time left, we'll take up the good news."

Subsequently Abrams broadened and expanded what had been almost exclusively a concentration on military aspects of the war. "What I have in mind here," he explained, "first of all, is to see if we can come to grips with a little bit more comprehension of what the situation is here in South Vietnam with respect to the enemy. In other words—the military campaign, that's one feature." But Abrams wanted more, "so we try to produce here next Saturday a reasonably comprehensive picture of the whole game Hanoi is playing in South Vietnam."

Soon detailed analytical briefings on North Vietnam's political and economic situation became prominent, as well as those of Laos and Cambodia, the status of negotiations in Paris, and cease-fire contingency planning. With respect to South Vietnam, the agenda grew to include pacification, expansion of territorial forces, manpower issues, economic reform, elections, and refugee assistance. Abrams was not neglecting the military campaign, but using the broadened perspective to facilitate use of forces to better advantage, to wage a smarter and more availing war. Soon attendance by Ambassador Bunker became frequent, whereas earlier the embassy had seldom been represented at these critical weekly planning sessions.

The J-2 was responsible for putting together the WIEU. From the summer of 1967 to the summer of 1969, that officer was Phillip B. Davidson, who served in this key post for a year under Westmoreland and another year with Abrams. Davidson left in the summer of 1969 and was replaced by William E. Potts. Davidson and Potts were both highly professional intelligence officers, but they were much different in style and personality. Davidson was the more freewheeling, willing to risk (sometimes unwisely) improvising the answer to an unanticipated question raised by the commander, not as punctilious in closing the loop on matters raised during the briefings, less self-disciplined in confining himself to his intelligence portfolio, and therefore more willing to volunteer opinions on operational and other matters. On the other hand, he was flexible and resourceful, qualities that enabled him to successfully restructure the weekly intelligence input when Abrams wanted to change the approach used under Westmoreland.

Davidson was under the cloud of having failed to warn the command of the enemy's Tet Offensive, a huge black mark on his career that could never be expunged. Though he had predicted an enemy attack at that season, he anticipated neither its size, its extent, nor the treacherous timing in the midst of the Tet observances. General Lung, the J-2 of South Vietnam's Joint General Staff, offered a comparison. "At the time of the 1968 Tet offensive," judged Lung, "the United States did not appear to be as capable in the production of intelligence as during the subsequent stages of the war."[4]

Abrams pushed hard for more comprehensive and more timely intelligence, and Davidson tried hard to please him. "Abrams was so sensitive to intelligence, he really knew so much about it, he considered it to be *the* most important aspect of his operation," Davidson recalled.[5]

While the WIEU always began with a weather briefing, these were not just cursory weather reports, but extended analyses of the seasonal weather as forecast and as compared with the historical norm, as well as the actual and anticipated impact of the weather on combat operations, especially air operations. This constituted a veritable banquet of weather for connoisseurs of winds aloft, cloud cover, visibility and ceilings, rainfall, monsoons, trafficability and soil conditions, temperature gradients, tide—all provided in current, anticipated, and historical versions.

The weather was an enormously important aspect of warfare in Southeast Asia, the whole enterprise being shaped by the recurring pattern of wet and dry seasons produced by the alternating northeast and southwest monsoons, and Abrams and his associates took the weather very seriously indeed. The weather briefers were intense, professional, and highly competent, even though perforce often the bearers of bad news. (During the first nine days of October 1969, for example, fifty-nine inches of rain fell at Hue–Phu Bai, greater than any *monthly* total recorded over the past thirty years at any station in Vietnam.) Abrams had only one complaint, that the weather officers sometimes seemed too damned cheerful in briefing the foul weather he then had to contend with.

Typically "out-country" developments, regional matters taking place outside the Republic of Vietnam, followed the weather. First came North Vietnam, both political and military aspects. Then Laos, same aspects, followed by Cambodia. Only then would the briefings turn to South Vietnam.

Beginning in the north, and moving southward, each corps tactical zone was reviewed in terms of recent enemy activity. Then the pacification briefer would cover his subject, followed by naval operations and air operations. A forecast of combat operations concluded the session, which typically lasted three or four hours overall.

Statistics were an inevitable part of the WIEU briefings—weapons captured, equipment operational, replacements assigned, ammunition expended, killed and wounded on both sides, refugees created and resettled, pacification estimates, budget figures, and on and on. Abrams, who once described himself as "constitutionally suspicious," often warned of the inherent limitations of statistical measures. "You've got to have the statistics, there's no question about that, absolutely no doubt about it," he said to the staff. "It's the way you get things pointed, and the way you commit assets and that sort of thing. But we've got to fight *all the time* to look *past* those, and bear in mind what the *real* purpose is, and then face the *real* results in a realistic way. And it's tough." So was the job ahead. "The thing that remains for us is completely *undramatic*," Abrams acknowledged. "It's just a lot of damn *drudgery*, in a way, in terms of military things and so on. But that's what we've got to do."

As implied by the name, the WIEUs were a weekly occurrence. They involved, besides a large and varied cast of briefers, some two dozen staff officers from MACV Headquarters and the supporting naval and air elements. The monthly Commanders WIEU also brought in the senior officers from each corps area, the three-star field force and corps commanders, the Marine amphibious force commander, and so on.

These were all-U.S. meetings, although portions often were subsequently presented to key South Vietnamese or other allied leaders, visiting dignitaries, and higher echelons in the chain of command in Hawaii or Washington. Following each session, the MACV J-2 prepared a comprehensive reporting cable for General Abrams to send to the Chairman of the Joint Chiefs of Staff.

"We devote Saturdays to wrestling with this thing," Abrams told a visiting officer. "We try generally to have one or two things that have been done in depth over a period of time, trying to challenge what we think. The *intelligence* is the most *important* part of this whole damn *thing*. And if that's good, we can handle *anything*."

Topics covered in greater depth included the enemy's infiltration program and efforts to combat it, for instance, or plans for redeployment of U.S. forces. There was virtually no topic that did not interest Abrams, and no one could ever be sure what would come up at the WIEU. One week, for example, he observed more or less out of the blue that in Vietnam "the only entrepreneur that I know of that's tried to play it straight is 'Coke.' I guess they want to make money, but they *have* played it straight." When each week's agenda had been completed, everyone in attendance was invited for lunch in the garden at General Abrams's quarters.

ABRAMS TOOK THE occasion of the first Fourth of July he was in command to convene a conference attended by his top commanders throughout South Vietnam and by the MACV staff. By then they had dealt with the second enemy offensive of the year, the "mini-Tet" of early May. Abrams had the briefers go through the current situation—enemy infiltration and apparent plans for future operations, allied units and logistics, a classic estimate of the situation. The conclusion was simple and unadorned. As far as the enemy was concerned, "the war is not going well for him." The enemy had designated 1968 "the year of decision," but those expectations were not being realized, nor would they be.

In the ensuing give-and-take Abrams revealed much about his own outlook on the nature of the war and how it should be fought. The key was of course security for the people in South Vietnam's villages and hamlets. And that was not yet the norm. Part of the difficulty was simply understanding the nature of the war. "The military—all of us in the military—we have a little *problem,*" pointed out Abrams. "We've got an *institutional* problem, I guess. We recognize *trouble,* you know, where people are *shooting* or *fighting* or *punching* or *rioting* and so on. And that's the kind—we know all about that trouble. You know, what it *looks* like, what it *smells* like, and what you *do* about it. But this trouble that nobody can *see,* and nobody can *hear,* and so on, but is just *meaner* than hell—just going around collecting taxes, quietly snatching somebody and taking him off and shooting him, and so on—." That took a lot of adjusting to deal with effectively. And the answer was not conventional military operations, or at least not those alone, not just attrition of enemy main force units, not just the war of the big battalions.

"What we've *been* doing," said Abrams, tellingly contrasting the new approach to previous tactics, "is sort of a treadmill. We have to find these same units, and they're always getting ready to hit Saigon or Tay Ninh, so we go after that, and we're whacking them with B-52s, tac air and artillery, and dumping in on them and piling on and that sort of thing. And the *history* of that is that we go ahead and mash it all up, but then he sends a lot more guys down and builds it back up and we mash it all up again and just—you know, cause a lot of casualties and so on. Now the way to put a *stop* to it, the way to get off the *treadmill,* is to go after this *other* part which always seems to *survive. This* is the *way* to *run* the *war! Our* war!!"

NOWHERE WAS THE excruciating nature of the war in Vietnam more apparent than in the efforts to reach a negotiated solution. And nowhere, it may be argued, was the enemy's manipulative skill more apparent. During the spring of 1968, following Lyndon Johnson's landmark speech opting out of the presidential campaign and cutting back on the bombing of North Vietnam, the Washington community worked toward anticipated peace negotiations. As they did so, concluded an official historian, "they became increasingly convinced that negotiations would be drawn out, with no immediate settlement of the war. This realization led to a rather sudden change in their priorities in June"—in other words, just as General Abrams was assuming command in Vietnam. LBJ wanted more prominence given to the role of South Vietnamese forces and substitution of those forces for American troops wherever possible. "Any measures that could reduce American casualties and muffle domestic criticism of the war effort were critical in a presidential election year," wrote Army Chief Historian Jeffrey Clarke. "While visiting Saigon in July, [Secretary of Defense Clark] Clifford personally communicated these views to General Abrams."[6]

While it seems logical that Clifford would not otherwise make the 10,000-mile trip, he later claimed a lapse of memory, then denied that was his mission in July of 1968. "I wouldn't remember that," said Clifford. "Instructions to General Abrams would be in writing, they wouldn't be oral." When asked if he said anything like "General, we're going to bring this army home," he answered, "I wouldn't think so." Asked if he conveyed any instructions about holding down American casualties, Clifford's answer was "I wouldn't remember that, either."[7]

These were the crucial issues at a point of genuine crisis in American politics. Clifford was the Secretary of Defense who, by his own contemporary accounts, turned LBJ around on his attitude toward the war. (It now appears, however, that Clifford did not so much turn LBJ around as isolate and undermine him, making it untenable for him to continue the policies he had brought Clifford in to prosecute.) Vietnamization and American casualties were the central issues. Perhaps an activist, even radicalized, defense secretary went to the war zone to confer with his field commander and had no instructions for him, but given the temper of the times it is hard to credit.

Andrew Goodpaster, then deputy COMUSMACV, remembered the Clifford visit well, relating it to a previous trip he had taken with the man, the same flight on which he had tangled with Averell Harriman. "I went over to Paris in a plane with Secretary Clifford and Harriman and Vance," said Goodpaster, "and we talked on the way over, and this was a real eye-opener to me, because Clifford started right out saying, 'Now, what you have to do over here is bring this thing to an end on the best terms that we can get.' And I said, 'Mr. Secretary, that's not the guidance we had from the President.' He said, 'No, in practical terms we've got to get out on the best terms that we can arrange.' And we had quite an argument over this."[8]

As a result, said Goodpaster, "I knew that this was in his mind, and when he came out to South Vietnam this is what he was stating. We had a meeting headed by Ellsworth Bunker, the ambassador, and Abrams and myself, and when Clifford came out with this—it was woven into what he was saying, but I brought it right out into the open—I pointed out that there was nothing in our guidance that said anything like that, that our guidance was really quite different than that."[9] Clearly, at least from Goodpaster's perspective, Clifford was freelancing, and in Paris it would soon become apparent that Harriman was doing the same.

In his memoirs Clifford says only that during the visit to Saigon he told Bunker and Deputy Ambassador Sam Berger "that we would be derelict in our duty if we failed to make use of the six months left in the Johnson Administration to seek an honorable end to the war," and that "Bunker and Berger were startled by my vehemence and unalterably opposed to my suggestions." As a result, added Clifford, "when I left Saigon for Hawaii I was depressed. With the exception of Nick Katzenbach in Washington and Averell Harriman and Cy Vance in Paris, I was an isolated voice among senior people in the Administration."[10] Goodpaster had had it right.

Major General Charlie Corcoran briefed Clifford during that visit. "It was clear that from then on the national policy was to tear that thing down and get out as gracefully as we could," he recalled. "Abe knew that. Wheeler knew that. But Abe still had to do the best he could." And, said Corcoran, "the most significant thing that happened during my tour was the Clifford visit. He got mad because we weren't promoting the Vietnamese to general fast enough," devastating evidence of his tenuous grasp of the problem.

IN THE LATE SUMMER of 1968, Tet and the ensuing mini-Tet of May had quieted down as the enemy prepared for yet another such operation, what came to be called the Third Offensive. Douglas Pike, then a political officer in the American embassy in Saigon, believed that the enemy was at that point going through "a period of great doctrinal indecision." Nothing tried to date had brought the expected victory, and factions in Hanoi were advocating a range of adaptations. One, led by Foreign Minister Nguyen Duy Trinh, favored negotiated settlement. An-

other, following Truong Thien, was for protracted war along
Maoist lines. General Giap advocated "more of the same," a
continuation of the current course of action. Pike, reported
Ambassador Robert Komer, "feels in the end the protracted war
school will finally prevail."[11]

There came a point where the enemy was indeed changing
tactics, at least to a modest extent, motivated in part by an apparent need to hold down casualties after the heavy losses sustained at Tet 1968 and in the May 1968 "mini-Tet." Thus, when
he finally launched the Third Offensive in August, after a series
of delays imposed by preemptive allied operations, there were
some differences. For one thing, pointed out a MACV briefer,
the enemy was employing primarily what were called "attacks
by fire," artillery and rocket and mortar barrages directed at
friendly positions, but with few accompanying ground assaults
and "no attempt to launch a simultaneous countrywide offensive. The enemy seems to be purposely staggering his attacks to
stretch out this offensive," MACV concluded. "I'm frankly baf-
fled by what the enemy's up to," confessed Ambassador Komer.

Abrams detailed what *MACV* had been up to, and what that
might have had to do with the enemy's actions. "Some time
ago we thought there would be a third offensive," he began.
"We thought that the enemy was *prepared* for it. So, rather than
wait for it to *come,* the most intensified intelligence effort *yet—*
more patrolling, *more* focusing—and applying B-52s, tac air,
searching and getting caches, probably on a scale which we
haven't done before." Thus what the enemy had done, said
Abrams, "I choose to believe is not *his* plan. It's what he's been
able to do with his plan, with the efforts that we've made against
it in all the days and weeks preceding it. In his plan he's bound
to have provided in there for disruption of this and loss of that
and some *contingencies,* but I think he had a *better* plan than what
we have now seen executed, and it's been *screwed up* on him,
and this is the *best* he could do with what he *started out* to do—
so far."

With all this going on, Abrams continued to hammer on the essence of his new approach to conduct of the war. "The body count does not have much to do with the outcome of the war," he stressed to senior commanders. "Some of the things I do think important are that we preempt or defeat the enemy's major military operations and eliminate or render ineffective the major portion of his guerrillas and his infrastructure—the political, administrative and para-military structure on which his whole movement depends." And, added Abrams, "it is far more significant that we neutralize one thousand of these guerrillas and infrastructure than kill 10,000 North Vietnamese soldiers."[12]

It soon became apparent that the troops were getting the word. Caches captured in the month before the Third Offensive began were nearly 40 percent greater than those taken in the month preceding the May offensive. In the I Corps area they were nearly double, while in IV Corps they tripled. Secondary explosions produced by B-52 strikes followed a similar pattern— more than doubled countrywide and quadrupled in III Corps, signifying widespread destruction of precious ammunition and fuel. Clearly these losses of his carefully prepositioned military wherewithal were having an impact on enemy capabilities.

Some huge cache recoveries underscored the magnitude and probably the long-term duration of the enemy's preparations for combat in the South. At a place nicknamed the Pineapple Plantation, a Communist base area less than twenty miles from Saigon, searchers found a 4,000-bed hospital that even had refrigeration and whole blood. In the complex were 3,500 bunkers, a thousand of which had two feet of overhead concrete protection. "Well, this isn't any monkey business—this is for real," observed Abrams. "These things were not built in one night." Pleased with the discovery of this extensive complex, Abrams emphasized that finds of this kind were "just as important as defeating a communist battalion. In fact it is more important, because it never winds up in a big battle with a lot of destruction."[13]

Given the resulting situation, thought Abrams, the enemy commander was being profligate with the lives of his men. "I think he's one of the few guys in the world right now who would try to run a military campaign down here in *any* kind of shape. He hasn't got the *tickets* to make it work. And what he's doing right now—it's just an *expenditure* of men. He's *groping*."

There remained a question, too, as to what the enemy leadership in Hanoi really knew about what was taking place on the battlefields of South Vietnam. Long after the war was over, for example, a study of the war published in Hanoi claimed that during the 1968 Tet Offensive, Communist forces had killed 43,000 Americans.[14] Given that about 58,000 Americans died during the entire war (some 47,000 of them due to enemy action), that was an astounding figure, one it is hard to imagine they really believed, especially long after the fact. But perhaps they did. If so, the leadership was making decisions on the basis of some extraordinarily flawed data.[15]

Meanwhile, the enemy's attacks came up against a much differently arrayed defending force. One journalist—noting that the 3rd Marine Division was now deployed horizontally along the border with North Vietnam, the 4th Infantry Division vertically along the western border with Laos and Cambodia, and the bulk of the remaining forces, some eight divisions' worth, in the critical region of Saigon and its environs—called the new dispositions "a strategic somersault." A year earlier, he observed, "these allied units were sweeping the remote Communist strongholds near Vietnam's borders."[16]

DURING THE SUMMER the enemy was positioned in the DMZ (Demilitarized Zone) with a lot of heavy artillery and rockets, causing great difficulty for allied forces within range. A lot of fuel was blown up at Cua Viet, and a big ammunition dump went up in Dong Ha. "They were giving us *hell*," said Abrams, "but we had so many problems down here, we just had to kind of *take* it." But, while that was going on, a lot of intelligence and photography and so on were being collected, and a surprise was being prepared.

B-52 strikes at that time were conducted in waves, typically with an hour and a half or two hours between one wave and the next. Abrams went to General Spike Momyer and asked him whether there was "any way you could cut that out and just kind of line them all up and have them come one right after another, just keep it *up?*" Momyer worked something out with SAC, a kind of *compression* thing. The sortie rate was then sixty a day and, using this technique, you could do forty-eight in the morning and forty-eight at night, then the next day down to thirty-six to accommodate the needed recycling, maintenance, and so on, and you could compress each wave into about an hour and forty minutes.

When this was all ready, Abrams told them to take it up to the DMZ and see how the enemy gunners liked it. About seven o'clock the first morning, in came forty-eight B-52s, all dumping their loads within an hour and forty minutes. "Then," recalled Abrams, "the artillery, the tac air, the naval gunfire took up and had a great time all day. And then, about 1600 in the afternoon, here came forty-eight more and did it. We did that for seven days. It costs you sorties—you lose them. It's *expensive*. We did it for seven days. I want to tell you, it was forty-five days before there was ever a fucking *round* fired out of the DMZ! Forty-five *days!* And Xuan Thuy told Ambassador Harriman, 'This bombing is *insane!*' Best BDA we ever had!" That meant Xuan Thuy was providing gratifyingly authoritative bomb damage assessment. Abrams had commanded a tank battalion in the World War II breakout from Normandy, a classic use of thunderous bombing to pave the way. The DMZ raids, he thought, made that earlier campaign look like "sort of an *experimental* thing."

4

Intelligence

ABRAMS THOUGHT incisively about the enemy, about his objectives and what motivated him, and in the course of it developed substantial respect for him. Critical of missed opportunities on the part of enemy commanders, and of their willingness to waste lives in losing situations, Abrams nevertheless admired their tenacity, logistical resourcefulness, and planning ability. "He always has something fairly long-range," he observed of the enemy. "I mean, he doesn't plan just for Monday." And, he once observed, "adversity does nothing but strengthen him."

The political regime in the North was viewed much differently. There American prisoners were tortured and abused, sometimes even murdered, by their captors.[1] Military facilities, such as the antiaircraft gun on which Jane Fonda posed, were deliberately crowded in next to civilian areas, almost ensuring extensive collateral damage if they were attacked, thus using American scruples against causing such injuries to inhibit attack. Secretary of State Dean Rusk, remarking that Americans were frequently criticized for civilian casualties in North Vietnam, said, "I have on my conscience the additional American casualties that we took in an effort to prevent civilian casualties in that struggle—in the North as well as in South Vietnam—under the rules of engagement."[2]

North Vietnam's treatment of its own people was consistent with how it fought the war. "When I first went to Hanoi in 1967 I didn't want to see what the regime was like, and I didn't," admitted French journalist Olivier Todd. "When I went back to Hanoi in 1973, it struck me forcefully—these people are red fascists."[3] In an incessant terrorist campaign against civilians in the South, the enemy showed this true nature even more clearly. While loudly protesting civilian casualties in North Vietnam supposedly caused by allied bombing, casualties that were minuscule by any reasonable measure, North Vietnam's agents in the South systematically murdered, wounded, kidnapped, and impressed thousands of South Vietnamese civilians. At Hue, temporarily under his control during the 1968 Tet Offensive, the enemy seized the opportunity to execute, hands tied behind their backs, some 3,000 civilians whose bodies were then dumped in mass graves. Rockets fired indiscriminately at cities, grenades thrown into school yards, bombs in churches—all these and more were part of the North Vietnamese way of war. And of all this the antiwar movement had little or nothing to say, then or later.

These enemy proclivities—indifference to their own combat losses and to the harm done to innocents alike—produced a disparate pattern of casualties. South Vietnamese armed forces, while suffering substantial losses, to be sure, inflicted greatly disproportionate casualties on enemy armed forces. In the civilian populations, just the reverse was the case. Since no ground combat took place in North Vietnam, and the allies structured their bombing there to minimize civilian casualties, relatively few civilians were killed in the North. In the South, meanwhile, enemy terrorism and the rocketing and shelling of cities ensured a high civilian death toll. Douglas Pike estimates that South Vietnamese *civilian* casualties reached the staggering total of 465,000

killed and 935,000 wounded, those in the North only a tiny
fraction of that.[4]

IT WAS WIDELY believed that the enemy had numerous penetration agents in South Vietnam's government and armed forces,
and indeed there were frequent indications that this was in fact
the case. South Vietnamese commanders also were notoriously
careless about operational security, providing in the process
much valuable information to an alert and watchful enemy.
What is less well known, however, is that the enemy was similarly at risk. General Le Nguyen Khang, while commanding
ARVN III Corps, had an agent in the 9th VC Division and was
tapping him weekly for information. Davidson often referred to
a highly trusted agent who in early August 1968 reported that
allied operations had caused the enemy to postpone an expected
offensive. "As much credibility as we give to the gold-plated
agent's report," Davidson told Abrams, "we would still like a
little confirmatory evidence."

   That confirmation was often available from other well-
placed sources, one of them in COSVN (Central Office for
South Vietnam), controlling headquarters for enemy operations
in the southern provinces of South Vietnam. "I think the most
dramatic proof" of how intelligence had improved from a year
earlier, Davidson told a conference on intelligence collection,
"has been the breakthrough in the high-level agents. The
COSVN guy, the A-22, Superspook, 23, 24—the guys that are
really giving it to you the way it is! You don't have to say, 'Gee,
I wonder if this is right or not.' You know *that* guy's telling you
the truth." For this the South Vietnamese deserved the credit,
Davidson said. "That is an ARVN contribution, first rate."

THROUGHOUT THE earlier years, when General Westmoreland
was still in command, efforts to track and calculate infiltration
of enemy troops down the Ho Chi Minh Trail were both

difficult and controversial. Often there was a lag of months before intelligence officers could identify with any assurance the
number and destination of those who had come down the trail,
information painstakingly assembled from prisoner-of-war interrogations, captured documents, and agent reports. Repeated re-
calculations and revisions of earlier figures, as more information
was obtained, undermined the credibility of MACV infiltration
estimates and contributed to the order of battle controversy that
raged during the latter stages of Westmoreland's tenure, then
erupted again some years later as a result of the CBS Television
documentary *The Uncounted Enemy: A Vietnam Deception* and
Westmoreland's ensuing ill-fated libel suit against the network.

This frustrating situation was dramatically, almost magically,
swept away just at the beginning of General Abrams's tenure by
acquisition of a new and remarkably accurate means of determining details of enemy movements south. U.S. intelligence began to intercept, break, and read encoded enemy radio traffic
that accurately and consistently reported the numbers, progress,
and destinations of infiltration groups moving down the Ho Chi
Minh Trail.

Traffic on the trail was controlled by the General Directorate
of Rear Services (GDRS) in Hanoi and administered by the
Commo-Liaison Bureau through a series of military way sta-
tions, known as *binh trams*, at intervals along the route. Each
station was numbered, and therefore individually identifiable.
Binh Tram 33 in Laos, for example, was in the vicinity of Base
Area 604 near Tchepone. The system of *binh trams*, later further
expanded, extended initially from Hanoi through North Vietnam and Laos to the area where North Vietnam, Laos, and
South Vietnam meet. "Almost the entire Cambodian–South
Vietnamese border area is one continuous staging area," a
MACV analyst later concluded, with twenty or so bases in the
complex.

The *binh trams* controlled a second type of facility associated
with the trail, known as commo-liaison stations, or T-stations

for short. These also were numbered—for example, T-10. The mission of the commo-liaison people was to facilitate movement of those traversing the trail. There were also what were called K-facilities, providing permanent supply warehouses at intervals along the route. And there was one other feature of the trail, recalled Bui Tin, who had twice traversed the route—near each military staging post was a cemetery for those who perished along the way.[5]

A headquarters designated the 559th Transportation Group, located in Base Area 604, operated the trail in Laos under direction of the GDRS. Each *binh tram* exercised operational control over its supporting security forces, transportation, antiaircraft, medical, and engineer units, as well as the commo-liaison stations, an aggregation that reached approximately regimental size for each *binh tram*. Altogether an estimated 40,000 people were engaged in operating the trail under the 559th Group.

Suddenly the allies gained access to a tremendous source of information on all this activity, one whose significance went far beyond logistics. "Through interception of Rear Services messages," said a MACV analyst, "we've been able to determine the rate at which infiltration groups are put in the pipeline for movement south and their probable destinations in South Vietnam."[6]

Calling it a "new dimension" in knowledge of enemy infiltration, MACV's infiltration expert noted that this all began on 1 November 1967 with the first recorded intercept of a North Vietnamese Rear Services communication containing references to a numbered infiltration group. It took several months to grasp the significance of this new source, but by mid-March 1968, when fourteen groups had been detected, the analysts realized that a large infiltration effort was under way. During March and April, following the 1968 Tet Offensive, 114 groups, totaling nearly 66,000 men, were reflected in intercepted communications as commencing infiltration. Then, beginning in mid-June 1968, groups containing large numbers of sick and wounded were detected in apparent northward movement. Some of these groups included substantial numbers of apparently able-bodied men, and the analysts at MACV concluded that this represented withdrawal of the 304th NVA Division.

During the summer and into autumn, infiltration tapered off dramatically. In subsequent years similar cyclical variations in the traffic were observed, leading to the conclusion that the enemy anticipated periods of peak offensive activity, as well as the need for substantial replacements in the wake of them, and put troops into the pipeline accordingly. He apparently also was careful not to ship men down too soon, lest he have to provide rations and other support for them over a longer time than necessary, thereby increasing his logistical burden.

THIS DETAILED information on enemy infiltration depended on intercepts of communications emanating from Binh Tram 19, one of the way stations on the trail. Later the communications link between Binh Tram 8 and T-12 would be the principal source of information on infiltration of both personnel and matériel.[7]

Since each infiltration group was identified by a four-digit number, it was possible to keep track of them sequentially. During 1968 there were 247 groups identified in communications intelligence, plus 77 probable gap groups—groups not picked up in COMINT but believed to exist because groups with higher and lower numbers had been identified.

In making estimates of infiltration, then, MACV J-2 reported all the groups identified as having entered the pipeline, then gave another figure that included the gap groups, the premise being that those groups would in all probability turn up eventually; in fact a formal set of criteria for acceptance of gap groups was eventually developed and applied. In late September 1968, for example, MACV J-2 estimated that 191,000 men had infiltrated south from North Vietnam since the beginning of the

year, and projected an additional 16,000 for arrival during October–December, giving a total for the year of 207,000. If the
gap groups were added in, pointed out MACV J-2 Phil Davidson, the total would reach 229,000.[8]

The importance of this intercept capability was underscored
by Davidson at a conference on intelligence collection in the
autumn of 1968. "I think unquestionably one of the things that's
caused success is communications intelligence, perhaps the biggest," he said, especially the newfound capability to monitor
infiltration. "That's *really* changed a hell of a lot of things."
Abrams agreed. "Replacements are a thermometer of anticipated
combat activity," he observed, and with the new intelligence
capability it was possible to know where those replacements
were headed, in what numbers, and on what schedule. Such
information was invaluable when it came to arranging a proper
reception.

Using accumulated historical data on travel times to the various destinations, MACV intelligence could predict with impressive accuracy and assurance how many enemy troops would
arrive on the battlefield, and when and where they would appear. "Now we're getting even ahead of them getting in the
pipeline," an intelligence briefer exulted at one of the first
WIEUs after Abrams took command, meaning that with this
new capability they could identify the size, timing, and composition of infiltration groups even before they began their journey to the South.

This intelligence was also useful in assessing both enemy
intentions and capabilities. In early July 1968, for example, after
the enemy's Tet Offensive and a second round of attacks in May
had been turned back decisively, it was apparent that the enemy
still had not abandoned his tactic of mounting a coordinated
series of attacks at many locations throughout Vietnam, for the
infiltration data gave evidence of a buildup for yet another round
of such assaults. "I have put considerable reliance on keeping
track of these groups as a measure of the size of the problem

we're going to be facing down here in South Vietnam," Abrams told his intelligence officer once the new tracking system had proved itself.

Infiltration groups were observed to travel down what was called by the North Vietnamese their "strategic transportation corridor"—otherwise known as the Ho Chi Minh Trail—at an average rate of 12.2 kilometers per day, except for those going to the COSVN area, the Communist headquarters for the most southerly regions of the battlefield, who averaged only 10.5 kilometers a day. MACV intelligence initially used a figure of 565 men per group as the average, a number adjusted at later times to 568 and then 570. That was going into the pipeline. For arrival estimates they used 420 men per group, reflecting estimated attrition due to bombing, illness, and desertions. At other times a 15 percent trail loss was assumed, a figure that appeared conservative when a captured journal provided a detailed account of a 22 percent loss. In other cases, the MACV J-2 noted, groups lost as much as 50 percent during their journey down the trail.

Using the intelligence collected, MACV constructed a typical infiltration pattern that depicted groups starting from the general area of Hanoi with a one-day train trip to Vinh, then moving by barges down river to commo-liaison station T-12, about thirty-five kilometers farther south. From T-12 groups continued, some by truck but most on foot, through Laos to their eventual destinations. Time en route was calculated to be 20–25 days for those headed for the western DMZ, 45 days to Military Region Tri-Thien-Hue, and 60 days to the B-3 Front in the Central Highlands. Those headed for COSVN could expect to be on the move for 120 days.

Detailed knowledge of infiltration led Abrams to conclude that the enemy system was relatively hidebound. In preparing for an August 1968 general offensive, he pointed out, the enemy "planned the infiltration for July several months ago, in line with what he thought he'd do operationally, and a realistic estimate of his casualties, so on. And that's what's been getting down here. It's *really* sort of an *inflexible* system. All that gets here is what he decided five or six months ago, seven months ago, to send."

If the enemy's calculations about the state of the war turned out to be off the mark, there was little he could do to adjust. Abrams was doing all he could to upset those calculations. "We have *not* been *acting* like we've always *acted*," he reminded the staff. "The way we've hit this fellow with B-52s, the extent to which forces are out here patrolling, ambushing, and so on. The improvements in the ARVN—at least some of it."

SOME TIME AFTER acquisition of the new tracking capability there occurred a troubling development. Apparently there was some kind of a pause in enemy activity, one reflected in a significant reduction in the number of infiltrators coming down from the North. "We have seen peaks of infiltration activity in March, April, and May, followed by a lull during the first three weeks of June," said the WIEU briefer in late June 1968. "Now it appears that a relatively stable flow of replacements is being established." Abrams wanted to tie in the dates on which groups had entered the pipeline so as to be able to calculate what he would be facing on the battlefield.

Abrams stressed that, despite the absence of offensive actions at the moment, the enemy was far from idle. He was busy making preparations to receive and employ those forces moving through the pipeline. While they made their way south, "a lot of other fellows are carrying the ammunition up and putting it in caches, and they're getting the radios set up, and getting communications and dispensaries, this sort of thing. And *that's* going on up in the *forward* area. I think *that's* the way he *does* it. And *then*, at the last *minute*, he moves the *units* in."

While the enemy was making these preparations for future operations, his combat activity declined. That visible result led

antiwar elements in the United States to claim that these battlefield "lulls," low levels of enemy-initiated activity, were evidence of enemy goodwill or desire to deescalate the level of
hostilities. Thus, it was argued, U.S. forces should reduce their
own operations reciprocally, thereby winding down the war. At
MACV it looked like these pauses were being imposed on the
enemy by the success of the new tactics.

At the time of mini-Tet in May 1968, Abrams had commented on how "the Americans . . . are not fighting the way
they were a couple of years ago. Night operations by large units
are at an unprecedented peak. A lot of American units have not
done that in time gone past. And the Americans are using a lot
more long-range patrolling and reconnaissance. They're making
more effort now at developing solid intelligence before committing their forces."[9] That approach was paying off. On 15
October the Director of Central Intelligence, Richard Helms,
reported at the President's Tuesday Lunch that CIA had that day
issued a report on the situation in Vietnam. "No enemy military
objectives achieved," it stated. "Enemy forces badly mauled.
There will be a forced 'lull' because of it." In just six weeks of
the Third Offensive, the enemy lost 22,000 killed in action.[10]

That put the enemy in a rebuilding mode. "We see no major
coordinated [enemy] activity in the foreseeable future," reported
a MACV briefer in early November. Abrams reminded his staff
that while there might be a low level of enemy offensive activity,
this did not mean he was idle. Far from it. During such periods
"they go out and get the bunkers built and dug, and the dis-
pensary put in, the supplies brought in, and all that sort of thing.
And that's the part of the thing we ought to be working against
now!" When a briefer noted that during the preceding week
there had been eighty-three enemy attacks by fire throughout
South Vietnam, Davidson replied that by their former criterion
of reporting only attacks of twenty or more rounds, only one
of these eighty-three attacks would have qualified. "We've *es-*

calated. We've escalated the *reporting!*" Abrams erupted, provoking general laughter.

"We must work against the *whole* system!" Abrams told his
field commanders over and over again. Ambassador Charlie
Whitehouse recalled it well. "Abe was constantly trying to get
people to understand the enemy system," he said. "He must
have preached that sermon fifty times, week after week, month
after month, up and down the country."

Later Abrams would say privately he was convinced that the
withdrawal of substantial enemy elements during the early autumn of 1968 "was forced on them by the *exhaustion* of the
logistics system. And that was a combination of the interdiction
program and the torrential rain in the panhandle of North Vietnam, so virtually nothing—in September and October they
weren't getting enough stuff into Laos to feed the service troops
that were in there, by our estimates."

At the same time, inside South Vietnam vigorous action by
the Marines, the 101st Airborne, and the 1st Cavalry was depriving the enemy of large quantities of ammunition, food, and
medical supplies being taken from captured caches. For an enemy that was routinely employing heavy rockets, automatic
weapons, large mortars, and antiaircraft machine guns, the ton-
nages required to sustain his forces were substantial, and under
the circumstances they were not being delivered. "These people
were subsisting down here on rice gruel—the troops that were
left," said Abrams. "That was the situation on the first of November. And these withdrawals had all occurred by that time.
And, as I say, I'm convinced that it was not the fighting alone,
but the *exhaustion* of the logistical system."

In mid-November 1968 Admiral McCain went out to Vietnam
for one of his periodic visits, finding a very frustrated Abrams
on hand to greet him. There were the enemy's forced withdrawals, and his horrendous casualties: 250,000 so far in 1968

by MACV calculation, and nearly 600,000 since October 1965. As a consequence, noted a senior staffer, "There's not much going on in large-scale operations. The emphasis is on the pacification effort, the effort against the infrastructure."

Abrams wanted to follow up aggressively. "Washington has been very stubborn about getting on board with all of this that's going on," he told McCain. "And, in my viewpoint, this can *no longer* be tolerated. We're getting a military situation here that's got to be faced up to—and realistically—by our government and by our policies." Abrams, rapping the map, showed McCain where the enemy 9th Division had been pulled back, where the 5th was, the 7th, the 1st. "This is the *last* really significant military potential that he's got threatening South Vietnam," he stressed. "And *I* believe it has *got* to be defeated. And it will be *decisive* in the outcome of this war. But it *does* mean that, in order to do it, the policies on Cambodia have got to be changed, in my opinion."

A newsman once observed that Abrams could "inspire aggressiveness in a begonia." Now he longed to engage the remaining enemy in decisive battle, not let them retreat into border sanctuaries and refit for their next offensive. "I think it's criminal to let these enemy outfits park over here, fatten up, reindoctrinate, get their supplies, and so on," Abrams complained. "Also, we're giving them a *cheap* way of bringing it in," a reference to the port of Sihanoukville, long known to MACV as a major point of entry for enemy supplies that were then distributed throughout Cambodia and across the border into South Vietnam. The administration, of course, was pursuing an opposite political course. Authority to go into Cambodia after the enemy forces and base areas there would not be granted for almost two years, and even then it would be severely constrained in duration and depth—a mere raid, really.

Nevertheless, Abrams refused to take liberties with what authorities he was granted, including the right of self-defense. "I am concerned," he cabled Lieutenant General Ray Peers at I

Field Force, "that we may have a tendency to overreact and take targets under fire in Cambodia in addition to those which have fired upon friendly forces. In order to avoid this, our artillery and air when delivered into Cambodia should be precisely applied. Counterfires must be directed only in self-defense and against targets which are attacking friendly forces. We must exercise extreme caution in order to avoid exceeding this authority."[11]

Abrams observed that, in order to get one ton of matériel down the Ho Chi Minh Trail, the enemy had to put approximately ten tons into the pipeline, since interdiction would destroy or block 90 percent of what he tried to move. But to get one ton in through Sihanoukville, he had to put only one ton into the system because there was no interdiction in Cambodia. Yet, tempted as he was, Abrams was a soldier, and a disciplined and obedient one as well. "I want to say also we're playing the game *straight*," he told Admiral McCain, and they were.

At MACV, of course, it was apparent that the supposed "lulls" were in reality intense periods of enemy preparation for the next offensive, a reality underscored by intelligence of large numbers of replacements in the infiltration pipeline. Since knowledge of such infiltration was dependent on a very sensitive source, and any hint of what that was, or even that the knowledge was being acquired, might alert the enemy and lead to the source's being compromised, it was difficult to rebut those who claimed the "lulls" were politically rather than tactically motivated. Eventually the evidence would present itself on the battlefield in the form of the next enemy offensive.

BY OCTOBER 1968 Davidson could tell the visiting Secretary of the Navy, "I think the intelligence is many times better than what it was six months ago." First, "the breakthrough that we got on infiltration gave us a great lead on the enemy we never had before." And for the first time, he added, they had agents in the right places who were giving invaluable information.

Increased computer capabilities were beginning to have an impact, and the command's analytical capability had increased as a result. And, Davidson told a conference on intelligence collection, in contrast to previous years, "the commander is pleased with his intelligence, acts upon it, and has forced the staff to act upon it. That is what has changed in the last four or five months."

Charlie Corcoran remembered the controversies over intelligence "and whose intelligence you would accept" that swirled around MACV when he was Chief of Staff early in General Abrams's tenure. "Efforts were made to make MACV intelligence estimates agree with CINCPAC intelligence estimates agree with CIA intelligence estimates," he said. "In other words, to have the intelligence community as it was structured speak with one voice." Corcoran recalled that Abrams's view was "that every commander should be responsible for his own intelligence." Corcoran saw it the same way. "I think insistence that all intelligence agree is a very dangerous thing," he concluded, "particularly for the battlefield commander."

Abrams was seeking and using intelligence to fight the war. In other quarters intelligence was sometimes used for different purposes, including political ones. During the earlier years of the war, particularly the ill-fated "progress offensive" of 1967, battlefield reports of progress were subsequently undermined by renewed enemy offensives. The result was severe loss of credibility by government spokesmen, from the President on down.

Wary of politicized intelligence, Abrams insisted on MACV's right to control its own and—perhaps another aspect of the same outlook—that events in Vietnam should speak for themselves. This latter abhorrence of press agentry may explain in part why so much of what was achieved during the later years is even now little known or ignored.

5

Pacification

CREIGHTON ABRAMS understood that population security meant not only protecting the people from enemy main force, local force, and guerrilla elements, but also ridding them of the coercion exerted by the enemy's covert shadow government. "That infrastructure is just *vital,* absolutely *critical,* to the success of either the VC military *or* this political" campaign, he stressed to his senior associates. "They just *have* to have it." What was also clear was that, to this point, nothing much had been accomplished in terms of depriving the enemy of this critical resource.

Roger Hilsman, a former Assistant Secretary of State then teaching at Columbia, recalled going out to Vietnam in the fall of 1967 and coming back convinced of two things. "First, it was perfectly true that there had been major military victories. But second of all, they were irrelevant. The political infrastructure was intact."[1] Later Abrams, expressing a confirmatory view, told a regional conference of American ambassadors that "in the whole picture of the war, the *battles* don't really mean much."

The significance of these supposedly lower-level enemy forces was illustrated by an astounding comparison offered by General Fred Weyand. In III Corps, where his troops were operating, the enemy was at one time assessed as having a main force strength of thirty-two battalions. At that very same time, said Weyand, "his local force squads, platoons and companies, in toto, equated to *45* battalions of infantry!" Added to that were the guerrillas and infrastructure now being targeted.

U.S. forces supported this campaign by keeping large enemy elements away from pacification areas, destroying local forces and guerrillas, and helping to find and neutralize the enemy infrastructure. The results were significant in both tactical and pacification terms. "Denied access to these formerly contested or VC-controlled hamlets," observed a National Security Council study, "the enemy's main forces lose sources of food, recruitment, intelligence, and concealment."[2] Observing that the involvement of U.S. forces in this campaign was a radical departure from past practice, pacification official Clay McManaway concluded that "Abrams understood the war. Westmoreland never did."[3]

Leading a stable of energetic and aggressive subordinate commanders is challenging, and Abrams understood that it involved more convincing than ordering. "I watched Abrams turn the corps commanders around on the primacy of the pacification program," recalled McManaway, who found it a liberal education. "It was clear that he had to bring those guys around. Any notion of the Army as a dictatorial hierarchy was dispelled by watching that. Simply ordering a thing done was not enough."

When the new approach was presented for the first time, some commanders were not enthusiastic. One, Lieutenant General Julian Ewell, later demonstrated how Abrams had converted him. "The conventional theory was that we, being strong and mobile, were taking care of the main forces, and somebody else would take care of the rest," he explained. "But that was not what was needed. The enemy operated at many levels, and to defeat him you had to beat them up wherever they were found." In III Corps, Ewell reported, he was targeting local force companies on the premise that "it will tend to expose more VCI [the Viet Cong infrastructure in the villages] than any other

single thing, because you sort of take the protective mantle off
the VCI." And, he added, "I have a hunch if you clobber the
local force unit, the local guerrilla will *chieu hoi*" (rally to the
government side). Operationally, said Ewell, "we are trying to
drop the level of tactical operations down to company level,
both U.S. and ARVN. I'm perfectly willing to admit pacification's my primary mission."

NOT COUNTING the time he worked on the problem as a White
House staffer, Robert Komer had been at the pacification business since being sent out to Vietnam in May 1967 to serve as
deputy to the MACV commander for what was called CORDS
(Civil Operations and Revolutionary Development Support),
the U.S. element in support of South Vietnam's pacification program. By the end of 1967 the gains were, by Komer's own
admission, pretty slender. There were 12,700 identified hamlets
in the country, he said at a news conference only a week before
the 1968 Tet Offensive broke, and during 1967 only 640 hamlets
had been added to the relatively secure categories. "That's a
pretty modest increase," Komer admitted. In gross numbers,
about 11.5 million people out of a total population of 17.2 million, or about 67 percent, were then "living either in the secure
cities and towns or under reasonably good security conditions
in the country," an increase of only 4.8 percent over the past
eleven months. Even that modest gain was partially due to refugees moving out of the line of fire and other people migrating
to the cities in search of better jobs and better security.[4]

Komer made one other statement he probably soon came to
regret. Police strength had increased by several thousand, he reported, and as a result "our intelligence was significantly better
in the countryside."[5] When, only days later, the Tet Offensive
exploded all across South Vietnam, that assertion sounded hol-
low indeed. General Abrams, said an aide, always thereafter
blamed Komer for much of the surprise of Tet. Komer had
argued for his own intelligence network serving the pacification

program, a fragmentation of the intelligence effort that Abrams
had opposed. But Westmoreland had backed Komer, who now
had little to show for his independent intelligence operation.
"In the immediate aftermath of Tet," said an aide, "Abrams
wanted to fire every intelligence officer in Vietnam. He was
particularly upset with Ambassador Robert Komer."[6]

Komer proved to be at best a transitional figure in the pacification program for Vietnam. His days as head of U.S. support
for it were numbered as of the moment Abrams assumed command. "Abrams was deeply suspicious of Komer and believed
he provided rosy estimates of progress to please his political mas-
ters in Washington," recalled Abrams's aide Zeb Bradford,[7] and
it didn't take long for the drama to play out. Indeed, from the
time of their flight out to Vietnam together, recalled General
"Dutch" Kerwin, who was also aboard, the eventual outcome
was obvious. "By the time we got to Hawaii," he said, "it was
quite evident that Abrams and Komer were not going to be
friends. And that's a massive understatement."

The reasons were obvious. Komer was, in Kerwin's assessment, "one of the most egotistical, self-centered individuals that
you'll ever run across. Brilliant man, tremendous ideas. His only
problem is two-fold: he can't implement his ideas; he can't sift
the ones that are not good from the ones that are good. He just
antagonizes the hell out of everybody, openly, to the point that
he denigrates the tremendous intellect that he has."[8]

Heavy-handed and insensitive, Komer was also destined for
trouble with the South Vietnamese. Although he later prided
himself on having bulldozed them into doing things his way, the
cost—even if his assessment is correct, which is doubtful—was
high.[9] "The pacification in South Vietnam by Komer's team
during 1967–1968 was a clear quicksand," wrote Major General
Hoang Lac, who had worked in the program on the Vietnamese
side. "Ambassador Komer can't even pacify himself. How can
he lead the 'hearts and minds' program, pacifying the mass?"[10]
Brigadier General Tran Dinh Tho, author of a postwar mono-

graph on pacification, was equally critical, citing Komer's "ob-
sessive preoccupation with appearances which led to the
tendency of substituting statistical results for true achievements."[11]

In mid–1968 Thomas Scoville asked Komer when he was
coming back to Washington, to which Komer replied, "I've
come out to do a job; I'm going to stay until it's done."[12] That
was not, however, the way it turned out. If there was a single
defining moment, it came during a briefing soon after Abrams
took command. Komer was describing the status of pacification
when a map was put up. Abrams studied what that portrayed
for a moment, then brought Komer to a halt. "Do you mean
to say that, after all these years, and all this expenditure, we still
have within firing range of this base a VC hamlet?" he asked
menacingly. On the way out of the briefing, one officer asked
another in low tones, "Do you think Komer knows he just got
fired?"

When he went home for good, Komer later conceded, "I
left with my tail between my legs," an uncharacteristic admission
perhaps explained by the fact that he was under oath at the
time.[13] Said General Fred Weyand flatly, "Abrams got rid of
Komer."[14] When Abrams was the deputy commander, recalled
his aide Jim Ellis, "that was a difficult year, and Komer exacerbated a bad situation." General Robert Baer, who spent a year
working in CORDS, also formed some fixed opinions relating
to Komer. "I think General Abrams had a strong mistrust of
anything Komer was doing," he said, "and that he thought it
was all a paper exercise, and having been part of it I strongly
agree. I don't think it was until Colby came in and started to
deal with the infrastructure itself that we really started to make
progress."

IN LATE SEPTEMBER 1968, an agent report indicating that the
enemy continued to plan for an all-out attack was reported to
be "borne out by piles of evidence—documents, PWs, *hoi chanh*

[enemy defectors, also known as ralliers], and other sources that speak of preparations for major attacks, the coming climactic phases, the imminence of the new winter–spring campaign. Thus," said MACV, "we see no hint that the enemy intends at this time to abandon or seriously modify the type of military operations he launched at Tet [1968]." At least for the time being, even after three unsuccessful Communist offensives during the year, Giap still seemed to be calling the shots.

Abrams assembled his commanders for an analysis of the broader implications of the war. The heart of the briefing was presented by William Colby, soon to succeed Komer as head of CORDS. (CORDS pulled together, under MACV direction, the multiple aspects of support provided to the Vietnamese pacification program.) Colby described an ominous current situation, one that saw the enemy trying to establish "Liberation Committees" throughout South Vietnam with what he called a "particular sense of urgency." At this point the Hamlet Evaluation System (a periodic statistical compilation designed to reflect the current status of pacification), while admittedly imprecise, suggested that more than 46 percent of the population was under some degree of Viet Cong influence. Thus, said Colby, "in the event of a cease-fire, the enemy might claim political control of about one-half of the population of South Vietnam."

Colby then turned to means of reversing this unsatisfactory situation. The Accelerated Pacification Campaign—of which he was the architect, although he did not say so—would seek to eliminate enemy base areas and the command centers of his political effort. A program called Phuong Hoang—known as Phoenix in English and designed to neutralize the Viet Cong infrastructure—would serve as "an essential tool for this action." A preemptive campaign would be targeted against those areas controlled by the Viet Cong, contested, or heavily infested by VC; its objective was to plant the government's flag, saturate the areas with military forces, and purge the enemy's underground shadow government. Territorial security, VCI neutralization, and supporting programs of self-help, self-defense, and self-government would thus constitute the counteroffensive.

With negotiations with the Communists under way in Paris, concern had developed that the Saigon government's influence did not extend into many parts of the country, a potentially serious problem if some near-term cease-fire in place were negotiated. This had led to Colby's concept of "vigorous extension of security and political presence by the Government, with American support, in order to preempt the areas not yet penetrated by the Communists and to spread the Government presence into the contested areas." This was, Colby made clear, a job for the Vietnamese, but one in which American forces could help by screening the pacification areas from enemy assaults and conducting spoiling operations against enemy forces.

Having spent the past several months developing this approach, Colby now addressed his presentation most directly to Abrams. "I was not disappointed," he said later. Abrams "listened intently, following each point with obvious understanding of the essentially political analysis I was giving." At the end he gave his full approval for such a campaign to be worked out with President Nguyen Van Thieu.[15] The Accelerated Pacification Campaign began 1 November 1968, a day that marked a new departure in the war—the United States stopped bombing North Vietnam and the South Vietnamese launched a serious pacification program. The two events together dramatically changed the way the war was fought. Abrams considered it the turning point at which the government "took the initiative in South Vietnam, the initiative in the larger sense of the total war."

What evolved was a three-month blitz. The central goal of the APC, as it was called for short, was to raise 1,000 contested hamlets to relatively secure status in a ninety-day period. It was not complicated, said Colby, basically just "spread out and move into the countryside." When the campaign showed greater than expected success early in the process, the number of targeted hamlets was raised to 1,330, and by early January 1969 some force had been moved into 1,320 of them.

The plan integrated military and civilian approaches to an unprecedented degree. Commanders were encouraged to take forces from areas of light contact and put them where they could do the most good in helping to ensure the success of this offensive or extend it to additional target hamlets. And, Abrams added, "there is no restriction against overfulfilling this plan." He urged his commanders to "keep a sharp eye out for the enemy via reconnaissance screens while working behind that screen to keep the enemy from ever recovering. Let's move out on this."[16]

The priority given to pacification, even when it came to military operations, was an essential condition. The failure to do so in earlier years largely explained the numerous failed pacification efforts that littered the way. George Jacobson, an "old hand" who altogether served eighteen years in Vietnam and was a mainstay of the pacification program in these later years,[17] often observed that "there's no question that pacification is either 90 percent or 10 percent security, depending on which expert you talk to. But there isn't any expert that will doubt that it's the *first* 10 percent or the *first* 90 percent. You just can't conduct pacification in the face of an NVA division." Nor could you conduct it in the face of an entrenched and active Viet Cong infrastructure, and that was the other end of the spectrum.

PHUONG HOANG—roughly "all-seeing bird" in Vietnamese—was the part of pacification designed to identify and neutralize members of the Viet Cong infrastructure.[18] The VCI constituted a kind of covert shadow government in the villages and hamlets of South Vietnam, using terror and coercion to maintain control over the rural populace. Colby himself wrote the first directive for Phoenix, and in it he included the prescription that "this program will be operated under the normal laws of war." The concept was, he said, "let's at least get our intelligence organi-

zations to talk to one another."[19] Later he described it more
formally as "a program of consolidating intelligence and exploitation efforts against . . . key individuals" in the enemy infrastructure.

"This was an attempt to regularize the intelligence coverage," emphasized Colby, "decent interrogations, decent record-
keeping, evidence, all that sort of thing, the whole structure of
the struggle against the secret apparatus. This was Phoenix."[20]
Soon MACV shifted 250 people into intelligence support of
Phoenix. "It was a hard price to pay," said Deputy MACV
Commander General Andrew Goodpaster, "but it was quite obviously the thing to do."

The program never really got off the ground, admitted
Colby, until President Thieu signed a decree in July 1968. Other
senior Vietnamese understood the importance of dealing with
the enemy infrastructure, though, and once Thieu gave it his
blessing they supported the program. "It was the VCI, not the
guerrillas or local forces, which was the foundation of insurgency," wrote Generals Cao Van Vien and Dong Van Khuyen.
In fact the guerrillas were dependent on the infrastructure for
essential support. "Death of the VCI, therefore, was the primary
condition of security for national priority areas."[21]

During his tenure General Westmoreland had persistently
denied the importance of the enemy's "Self-Defense Forces" and
"Secret Self-Defense Forces," categories that were part of the
VCI.[22] Indeed, he ordered his intelligence officers to remove
them from order of battle calculations, where they had always
been carried, thus arbitrarily reducing the estimate of enemy
strength. Many saw this as a cynical move to demonstrate greater
progress than was actually being made, and to buttress his contention that the elusive "crossover point" had been reached.
Perhaps, though, it simply revealed Westmoreland's limited grasp
of the nature of the war and his inability to understand the
crucial role of the enemy's clandestine network in controlling
the rural population. William Colby observed that the more

serious flaw of the truncated order of battle was "its failure to perceive that the situation they faced was a people's war."[23]

During Tet 1968 the multiple tasks performed by the infrastructure were apparent to anyone who paid attention. "During this time," noted Colonel Hoang Ngoc Lung, J-2 of the Joint General Staff, "the Saigon VCI proved to be extremely active. Many of its members served as guides for the attacking units. A few of them were actually holding jobs in U.S. and GVN agencies." Others worked as informants, helped arrest and search government officials, acted as propagandists. "As a result of these supporting activities, the enemy local forces that attacked Saigon and Cho Lon were able to move around in a metropolitan area that was obviously too large, too populous, too strange, and whose modern facilities and civilization remained beyond their realm of knowledge."[24] Abrams thought it was absolutely the case that "the VCI *permits the main forces to operate.*"[25]

General Cao Van Vien, Chief of the Joint General Staff, also understood the importance of eliminating the infrastructure. "As long as the VCI continued to exist," he acknowledged, "total victory could not be achieved." Thus "destroying an enemy unit . . . amounted to just a short term military victory. In that sense, it is not an exaggeration to say that the destruction of an enemy company or battalion did not matter as much as the elimination of a VC district or province commissar."[26]

Identifying and rooting out the Viet Cong infrastructure was a challenging task. It is often said that during the 1968 Tet Offensive the enemy's underground elements surfaced and were cut down, effectively eliminating the infrastructure, but that claim does not stand up under analysis. Large numbers of the enemy's forces were indeed exposed and killed during the fighting at Tet, but they were not the infrastructure, certainly not the bulk of it. Recalled Davidson, "We captured 34,000 prisoners in the Tet Offensive, and not a one of them was SDF or SSDF."[27] MACV estimated that net enemy losses through 16 February amounted to 38,454, of which 5,000 were attributed to the infrastructure, while stating that "not one prisoner thus far upon questioning has admitted to being a member of a self defense, secret self defense, or assault youth" element.[28]

It *is* correct that the Viet Cong's forces were decimated during Tet 1968, as demonstrated by the consequent necessity to bring NVA forces from the North to fill formerly VC units. Over a relatively short time the enemy's fighting forces in the South went from three-quarters VC to three-quarters NVA, a dramatic reversal of the mix that also essentially terminated the Viet Cong's influence in the Communist movement. But those forces were not the infrastructure, which continued to flourish until painstakingly rooted out over a period of years.

One of the few specific subsequent claims of the damage done to the infrastructure was published at the end of April 1968 in the Chief of Staff's *Weekly Summary,* which reported "that many members of the VC infrastructure surfaced during Tet— more than 600 key infrastructure members were eliminated during February and more than 1,300 were eliminated during March."[29] Those numbers, too, indicate that, far from wiping out the infrastructure at Tet, the South Vietnamese had much work left to do.

ABRAMS NOTED THAT President Nguyen Van Thieu agreed on what had to be done to advance pacification, and that General Vien understood it as well. However, "I would have to say that there is some concern," Abrams acknowledged, "as to whether or not their military commanders recognize this *and* are personally disposed to lend their—not only their good offices, but their *muscle* to some of the things that have got to be done in here." It could not be done by government officials alone, he said, and military commanders—the same point he had been emphasizing to *American* commanders—had to realize that "there is more to the *problem,* there is more involved *in* the war, than just that [military] part."

John Paul Vann, by this point already a key figure in the
pacification program, saw the significance of what Abrams and
Colby were suggesting, calling it "a basic policy change in-
country." Vann's comments were of particular interest in that,
during earlier duty in Vietnam as a military officer, he had been
unrelentingly pessimistic about what was being accomplished
and not shy about saying so. His views carried weight, then and
later, because of his ability and his candor. "I think he was as
good a soldier as I've ever served with," said General Bruce
Palmer, Jr., who had known him since Vann commanded the
regimental heavy mortar company under Palmer in the 16th
Infantry.

WITH AMBASSADOR William E. Colby in charge of pacification,
the leadership triumvirate was complete. General Bill Rosson,
by now MACV's deputy commander, liked what he saw in
Colby, a man who "was soft-spoken and—unlike Komer—
spent a lot of his time in the field, so he didn't have to rely on
reports and knew what was going on." Ambassador Bunker welcomed Colby's appointment, too, citing "his ability to get things
done, also his judgment, his analytical powers . . . his experience."[30] Said a colleague, contrasting the new man with his
predecessor, "Komer was always trying to convince you pacification was working, but Colby was trying to make it work."[31]
    "Shortly after Komer left," Colby remembered, "Abrams
drew me aside. 'You know, I think our relationship is going to
be a good one,' he told me. 'I'll make sure it is, general,' I
responded." And, added Colby, "I was enormously impressed
by his grasp of the political significance of the pacification program. Finally we had focused on the real war."

BY THESE LATER YEARS a revised set of statistical measures, known
as the Hamlet Evaluation System, was being used to chart the
progress of pacification. A U.S.-developed and -administered
system, it was based on input from the network of Americans

serving as district advisors. "Many of them don't speak Vietnamese very well," acknowledged William Colby, "many of them haven't been there very long, so it's an imperfect system. But it's just an awful lot better than anything we used to use."

The system placed hamlets in one of six categories: A, B, C, D, E, or VC. The A, B, and C categories indicated degrees of being relatively secure, while D and E meant contested. Those designated VC were considered to be under enemy control. The ratings were calculated by using the advisors' answers to a comprehensive set of questions on both security and development. Among the specifics were such things as whether the hamlet had an assigned Popular Forces platoon, an elected government, a People's Self-Defense Force unit, and an ongoing self-help project. While acknowledging that individual ratings might be suspect, Colby observed that the trends over time were useful and valid. John Vann agreed. "What the HES does is give you a valid measurement of trend," he told a college audience. "I use it in this fashion, and most other people who know this system use it in this fashion." By February 1969, said Vann, "using it in that sense we are at the moment in the most favorable position that we have ever been."[32]

A postwar study by the BDM Corporation observed that HES "replaced the biased, inaccurate, exaggerated, and often self-serving Joint GVN-US reporting system" of the earlier period and that, while it "contained some inaccuracies . . . US advisors had the final word, and higher echelons could not make changes in the advisors' evaluation of hamlet security. As a consequence, the HES system provided very good data on trends and was generally considered to have been the most effective system that could have been implemented."[33]

Army historian Richard Hunt added, in his study of pacification, that "no one in CORDS relied solely on HES figures for information on conditions in the countryside." Rather, they analyzed those data "in conjunction with Chieu Hoi rates, incidents of terrorism, reports from CORDS evaluators and province advisers, and intelligence information. The HES was only the most visible and notorious indicator; it was by no means the only one."[34] Said Colby, "My evaluation of how strong the infrastructure was, and how strong the enemy was, was more learned by my frequent visits to the countryside and driving up the roads . . . than by reading the numbers in Saigon."[35]

Before the 1968 Tet Offensive the ratings had put 67.2 percent of the population in the relatively secure categories; the figure was knocked down to 59.8 percent during the offensive but rebounded to 65.8 percent by August. Also, to the surprise and delight of the South Vietnamese, it was discovered that of 5,000 or so small outposts and watch towers fewer than 480 had been abandoned or overrun during the enemy offensive.[36] In other words, the damage to the government presence in rural areas had been far less severe than originally believed. That set the stage for the Accelerated Pacification Campaign devised by Colby, accepted by the South Vietnamese, and launched in November 1968.

COLBY HAD ALSO identified improvement in the Regional Forces and Popular Forces—components of the Territorial Forces whose mission was to remain in place in their home provinces and districts so as to provide local security—as key to gains in pacification. Abrams had made their expansion and improvement his special concern, achieving particular success by sending out small military advisory teams to work with the RF companies and PF platoons. By October 1968 there were 250 such five-man teams at work all across the country, and the RF and PF had been expanded by about 86,000 since the beginning of the year.[37] Three months later the increase had reached 91,000 and there were 350 advisory teams living and working with RF and PF units. Further, 100,000 M-16 rifles had been issued to these forces, reflecting the emphasis being given to their importance in upgrading village security. "The RF and PF received the highest priority of anybody. That's where the first M-16s went, *before* ARVN," Abrams later reminded his field commanders. "They've been given, for over a year, the very *highest* priority."

In the Delta, Vietnam's most populous region, Regional Forces and Popular Forces comprised 80 percent of the government's armed strength. Greatly expanded during these later years, they eventually came to comprise half of South Vietnam's total armed forces nationwide. In every area of the country they were an important part of the security environment. Patrolling, conducting night ambushes, on bridge security, the RF and PF inflicted a substantial amount of damage on enemy forces—and in turn suffered serious losses—while denying them easy access to the population. Abrams observed of the RF and PF, along with the People's Self-Defense Forces, that "there isn't *anybody* in this country who can work as well with the people and get along as well with the people, enjoy the *confidence* of the people, the way those people can." One reason was that "the RF and PF don't have the military mind. They're really kind of home folks. It just works better."

"Gradually, in their outlook, deportment, and combat performance," said Lieutenant General Ngo Quang Truong, "the RF and PF troopers shed their paramilitary origins and increasingly became full-fledged soldiers." So decidedly was this the case, Truong concluded, that "throughout the major period of the Vietnam conflict" the RF and PF were "aptly regarded as the mainstay of the war machinery."[38]

In terms of assets invested, the RF and PF provided a very high payoff, especially for those who thought in terms of cost-effectiveness. Systems analyst Thomas C. Thayer, concluding that the RF and PF, "by their combat performance, and by their permanent presence in the countryside, had a profound and perhaps decisive effect on improving the security of the rural population," also calculated that they consumed less than 5 percent of the total costs of the war.[39] Expanded in size, better armed and better trained, the Territorial Forces were coming into their own, earning the respect of even so tough a critic as Julian Ewell. "They were the cutting edge of the war," he said admiringly.

COLBY THOUGHT the Accelerated Pacification Campaign's most important effect was to "energize the Government and local officials to take the offensive in the war and to do so at the level of the people's war."[40] No sooner had the APC been completed with gratifying results than the South Vietnamese decided to follow up immediately with a further ambitious push. What was being accomplished was really quite straightforward: establishing a continuous government presence in rural villages and hamlets so as to bring security and economic and social benefits to the people. The follow-on plan, set to begin in February 1969, aimed to put 90 percent of the population into relatively secure status, to double the recently created People's Self-Defense Forces to two million members, to establish an elected government in every village, and to resettle a large number of refugees.

Colby wrote to his parents that "the situation does seem to be moving. The enemy seems unable to crank up his big units to hit us hard, and our Vietnamese local forces are doing better against his guerrillas. So if we can keep the pressure on we may achieve what I've spent the last *10* years working on . . . helping the Vietnamese find ways to defend themselves against their brothers from the North. We seem to be on the right track now, at least, so we'll keep the pace up."[41]

Perhaps the strongest evidence of the new approach's successes came from the other side. "Because we did not reassess the situation in a timely fashion," noted a history of the People's Army of Vietnam, "especially when the balance of forces between our side and the enemy and the form of development of the war both had disadvantageous elements for our side, we did not in a timely fashion change the direction of our attacks. We continued attacks into the cities and left gaps in the defenses of the rural areas.

"When the enemy turned back to the defensive," said this document, "striving to defend the cities and block our main forces in order to concentrate his own forces to carry out rural 'pacification,' we again did not fully appreciate the enemy's scheme and the new strength of his 'clear and hold' strategy." Thus "our main force units in South Vietnam endured continuous waves of vicious combat; they suffered losses, and their combat strength declined." Admitting that the summer and fall offensives of 1968 "did not achieve the military and political goals which they were assigned," the Communist historians nevertheless concluded that they had paid off in another realm because "they rained new blows on the already shaky will of the American imperialists."[42]

The top Americans recognized President Thieu's importance to all of this, Abrams observing that "he knows more about pacification than any other Vietnamese" and Colby calling him "the number one pacification officer." On a number of occasions Thieu invited Ambassador Bunker to go along on visits to the countryside, where Bunker heard him emphasize restoring local government, holding village and hamlet elections, training local government officials, and land reform. At Vung Tau 1,400 village chiefs, representing about three-quarters of all the villages in South Vietnam, went through training during the first nine months of 1969. President Thieu visited every one of those classes, giving the village chiefs the incomparable cachet of being able to go back home and speak about "what President Thieu said to me—."

Hamlet and village chiefs going through that training got essentially two messages, said Colby. The first, promulgated by Colonel Nguyen Be—"the very brilliant officer who runs this program down there"—had a revolutionary theme: "You live in a corrupt and antiquated society, and you've got to go out

and change it—and make it a better one." Complementing that
was the message President Thieu offered on his visits to Vung
Tau: "*You* are important. You are a little president in your community. You are responsible both to lead and protect and help
your people. And our job is to help you." Thieu knew how to
talk to the hamlet and village chiefs, Abrams said, "because his
father was a village chief for a long time."

Important personnel changes also advanced the overall success of pacification. John Vann, then assigned in III Corps, described what had happened there. "In the last year I have had
nine of my eleven province chiefs replaced," he told a college
audience during a visit to the United States. "Eight of them
were substantial improvements over their predecessors. I had
forty-three of my fifty-three district chiefs replaced. All but three
of them were substantial improvements over their predecessors."[43] Coupled with the better-trained and -motivated civil
officials coming out of Vung Tau, this contributed to improved
rural life.

ALONGSIDE EFFORTS to upgrade the security of hamlets, the
Chieu Hoi (Open Arms) program, aimed at inducing the enemy
to "rally" to the government side, was gaining momentum. The
three-month APC goal of 5,000 *hoi chanh,* as the ralliers were
called, had already been exceeded by year's end, with more than
3,000 coming in during December 1968 alone. That in itself
was an affirmation of how pacification was taking hold, for, as
Davidson observed, "your Chieu Hoi rate goes up not as a result
of sweeps, but as a result of getting in an area and staying in it."
During 1969, more than 47,000 enemy rallied to the government side, half again as many as during 1968.

Pacification also encompassed assistance to the large number
of refugees from the fighting. By early 1969 some four million
people had been refugees at one time or another, nearly a quarter of South Vietnam's population. Tet 1968 alone generated
three-quarters of a million temporary evacuees, and another

quarter-million were created at mini-Tet in May, along with 150,000 homes damaged or destroyed in those battles. This was a huge task for the governmental ministries to deal with in the midst of a war, but successes achieved built up credit in the eyes of the people. During 1968 a quarter-million people were returned to their own villages.

While that left a very large number of refugees—1.3 million—still needing assistance, better security meant many of these people could go back to their homes rather than, as in earlier years, being sequestered in resettlement projects. Ambassador Bunker observed that an important measure of the security situation was the refugees returning home. "I think that's one of the *best* indications that you could have, a feeling of assurance on the part of the people," he said.

Abrams speculated that the enemy—who appeared to have been slow to grasp the significance, and the danger to him, of the energized pacification program—would be forced to react to it. "I think this strikes at the real *root* of his strength," he said. "His strength is *not* in these divisions. His strength is inside this [VCI] program. It's the part he *can't* let go down the drain." And there was little doubt that the enemy knew, or should have known, what he was up against. "He's got copies of the GVN Pacification Plan, complete with all the annexes," Abrams believed. "It generally takes him forty-eight to seventy-two hours to get it."

PACIFICATION'S PROGRESS was further illustrated by President Thieu's confidence in his people and their loyalties, confidence demonstrated in his decision to arm the populace through creation of the People's Self-Defense Force. Against the advice of virtually all his advisors, Thieu activated the PSDF in April 1968, arguing that "the government had to rest upon the support of the people, and it had little validity if it did not dare to arm them."[44] The acceptance of arms constituted an act of commitment to the government side, and ultimately four million people equipped with some 600,000 weapons participated in their own defense.

No government in doubt of the loyalties of its people would have dared such an approach. Thieu's confidence was repaid by the performance of village defenders throughout the country. Indeed, it might be argued that it was this experience which demonstrated, as the government later decided, that "pacification" was an outmoded and no longer appropriate term. What the people needed, and wanted, was security, freedom from coercion by the Viet Cong infrastructure, and improvement in their ordinary lives, and they were willing to take risks to achieve them. A priest told Colby that at the most recent armed retreat of his diocese, during planning for a village defense force he was organizing, they had even discussed the relative merits of the M–16 and AK–47 assault guns. The term "revolutionary development," later revised to "rural development," recognized those realities while at the same time reflecting where the underlying loyalties of the people lay.

The Communists were critical of their failure to gain the support of the South Vietnamese people. "Our armed forces failed to adequately perform their role of creating favorable conditions to induce uprisings by the people in the towns," said COSVN Resolution 6 dated March 1968 in discussing the Tet Offensive. In fact, there was *never* any popular uprising in support of the enemy in South Vietnam. "He's got a wonderful cadre machine, absolutely magnificent cadre machine," Colby said of the enemy, "but it hasn't turned into mass political support." And it never did, an outcome not too surprising in view of the enemy's record, year after year, of assassinations, kidnappings, terror bombings, impressments, and indiscriminate shellings of population centers throughout South Vietnam, actions hardly calculated to win the hearts and minds of the victims.

The enemy's response to the success of pacification, said General Harold K. Johnson, was "cut throats faster, cut throats faster." Abrams recalled an incident in which a ten-year-old boy pushed his bicycle, loaded with an explosive device, into a school yard filled with young girls. The device went off prematurely, killing the boy and injuring several of the girls. "It's very difficult to understand why anybody on either side would feel that it had somehow advanced their cause," Abrams commented somberly.

As 1968 neared an end, with the Accelerated Pacification Campaign roaring along, Abrams gave Colby some well-deserved recognition, saying at the WIEU that "this pacification program really bears no resemblance to what was going on last year—as far as results and so on."[45] And Abrams viewed this as the critical battlefield, cabling General Wheeler that in pacification "we are making our major effort; so is the enemy. In my judgment," he added, "what is required now is all out with all we have. The military machine runs best at full throttle. That's about where we have it and where I intend to keep it."[46]

6

Interdiction

ONE OF THE CLEAREST absolutes of the war was the essentiality to the enemy of his logistics and personnel replacement lifeline, the complex of routes from North Vietnam down through Laos and Cambodia known as the Ho Chi Minh Trail. Acting on this realization, allied forces devoted an extraordinary amount of attention and effort to interdicting those vital flows of men and matériel.

The Ho Chi Minh Trail had begun life in 1959 as a genuine trail, a rutted and primitive pathway south through the Laotian panhandle and on into the border areas of Cambodia adjacent to South Vietnam. With every passing year, however, the route became less a trail and more a highway, then a superhighway, all this in the face of unremitting attack by allied air forces. "Building and maintaining the trail was a huge effort," said Bui Tin, "involving tens of thousands of soldiers, drivers, repair teams, medical stations, communications units."[1]

Painstaking effort was the norm on both sides. North Vietnamese laborers, described admiringly as "ants" by some, had over a decade transformed primitive paths into a network of serviceable roads and a supporting complex of way stations, repair facilities, and air defenses. All this was largely concealed beneath the jungle canopy and camouflage. Meanwhile, the allies labored just as hard to find and destroy the trucks plying this route, employing staggering quantities of munitions in the process. All this was, of course, only a less desirable and less effective substitute for ground operations that might have cut the trail permanently and isolated the South Vietnamese battlefield. Successive MACV commanders and the Joint Chiefs of Staff had long sought permission to conduct such an incursion, but were in every case denied.

The enemy's buildup for the 1968 Tet Offensive had started the previous September, peaking in the immediate pre-Tet period. Another peak preceded the May 1968 mini-Tet offensive. By June, when the next such buildup started, preparatory to the Third Offensive planned for August, Abrams was in command and stimulating a greatly intensified effort to interdict the enemy's critical logistics operations.

The new campaign was quite different in concept from earlier interdiction efforts, which had concentrated on "killing" trucks—damaging or destroying them. (Killing trucks, frustrating and expensive at best, was also only a temporary solution. MACV later estimated that the enemy imported 5,600 trucks during 1969, about what was needed to replace losses.) The new emphasis was on keeping known choke points and bypasses closed.

Concentrating on the southernmost provinces of North Vietnam and the Lao panhandle, the air effort targeted a number of key interdiction points. Six water crossings were included, one a point where the enemy floated a pontoon bridge out from a cave every night. Allied aircraft destroyed that bridge, confining enemy traffic there to individual ferries, then picked those off one by one as they could be located. Mines were placed in the waterways and, when a B-52 strike uncovered an underwater rock causeway, a cable bridge, and a cable ferry, those were interdicted as well..

Seventh Air Force systems analysts calculated the relative costs of impeding the flow at about $13,000 a ton using the truck killing approach and $1,000 a ton using the blockage method. Even so, the necessary air effort was huge. From 3,000 sorties in May the commitment had soared to 6,500 in July and 8,000 in August before tapering off to 6,400 in September. When at one point the enemy succeeded in reopening the Ban Laboy ford, which had been closed for thirty-two days, MACV put in 50 to 100 fighter sorties a day to reclose that point.

The results were dramatic. In mid-July 1968 the enemy had been moving more than 1,100 trucks a day, the most traffic ever observed on the trail. One week into the new interdiction campaign, that had been cut in half, and less than a week later by half again. By early November it was down to a trickle, if that, with the calculated throughput tonnage only 10 percent of what it had been. Brigadier General George Keegan, Seventh Air Force's intelligence chief, suggested that this represented the most effective interdiction thus far in the war, the product of air attacks on the supply routes from North Vietnam and attrition of in-country caches within South Vietnam by raids, spoiling attacks, and bombing whereby enemy supplies were "being consumed, attrited, discovered, and spoiled in the battle area."

"We believe the net effect has been a very serious, if not disastrous, impact logistically upon the enemy," said Keegan. "We believe the forced exodus is related in part to these . . . operations." That exodus—a wholesale withdrawal of enemy regiments from the northern provinces of South Vietnam—would soon become a key issue in the controversy over enemy "understandings" and the cessation of bombing in North Vietnam.

DEBATE OVER THE bombing of North Vietnam was a constant almost throughout American involvement in the war. In the spring of 1968 Lyndon Johnson, in the same speech in which he renounced his candidacy for reelection as president, restricted such bombing to below the 20th parallel. What that meant was that henceforth North Vietnam could be bombed only in its southernmost regions adjacent to the DMZ and South Vietnam;

meanwhile, bombing within South Vietnam itself, and along the Ho Chi Minh Trail in adjacent Laos, continued without restriction.

That partial suspension was of little moment to those conducting the war in South Vietnam. Before LBJ ordered it, he had brought Abrams, then on the point of being named Westmoreland's successor, back to Washington to discuss the matter. "President Johnson asked our opinion—the Joint Chiefs of Staff, and General Abrams and General Westmoreland—as to what the effect would be," recalled General Earle G. Wheeler, then Chairman of the Joint Chiefs of Staff. "And we had, in all honesty, to tell him it would have very little effect on what happened in South Vietnam."[2]

While exempting Hanoi and most other parts of North Vietnam from bombing may not have had an enormous effect on the course of the war in South Vietnam (as distinct, it should be emphasized, from the effect a *total* suspension of bombing in the North would have had), it is clear that the North Vietnamese were eager indeed to get especially their capital out from under the bombing for which, recalled Major General Lu Giang, commander of the Hanoi capital region, "the capital's armed forces and people were honorably awarded the determined-to-defeat U.S. aggression banner by Uncle Ho."[3]

Although most of the controversy over bombing during the war was occasioned by bombing in North Vietnam, that is somewhat ironic given the distribution of bombing operations. About 75 percent of Air Force missions during the war were flown in South Vietnam, to include close air support, airlift, search and rescue, defoliation, and courier missions. Another 15.2 percent consisted of interdiction and close air support in Laos, and 3 percent more in Cambodia, leaving just 6.7 percent applied in North Vietnam.[4]

For the allies, at least as Ambassador Bunker saw it, the partial bombing halt had positive results. "President Johnson's statement of March 31st," he said, "followed by the partial cessation of the bombing, brought the Vietnamese face to face with the fact that our commitment was *not* open-ended, and that one day they'd be on their own. This realization, I think, had an important and subtle impact on the development of Vietnamese attitudes and events."

By autumn, an intense discussion was under way concerning suspending bombing in North Vietnam *altogether,* a much different matter, since this would put out of reach of allied bombardment enemy forces positioned threateningly just above the border with South Vietnam. In a key White House session of 14 October, the President, meeting with Secretary of State Dean Rusk, Secretary of Defense Clark Clifford—who had succeeded Robert McNamara in the post the previous March—General Earle Wheeler, and others, asked why Abrams now felt a *total* bombing halt would be acceptable when only the previous August he had opposed it. At that time, recalled George Christian, Abrams had "built a strong case against halting the rest of the bombing of the North without guarantees from the enemy that the DMZ would be restored."[5] LBJ was told that Abrams now thought it would be worth it if the enemy indeed respected the DMZ (a part of some supposed "understandings" about what he would do if a bombing halt were ordered), and also that the weather was turning much worse now and thus less would be lost by halting the bombing (this latter apparently reflecting a belief, subsequently shown to be incorrect, that the bombing could later be resumed if deemed militarily desirable—for example, when the weather turned good again).

With a steady stream of optimistic reports issuing from Westmoreland in Vietnam, LBJ had first stated conditions for halting the bombing during a September 1967 address in San Antonio: "The United States is willing to stop all aerial and naval bombardment of North Vietnam when this will lead promptly to productive discussions. We, of course, assume that while discussions proceed, North Vietnam would not take advantage of the bombing cessation or limitation."[6] The qualification would lead to all manner of controversy, especially when Ambassador Harriman, chief American delegate to the Paris peace talks, maintained in the face of repeated North Vietnamese denials that the enemy had indeed agreed to some restraints in the event the United States suspended bombing of their country.

The North Vietnamese rejected this overture, but General Wheeler was still concerned about the implications of the offer should it be accepted. Accordingly he commissioned a study, known by the code name "Sea Cabin," to "consider the implications of the 'assumption' it made that North Vietnam would not 'take advantage' of a halt in the bombing" and "identify the dangers to the US military position in South Vietnam resulting from a bombing halt." Faced with the crude methods for monitoring and measuring enemy infiltration into South Vietnam then available, the study concluded that any increased infiltration "could not be discovered until four to six months after the event. As a consequence, the enemy could increase infiltration during protracted talks with confidence that detection would be too slow and uncertain for the United States to justify stopping negotiations or resuming the bombing."[7] Thus, even though he went along with the proposed bombing halt, Wheeler had reason to know it depended critically on North Vietnamese good faith.

IN THE INTERVAL between the partial and full bombing halts, a pertinent political event took place. Jack Albright was then an Army colonel in charge of the White House Communications Agency, a job he had held for three years and in which he saw a lot of Lyndon Johnson. In late August he was sent to Chicago to prepare for the Democratic National Convention. Among other things he supervised the installation of a forty-foot screen that could be lowered from the ceiling, a device intended to be used in screening a documentary tribute to Lyndon Johnson.

On the third day of the convention, Albright was in a hotel room with LBJ operatives Marvin Watson, Jim Jones, and Jake

Jacobson. Watson took Albright with him into another room while he placed a call to LBJ, who was at his Texas ranch. "As you know," Watson told the President, with Albright listening on an extension, "we made plans and provisions that there'd be a groundswell, and they'd nominate you by acclamation, but we now see that this won't happen, and that is confirmed by those here with me." LBJ had only one comment: "Those ungrateful son of a bitches!"

Then the President spoke to Albright: "You get your people out of there, no more than two through any airport. And don't let anybody know that you were there in preparation for my arrival." Those preparations, said Albright, had included having the President's airplane and pilot, normally kept at Bergstrom Air Force Base, standing by at the ranch. The much publicized LBJ withdrawal, then, had been a tactic, one the President never expected to have to make good on. Whatever Johnson hoped, his withdrawal freed him to move forward on a total bombing halt without regard to political consequences.[8]

BEFORE FINALIZING his decision on halting the bombing altogether, President Johnson met once again with his senior advisors, including Abrams, brought back on short notice from Vietnam. Abrams had assented to the proposed bombing halt after having been assured that any enemy violations of the "understandings"—that there would be no violations of the DMZ and no shelling of cities—would be met by resumed bombing. This was a crucial point, for only recently Abrams had cabled General Wheeler to say, "It would be my estimate that an announcement of a bombing halt without any compensating move by the enemy would come as quite a shock to some of the troops and their commanders."[9]

At the White House, LBJ asked Abrams a question with a key conditional: "If the enemy honors our agreement, will this be an advantage militarily?" That was easy. "Yes, sir," he answered.[10] Abrams, in turn, asserted a condition of his own: "If the bombing were stopped and the North Vietnamese then precipitated some emergency, the situation could be handled easily by the military until the political decisions were made to resume the bombing."[11] That reinforced the position Abrams had stated unequivocally only days earlier, when he cabled Wheeler that "it must be clearly understood that initiation of ground attacks or attacks by fire against major population centers in SVN may be considered as justification for resumption of bombing in NVN."[12] On that basis, he agreed to ending the bombing.

Before Abrams departed the White House, LBJ handed his field general a letter that Abrams put in his pocket to read on the way back to Vietnam. When he took out the pale green White House stationery and read a message that began "Dear Abe," he saw that the President still hoped the war might be won, and on his watch. He told Abrams to "follow the enemy in relentless pursuit. Don't give them a minute's rest. Keep pouring it on. Let the enemy feel the weight of everything you've got." Such advice was probably superfluous in the case of Abrams, a warrior through and through, but LBJ's objective was revealing. "With luck and with Abe," he concluded, "we shall conquer ourselves a peace in the next three months."[13]

This admonition served to demonstrate dramatically the ambivalence of Lyndon Johnson toward conduct of the war. At the same time he was contemplating a total bombing halt, he was urging Abrams to go all out in the ground war in South Vietnam in quest of an early victory. One conclusion that this dichotomy, even schizophrenia, suggests is that by this point LBJ was far from a free agent even within his own administration. In Clark Clifford he had gotten a defense secretary who, contrary to Johnson's expectations, was more interested in manipulating the President to disengage than in helping him prosecute the war. Clifford boasted in his memoirs of how he had carefully crafted "the next steps in moving the President toward de-escalation."[14]

And Townsend Hoopes credited Clifford, Harriman, and Vance
with bringing off the total bombing halt.[15]

PRESIDENT JOHNSON's order to halt the bombing of North Vietnam, in fact all "air, naval, and artillery bombardment," effective
1 November 1968, drew worldwide attention. In Vietnam, the
English-language *Saigon Daily News* headlined "LBJ Orders
Bomb Halt As Reds Rocket Cities." Beyond that spectacular
enemy disregard for any reciprocal restraint, there were other
immediate military repercussions. For one thing, noted a MACV
briefer, "The bombing halt in North Vietnam will release additional experienced antiaircraft units for employment in the Laotian panhandle." A sharp rise in sensor-detected activity—
southward movement of enemy men and matériel as monitored
by allied sensors—followed the bombing halt, with "near-
capacity transshipment activity" (unloading of inbound cargo
from ships and railroads) observed in North Vietnam, intense
activity in repairing interdiction points, and the anticipated re-
location of antiaircraft units. Conversely, the halt made allied
aircraft that had been involved in the Rolling Thunder campaign
against the North available for use elsewhere, such as in the
interdiction campaign in Laos.

Abrams, back from his Washington meeting with the President, sent an important message, titled "Special Guidance for
General Officers Commanding," to his field commanders. "As
the enemy's main forces are defeated and forced to withdraw,"
Abrams observed, "the original and underlying war against the
basic VC/NVA structure in SVN comes to the fore. It must
now be carried forward with greater intensity . . . , getting into
his base areas, confiscating his supplies, and rounding up his
infrastructure. The order of the day," concluded Abrams, "is to
intensify your offensive against infrastructure, guerrillas, and local force units, while maintaining unrelenting pressure on the
VC/NVA main force units. We must carry the fight to the
enemy and complete his destruction."[16]

"In the summer and early fall of 1968," Abrams later recalled, "during the northeast monsoon season in North Vietnam, the interdiction program from the 20th parallel down was *so* effective he was not getting six trucks a week into Laos—a combination of the interdiction program and the weather. And that's the situation you had when the bombing halt occurred."

Things changed in a hurry. Two weeks into it Abrams cabled an assessment to General Wheeler. "The enemy's actions since the bombing halt reflect as much his political and psychological warfare schemes as they do the pursuit of his military goals," Abrams said. "He seeks to popularize the idea at home and abroad that he forced the bombing halt on the US without reciprocal commitments on his part. He tries to give the impression that he retains the initiative on all fronts. And he probes the limits of allied patience to determine how far he can go."[17]

During the first week after the halt there were 262 trucks detected by sensors in Route Package 1—the complex of roads and trails in the southernmost provinces of North Vietnam, just north of the DMZ—and 778 trucks by sensors in the Laotian panhandle, with 165 seen visually. By the third week 2,220 trucks were detected by sensors and 1,651 observed in Laos. The bulk of the tonnage was ammunition, 70 percent or more— 1,125 tons of it in a week. Most of the rest was POL—petroleum, oil, and lubricants—and high-priority construction of a new POL pipeline in southern North Vietnam was also observed. Meanwhile, the North Vietnamese had stepped up use of coastal sea-lanes and inland waterways to move matériel in North Vietnam, an average of seventy-five ships a day versus nineteen a day in the month before the bombing halt. In southern North Vietnam heavy tonnage vessels not seen since 1965 were back in use.

BY THE TIME ABRAMS took command, exploration of a negotiated settlement of the war was an important part of the overall calculus. Averell Harriman had represented Lyndon Johnson's administration in the early sessions with North Vietnamese negotiators in Paris. Harriman had his own agenda, one not revealed when he attended the first meeting of the "Wise Men" with President Johnson at the White House in November 1967. Wrote Clark Clifford of Harriman: "Hoping to cap his long and distinguished career by heading the negotiating team, he had no intention of losing his access to the President by prematurely revealing the depths of his opposition to the war itself." Instead, Harriman told LBJ simply that negotiations were "inevitable and necessary."[18]

Harriman did indeed get the Paris assignment, being posted there in May 1968 with Cyrus Vance as his deputy, Phillip Habib as political advisor, and Lieutenant General Andrew J. Goodpaster as JCS representative. Potential problems surfaced as early as the plane ride to Europe—indeed, even before the mission began—recalled Goodpaster. "From the outset Governor Harriman tried to get approval for offering a 'scaling back' of our military operations in Vietnam as a negotiating gambit with the North Vietnamese, hoping they would reciprocate. I opposed this at all times, beginning with our delegation's meeting with President Johnson, who disapproved Governor Harriman's proposal, and approved my position."[19]

But Harriman apparently had no intention of being constrained by anything so mundane as instructions from the President. Soon after the delegation's aircraft departed Washington, he offered the view that "now it's our job to end this war—to get the best terms we can, but to end the war." Goodpaster immediately objected. "That's not my understanding," he retorted, recalling LBJ's statement that the delegation was to negotiate, but not in any way compromise the "maximum pressure" he wanted put on the enemy. "That's not right, General," Harriman countered. "I think it's clear what our position is—what the president ordered." Goodpaster would not be intimidated. "No, sir," he shot back. "The president would not want us to endanger American lives. We have not been in-

structed to end the war on the 'best terms we can.' " By this
time the autocratic Harriman, not accustomed to being contra-
dicted, was angry. "We're going to end this war," he insisted.
"That's what the president said we should do." Goodpaster had
the last word. "Sir," he said in acid tones, "that is not what the
president said. Those are *not* our instructions."[20]

Within a few weeks Goodpaster was recalled from Paris,
promoted to four-star rank, and sent to Vietnam as deputy to
General Abrams. Lieutenant General George M. Seignious II
joined the Paris delegation as his replacement. General Earle G.
Wheeler, Chairman of the Joint Chiefs of Staff, sent Seignious
off with this message: "You're approved by the President with
only the following instructions: 'Keep steel in the backbone of
Averell Harriman.' "[21]

AFTER LONG DEBATE over procedural matters, discussions with
the North Vietnamese concerning a negotiated settlement of the
war had begun. At MACV, little was known about the process.
"I don't know what instructions the men in Paris have," Abrams
wrote to General Harold K. Johnson, "but I don't need to know.
I do know what needs to be done here and I have faith that
our government will do what's best."[22]

One thing that soon became apparent was the enemy's success in using "negotiations" as just one more weapon of war.
"It seems to me," said a participant in a discussion of expected
enemy action in August 1968, "that we've jockeyed ourselves
into a funny position in Paris vis-à-vis this projected offensive
of the enemy that, if everything goes well for the enemy and
he's able to mount the offensive, then he gets credit in the head-
lines for power and so on, like he did at Tet. On the other hand
if, by virtue of our efforts here, we succeed in preempting him
and preventing his offensive, then he gets credit for deescala-
tion." That was it exactly, an excruciating problem for the field
command. "You've described the problem quite well," Abrams
told his colleague to accompanying laughter.

In Saigon there was great concern about what Averell Harriman as chief U.S. delegate to the Paris peace talks was up to. "There have been several press announcements or interviews by Secretary Clifford and by Ambassador Harriman which seem to me to indicate considerable misunderstanding, or at least terribly wishful thinking on their part vis-à-vis a possible NVN . . . de-escalation," noted a MACV staffer in late August. Thus he put a question to General Goodpaster, based on his recent experience in Paris, as to whether it was understood there that the enemy had earlier that month attempted a major offensive, but U.S. operations had successfully delayed and diminished the attacks when they came. Did anyone in Paris recognize that, far from showing goodwill or restraint, the enemy was doing its best to continue the war at full force? "It seems to me very important that our negotiators not be given *any* chance to misinterpret the fact that we have successfully preempted this guy as in *any* way a de-escalation on his part."

Goodpaster understood that concern very well indeed. "I think the pressures that were mounting during this so-called 'lull' were very, very great," he said, "and if it hadn't been for two men, probably, we would have interpreted the lull as this restraint. And those men are Dean Rusk and the President, with of course the advice of General Wheeler." There was a related point concerning the Third Offensive: "If the enemy had *not* started this thing when he did, prior to the Democratic convention, it would be just a *damn* close thing as to which way that resolution [on the antiwar platform plank] would have gone."

When the Third Offensive of August 1968 accomplished very little for the enemy, who had hoped for a great deal from it, the obvious question was what that would mean in terms of negotiations, and especially the enemy's attitude at the talks. Abrams observed that the enemy "really had planned on a *humdinger*," a judgment confirmed by his intelligence officer. "Bigger than *ever* before, according to their documents," said

General Davidson. "And that would fit *so well* with the Communist as he picks up his suitcase and goes off to the negotiations," concluded Abrams. "And probably has a lot to do with the intransigence that they have shown. Now, if there's any validity to *that,* what form is the *next* shoe going to take that's dropped?"

Abrams was keenly aware of the leverage the enemy derived from antiwar elements in the United States. "Did you see that *plank* that was defeated by 1,500 to 1,000?" he asked, referring to the platform debate at the Democratic National Convention in August. There the antiwar faction's plank had advocated unconditional termination of bombing in North Vietnam, mutual withdrawal of U.S. and North Vietnamese forces from South Vietnam, a coalition government in South Vietnam, and reduction of U.S. offensive operations.[23] "*I* would say that he's got *substantial* negotiating material. He's got 1,000 Democrats that were at that convention that would have *emasculated* the position over here." Given that background, speculated Abrams, were Xuan Thuy to propose a cease-fire, "with things the way they are in the United States, he could get a damn good deal out of it. A *lot* better than he *deserves,*" meaning better than battlefield results entitled him to.

Later such authoritative voices as Bui Tin's testified to the importance the North Vietnamese attached to the antiwar movement in the United States. "It was essential to our strategy," said Colonel Tin. "Every day our leadership would listen to world news over the radio at 9 a.m. to follow the growth of the American antiwar movement. Visits to Hanoi by people like Jane Fonda and former Attorney General Ramsey Clark and ministers gave us confidence that we should hold on in the face of battlefield reverses. We were elated when Jane Fonda, wearing a red Vietnamese dress, said at a press conference that she was ashamed of American actions in the war and that she would struggle along with us."[24] After the war Admiral Elmo Zumwalt visited Vietnam and talked with Communist leaders. "General

Giap was very clear," said Zumwalt. "They always knew they had to win it here [in the United States] and the Jane Fondas of this world were of great use to them."[25]

As 1968 NEARED an end, the evolving calculus was, as seen from MACV, increasingly favorable. Enemy combat losses during 1968 had to be made up through further recruitment in the South or infiltration from the North. Douglas Pike estimated that General Giap began the winter–spring campaign with about 195,000 troops and lost 85,000 of them killed or permanently disabled in just that one offensive.[26] Then, as the pacification program extended government control to more of the rural population, recruitment or impressment in those areas became more difficult. In addition, in the aftermath of the Tet Offensive a large number of Viet Cong rallied to the government side, constituting more losses that had to be covered. By year's end, concluded MACV, enemy losses had reached the staggering total of "289,000 men, or more than 100 percent of his total present military strength."

Said Bui Tin, "The second and third waves in May and September were, in retrospect, mistakes. Our forces in the South were nearly wiped out by all the fighting in 1968. It took us until 1971 to re-establish our presence, but we had to use North Vietnamese troops as local guerrillas. If the American forces had not begun to withdraw under Nixon in 1969, they could have punished us severely. We suffered badly in 1969 and 1970 as it was."[27] These admissions underscore dramatically the incalculable cost to the allies of General Westmoreland's having squandered four years of public and congressional support for the war with his unavailing schemes.

John Vann provided a year-end assessment in letters to various correspondents. "The situation in Vietnam today gives cause for more optimism than at any time since 1961," he wrote. And the RVNAF, Vann told San Francisco Mayor Sam Yorty, "has improved substantially since the arrival of General

Abrams and the greatly increased interest in the RF/PF that he was able to stimulate." Yorty sent a copy of the letter to Richard Nixon—"as I expected," Vann wrote to a friend.[28]

At a commanders conference General Abrams invited Ambassador Bunker to comment. Bunker called the year 1968 "perhaps the most momentous one we've seen since the decision in 1965 to come in here in force." Acknowledging that there were still many problems to be solved, he commented on the "*very great progress*" made during 1968, progress not always appreciated in the United States. "I went back for three days in April to report to the President," he recalled, "and I was *shocked* to see the effect the Tet Offensive had had at home. There was no panic *here,*" he added, implying that that had perhaps not been the case in Washington.

Bunker also mentioned the constructive results of Tet 1968 in South Vietnam. One step taken was full mobilization, and Bunker illustrated the significance—and burden—of that by comparing South Vietnam's force of one million people under arms with what a like percentage of America's population would produce—an armed force of some 18 million. He also mentioned the People's Self-Defense Forces and the Accelerated Pacification Campaign, the Chieu Hoi program, and the beginning of efforts to root out the enemy infrastructure. "My yardstick of success here," Bunker concluded, "is what the Vietnamese can do themselves, because that eventually is the ultimate test. They've got to take over someday. It's quite clear that we're not going to be here forever. And what *we* can get them to do— through instruction, through persuasion, through pressure, in whatever way—to do the job themselves is the ultimate yardstick of success."

AT YEAR'S END General Abrams offered an imaginative gift to General Wheeler. "I have developed a clandestine capability to fire the 107, 122, and 140mm enemy rockets," he revealed. In a project called "Pot Luck," a firing team of one officer and ten enlisted men from the 525th Military Intelligence Group had been trained in all aspects of laying and firing rockets. Said Abrams, "Their accuracy ranges from two hundred to eight hundred meters at a range of seven thousand yards."[29]

Abrams had picked out a likely target, an enemy base area in the Fishhook area of Cambodia west of Saigon, where he thought 122mm rockets with delay fuses could be very effective. Radio direction-finding indicated that major elements were almost always in residence, and danger to Cambodian civilians was deemed minimal. "Even if Sihanouk complains (and the ICC investigates)," Abrams said reassuringly, "there will be no evidence of US weapons being used." Noting that Ambassador Bunker concurred in his recommendation, Abrams asked for permission to lob twenty rockets into the enemy camp.

The reaction in the Joint Chiefs of Staff must have been "not only no, but hell no," because before long Abrams was sending a message instructing all those who had gotten his earlier communication to destroy all materials relating to "Pot Luck."[30] The war continued in more pedestrian fashion.

7

Tet 1969

EARLY IN THE NEW YEAR Abrams began getting some welcome mail. "Some of these loyal Vietnamese citizens down here in Saigon began writing me about generators making too much noise or black smoke coming out of the diesel generators and all that," he exulted. "It was *great!* Before that, of course, they were yelling about the *rockets.*"

More ominously, in early January 1969 MACV intelligence reported that "right now we probably have more hard indications of an imminent offensive than we have ever had before. Their most significant aspect, however, is their contradictory nature."[1] The enemy had, MACV calculated, lost 42,000 at Tet 1968, 40,000 in the mini-Tet attacks of May 1968, another 26,000 in the Third Offensive of August 1968, and a surprising 53,200 in the final quarter of 1968—161,200 dead in just that one year—and now it seemed that he was stubbornly, foolishly, incredibly going to have another go at the same unavailing approach. Abrams and Bunker sat down together for a special assessment briefing that considered three enemy options: a DMZ attack, a Laotian–Military Region Tri-Thien-Hue attack, and a Cambodian option slicing into Vietnam from the flank.

Clearly the enemy was building up for something significant, as signaled by an accelerated flow of infiltration. Several groups

were moving by train, and by late December the rate of input
into the pipeline had been exceeded only during March–April
1968. There were now more than 37,000 troops moving south,
the bulk of them destined for the I and III Corps areas, and the
analysts thought they included the 304th NVA Division. "In
summary," they observed, "we are currently observing a movement of unusual proportions, comparable to that which occurred during the same period in 1968."

A comparable large-scale logistical buildup was also under
way. Soon after the bombing halt of 1 November 1968, the enemy had begun reconstructing fords, bridges, and ferry crossing
sites on his lines of communications in the southern provinces of
North Vietnam, extending a rail segment to Vinh, and stockpiling
matériel—an estimated 300 tons a day—near the DMZ. MACV
looked ruefully at a photograph of more than fifty enemy trucks
waiting to cross at one of the two Quang Khe ferries. That had,
observed the briefer, been "one of our key choke points in the
summer interdiction campaign. Employment of hard bombs, an-
timatériel and antipersonnel munitions, plus seeding of the river
with Mark 36 mines bottled up the traffic." Now it was wide
open.[2] In addition, foreign vessels were observed at the port
facilities near Vinh for the first time in many years.

With all this under way, interdiction of the Ho Chi Minh
Trail thus continued to be an allied obsession. Now, though, the
task was made infinitely more difficult by the termination of
bombing in North Vietnam. Whereas before there had been
within North Vietnam that small number of well-defined choke
points which, if kept closed, effectively blocked traffic to the
South, now the bombing effort had to be shifted to Laos, where
most of the choke points could be bypassed, and the farther
south one got, the more the route structure expanded.

The two prime access routes into Laos from North Vietnam
went through defiles known as the Mu Gia Pass and the Ban
Karai Pass. Interdiction efforts concentrated on these choke
points. Once they were beyond the choke points, enemy truck

convoys could be brought under attack on flatter and more open terrain, where more truck kills were recorded, but it continued to be extremely difficult to halt the influx by taking trucks out individually.

By early January 1969 sensor detections were running at the highest level since before the previous year's May attacks, further evidence that a serious offensive was in the offing. Killing these trucks had, however, become easier in November and December 1968 with the introduction of AC-123 and AC-130 gunships. Initially there were two of each type of aircraft, a total of four out of some 300 aircraft devoted to interdiction. By January 1969 these four gunships were, according to the Seventh Air Force commander, General George Brown, accounting for an astounding 27 percent of the truck kills.

A later history of PAVN reflected the enemy's view of this terrifying new weapons system. "Over the Ho Chi Minh Trail," it observed, "AC-130E aircraft, equipped with sensors to locate targets and 40mm rockets [actually cannon] to destroy these targets, flew constantly throughout the night. They destroyed many of our trucks. Our combat fighters who drove the trucks courageously, resolutely, and cleverly overcame horrendous obstacles to bring supplies to the front lines, and some comrades sacrificed their lives in the cabs of their trucks. At the same time, faced with the blood and fire of combat on the supply route to the South, some drivers wavered, and there were even some who abandoned their vehicles when they heard just the sound of the enemy's AC-130E gunships flying overhead."[3]

In December 1968, 857 trucks had been taken out, and it looked like the total in January might reach 1,000. But even that did not stem the tide. General Brown reported that of 1,800 Arc Light—B-52 bomber—strikes a month, almost half were being put into Laos, along with 450 to 500 Navy and Air Force tactical air sorties a day. "And he's still pushing trucks through," Brown admitted. "He's got quite a stockpile now down as far as Tchepone."

What the enemy was moving was ominous. Bombing the
trail was producing large numbers of secondary fires and explosions—reciprocal reactions caused by the bombs being
dropped—and, said Brown, "there're only two things moving
through there that'll burn and explode—that's ammunition and
POL. It's the most frustrating experience *I've* ever had chasing
these things [trucks]," he exploded. "I can't stop trucks one at
a time." Clearly the enemy was preparing for heavy combat, not
just hauling rice to feed the troops, and everyone knew it.

Despite the frustration, an impressive number of trucks was
in fact taken out, an estimated 7,000 damaged or destroyed during January–July 1969. During the same period the enemy
brought 2,600 new trucks into North Vietnam by sea—more
than double the number during the same period in 1968—most
of them from the Soviet Union, and an unknown additional
number by rail or road from China.

The enemy acknowledged grave difficulties due to allied interdiction during this period. During several months of 1969,
noted a history of PAVN, some main force units operating in
forward areas, replacement troops traveling down the Ho Chi
Minh Trail, and the 559th Transportation Group that administered the trail were reduced to eating only two or three *lang* of
rice per day, a *lang* being about an ounce and a third. One unit
in particular distress, the 6th Engineer Battalion stationed at Binh
Tram 35, "was forced to eat sycamore berries, roots, and weeds
in place of rice, and they burned straw and ate the ashes in place
of salt." Troops were diverted from military tasks to search for
food, some even developing the slogan "Producing food is the
same as fighting the enemy." In the Central Highlands, claimed
this account, "each cadre and soldier planted 1,000 manioc
plants."[4]

WHILE THE HO CHI MINH Trail was under fierce and continuous
air attack, access to the South Vietnamese coast from the sea had
since mid-1966 been effectively sealed off through intensive pa-

trolling by South Vietnamese and U.S. ships. But there was a flood of supplies coming into the Cambodian port of Sihanoukville and then through Cambodia into III and IV Corps of South Vietnam and even up to the southern portions of II Corps. By January 1969 it was clear to MACV analysts that Sihanoukville was "the primary point of entry for supplies, especially arms and ammunition, destined for enemy forces in southern South Vietnam." This traffic had been monitored since November 1966, and so far thirty-four ships suspected of unloading ordnance had docked at Sihanoukville. Twelve that were well documented had delivered more than 14,000 tons of ordnance from November 1966 to October 1968.

Those deliveries were ostensibly made in fulfillment of military aid agreements Cambodia had concluded with China and the Soviet Union, but the quantities were grossly more than FARK (the Cambodian armed forces) could need, perhaps 14,000 tons delivered as against an estimated requirement of 800 tons. Clearly a lot of extra ordnance was floating around somewhere. MACV intelligence officers had built up a very complete picture of this traffic from a wealth of prisoner of war interrogations, ralliers, and agents. "The magnitude of the arms traffic, and its efficient working apparatus, suggest the knowledge, if not active participation, of high-ranking Cambodian military and political figures," they concluded.

Cambodian military trucks were found to be engaged in distributing the arms and ammunition landed at Sihanoukville, as were those of a Hak Ly Trucking Company.[5] There were even reports of regular Sunday meetings in Phnom Penh at which representatives of FARK, the Sihanouk regime, the Hak Ly enterprise, and the National Liberation Front arranged distribution of the goods. This and other evidence, MACV concluded, left no doubt of "FARK's complicity with the enemy." Indeed, said Davidson in early January, an intelligence task force from Washington "now agree with us specifically as to this, that there *is* high-ranking Cambodian complicity in the movements of arms and ammunition through Cambodia. They're inclined to take a disclaimer that Sihanouk himself is involved, although whether he *knows* [about it] or not they—I *think* they're inclined to believe he does, as we are." In any case, added Davidson, "there is high-level complicity. It may go as high as Lon Nol, the acting prime minister."

The distribution system was well organized and efficient. After leaving Sihanoukville, the munitions were transported to an arms depot at Kompong Speu, about twenty-five miles southwest of Phnom Penh, or to warehouses in the capital city. From there they were distributed to enemy base areas in the border region, and eventually to troop units in South Vietnam.

At CIA this picture of the enemy supply system had for a long time been vigorously disputed. There the "intelligence analysts at the Washington level" really came down to one man, a veteran CIA officer named James Graham. The lead analyst on the problem, he stubbornly refused, year after year, to be convinced that any significant amount of military wherewithal was reaching the enemy through the port of Sihanoukville. Within MACV, the "Graham Report" staking out that position became infamous. MACV was incensed by its obtuseness, as they saw it, or worse. Later Davidson, who had struggled with this problem when he was MACV J-2, recalled that Graham once said to him, "Sometimes you've got to find what you've got to find."[6]

THE NEW TACTICS were by now widely in evidence. In the 25th Infantry Division during this period, said its commander, Major General Harris Hollis, tactical deployment consisted of a huge number of small operations that were decentralized in execution but highly centralized "in terms of target acquisition, intelligence and surveillance, and in the provision of aviation and other combat support." This approach inhibited enemy movement, both day and night, while serving to "disrupt his communications, uncover his caches, interrupt his supply, fragment his units and take out his guides in increasing numbers." Hollis came to think of his command as a "reconnaissance division."[7]

In the 1st Cavalry Division its commander, Major General Elvy Roberts, reported a similar approach. Describing a number of shifts in small unit tactics over the past year, he identified as the most important "the use of infantry companies, operating alone, as light scouting forces whose mission is to search out the enemy, locate him accurately, and bring all possible heavy firepower down on him." In the XXIV Corps the situation was pretty much the same, said Lieutenant General Melvin Zais, "characterized by intensive patrol and ambush activities to deny the enemy access to the population, and by limited offensive operations to thwart enemy efforts to build up for attacks, particularly during Tet. This use of forces permitted an intensified effort to accelerate the pacification program in Thua Thien and Quang Tri Provinces."

In February 1969 an Army liaison team visited Vietnam. One of its members, an experienced infantry officer who had served two previous tours in Vietnam as a battalion commander in the 1st Infantry Division, as an operations staff officer in MACV Headquarters, and as a regimental advisor to the ARVN, reported his impressions after extensive visits by the team to nearly all major Army units in Vietnam. His first words told the story: "It's a new and different war!"[8]

Colonel Richard Prillaman cited as the key changes that "US Army units are fragmenting, with small unit operations replacing searches by battalions and brigades; and second, we are now working with the Vietnamese to an unprecedented degree, targeting on the enemy among the population rather than forces hiding in the jungle." He recalled a conversation with a brigade commander who had been told that if a given bridge in his area of responsibility got blown up, "my best position would be right in the middle of it."[9]

"Had I been told of these new developments in higher headquarters briefings," Prillaman said, "I might have dismissed them as being colored by wishful thinking, but my information was gathered from battalion commanders, company commanders, sergeant majors, and working men. . . . I put my faith in the off-the-cuff comments of C-ration consumers, and these men are unanimous in their opinion that a new situation exists and that our response is effective."[10]

ANTICIPATING THE enemy's winter–spring offensive, Abrams coached his commanders on how the enemy did business, emphasizing the opportunities such knowledge presented. "First, he will set his objectives. Second, he will establish his axes of advance, all based on areas in which guerrillas and VC infrastructure are strong. Third, he will work with the VC infrastructure and guerrillas to establish his supplies in depots or caches. Fourth, he will maneuver his main force units to take advantage of the supplies, security, reconnaissance, and guides provided by the guerrillas and VC infrastructure. So the best thing to do is to get out and beat the hell out of the cadre and local forces," Abrams stressed, "so that the ability of the big units to move, or do anything, is militarily impractical. This is the real meat and potatoes."[11]

All this enemy activity could be detected early by relatively small forces, Abrams pointed out, while "simultaneously, the attack against enemy base areas, supply points, main and local forces, and the VC infrastructure can continue unabated." Keep the pressure on, Abrams urged, and do it intelligently, paying attention to how the enemy operates. "Then, utilizing the knowledge thus gained, go after the enemy's machinery, crack his engine block, drain his oil, strip his gears, break his fuel lines, remove his spark plugs, and otherwise put his engine beyond repair or rebuild."[12]

ON 23 FEBRUARY the enemy buildup reached its logical conclusion. That was right on schedule; Bunker and Abrams had only the day before "warned Washington that large-scale attacks were expected that day or the following."[13] The new offensive was much more intense than any in the previous year. Separate incidents totaled a third more than at Tet 1968, as did ground attacks, along with nearly 600 more standoff attacks by fire. Most proved short-lived. Colonel Hoang Ngoc Lung observed "the conspicuous absence of local forces and the exclusive use of main force units in all attacks," judging this to be a consequence of the heavy losses inflicted on local forces during the campaigns of the previous year, also reflected in the enemy's "inability to launch any infantry attacks against Saigon" during this offensive.[14]

There were other major differences. This offensive struck primarily military units and facilities, whereas earlier offensives had targeted population centers. And now, rather than a coordinated countrywide offensive, the attacks were concentrated in just two areas, near Saigon and near Danang. Consequently, Tet 1969 generated very few refugees, a scant 2.5 percent of the number produced by Tet 1968. Summing it up, a MACV analyst called this "a well-coordinated and widespread effort, but one designed to be least costly to the enemy. Many small ground attacks, but relatively little significant ground action. Instead, primary reliance on attacks by fire. And these, though numerous, have been comparatively light in munitions expenditures."

During the 1969 Tet Offensive, just as before, the enemy took terrible casualties. A chart depicting enemy KIA—categorized by the allied elements that caused them—drew a reflective responsive from Abrams. "*Well*—in a way that's a very sad chart," he began, "because there're so many people killed. But, looking at it dispassionately if you can, that is the most favorable balance of affairs that we have yet seen." The data showed that in III Corps 31 percent of the KIA had been inflicted by U.S. forces, 67 percent by the RVNAF. And in I Corps, where there was still a heavy U.S. commitment, 51 percent was credited to RVNAF. "*Ah*—you know, there's a *story* in that chart. Talk about ARVN, whether they're in the game.

As I say, it's a *sad* thing. There's no—it sounds kind of disre-
spectful to gloat over it, but in the business of who's getting in
the war, I think that's an important chart."

Meanwhile, although the stated intent of the enemy was to
inflict heavy casualties on U.S. forces, those casualties were
down substantially from the comparable offensive of the year
before. Abrams credited better intelligence. "I think that for this
offensive we were far better served by intelligence as we approached it, which meant that we were able to target our resources against his preparations in a far better way, a far more
effective way, than we were in any of the other—although I think
in the Third Offensive we had *that* pretty well knocked."[15]

During this offensive Saigon took a number of rockets, and
afterward it was determined that a patrol from the ARVN 6th
Ranger Group would have been fifty meters from the launch
site if it had gone where it was supposed to go. Instead, it had
stopped a kilometer and a half short. The patrol leader was
court-martialed and, reported Abrams to Admiral McCain,
"the commanding officer of the 6th Ranger Group has been
guaranteed forty days in jail if a single rocket is fired out of his
area of responsibility against Saigon." Abrams was encouraged.
"This is new around here," he noted. "They're getting serious
about this. It's a little crude, but I'm sure they'll get the message."

THESE ENEMY ACTIONS completely demolished the notion that,
in exchange for cessation of bombing in North Vietnam, they
would exercise any restraint in the South. Abrams and McCain,
strongly supported by Ambassador Bunker, recommended retaliation. "If US forces did not respond promptly," Bunker told
the Secretary of State, "the enemy would be encouraged to
continue the attacks, some of which clearly violated the understandings made with Hanoi at the time of the bombing halt three
and a half months earlier." But, reported JCS historians, "avail-

able sources provide no evidence that the . . . proposal was considered at the policy level."[16]

Later Nixon was his own apologist for the failure to act. "Ideally," he wrote, "we should have dealt a swift blow that would have made Hanoi's leaders think twice before they launched another attack in the South. But I was stuck with Johnson's bombing halt. I knew that even though we could show that North Vietnam clearly had violated the 'understandings,' bombing North Vietnam would produce a violent outburst of domestic protest. This, in turn, would have destroyed our efforts to bring the country together in support of our plan for peace."[17]

Henry Kissinger also critiqued this lack of response, later telling William Safire that when the North Vietnamese started this offensive "we should have responded strongly. We should have taken on the doves right then—starting bombing and mining the harbors. The war would have been over in 1970."[18] That was a judgment Nixon also came to in retrospect, suggesting that "if we had done that then, I think we would have ended the war in Vietnam in 1969 rather than in 1973." Instead, concluded Nixon sorrowfully, "that was my biggest mistake as President."[19]

THE CENTERPIECE of Averell Harriman's eight-month assignment to Paris was his assertion that he had reached an "understanding" with the North Vietnamese that if the United States stopped bombing North Vietnam, the North Vietnamese would not "take advantage" of that cessation. What that meant, it was later claimed, was that the enemy would not attack South Vietnam's cities, would not increase infiltration into the South, and would not violate the demilitarized zone.

From the first articulation of this proposition there had been widespread skepticism about the supposed understanding, not least because the North Vietnamese repeatedly and vociferously denied that any such understanding existed. Reporting to the President in mid-February 1968, Walt Rostow had noted that efforts to negotiate a peace in Vietnam had "yielded no constructive results" and that, "in particular, Hanoi apparently is not prepared to accept our assumption that, if bombing of the north should stop, no advantage would be taken of that situation."[20]

Abrams observed in early 1969, after the administration had changed and Harriman was no longer in Paris, that a North Vietnamese scam "isn't going to be so easy to run the second time, because the United States has now had quite a little experience about 'understanding.' And it hasn't been *good*." A prominent exhibit was the 1969 Tet Offensive. Abrams cabled General Wheeler in late February, saying, "I believe it appropriate to review the enemy's current offensive activity, particularly his attacks against Saigon and other populated areas and his abuse of the DMZ."[21] Those were, of course, key elements of the supposed understanding, now flagrantly ignored, or rejected, by the enemy, as Abrams noted in laying it all out. Soon he followed up with another message to Wheeler, observing that "since the enemy knowingly disregarded the 'understandings,' we should speculate as to why he did so. First, he may have wanted to show the world that the 'understandings' have no basis. He has consistently said that our bombing halt was unconditional and has stated that the 'understandings' do not rpt not exist."[22]

Only days before the Nixon administration took office, Ambassador Bunker had offered his assessment of the prospect for the negotiations. "*My* view is that the talks are going to be complex, and difficult, and long, and arduous," he said. "And I don't think we're going to reach conclusions easily or quickly." That, he suggested, had its good side: more time to make progress in building up the South Vietnamese, both militarily and politically. As President Thieu "said to me—what, six months ago?—he could hardly talk about peace or talk about negotiations or anything other than a military victory. Now he can talk

about the fact that there has to be a political settlement sometime, and that the context *will* change from military to political."

Goodpaster was able to provide some wary insight in Saigon.
Davidson, the MACV J-2, had in early February 1969 studied
a sheaf of incoming State Department documents and perceived
that he "had been working on what's at best a questionable
premise, and perhaps a false premise." He had believed that the
claimed "understanding" with the enemy included prohibition
of ground attacks on cities. Now he realized "that the North
Vietnamese do not understand that a ground attack on Saigon,
without 'indiscriminate shelling,' is a violation of the understanding." Cautioned Goodpaster, "Well, that's fairly finespun
stuff, Phil—what they understand, what they don't understand,
do we understand that they understand, and so on. You get into
fairly wispy stuff there." From Abrams: *"That's right!"*

Repeatedly the shaky basis for there being any "understandings" became clear in the one place it really mattered—on the
battlefield. The Nixon administration had continued the total
bombing halt ordered by LBJ, and there continued to be frequent references to the understandings. "As you know," Abrams
later told a visiting General Charles Bonesteel, "one of the understandings in the bombing halt was that everyone would observe the DMZ. And these characters in there—when pressed
on this, they always said, 'You will see. You will see. We will
understand and we will do appropriate things' and so on. So this
sort of *bullshit* developed into an 'understanding.' Well, it turns
out that the understanding was quite different. Now, *we* wanted
to have freedom to the Ben Hai—in other words, to the demarcation line. And I can tell you that at the meeting in Washington when this decision was made, I *lost* that, because *they* said
that our—the understanding was that we would *both* keep out
of the demilitarized zone. Well, this handicaps—. We've stood
against this *forever*, because it *handicaps* us."

Soon after the change of administrations, a copy of COSVN

Resolution 8 was captured and analyzed. What it revealed about the enemy and negotiations, MACV concluded, was that "it is here that he believes he had made his greatest progress—the bombing limitations, then the complete bombing halt, the admission of the NLF to the Paris discussions." Beyond that, "negotiations are now his main arena. We hold that all his political, military and diplomatic actions are directly or indirectly related to their outcome."

IN LATE MARCH 1969 another crisis erupted when there was a further hiatus in intercepted communications from the *binh trams*. It was always possible that there simply had been no new infiltration groups entering the pipeline, but the fact that logistical traffic continued unabated seemed to indicate otherwise.

Abrams had only recently been told that the enemy was not limited by manpower shortages, a crucially important judgment, and now he challenged his new intelligence officer. "The study that you cited for me the other day—they could go on indefinitely at the 1968 level," he reminded William Potts, "that's supposed to be an authoritative study." If infiltration really had ceased, as the absence of communications intelligence suggested, perhaps a different conclusion was warranted. But by mid-July a MACV analyst could report that "collateral evidence," meaning such things as document exploitation and prisoner of war interrogation, "now provides evidence that infiltration from North Vietnam has in fact continued." That was very interesting, but extremely worrisome as well. "The real question here," Abrams pointed out, "is whether COMINT [communications intelligence] any longer gives us a hold on this."

"This matter of infiltration has tremendous political implications to our government," Abrams emphasized. "We've grown unsure now that we *know* a reasonably good picture. We're *unsure* of that. And it's been brought out by this prisoner and document effort that we *had* missed something. If we read this wrong, or our *government* winds up reading it wrong, it's possible to make *quite* a tragic mistake. That's what we don't want to do."

The fact of the apparent lull had been reported, then leaked, so "everybody in Washington knows this, including Joe Alsop," said Abrams, and "*tremendous* political significance has been attached to it." Particularly was that the case with "a large body of people that think that these fellows are really pretty nice guys, honorable chaps, and they're *really* trying to show us that they really want to call this thing off. But they have so much pride and so on that they can't afford to announce it publicly. They're just sending discreet—ah—signals.

"I'm not anxious to cling to *anything*," Abrams emphasized. "If our estimates have been off, then we will *say* that our estimates have been off. There's nothing *sacred* in this. The only thing that's sacred is try to know the truth. *That's* the thing that's sacred. We've got to—we've *got* to put our best work into this! And we've got to look at it, because our own government is just going haywire on the *dreams* that they're manufacturing out of no infiltration. It's of *strategic* impact."[23] Potts suggested that people in Washington looking at the lull were "trying to read into it what they want." Abrams agreed: "It shows you what *weak* men will do—what *weak* men will do!"

8

Drawdown

EARLY IN 1969, many months before the first redeployments of U.S. forces from Vietnam, Abrams had described for the staff the pressures that existed. Maybe they would be asked, "What should you do?" Suppose they answered, "Well, just keep on doing what we're doing." And the next question would be, "How long is that going to take?" Then, "What's *that* going to do? What's the *price* tag on that? How many *lives* are you talking about? Another 30,000? I mean, where is this thing going to wind up?" Abrams, with the understatement he often favored, concluded simply: "It could be quite a problem."

Newly appointed Secretary of Defense Melvin Laird arrived in Saigon for his first visit just hours after enemy rockets struck the city. Naturally the topic came up at his airport news conference, prompting Laird to state that "such sadistic attacks against the civilian population are, in my view as Secretary of Defense, a violation of the understanding between the United States and North Vietnam."[1] According to Averell Harriman, though, this was all the fault of the Americans. "If the United States would take the lead in scaling down the war," he was quoted as saying, "the enemy would follow suit."[2]

During Laird's four years in office the American presence in Vietnam would be progressively reduced, then terminated altogether, and Laird was the strongest advocate of accelerating that process. In Saigon he laid out his perspective for Bunker, Abrams, and others. It was important, he said, to develop some sort of a program that would demonstrate that American troops were being protected, and that real progress was being made toward the overall objective of self-determination for South Vietnam, while at the same time reducing the American contribution in terms of men, casualties, matériel, and dollars. And, Laird emphasized, there was not much time to come up with such a plan, since "that program has to be laid out by our President probably within the next three or four months."[3] This was, apparently, going to be what Nixon needed to make good on his "I have a plan" assurances during the recent election campaign.

The centerpiece of the new approach was unilateral withdrawal of American forces from Vietnam. That was, contrary to many later assertions, wholly acceptable to the U.S. command. In fact, Don Marshall's new long-range study, published as the *MACV Objectives Plan,* included an assertion, labeled "the heart of the matter," that "the reduction of American forces is required, not simply as a ploy to 'buy' time, but also as a necessary method of compelling the South Vietnamese to take over the war. They must!"[4] One field commander, confronted with that prospect, described the difficulty of implementing force reductions. "Unfortunately, every time we get to that point, the terrain and the enemy foul us up," he complained. "Well, of course that's been the problem right along, the enemy," Abrams sympathized.

Ambassador Bunker described to Laird how it looked from his perspective. "We're engaged in fighting a limited war, for limited objectives, and with limited resources. At the same time we're advising and supporting the Vietnamese in their efforts to carry out—carry through—a social revolution." Under those circumstances, "when we talk of winning the war, we mean it in the sense of an acceptable political settlement which gives the

Vietnamese people the opportunity to choose freely their own government."

Looked at from the opposing side, said Bunker, "the current offensive has gained nothing for the enemy militarily, and he must, I think, have known this before he started. The real target of the offensive is political and psychological—psychological effect on American opinion, and on the Paris talks, to prove the bombing halt is unconditional, to raise the morale of his own forces, to convey an impression of strength, and our own ineffectiveness, to try to create divisions between us and the Vietnamese, and I think to test out the new administration."

All of a piece with this, at least as seen from Saigon, was the enemy's skillful manipulation of American opinion on the war. When a briefer quoted a warning from *Quan Doi Nhan Dan,* the North Vietnamese Army's newspaper, that "a summer of active struggle will certainly occur in the United States," Abrams reacted strongly. "They have *direct* contact with leadership of groups in the United States, and they go ahead and hold meetings on how to step up, *in the United States,* the summer offensive," he maintained. "And the *doctrine* and the *tactics* and all of this goes out and so on. We're *involved* on a lot of fronts, and so are *they.* It's no exaggeration to say that they *are* in the United States."

According to a captured document, the enemy concluded—as though to reinforce Bunker's point—that "the most significant success of the 1969 spring offensive was that it boosted the anti-war movement in the US which seriously affected the American plan of aggression." Abrams passed that word to McCain, along with the enemy's observation that "the general offensive and general uprising is a hard and difficult campaign, full of rigors, sacrifices and hardships."[5]

Abrams also gave McCain his assessment of how the South Vietnamese were performing. "The divisions down in the delta are doing very well," he confirmed. "I think you can say that of all three of them. We've put a lot more helicopters down there, and it's paid off. Those three divisions down there have been doing damn well in offensive operations, preemptive operations. I'd have to say that II Corps is satisfactory, too. The *best* performance of ARVN is up in I Corps. Next, I would say, is IV Corps, with II Corps right in there. Our problem is in III Corps, and it's limited to the three divisions. The Airborne Division's done well, the Marines are doing well, the Rangers are doing well *everywhere*."[6]

BY THE TIME OF Laird's first visit to the war zone, Phil Davidson was an old hand. As the visit neared, he observed for the benefit of some of the less experienced that every Secretary of Defense visit had a point of emphasis. Robert McNamara's last visit concentrated on what use General Westmoreland was making of the troops at his disposal. Clark Clifford's one visit keyed on what could be done to improve ARVN. And, like the good intelligence officer he was, Davidson accurately predicted what Laird would be interested in. "My guess is that the hidden theme this time, and there's no word of it on the agenda, is 'When can you start withdrawing troops?'"[7] That was right on the button. As Laird's plane lifted off at the conclusion of the visit, Abrams turned and remarked to someone that Laird "certainly had not come to Saigon to help us win the war."[8]

Lieutenant General Robert Pursley, who was Laird's military assistant, offered some insight into Laird's situation. "Nixon had campaigned on having a plan to end the war," Pursley recalled. "The fact is he did not. Administration policy was largely formulated on Laird's first trip to Southeast Asia." Laird saw in Vietnamization the key to resolving the problem, turning the war back over to the Vietnamese. That would, he reasoned, send a signal to the North Vietnamese that the United States was going to help build a force in the South that could last as long as the North could. At the same time it would send a message to the Congress that there was another way than just sending more U.S. troops and taking more casualties. Laird, added Pursley, "felt he had a receptive audience in Abrams, and a supporting military commander for that line of strategy."

The rate of troop withdrawal would become, and remain, one of the most divisive issues among senior administration policymakers. Laird aggressively pushed for the fastest possible withdrawal, whereas Nixon was more disposed to take troops out only as rapidly as necessary to pacify domestic opposition to the war. Abrams took the brunt of this, remembered Al Haig, "because he was clearly being whiplashed between the White House on one hand and Mel Laird on the other."[9] Henry Kissinger commented that "Laird would think nothing of coming to a White House meeting with the Joint Chiefs of Staff, supporting their position, then indicating his reservations privately to the President and me, only to work out a third approach later with his friend Chairman Mahon. The maneuvers of Nixon and Laird to steal the credit for each announced troop withdrawal from Vietnam were conducted with all the artistry of a Kabuki play, with an admixture of the Florentine court politics of the fifteenth century."[10]

Colby—and this is compelling testimony, given Colby's desperate push to achieve pacification before the American troops were all pulled out—argued that "Laird was the unsung hero of the whole war effort. A clever midwestern politician, he saw the need to adjust American strategy to maintain the support of the American people in political terms—'the art of the possible.' "[11] It is arguable that Laird—who opposed the Cambodian incursion and the resumption of bombing in the North, and lost on both—had the more perceptive view of the rapidly waning patience of the American public and that, through skillful bureaucratic maneuvering, he did eventually win out on the key issue in contention, the pace and magnitude of American withdrawal.

"I do not want to be an obstruction to this thing," Abrams

told Colonel Donn Starry, his key associate during the initial close-hold redeployment planning. "It's going to happen whether you and I want it to happen or not. I do not want to be an obstructionist, but I do want it to be done in a way that does not completely bug out on the Vietnamese and leave them flat and unable to defend themselves." Both knew there were strong forces pulling the other way.

As EARLY AS THE autumn of 1968 Abrams had begun urgently requesting additional authorities that would permit extensive cross-border reconnaissance into Cambodia. "The Cambodian problem is of vital importance to this command," he cabled Admiral McCain. "The enemy's logistic system depends on use of Cambodia, and this use increases daily." This was particularly significant because it came at a time when—by means of an intensive air campaign, supplemented by aggressive cache seizures in South Vietnam—Seventh Air Force reported having reduced the throughput of enemy matériel by 90 percent. "The authority requested, we realize," Abrams acknowledged, "is much greater than anyone has asked for in the past. It is necessary and is commensurate with the growing magnitude of the problem. Partial measures will not suffice."[12]

Then Abrams asked for authority to conduct bombing of enemy forces in Cambodia. Washington approved the request, and Nixon ascribed great significance to commencement of the Cambodian bombing. "It was," he later reflected, "the first turning point in my administration's conduct of the Vietnam war,"[13] a judgment probably based on a sense that the operation shifted the administration to a more proactive stance. B-52 bombing of enemy base areas in the Cambodian border region began in mid-March 1969 and continued periodically for the next fourteen months. At MACV the operation was considered highly effective in disrupting the enemy logistics system, destroying stockpiled supplies, and preempting offensive actions.

"The raids were kept secret," wrote William Duiker, "in order to avoid alerting the media and antagonizing public opinion."[14] There had been another, perhaps more important, reason for bombing in secret: to shield Prince Norodom Sihanouk from having to defend his allowing it to happen. "Sihanouk tacitly let it be understood that as long as we didn't bomb civilian areas and kept our bombing to the sanctuaries that he didn't really object to it, although he wasn't going to say so," recalled Ambassador Bunker.[15]

The secrecy led to establishment of a complex system of dual reporting under which a B-52 strike on a target in South Vietnam was requested in the normal manner, while at the same time a strike on the nearest Cambodian target was requested through restricted channels. When the strike was flown, the aircraft would be routed to pass over or near the nominal target in South Vietnam, then continue on to drop its bombs in Cambodia. When the aircraft returned to base, the crew filed reports indicating that the target in South Vietnam had been struck and then, through separate and closely held channels, reported the Cambodian strike. A number of congressional leaders, among them Gerald Ford and John Stennis, were kept informed of the operation.[16]

Nixon later recalled how he had "directed that a cable be sent to Bunker through regular channels saying that all discussions of bombing should be suspended. I simultaneously sent a top secret 'back-channel' message—a routing outside the official system—to General Abrams telling him to ignore the message to Bunker and to continue planning the B-52 strikes on a contingency basis."[17] Laird had refused to send such a message to Abrams, insisting that it come from the President and go through Bunker, because he "didn't want Abe to have that kind of an order."[18] Laird was sympathetic to the situation that such a "dual reporting" requirement created for military officers. Later General Bruce Palmer described why he agreed: "It placed the military in an impossible situation, having literally to lie publicly about a perfectly legitimate wartime operation."[19]

Asked why the system of dual reporting for the raids had been set up, Abrams replied: "I just don't know. From a purely administrative viewpoint, this whole thing had become so complicated that I couldn't keep those things straight in my own mind. We had to have specialists to keep track of this thing and that thing."[20] For all the machinations, the secrecy didn't last long; the bombing began in March 1969 and became known publicly in May.

Of course critics of the war found in this bombing—once it was revealed—a new cause célèbre, but the operation was soundly based in international law. Nixon quoted the Hague Convention of 1907: "A neutral country has the obligation not to allow its territory to be used by a belligerent. If the neutral country is unwilling or unable to prevent this, the other belligerent has the right to take appropriate counteraction."[21]

Abrams remembered a talk in which Prince Sihanouk had said, "If the Americans bomb where the VC are, that's none of my business. Just as long as there're no Cambodians there, then there're no Cambodians to report it. I wouldn't even know." And, per Abrams, Sihanouk added, "I can't *imagine* the Hanoi representative coming to my Minister of Foreign Affairs and saying, 'I have the honor to inform you that the Americans have bombed my forces who are in your country without authority.' "[22] Significantly, on 16 April 1969, just a month after the bombings in Cambodia began, that country reestablished diplomatic relations with the United States after a four-year break.[23]

The whole matter had a surrealistic cast to it. The Cambodians pretended that the North Vietnamese had not taken over the border areas of their country, the Americans pretended that they were not bombing those enemy sanctuaries, the Cambodians pretended not to notice the bombing, and the North Vietnamese pretended that they weren't there in the first place, the latter stance a decided inconvenience in that it prevented their complaining about the bombing.

THE WAR, OF COURSE, was a Southeast Asian war, not just a war in Vietnam, despite the failure to treat it as such in the fractionated American command structure. Abrams lacked control over some of the key elements in his conduct of the war—but not, as had been the case earlier in the war, of the B-52s. Since the cessation of bombing of North Vietnam, the B-52s were employed where and when Abrams specified—*except* when Ambassador William H. Sullivan and later Ambassador G. McMurtrie Godley in Laos were able to end-run Abrams and force allocation of Arc Light strikes to their battlefield.

This absolutely infuriated Abrams, who thought most of this bombing was wasted effort because Vientiane was simply incapable of developing the timely intelligence on which good targeting could be based. He was also incensed because Vientiane had authority to disapprove strikes in Laos and frequently used that power to thwart attempts to bomb enemy base areas, especially around Tchepone, a key terminus on the Ho Chi Minh Trail. General George Brown complained that "Vientiane's got the idea that the [Base Area] 604-Tchepone area is populated by a bunch of good, stout Lao patriots, and we shouldn't be bombing up there." "Our problem is Vientiane," Abrams agreed. "That gets us back to the basic problem again of responsibility."

But when the ambassador to Laos *wanted* bombing, he wanted it in quantity and without delay. Abrams understood the importance of what Vang Pao and other indigenous commanders were accomplishing in fighting a rearguard action in northern Laos, but he hated to see assets go to waste. His view was that, without good targeting intelligence, it made no sense to just fly out and dump bombs in the jungle. "At some point in time I'm going to have to say it," Abrams concluded, "that I'm not going to put up with using resources that are available to fight *this* fight over there with a headquarters that has *established* and *proven* incompetence in the conduct of military operations. Their intelligence has been *rotten*. They have attempted to pussyfoot with the problem. And that's why they're where they're at." Then he added, "One of the principles that I've followed ever since I've been in the Army is *never reinforce disaster!* And it's stood me in good stead." The headquarters in Vientiane, he thought, was such a disaster.

The embassy was attempting to conduct a fairly robust war by using only the resources available in its attaché office and the CIA station. That was not, as seen from MACV, getting the job done. And Ambassador Godley—in the absence of compelling targeting intelligence—was not above trying to coerce Abrams by appeals to authority. During one of Secretary Laird's visits to Saigon, Abrams invited him to dinner. Laird drew Abrams and General Wheeler into Abrams's private office and pulled out a message. "He's got this goddamn thing *direct* from the ambassador," said Abrams. And neither Abrams nor his air officer, George Brown, was even an information addressee. "And he's talking about Arc Light" (B-52 operations). "*Here's* the Secretary of Defense and B-52s and—aaahh—and the imminent collapse of Laos and so on. Well, it's fairly heady wine. I've told them over and over again about the system. And then the next morning he's got *another* message from Godley which, among other things, *implores* the Secretary of Defense to use his good offices to put in the maximum tactical air effort. Frankly, quite frankly, it's not even a thing for *me* and Ambassador Godley to arrange. The *system's* got to do it. And the *system will* do it. And it will do it better than anything else we've got." Here Abrams was referring to the established staffing system through which competing air requests, targets, intelligence, and available aircraft were evaluated and, as a result of that complex calculus, bombing missions were allocated. "But this thing of solving it all between Ambassador Godley and Secretary Laird—B-52s and tac air and 105s and F-4s—it's getting too big of men involved in too little of a problem," insisted Abrams. A lot of the war was like that. General Brown assured Abrams that the thing had gotten back on track. "The only regrettable thing," he added, "is that I think the ambassador wound up looking like a guy who was sort of panicking and didn't know what he was doing."

As for those crucially important B-52s, they now belonged essentially to MACV, a major change from earlier in the war. "Back in the days when they were bombing around Hanoi and Haiphong," Abrams observed, "that was run from CINCPAC." But when the bombing was cut back, what had been Route Packages 1 and 2 were turned over to MACV. "So when you got south of the 20th parallel," said Abrams, "CINCPAC was then out of the air war and it was all run from here." Abrams viewed the B-52s as all-important, describing them as "the theater commander's reserve, his artillery, his interdiction tool, his means for influencing the battle, and in some instances his only means for meeting the enemy immediately upon discovery."[24]

The endorsements from the victims of all this firepower were, if anything, even more heartfelt. Recalling "the great B-52 deluges of 1969 and 1970," Truong Nhu Tang, a former Viet Cong, wrote that "we lived like hunted animals, an existence that demanded constant physical and mental alertness. In the Iron Triangle, wariness and tension were the companions of every waking moment, creating stresses that were to take an increasing toll on our equanimity as the American bombers closed in on the bases and sanctuaries in late 1969 and 1970." The B-52s, "invisible predators," produced "an experience of undiluted psychological terror into which we were plunged, day in, day out, for years on end."[25]

BUNKER, ABRAMS, AND Colby found no shortage of outsiders eager to contribute their ideas as to how the war should be fought. Indeed, there was a constant stream of visitors with proposals of every stripe. An example was Herman Kahn, known primarily as a civilian theorist on nuclear war issues, who wanted to establish a Saigon branch office of his Hudson Institute. (Among the schemes proposed by Kahn was digging a ditch, or moat, entirely around Saigon.) Abrams asked General Wheeler to head off any Kahn proposals in Washington, assuring him that "MACV has developed adequate in-house talent to work areas of interest to this command."[26] A prominent part of that capability was the small but high-powered long-range study group that had, since the previous autumn, been at work directly for Abrams under Lieutenant Colonel Don Marshall.

Before Abrams arrived, U.S. objectives in Vietnam had been at best uncertain. Army generals who commanded there, polled by Douglas Kinnard, responded overwhelmingly that before 1969 those objectives were neither clear nor understandable. Commented Kinnard, "That almost 70 percent of the Army generals who managed the war were uncertain of its objectives mirrors a deep-seated strategic failure."[27] As the new commander, Abrams later said, "I wanted to look seriously at what my job was, what my mission was, what they wanted me to do, what they expected me to get done. So I immediately put some people to work gathering me official documents so I could study it and get myself oriented on the chain of command and so on. That is a very frustrating story." Abrams studied the documents, and he had the staff explain them. "And it was so unreal, what was going on, compared to that—that I then organized a study group to determine what my mission *should* be."

By March 1969 the result, Don Marshall's new long-range study, was complete and, published as the *MACV Objectives Plan,* ready for implementation. It emphasized security for the population, destruction of the enemy's infrastructure in the hamlets and villages, and more effective territorial forces and police. Progressive replacement of appointed military officials by elected civilian officials and transfer of local security from the army to local forces were also key objectives, all designed to provide for eventual withdrawal of U.S. forces. The long-range plan also included a final, realistic caution: "It must not be [taken as] a foregone conclusion that the United States has the capability of reaching our stated objectives in Vietnam simply because of our enormous wealth, power, and drive to use both."

A key aspect of the new tactics devised by Abrams was restraint in the application of firepower in and near built-up areas. His long-range study group had emphasized that the villagers of South Vietnam were, naturally, just as afraid of bombs and bullets from friendly forces—the "collateral damage" caused by spillover from combat actions—as they were of enemy attacks. "My problem is colored blue," Abrams observed ruefully, meaning that he had to rein in the destructive effects of friendly forces, those traditionally depicted on battle maps in blue. "Abe was always trying to get everybody to use *appropriate* levels of force and violence," recalled Ambassador Charlie Whitehouse, and that was not an easy task. "One day he had been up somewhere and saw a patrol discover two unarmed VC in a field. 'And what do you think they did?' he asked. 'They called in an air strike, goddamn it!'" Besides that, Abrams kept emphasizing, the key was population security. As for the enemy, concluded Abrams, "I don't think it makes any difference how many losses he takes. I don't think *that* makes any *difference*."

While these battles were under way, MACV was fighting yet another, this one aimed at staving off budgetary decisions that would curtail the forces available in Vietnam. The individual services, under intense pressure to reduce expenditures—cuts of $1 billion each in Fiscal Year 1970, mandated by the administration to "cool off the economy"—were trying to bring some expensive units back from Vietnam. The Navy cut ships on the gunline by half, and Secretary Laird announced, without any coordination with MACV, that B-52 and tactical air sorties were being reduced. Then the Air Force pulled out four Air National

Guard tactical fighter squadrons and replaced them with only two, another budget-driven decision.[28]

Abrams objected vehemently to these unilateral moves. Tet 1969 was a serious matter, he emphasized, and he had no resources of his own. "The sum total of our combat power is what the services give us," he reminded Wheeler and McCain. "Quite frankly it makes my position as an operationally responsible commander in the field most difficult if the services proceed to carve out on their own my operational capability." And, Abrams observed prophetically, "once the erosion sets in, it will be hard to stop." What the services had accomplished to this point had been "magnificent," he added. "I ask only that I be consulted and given a chance as they, the services, begin to cut and run."[29]

LIKE COLBY, Ellsworth Bunker witnessed firsthand the progress in the countryside. When Secretary of State William Rogers came out in May 1969, Bunker took him to see an area in the Delta with an elderly Vietnamese as a guide. It was a hot and sticky day, and they walked about two miles to a remote hamlet. At the end, remembered Rogers, Bunker, in his Brooks Brothers seersucker suit, still looked fresh and cool. The old Vietnamese was totally exhausted, and somebody remarked on how well he had done to make it. After some discussion it was determined that he was sixty-eight years old. "Bunker," said Rogers, "was seventy-five. It was a wonderful thing."

ABRAMS HAD TAKEN command in Vietnam only a few months after America had decided, in the wake of the Tet Offensive, that the war should be abandoned as unwinnable and not worth pursuing. Soon thereafter planning began for withdrawal— transparently described as "redeployment"—of successive increments of American troops. "The Nixon administration began talking about unilateral troop withdrawals at the NSC meeting five days after the inauguration," said Alexander Haig.[30] In the Pentagon the change was reflected by renaming the *Army Buildup Progress Report,* a detailed weekly compilation of data on the forces deployed, the *Southeast Asia Analysis Report.* There would be no more buildup.[31]

Clark Clifford, Secretary of Defense in the last months of LBJ's presidency, had wanted to begin withdrawing U.S. forces from Vietnam soon after the 1968 Tet Offensive, long before the programs to improve South Vietnamese armed forces had begun to take effect. When he went out to Vietnam and advocated that, Ambassador Bunker reacted strongly against the idea. "I objected to that because I thought it would have a very demoralizing effect," he said. "And [I] was upheld. We subsequently met in Honolulu, and the President agreed that we would not begin to pull out."[32]

After that July 1968 visit to Saigon, Clifford told LBJ that he was pleased with the leadership and outlook he found in the U.S. command. "I am most favorably impressed by General Abrams," Clifford wrote to the President. "He is intelligent, experienced and resourceful. He appears to have the quality of flexibility which will be so necessary in the days ahead." And Clifford had gotten Abrams to put in writing that which he most wanted to hear. "General Abrams said in a written report to me: 'The present and programmed U.S./Free World Forces are adequate to cope with the enemy forces in South Vietnam and those known to be infiltrating.' " And, Clifford emphasized to the President, "in no quarter, at any level, did I find any suggestion that . . . additional manpower should be rushed to Vietnam."[33]

Clifford appeared to think he had wrung some sort of concession on the troop issue from Abrams, but that was far from being the case. Abrams had always maintained that the problem was not lack of manpower, but how the existing manpower had been used. Called back to Washington to confer with LBJ in the wake of the Tet Offensive, Abrams had told the President, "We've got plenty of troops." He never wavered from that, never requesting more troops at any time during his four years in command in Vietnam.

EVEN BEFORE THE drawdown of U.S. forces began—in fact as early as the summer of 1968, more than a year before the first increment of American troops left for home—it was apparent that severe financial constraints were going to constitute another impediment to conduct of the war. General Ralph Haines, who had recently left the position of Army Vice Chief of Staff, visited Saigon in July 1968. There he tried to give Abrams and the MACV staff some insight into what they were up against. "In the Department of Defense right now there's a great exercise going on," he reported, "the so-called 69-3, which is Fiscal 69 budget, give up $3 billion for blackmail to Mr. Mills and company." (Congressman Wilbur Mills was at the time chairman of the House Ways and Means Committee.) "And that impact will be felt *even* here. Today you can't touch anything that is Vietnam or Vietnam-related, but the name of that game has changed a little bit, because there's just not enough in the service budgets." Thus there loomed reductions in the training base, reductions in the sustaining base, reductions in hospital support in Japan, limitations on expenditures. "And," concluded Haines, "I don't think there's going to be an FY 69 supplemental to bail us out, regardless of *who* is elected."

Abrams reacted typically, thinking first of the impact on the soldier. "We've got to be careful what we put out here on saving money and saving expenditures. There—at least there's a *part* of the people who are over here—that doesn't *sound* very good to them. Guys at a fire support base, you know, they don't think much about this saving of money. They want to feel they've got *full* support. I just hope it doesn't get to the point where there's a clear competition between the priority to economize and the

priority to support the forces in Vietnam. I can't see how the
Army, or the country, can afford to get into *that* kind of an
argument."

BY THE TIME HE WAS elected, Richard Nixon later wrote, "it
was no longer a question of whether the next President would
withdraw our troops but of how they would leave and what
they would leave behind."[34] Both Bunker and Abrams understood that imperative, as confirmed by Deputy Ambassador Sam
Berger. "Ambassador Bunker and General Abrams and I agreed
that following Tet it was essential that the American presence
be reduced as quickly as possible and that the Vietnamese
be given every opportunity to develop with arms and equipment and training," he said. "After Tet it was impossible for us
to continue to stay there on the old basis, and that was fundamental."

It is often asserted that Abrams fought the drawdown, striving to hang on to as many troops as he could for as long as he
could, but this competent testimony establishes otherwise. "We
talked a lot about the consequences of Tet," added Berger of his
conversations with Abrams, "and the necessity to start thinking
about reducing the American forces and turning over the responsibility to the Vietnamese. He regarded the last as essential—
something that had to be done."[35]

When Presidents Nixon and Thieu met at Midway Island
on 8 June 1969, they jointly announced that an initial increment
of 25,000 U.S. troops would depart Vietnam during July and
August. This came just three and a half weeks after Nixon had
said, in a 14 May televised speech on Vietnam, that "we have
ruled out a one-sided withdrawal."[36] Nixon stated that this step
was being taken "as a consequence of Thieu's recommendation
and the assessment of our own commander in the field." Only
later did he admit that to be untrue, that "both Thieu and
Abrams had privately raised objections to the withdrawals."
Even then Nixon described the lie as a "diplomatic exaggera-

tion."[37] Such maneuvers helped illustrate Admiral Zumwalt's observation that "it wasn't easy to keep hold of your integrity or honor or pride when you worked for Richard Nixon."[38]

Some crucially important issues were debated during planning for the first withdrawal increment. One of the most significant involved who should be sent home. Abrams strongly favored redeploying units as units, sending them intact with the people currently assigned. In Washington, Army Chief of Staff General William C. Westmoreland argued for sending home the people who had served longest in Vietnam. This meant that there would have to be wholesale transfers of people in and out of redeploying units to repopulate them with only the longest-serving people. That was, insisted Westmoreland, the only fair way to do it.

It was also, and this was not hard to figure out, the most disruptive thing that could be done to the remaining forces. Ripped apart by having all their most experienced people taken out, they were then reconstituted with a collection of individuals whose only shared attribute was relatively less experience in Vietnam, a formula for destroying any semblance of unit cohesion. "Our fear was that the turbulence rate would be so high that units would become ineffective," said Donn Starry, who worked on this issue directly with Abrams. "And that's what happened. I believe it caused most of the indiscipline in units which plagued us later."

There was no doubt where the responsibility lay. "The confrontation was a direct one between Abrams and Westmoreland," said Starry. After an extended struggle, Westmoreland was able to override Abrams on the issue. "The night of the final rejection of our proposal to redeploy units instead of individuals," said Starry, "Abrams and I sat long over scotch and cigars. Finally, his eyes watering, he turned to me and said, 'I probably won't live to see the end of this, but the rest of your career will be dedicated to straightening out the mess this is going to create.' How right he was."[39]

The result was to saddle the command in Vietnam with much more difficult leadership challenges, and to do so at a time when serious problems of racial strife, drug abuse, and indiscipline were already beginning to afflict the forces both in Vietnam and elsewhere. "In the end," said Starry, "it caused leaders to go forth to battle daily with men who did not know them and whom they did not know."[40]

Starry reached the rank of full general and, as Abrams had predicted, struggled for years to help overcome the disruptive effects of Westmoreland's decision. General Max Thurman, another officer who played a key role in the Army's postwar rebuilding process as the reformist head of Recruiting Command, experienced the same effects. General Westmoreland's "fair and equitable" redeployment policy, he affirmed, was "a disaster."[41]

9

Higher Hurdles

ABRAMS WAS PASSIONATE about good intelligence. Once visiting General Charles Bonesteel suggested that intelligence was "what—half the game over here?" "W-e-l-l," Abrams responded, "sometimes I get it up around 90 percent. But I've *never* gotten *below* 50! This is your lifeblood. It's your lifeblood!" In April 1969 Brigadier General William E. Potts took over MACV intelligence. "When I reported to General Abrams to be his J-2," recalled Potts, "he said to me, 'We call it like we see it!' He told me to be absolutely factual, including on enemy strength."[1]

Potts was de facto master of ceremonies for the Weekly Intelligence Estimate Updates, and he proved to be a master indeed. More buttoned-up than his predecessor, more careful by nature and by training, very precise, very structured in his approach, Potts was serious about the job. Officers who served with him can remember the punctilious Potts, sitting with a stack of papers in front of him, compulsively straightening them, side to side, then top to bottom, over and over and over again. And they remember Potts with a small notebook of particularly sensitive information that he consulted guardedly, close to his chest, much like W. C. Fields taking a peek at his cards during a high-stakes poker game.

Asked in one meeting when the last enemy battalion-size
attack had taken place, Potts responded without an instant's hesitation: "You've had eleven since the first of July. One this past
week was reported as battalion-size, but after the reports all got
in, it was a company-size." That was vintage Potts, as was another occasion when General Abrams wondered what it would
look like if certain data were displayed in graphic rather than
tabular form. "Put up backup slide 5," said Potts, and there it
was, as though by magic, shown the other way. Even Abrams
was impressed. Not surprisingly, Abrams told Potts that he was
going to be the MACV J-2 for as long as Abrams continued in
command, and so he was, outlasting in the process five MACV
Chiefs of Staff, seven J-3s, and six J-4s.

At one WIEU the matter of intelligence reports on suspected
enemy tanks was raised. "I think I have a report on that," said
Potts. "Step out, please." Instantly a new briefer appeared and
gave a complete rundown on the subject. When Abrams asked
for a comparison of enemy input and throughput during his
logistics offensives for two years, Potts said, "Put up slide 206,
please." Then, to Abrams: "We had this updated for you last
night, sir." Indeed, Potts often seemed almost capable of reading
Abrams's mind. "Bill, do they have the—?" began Abrams. Before he could finish the sentence, Potts inserted "bar graph?"
Abrams: "Yeah, can they show that?" Instantly Potts instructed,
"Slide 201, please."

None of this was accidental. Unhappy with the response
time on one occasion, Potts gathered his staffers for some guidance after the session. "See," he explained, "when the COMUS
has his briefings, anything he's heard for the last six months he'll
call for." Potts prescribed a rehearsal with the slide list. "Call for
209," he instructed. "See if it can go up within two seconds.
You just have to drill, drill, drill."

Potts himself seemed to have mastered every fact and detail
of the complex events confronting MACV. When, for example,
Abrams asked a question about Chinese manufacture of the T-

59 tank, Potts responded with a detailed and very well-informed discussion of eight models of the T-54, the last being designated T-55, and the Chinese version or copy, the T-59, "only one of which has been spotted so far." When, during a discussion, Abrams commented that during 1965 enemy forces in the South were about 25 percent NVA, Potts quietly supplemented with "26.74." After a holiday truce the J-3 said something about "thirty-seven major enemy violations." "Thirty-four," Potts observed, and the J-3 acknowledged that was correct. What he didn't have in his head, Potts had in his notebook. Once he consulted it to determine the number of tanks the enemy had committed during Lam Son 719, provoking George Jacobson to comment that "if there's anything he can't find in that goddamn book, I don't know what the hell it is."

When, during a briefing, questions arose to which Potts did not have the answer (a rare occurrence in any event), answers materialized from some member of his staff before the briefing was over. Sir Robert Thompson, visiting MACV, once asked about the enemy's 160mm mortar. Within minutes a briefer appeared to give a complete rundown, including pictures, on the weapon. After each briefing Potts conducted a careful personal critique with his senior subordinates, at the same time ensuring that they understood whatever future tasking had resulted from the session. He was in this role invariably courteous, patient, even schoolmasterly, and gracious in publicly giving credit to his intelligence analysts for work well done.

When on one occasion Abrams challenged a briefer's presentation, complaining that reports of enemy tanks destroyed had not been confirmed, Potts gathered the key analysts during a break. Ascertaining that there were pictures of the destroyed tanks, he arranged for them to be brought in and displayed. If, very rarely indeed, Potts was subject to correction, it was usually Abrams who corrected him. Abrams, too, seemed to have the whole war in his head, and not just currently but in historical perspective as well. When a briefer slipped up in identifying an enemy unit, Abrams pointed out that it was the 9th VC, not the 9th NVA, Division. Then when Potts got into the discussion and mentioned the 271st Regiment, Abrams said it was the 273rd instead and was proved right on both counts.

By this point there was a lot to keep track of, for captured documents had become a flood. During July 1969 alone, Potts reported, 780,000 pages of documents were brought into the Saigon exploitation center. Divisions were flying the material in every afternoon. "We work on it all night," said Potts, "and the next morning reports are flown right back to them. Of course they don't translate all of that, but they scan it quickly, pull out the significant ones, and then work with them intensively."

Potts was conspicuously devoted to Abrams, directing all the briefings to him personally, however large an audience of senior people was present. The J-2 was also responsible for taping all the briefing sessions. On one occasion, a discussion with the visiting General John Michaelis, someone screened the completed tape and remarked, "General Michaelis is hard to hear." Potts explained that he had had throat cancer some years before, and now "he whispers." Never mind that, said Potts. "The main thing we want's the COMUS. *COMUSMACV!*" Responded the staffer, "No sweat. We can *always* hear him!"

Major General Tom Tarpley, who served at one point as the senior advisor in Military Region 4, savored the occasions when he was invited up the night before a Commanders WIEU to stay with Abrams at his quarters. After dinner, when the local commanders and staff had departed, those staying overnight settled in for discussion of current operations. "Those were," Tarpley remembered, "the finest exchanges of thoughts on leadership, combat, and tactics that I have ever had the privilege to participate in."[2]

ABRAMS CONTINUED to be frustrated by the failure of some commanders, American and Vietnamese alike, to grasp the essentials of one war and the emphasis on population security. He cited the 22nd ARVN Division as one example, comparing it with one of his own units. "It's like the 173rd Airborne," he said. "They've got *rigging* equipment, and they've got TO&Es for air-dropping wherever in the world the United States wants to put them, and they're all airborne trained and they're all 'all the way, sir' and all that kind of stuff. We don't *need* it! We don't *need* it!"

"Instead," Abrams insisted, "what they've got to do is get out there and cream the *VCI,* get out there in little units muckering around at night, helping the goddamn villagers, seeing that the goddamn rice stays in the warehouse and so on, and—Christ, there isn't room for a *parachute!* The only thing you can do is use it for a picnic with the villagers or something. And, unfortunately, the 22nd Division can't *see* that. It isn't being a great division, going out battling with *regiments* and *battalions* and so on! *Goddamn it,* the name of the game that's got to be done is this *other* thing!! And that's what *needs* to be done in Binh Dinh! And that's what"—he banged the table—"the 22nd Division can't *see!!* And that's what the division commander is psychologically indisposed to do! And what *everybody's* got to do, instead of talking about going off to war and *battling* with the—Christ, they've been down there licking their chops waiting for the 3rd NVA to come back! Well, of course if the 3rd NVA came back, they'd clean their clock. But that's the day they're waiting for—when the 3rd NVA comes back! W-e-l-l, *bullshit!* The thing—you *can't* do what you're *organized* for, you *can't* do what you're *trained* for. You've got to go out to do what has to be done right now in this country! *Everybody's* got to do it!!"

That was the message Abrams had been sending from the beginning, and it was one he had to keep sending over and over again, both to convince the unbelievers and, as one cohort of commanders after another finished their tours and rotated home, to teach yet another group of newcomers what he, as the institutional memory, passionately believed was the only way the war could be won.

If some South Vietnamese divisions were not up to standard, neither were—in Abrams's view—all the U.S. forces. "I must be frank to say I'm not satisfied with the way the 4th [Division] has been operating," Abrams told his J-3 in April 1969. "They haven't got—they haven't been *smart,* haven't been *skillful.* Those two miserable [enemy] regiments caused us a lot of trouble up there. And goddamn it, we were flying around blind up there, too. We didn't know what the hell we were doing. *Ponderous!* Really not up on the bit."

DURING THE SPRING of 1969, with the new administration taking a fresh look at the war in Vietnam, Washington-level policy and expectations of what the South Vietnamese must be able to accomplish were drastically revised. The result was to make their already difficult tasks dramatically more difficult. At MACV, the first indications of impending change were derived from a classic source—newspaper articles quoting various American officials. "In designing their forces," meaning those of the South Vietnamese, Abrams told a visitor, "we've tried to design them to deal with insurgency, and *not* with an NVA force of the magnitude and kind that is present at the moment in and around South Vietnam. And that's the way this has been designed, that's the way it's been funded, and so on. In other words, the thrust of this whole thing has *counted* on, I would say, negotiating the North Vietnamese out of South Vietnam." But now it appeared that change was in the wind, or at least in the press.

The visitor, Ambassador Lawrence Walsh, suggested that the program for RVNAF improvement and modernization could always be accelerated. "No, no, I don't say that," Abrams objected— equipping and training and developing leadership for an expanding force could move only so fast, and accelerating beyond what was realistic would produce only illusory progress. "In fact, I would *always* recommend against that. That would be just a case of the United States kidding itself, and"— pounding the table for emphasis—"*by god* you mustn't kid yourself!!" Walsh was unmoved. "Well, I think that's what's going on to some extent," he observed. "Well, not from me," Abrams shot back.

Back in Washington after a July 1969 visit to Vietnam, Wheeler submitted a trip report to Laird in which he emphasized that the currently planned program for Vietnamizing the war, in part by upgrading military capabilities, would yield a structure "not designed to provide the South Vietnamese armed forces the capability to deal with both the full enemy guerrilla force in country and cope with the North Vietnamese armed forces." From that fact two imperatives derived: the requirement "to obtain the withdrawal of North Vietnamese formations and individuals from South Vietnam, Cambodia, and Laos to North Vietnam; and the strong probability that we will have to maintain a residual support force in South Vietnam for some years to come unless and until the withdrawal of the North Vietnamese is achieved."[3] Abrams and others frequently spoke of what had been done in South Korea, where two U.S. divisions were still stationed some fifteen years after a peace treaty, as a model for what might happen in South Vietnam.

At the same time there was, as Abrams saw it, real progress in the all-important factors of South Vietnamese self-confidence and morale. "What's going on is not so much how many divisions anybody's got, or how many artillery pieces anybody's got," he argued. "What's going on is whether the South Vietnamese can rise up above this, or whether they can't. Whether they can get it in *their* heads to stop and lick these fellows, and all the things they do, or whether they have to succumb to them. And *I* think it's *moving* in *their* favor, the South Vietnamese, clearly and unmistakably. I'm not trying to be Pollyanna about this," Abrams concluded, "*but* the truth of the matter is that since 1964 it has *never* looked so good. There has *never* been the confidence, there has never *been* the forward movement in terms of the people *themselves*, that there is today."[4]

THE CHANGES IN tactics under Abrams, and in the concept of the nature of the war, and even the enemy reaction to battlefield reverses, by no means meant an end to fierce combat, or even to large-scale military operations. On the allied side, understanding the enemy's dependence on a "logistics nose" made clear the benefits to be had from aggressive efforts to preempt enemy operations by depriving him of the laboriously accumulated wherewithal needed to support them. Enemy base areas, many of them previously considered sacrosanct, became a main target of the new tactical approach.

For example, in the remote western portion of I Corps Tactical Zone, the enemy was making extensive use of Route 922 from Laos into the A Shau Valley. In January 1969 as many as 1,000 trucks a day were sighted by allied reconnaissance, with dense enemy antiaircraft defenses protecting the traffic. The logistical buildup signaled impending enemy operations that would imperil Hue and Quang Tri to the east. Beginning late that month, the U.S. XXIV Corps, under command of Lieutenant General Richard G. Stilwell, mounted a series of brigade-force thrusts into the border area. The overall operation, designated Dewey Canyon, was designed to interdict enemy lines of communication, capture or destroy supply caches, and inflict casualties. In an offensive sustained for some eight weeks, the U.S. 9th Marine Regiment seized more than 525 tons of matériel, including a dozen 122mm artillery pieces, the first time these powerful new weapons had been identified in South Vietnam.[5]

The captured rockets and mortars alone totaled two and a half times what the enemy had expended during the entire 1969 Tet offensive. Abrams later told his staff about some calculations based on what had been seized from enemy stores. "Now assuming that he went ahead and distributed that, and fired it,

then you can say that Dewey Canyon saved us—what?—five–
six thousand in casualties. That's one of the ways of looking at
Dewey Canyon—if you want to be so optimistic as to assume
that he would distribute it, and would *shoot* it all, that would
have given us five times the casualties we've had."

Far to the south, similar operations in the U Minh Forest
constituted the first friendly penetration ever made there, even
as far back as the Viet Minh war. "Thus the sanctuaries are
gradually losing their invulnerability," observed a MACV analyst. And in the process the enemy was losing much of his laboriously accumulated wherewithal, losses that slowed or
preempted many planned operations.

In mid-April, Charles B. MacDonald, then the Army's Deputy Chief Historian, lunched with General Abrams at his quarters in Saigon. They talked about the nature of the war, what
worked and what didn't, and how to get the job done at least
cost in American lives. "General Abrams emphasized," said
MacDonald, "that it was essential to get out into the difficult
western part of Vietnam in order to meet the enemy even as
he begins his trek from sanctuaries in Cambodia and Laos. This
way we destroy his tediously-prepared logistical arrangements
and thus in the end deny large-scale attacks on the populated
areas. We have insufficient numbers to protect the population
centers in a passive defense. Furthermore, when we have maintained the initiative—whether the enemy is technically on the
offensive or not—our kill ratio is spectacular."[6] That combat
philosophy was about to be implemented in the A Shau Valley.

Guided by this concept of getting into the enemy's system,
the major battles now had a coherence they had lacked in the
earlier days of the war. It was in this context that a fierce and
bloody battle in the A Shau Valley drew attention—and criticism—from antiwar elements in the United States. When the
enemy's 29th Regiment sallied forth into the traditional assault
route toward Hue, ARVN and U.S. troops moved to intercept
it. At Hill 937—also known as Ap Bia Mountain, and soon to

become more widely known as Hamburger Hill—the battle was joined. That was on 10 May 1969, and it took ten days of extremely hard fighting before the enemy was dug out of prepared positions on the rocky slopes and crest of 937.

Colonel Joseph B. Conmy, Jr., was in command of the 101st Airborne Division's 3rd Brigade. A lean and capable combat leader, Conmy was one of the few men in history to earn three Combat Infantryman's Badges—in World War II, Korea, and now Vietnam. He commanded infantry troops in battle in those three wars, was wounded in three wars, was decorated for valor in three wars, and in Korea won two battlefield promotions.[7] Now, early in 1969, he received orders to plan for an operation that would take the A Shau Valley away from the enemy, who was using it as a major avenue of approach—branching off from the Ho Chi Minh Trail that snaked down through Laos—to the populated areas of the coastal lowlands. That preemptive move would turn out to precipitate, said one senior officer, "the last major U.S. battle in Vietnam."[8]

Conmy's brigade, along with five ARVN battalions, conducted the battle, early on making contact with the 29th NVA where it was established in a network of bunkers on Hill 937. Violent tropical storms punctuated the fighting, turning the steep slopes into rivers of mud. At one point two battalions of the 101st within sight of their objective were mistakenly strafed by U.S. helicopter gunships, taking heavy casualties. Eventually, after the enemy positions had been bombarded by everything from heavy artillery to B-52 bombers, the position was taken.

"We destroyed the 29th NVA Regiment as a fighting force," reported Conmy, "capturing many of their weapons and much equipment. Body counts are now in disrepute, but we found 691 of the enemy dead and five badly wounded. A Special Forces patrol on the Laotian side of Hamburger Hill saw some 1,100 enemy dead and wounded being removed from the hill during the battle."[9] The U.S. elements suffered 78 KIA and 546

WIA in the overall operation, 47 KIA and 308 WIA being attributed specifically to the capture of Hill 937,[10] but these were not the real measure of success. Rather, it was disruption of the enemy system, which prevented him from laying the groundwork for operations in the populated areas to the east. After driving out the 29th NVA, the 3rd Brigade stayed in the A Shau for months, then passed the mission to other units. "We and our successors," Conmy said, "controlled the area until ordered out of Vietnam three years later."[11]

In the United States, though, reports of the operation generated a torrent of criticism and provided a new rallying point for opponents of the war. Senator Edward Kennedy was among the most outspoken, calling the battle "madness" and denouncing it as "both senseless and irresponsible." Soon General Earle Wheeler cabled Abrams to say that the battle had "received extensive press coverage here and has evoked an unusual amount of high level interest in the operation." Clearly feeling the heat, Wheeler asked Abrams to detail the measures that had been employed to minimize casualties.[12] Abrams dutifully cataloged the torrent of artillery, mortars, napalm, tactical air, helicopter gunships, and B-52 bombers that had supported the assaulting infantry.

Lieutenant General Melvin Zais commanded the 101st Airborne Division during the battle, entitling him to share in the abuse the operation generated from certain quarters in the United States. "General Zais was a wonderful commander," said Conmy. "He could come onto the battlefield when things were really tough, give you a big smile and put his hand on your shoulder, and just lift all your troubles."[13] Soon after the battle, having moved up to command of XXIV Corps, Zais visited 3rd Marine Division for briefings. His hosts expressed sympathy over the criticism he had received in the United States, particularly that dished out by Kennedy. "Let me tell you something," Zais responded, "at least I evacuated my dead and wounded."[14]

In Vietnam, the results of this fierce battle contributed to Abrams's favorite objective of working inside the enemy system. The enemy's main means of supply and infiltration for southern I Corps was out of Base Areas 604, 610, and 611 into the A Shau Valley. "Now he hasn't been able to use A Shau for some months," Abrams commented in late summer. "We've been there—the ARVN and U.S.—and we're going to *stay* there."

Later Abrams also acknowledged the inevitability of criticism. "It's like the 29th Regiment," he said. "You fight them in the A Shau and they piss on you for that. You fight them in Hue and they raise hell about that. You can't find a good place to fight them. The *places* aren't good." As for himself, Abrams had no doubts as to the best place for the battle to be joined. "I think it's better to fight the 29th in the A Shau," blocking his moves through traditional invasion corridors, he told the staff, rather than waiting until he had gotten in among the populace. "We wouldn't get any less casualties fighting them in Hue. We took a lot of casualties in Hue. S-o-o-o, I don't know *why* these people can't—. Of course, Senator Kennedy does have military experience. He was a guard at Norstad's headquarters. I think he got to be a Speedy Four [Specialist Fourth Class]." "No, sir, PFC," someone corrected. "Yeah, but hell, it's serious *business*," Abrams concluded.

When, by mid-June 1969, allied forces had seized more ammunition in caches than in all of 1968, Ambassador Bunker asked whether it was the result of better intelligence. "Mr. Ambassador," Abrams responded, "I think that *all* of this is this whole business of trying to work on his *system*. And his system—it's the VCI, the guerrillas, it's the commo-liaison, it's getting out on the trails, it's patrolling, ambushing, and [our getting] out in the things that *he's* using to move the supplies in and make the liaison and that sort of thing." These preemptive tactics were paying off in many ways, one of the most dramatic being—as Ambassador Bunker reported to the President— reduction by a third of Americans killed in action during 1969 while inflicting virtually the same losses on the enemy as the year before.[15] The statistics demonstrated that the drop in American losses was a function of superior tactics rather than any decline in the tempo of combat.

SOME RECORDS WERE set in late July 1969 when the MACV analyst reported that during the period 23–29 July truck movement detected by sensors declined to fewer than fifty, the lowest weekly total ever recorded. On 28 July, in fact, there was a total absence of sensor-detected and visually observed truck traffic, the first time since emplacement of the sensor field in December 1967 that no movement had been recorded. These developments were attributed to the combined effects of air interdiction, heavy rainfall, and widespread flooding.

Summing up operations in recent months, in August 1969 MACV estimated that the average number of trucks entering the Lao panhandle had declined from thirty-four in May to nine in June and only four in July. An estimated 51 tons a day was being destroyed by air as it moved through the panhandle. Overall it was estimated that only 6.1 tons per day arrived in South Vietnam from Laos during June, and only 2 tons daily during July. As a consequence, MACV calculated, enemy stockpiles in Laos had a net decrease of 1,200 tons in June and 330 tons more in July.

The enemy had, nevertheless, accomplished an impressive amount in North Vietnam since the bombing halt. After rehabilitation and improvement of lines of communications in Route Package 1, new storage facilities were constructed, supplies stockpiled, and POL stocks built up. The North Vietnamese town of Vinh was the logistics hub for all this activity. Until weakened rail bridges could be shored up, rail-mounted trucks were often substituted for locomotives on those routes. Meanwhile, the rail system was being restored and extended to the south, antiaircraft defenses were increased, and development continued on a new entry corridor skirting the DMZ on the

west so as to provide traffic a longer route of safe passage before
being exposed to air strikes in Laos.

Sometime in 1969 the enemy also began construction of fuel
pipelines more or less paralleling the Ho Chi Minh Trail.[16]
When put into operation, these would greatly ease the burden
on the trail. One pipeline running from Vinh through the Mu
Gia Pass, for example, could pump an estimated 1,130 metric
tons per day, the equivalent of more than 400 trucks for movement of fuel, and another pipeline was installed west of the
DMZ. After the bombing halt the enemy began emplacing extensive fuel storage facilities just north of the DMZ, by the end
of 1969 reaching an estimated capacity of 5,800,000 gallons in
Quang Binh Province alone.

THE FACT THAT THE Viet Cong infrastructure had remained
largely intact after Tet 1968 was confirmed by continuation of
the enemy's ruthless campaigns of terrorism and assassination.
More than a year later, the newly installed Nixon administration's comprehensive survey of the situation in Vietnam also
reached that conclusion. Colby told Secretary Laird the same
thing on his first visit to Saigon in March 1969. "The war used
to be about North Vietnamese divisions," said Colby. "Now it's
about terrorists, and it's about economics. And it's about politics.
That's where the fight *is*."

The iron grip of the infrastructure on the rural population
began to be loosened only when the Accelerated Pacification Campaign and an effective Phoenix program were em-
braced and implemented by the South Vietnamese. Phoenix was
slow in getting started and gathering momentum. When General
Wheeler came out to Vietnam in July 1969, Colby told him,
"Frankly, we can't report any great success." The data on total
VCI strength were soft, but at that point only an estimated 1.5
or 2 percent were being neutralized each month, and many of
those could probably be replaced. Lieutenant General Herman
Nickerson, commanding III Marine Amphibious Force, rein-

forced that view. "On the VCI," he said, "I think our targets are much too low. I've told General Lam and all of his people that we're going to have to target more of these, not just 2 percent or 3 percent or 4 percent of the total, or we're going to be here a thousand years."

As was the case with just about everything else in Vietnam, good intelligence was the key to dealing with the infrastructure. A network of what were called census-grievance teams was sponsored and set up by the United States, ostensibly to survey the aspirations and grievances of people in the rural areas. "Their cover assignment," said General Truong, "was to collect intelligence on the VCI."[17] One VCI member captured in Binh Thuan Province was found to be the mimeograph operator in the province headquarters. "That little bastard was in there taking a copy of everything," Abrams said, prompting him to insist again that "the thing that we have to work harder and harder on in 1970 is an understanding of *this* part of it. You can go out here and beat the shit out of the 9th Division, but if you haven't advanced on this other front, it's *all* for naught. You *haven't* gotten *anywhere!* You just *think* you have. I know body count, you know—it has something about it, but it's really a *l-o-o-n-g* way from what's involved in this war. Yeah, you have to do that, *I* know that, but the *mistake* is to think that that's the central issue."

CRITICS OF THE WAR, as Colby had pointed out, denounced Phoenix as an "assassination" program, but the results showed otherwise. For one thing, enemy who had knowledge of the enemy infrastructure and its functioning were invaluable intelligence assets. The incentive was to capture them alive and exploit that knowledge, not bring in mute corpses. Congressional investigators who went out to Vietnam to assess the program found that of some 15,000 VCI neutralized during 1968, 15 percent had been killed, 13 percent rallied to the government side, and 72 percent were captured.[18]

In early 1969 Colby, briefing Ambassador U. Alexis Johnson,

told him that "of the infrastructure neutralized, *most* of them are captured. The emphasis *is* on capturing and interrogation." The following year, back in the United States to present testimony before Senator J. William Fulbright's Senate Foreign Relations Committee, Colby found that one of the few things about Vietnam they were interested in was the Phoenix program. "I went out very flatly on the point that the United States government is not associated with a program of assassination," Colby told his colleagues back in Saigon, "and that the government of South Vietnam is trying to make this a decent program, a normal internal security program conducted under decent standards."

The bulk of the infrastructure members who died were killed not by Phoenix operatives but by regular military forces engaged in combat operations. As Douglas Pike has explained, "The Vietnamese communists erased entirely the line between military and civilian by ruling out the notion of noncombatant. Their strategy precluded, by definition, the disinterested onlooker. Not even children were excluded—particularly not children, one might say. All people became weapons of war."[19]

Colby later described for Richard Helms the techniques being used to inject greater rigor into the Phoenix program. "We change the rules on them all the time," he said, "so we make it harder and harder to get the brownie points—the goals and so forth. The first year it was all VCI. The second year we left out the 'C' category. It was only 'A' and 'B' that counted. This year we put in the rule that it wasn't 'captured,' it was 'sentenced,' in order to put some heat on the sentencing process and make it work properly. And we'll invent something else next year to make it more effective."[20]

"Now you take a thing like that Phuong Hoang thing—we can't just turn loose of that, because it's driving the enemy crazy," Abrams told Secretary Laird. "But it's not just Phuong Hoang, it's the RF and the PF out there on these interdiction things at night, ambushing, and the VCI are just having a hell of a time moving around." Abrams explained how putting the pressure on could pay off in other ways as well. "It's not entirely how many you have eliminated or caught or jailed," he observed. "What's happened to some of this infrastructure is it's out in the jungle where it can gain the security of its forces, which means that it's *not* functioning in the population. Now, it's true they'll survive in the jungle. And it's always something that can come out again if the territorial forces, the police, the PSDF, and so on aren't up to snuff. But in terms of getting the job done, the only thing they're doing is surviving. They're *not* collecting taxes, they're *not* getting intelligence, they're *not* propagandizing the people, they're *not* twisting their arms, and this sort of thing. They're *dormant* where that situation exists."

The enemy knew both the objectives and the effectiveness of the pacification program, including Phoenix, saying it "combined political, economic, and cultural schemes with espionage warfare in order to eliminate the infrastructure of the revolution and build the infrastructure of neo-colonialism."[21] Except for the propaganda, that was it exactly. Stanley Karnow wrote that he was skeptical of the program's impact until after the war, when discussions with several North Vietnamese leaders convinced him of its worth. The Communist authorities in Vietnam, he told Colby, said that Phoenix was "the single most effective program you used against them in the entire war." Colby smiled at that. "I always thought they confused it with pacification," he observed.[22]

A MAJOR ELEMENT of the new initiative was the Police Field Force, "targeted specifically at the infrastructure." During 1968 nearly 10,000 men had been added to the police, bringing the total to 80,000. Even more important than expanding the forces was a change in outlook. "The thing is," said Colby, "that, frankly, six months to a year ago the police were operating in their world and the military were operating in the military, and there was very little common attention to the political command structure of the VC."

Dispersing police into the countryside was in fact a new departure for South Vietnam, another indication of change in its traditional society. Historically, the police had confined their operations to the cities, functioning primarily as a mechanism for keeping the ruling class in power. "Their tradition," said Colby, "was a colonial police whose function was to protect the administration. It is gradually turning into a police whose function is to give the *population* some protection in terms of law and order." The new idea of fanning out to provide protection and justice to the people at large had a powerful potential for beneficial change.

This development was viewed with approval by Sir Robert Thompson, the British counterinsurgency expert who was a frequent visitor to MACV during these years. Thompson, observed George Jacobson, considered Vietnam "a police problem rather than a war." To that Abrams responded, "I *agree* with that. I agree with it as far as it goes. Now when you—when they get down here with the 9th, the 5th, and 7th, and the 1st Divisions, *goddamn* it, there isn't any way to handle that with administration and police! I mean, I don't care *what* kind of a damn genius you are, you can't get out here and give them tickets or arrest them or what the hell ever you do with police. I mean, these are just mean bastards with a lot of firepower and a lot of strength." But with those elements fended off, police were essential to rooting out the enemy infrastructure and extending the influence of legitimate government. "It's the people in the end," concluded Abrams. "That's the critical thing of the whole business."

Another new departure was the involvement of U.S. forces in supporting the pacification program. Urging his commanders to expand their preemptive and spoiling attacks, Abrams specified that this included "an intensive drive against the VC infrastructure and political apparatus aimed at eliminating it just as rapidly as possible; not suppress, but eliminate." Thus it was essential that commanders "get moving on this phase of operations, bring it up to, and maintain it at, the tempo of our tactical operations."[23]

That soon became a major thrust of operations. General John Wright spent a year in the 1st Cavalry Division, went home in September 1966, then returned to Vietnam in May 1969 for another year as commanding general of the 101st Airborne Division. "I think the most significant difference," he said in contrasting the two periods of service, "and it was just a spectacular difference, was the involvement of the division in civic action and rural development programs in our area of operations."

WIDESPREAD ECONOMIC progress was meanwhile becoming both more robust and more readily identifiable. The multiple and bountiful crops resulting from the introduction of "miracle rice," IR-8 and other variants, were everywhere to be seen. Despite the disruption of the 1968 Tet Offensive, the year's goal of 40,000 hectares planted in IR-8 had been exceeded, and for 1969, 200,000 hectares was the target. Said Colby of one key province, "An Giang, in two years, is going to *double* its production." As the percentage of secure hamlets kept rising, so did what one Vietnamese called appreciatively "the refreshing green surface of rice seedlings" expand across the countryside. Rice production nationwide went up 700,000 metric tons in 1969 and another 400,000 in 1970, at 5.5 million tons surpassing 1964, previously the best year since World War II. During 1971 and 1972 the figure would climb to 6.1 million tons from over 2,650,000 hectares, some 42 percent of it planted in miracle rice producing three crops a year.[24]

AVERELL HARRIMAN's legacy from his brief assignment in Paris continued to cast a shadow. The question of whether or not there had been any actual understandings on the part of the North Vietnamese was important for the conduct and course of the war, not least because South Vietnam later positioned its forces in part on the basis of acceptance of the proposition that the enemy would respect the DMZ. Following his departure from government, Averell Harriman continued to be a frequent commenter on negotiations and the war itself, often taking stands contrary to the facts. In June 1969, for example, he was quoted in a *New York Times* editorial as insisting that "on 1 November after the President announced the bombing halt, NVN withdrew 90 percent of its troops out of the two northern provinces of I Corps." The implication was that the withdrawals were a reciprocal step induced by the bombing halt. But that was wrong, and Harriman knew it was wrong when he said it, as Abrams was quick to confirm to General Wheeler.

Harriman's statement, he cabled, "is incorrect. Virtually all of the enemy's forces that he was to withdraw from the northern two provinces of I Corps had departed prior to the president's announcement of the bombing halt. The enemy's greatest strength in the northern two provinces of I Corps was during the month of July 1968, when he had a total of 53 maneuver battalions. During the period 1 July–31 October 1968, 39 maneuver battalions moved out of Quang Tri and Thua Thien Provinces and relocated to NVN or Laos." Abrams then provided minute details of these redispositions. "By 1 November the enemy maneuver battalions in northern I Corps had been reduced by 74 percent or to 14 maneuver battalions. Subsequent to 1 November only 2 battalions relocated from Quang Tri Province to NVN."

Then, although the U.S. bombing halt continued, the North Vietnamese withdrawals did not. By early June 1969, Abrams confirmed, "23 of the 41 maneuver battalions which had relocated out of Quang Tri and Thua Thien Provinces during the second half of 1968 have returned to SVN."[25]

Lieutenant General Julian Ewell asked Abrams about Harriman's statements. "Harriman has—either consciously or unconsciously—distorted the facts that were given to him when he was the negotiator over there," Abrams stated. "*He* has used it to indicate it was their *response* to the bombing halt, and the *facts* are that it started in the summer and was virtually completed, except for one regiment, before the bombing halt." Ewell followed up: "As I understand Mr. Harriman's point, he's saying that each side made a move, and then because we were maliciously and deliberately aggressive in-country they had to kind of undo that gesture." "Yeah," agreed Abrams, "in a way you're right, but he's *twisted* the facts in order to support his thesis."[26]

The issue came up yet again when a citizens group visited Vietnam later in the summer. Among them, Abrams recalled, were several "that *admire* Mr. Harriman tremendously. You know, 'He's devoted a lifetime to this kind of thing—service and that sort of thing.' So I *joined* them in that. And they went and *saw* him before they came out here, spent five or six hours with him, at least some of them did." Abrams spoke with a mathematician in the group, a man he found most impressive. Eventually Abrams mentioned how difficult it was for him to understand why Harriman said these movements out of South Vietnam occurred after the bombing halt. "I said maybe it's because of his age, his memory," he recalled. "I said how I *know* he at one time *knew* better than that, because *I* was the one that was *reporting* it to him."

The mathematician offered his view of the reasons. "Well, I'll tell you," Abrams recalled his saying as they walked together, "I love him, but he has—this time, the whole thing came as a tremendous personal disappointment, that he hadn't wound up that negotiation. It would have been his last service and so on. So that has eaten on him. It has had a tendency to disturb the objective view that he usually—that used to be the *hallmark* of his service."[27]

Ambassador John Holdridge put it somewhat more directly. "Harriman wanted to believe things," he said. "A lot of wishful thinking was going on. If we were nice to them, Harriman suggested, the North Vietnamese would respond. That was obviously a lot of horseshit."[28]

THERE WERE MULTIPLE sources of perceived peril as far as Saigon was concerned, and one was in the Department of State in Washington. "I have just seen a secret letter from Deputy Assistant Secretary Sullivan to Ambassador Colby, dated 25 July," Abrams cabled McCain and Wheeler in early August 1969. "The letter states that Washington is working on a revised cease-fire paper for the NSC and that one of the questions to be addressed is the possibility of a cease-fire proposal initiated by our side. Such a cease-fire would not be explicitly linked to withdrawal of all non–South Vietnamese forces, but would be linked only to international supervision. Sullivan states that the problem is how to judge whether this sort of cease-fire would be in our interest, and has solicited Colby's personal, informal views."[29]

Abrams observed that such proposals always seemed to be based on an assumption that the enemy was about to propose a cease-fire, then progressed rapidly to consideration of a preemptive U.S. proposal to reap the supposed political and psychological benefits from what was inevitable anyway. "While it may be imprudent to argue this publicly," he observed, "those who are vitally concerned with the interests of the United States must not overlook the fact that we have got where we are by the exercise of powerful force. Current circumstances, e.g., pacification, RVNAF increasing effectiveness, the general state of security, and diminishing capabilities of the enemy, have been brought about by extensive use of tactical air, B-52s, artillery, helicopters, and so forth—by exploiting mobility and firepower in the application of force. We hold the initiative and the enemy is confronted with serious military problems. Any transition from the assumption that a cease-fire might be good for the enemy to the idea that it would be good for our side tends to ignore this current battlefield situation."

And, Abrams concluded, "Any scheme advanced under the hypothesis that there has to be an assumption of 'good faith' on the part of the enemy rests on thin ice. For twenty years, with remarkable tenacity and consistency, this enemy has failed to demonstrate one iota of good faith except to himself." The cease-fire idea faded away, at least for the time being.

10

Resolution 9

As 1969 PROGRESSED the enemy mounted—or sought to mount—a series of "high points," about once a month launching attacks at various places around the country. These short-lived operations were apparently intended to give the impression of widespread offensive activity while conserving manpower and resources. Typically they lasted only a couple of days, and more often than not involved only attacks by fire (shellings) rather than ground assaults.

If, as seemed to be the case, the enemy's shift to "high points" was intended to limit his casualties, that objective was not achieved. In early October 1969, a MACV briefer told General Wheeler, the enemy was "continuing to sustain high combat losses," so much so that by that point those losses had "already far exceeded his entire combat losses for any other previous year" except 1968.[1] By mid-November the toll had reached an estimated 153,800 killed in action, plus those who died of wounds, were permanently disabled, and constituted nonbattle losses due to disease and desertion.

A few months later General Abrams observed that comparative casualties had meanwhile taken on a more favorable balance. The enemy's killed in action had "stayed at roughly the same level over the past several months," he told Australia's visiting Minister of Defence. "So the cost to him has been fairly constant, while ours has declined substantially. In other words, I don't think that the policy of attacks by fire, standoff attacks, and sappers has really produced in concrete terms. He sees it as a way of saving his own manpower and increasing our losses, and I don't think—take the whole thing, it hasn't quite worked out that way."

AFTER FOUR FAILED general offensives and the terrible losses they occasioned, the enemy apparently—finally—took stock and decided a change was essential. By the end of May MACV's assessment concluded that if the enemy's next offensive should fail, as it surely would, "his alternative to defeat will be a severe reduction of the intensity of his fighting and the amount of force he can commit to South Vietnam." Indeed, "there are signs, though tenuous ones, that he's recognized this and already started his long-range readjustment." Thus "he must soon, or perhaps already has, abandon the general offensive/general uprising and revert to a type of warfare we saw before Tet of 1968." That proved to be right on the mark.

"He was whipped—I mean absolutely whipped—after the three offensives" during 1968, said Potts. Still he had another go at it during Tet 1969. "Then came COSVN Resolution 9," recalled Potts. In his judgment it was a reflection of the allies' effective interdiction of enemy lines of communication and the battlefield losses they had inflicted. "The *enemy* thought the war was won—by *us!*" remembered Potts. " 'Now let's outlast them,' they said in Resolution 9."

COSVN Resolution 9 was issued in July 1969. When a copy was captured in early October by the 199th Infantry Brigade it represented, recalled JGS J-2 Colonel Hoang Ngoc Lung, the most comprehensive enemy policy document ever acquired, forty-one pages in all. "All of our enemy's strategic approach, present and future, his vulnerabilities and shortcomings, his short and long-range objectives were there, laid out with unmistakable clarity," said Lung.[2]

Initially the allies captured not the resolution itself but a lesson plan for use in enemy indoctrination on its provisions. They got that—which proved very informative—sometime in September. Then a prisoner captured in Phu Yen Province revealed she was a member of a special action unit and had attended a three-day study session on COSVN Resolution 9. "The resolution directs the VC to preserve their strength in order to protract the war," said her interrogation report. "It also directs that large NVA units are to be broken down into smaller units and that they, along with main force units, are to employ sapper tactics and target themselves against U.S. troops and installations." Meanwhile, "all provincial local force units are to be divided into small cells and target themselves against Revolutionary Development teams and GVN cadre at hamlet and village level to break the GVN's control of the population."[3]

Thus what the document revealed was an enemy who had radically changed tactics. Compared with Resolution 8 of a year earlier, references to a complete military victory had been dropped. Emphasis was shifted from urban to rural areas, a change described as necessary to expand the political base in preparation for a coalition government. And, somewhat belatedly, perhaps, more emphasis was placed on disruption of pacification. Finally, stress was put on the need to inflict casualties on the Americans so as to increase pressure for rapid troop withdrawals.

"Thus COSVN Resolution 9," summed up MACV in a retrospective analysis, "heralded the return of protracted guerrilla war, with its emphasis on small-unit tactics, reliance upon sappers, terrorism, and increased reliance on attacks by fire, as the most efficient means of wearing down the fighting capability of ARVN, heightening demands by the U.S. public for withdrawal of U.S. forces, and eroding the Vietnamese people's faith in their government's ability to maintain their security."

Abrams saw in the document South Vietnam's seizure of the initiative, going back to the Accelerated Pacification Campaign in November 1968. The enemy was, he thought, "reacting to an initiative which has *now,* in his own estimate, begun to create a problem for him." Abrams continued in modest terms, saying, "I don't necessarily like the term 'forced.' He *is* a resourceful fellow, and he *is* an intelligent fellow. And just as he changed from what he'd been doing before to another level . . . he's doing the same thing *again.* But *maybe,* maybe for the *first* time his response, his guidance here, is . . . responding to the initiatives that have been exercised over almost the last year by *our* side, which no small part of is the GVN itself."

PERHAPS INEVITABLY, these positive developments in Vietnam were not mirrored in the United States, where—as described by General Wheeler on his next trip to Vietnam—a depressing environment had developed. The problem he faced, and the Joint Chiefs of Staff faced, he lamented, "is attempting to get the political leadership, past and present, to understand, really comprehend, what this military situation is in Vietnam the way it's developed over the past couple of years, and comprehend— I guess even more important—to comprehend what this really means as regards our own continuing actions, and the actions which are available to us." Wheeler described a situation in which the administration was "practically apologizing for our position, or the situation in Vietnam. It's a very, very curious, almost a phenomenal, situation."

Then Wheeler revealed his own deep pessimism: "Now I think probably it's too late to *correct.* The efforts of the American press, the attitude of a considerable segment of the Congress who are always shooting off their mouths about things they know nothing about, just have created a public impression, I

gather, that we're hanging on over here by our teeth, barely able
to stay in the stadium. Well, I'll be goddamned if I've ever—I
haven't been able to figure out any way to solve the problem. It seems almost impossible to get the Secretary of State,
the Secretary of Defense, equally or more important the President, to realize that they are dealing from a position of military
strength." Wheeler saw this adversely affecting not only the
war in Vietnam, but negotiations as well. "Christ," he said,
"they act and talk, on *many* occasions, the Commander in Chief
and particularly the Secretary of State, as though the damned
peace talks, or peace negotiations or whatever terminology
you want to use, in Paris, *we're* the guys that are doing the
suing."[4]

When Wheeler went to visit Charlie Corcoran, then commanding I Field Force, Corcoran was shocked by Wheeler's appearance. "He looked like a man who had had the course,"
recalled Corcoran. "He started to unload about what was going
on in Washington. I had the feeling he had just given up."[5]

Wheeler had raised the role of the press in determining the
course of the war, and that continued to be a topic of lively
interest and controversy for many years after the conflict had
ended. The press itself was conflicted on the matter, wanting on
the one hand to receive credit for its influence and importance,
but on the other to escape blame for the failed outcome. Walter
Cronkite illustrated the dilemma in his memoirs. "A generation of officers later," he complained, "there still lurks in the
Pentagon the belief that the media lost the war." But, a hundred
or so pages later, Cronkite states with some apparent pride that
"the daily coverage of the Vietnamese battlefield helped convince the American public that the carnage was not worth the
candle."[6]

Another challenge, at least in theory, was maintaining the
stance of impartial reporter while in the grip of settled opinion.
"My job," Cronkite later wrote, "was to try as hard as I could

to remove every trace of opinion from the broadcast. If people knew how I felt on an issue, or thought they could discern from me some ideological position of the Columbia Broadcasting System, I had failed in my mission."[7] That was the same Walter Cronkite who, back from a brief visit to Vietnam during the 1968 Tet Offensive, had solemnly informed the viewing public of his judgment that the war was stalemated and could not be won. Then it was back to reporting on that war for seven more years—even though, in his own terms, he had already failed in his mission.

And so, according to a detailed analysis by Ernest Lefever, had his network. Dr. Lefever, a longtime senior fellow on foreign policy at the Brookings Institution and founder of the Ethics and Public Policy Center in Washington, determined—based on content analysis—that during 1972 and 1973 CBS-TV News had presented an "overwhelmingly unfavorable portrayal of the U.S. Armed Forces, the Defense Department, and their activities." This "striking effect was achieved by omitting many readily available stories on positive military accomplishments . . . and focusing on criticisms . . . and by presenting neutral topics in a negative light." In addition, "CBS Evening News was far more critical of America's ally, South Vietnam, than America's enemy, North Vietnam." In the course of this coverage CBS News "gave 48 times more coverage to critics who wanted the United States to end military support of South Vietnam than to critics who wanted the United States to step up its military action against North Vietnam." Most of this was "advocacy . . . under the guise of straight reporting."[8]

Keyes Beech, one of the more experienced journalists covering the war, found it unlike his previous experiences. "We fought, shouted, shrieked, attacked, defended," he said of the media. "Ours was a babble of voices that lost all credibility." The camaraderie among the press corps of earlier wars was largely lacking in Vietnam, Beech lamented, and so was any sympathy on the part of the press for those conducting the war.

"As the bitterness grew," he remembered, "the press corps divided into two camps—those who wanted to win the war and those who wanted to lose it. I belonged to the former. Few members of the latter group would have admitted it, but only by losing the war could they be proved right."[9]

BY EARLY AUTUMN the situation in tracking infiltration had returned to "normal"; the allies were picking up communications intercepts on the infiltration groups as they entered the pipeline. Later Potts reflected on the recent crisis. "We *knew* that these people were coming in, but we weren't getting it out of the *air* any more." Intelligence analysts were again reliant on collateral materials. "And *then* we found that there *were* groups coming in," he said. "Men had diaries and so forth, and we could trace them all the way down."

It had been a difficult time. "We went through the *trauma* of when this went down—stopped picking them up—we went through the trauma of something was wrong with the system," recalled Abrams. The reasons for the hiatus in enemy radio traffic on infiltration were never discovered, but when, after several months, the revealing messages began again, proving just as reliable as before, MACV was both relieved and grateful. Meanwhile Potts had been confident of the interim deductions based on collateral evidence because of the exceptionally able analysts working on this and other intelligence accounts. At a subsequent meeting Abrams asked the young briefer, "Are you the infiltration man?" He was. "How long have you been here?" Abrams wanted to know. "Three months now, sir," was the reply. There was a pause, then an addendum. "I have a *very* good feel for this subject, sir."

THE DRAWDOWN OF U.S. forces, begun in July and August, soon became an essentially continuous process. "The critical phase is Phase III," Colonel Donn Starry briefed in early September

1969. "We no longer have parity with the enemy in maneuver battalions, and we begin to see a degradation in helicopters, artillery tubes, and—again, after Phase IV—in tactical air sorties." To compound the problem, budget reductions imposed by Washington took more sorties from the tactical air support capability than MACV had planned to lose in the entire first five phases of Vietnamization.[10]

The danger of successive withdrawals was underscored by the fact that, before the first increment departed, U.S. maneuver battalions had made up about one-third of the total allied combat force in South Vietnam but accounted for more than two-thirds of the operational results in almost all categories, including the two key factors affecting the enemy's combat capability most directly—enemy killed in action and cache finds. This reality no doubt informed MACV's conclusion in the autumn of 1969 that "unless North Vietnamese forces return to North Vietnam, there is little chance that *any* improvement in RVNAF or *any* degree of progress in pacification, no matter how significant, could justify significant reductions in U.S. forces from their present level."[11] In other words, their assessment was that, despite the gains being made by South Vietnam's forces, their situation would become untenable if the NVA were permitted to remain in the South while U.S. forces withdrew. That conclusion was, of course, going to vanish in the wind of domestic pressures for withdrawal.

The effect of troop withdrawals was exacerbated by the failure of the Army to provide the required number of replacements for troops rotating home at the end of their tours. In early November 1969, for example, Army elements in Vietnam were short 7,000 of the 25,000 replacements they should have received the preceding month. There was a certain irony in the situation, for it was General William C. Westmoreland—whose tenure as U.S. commander in Vietnam had been marked by incessant requests for more and yet more troops—who was now

responsible for providing troops to meet the Vietnam requirement, and failing to do so.

SIR ROBERT THOMPSON was an astute observer of the war in
Vietnam. A former British soldier who won the Military Cross
and the DSO during World War II service in the Far East, in
the postwar years he made a career in Malaya. There, over the
next fifteen years, he held increasingly responsible posts as the
fight against Communist insurgents was successfully prosecuted.
Then, during the period 1961–1965, he headed the British Advisory Mission to Vietnam.[12]

Thompson was a frequent visitor to Vietnam in subsequent
years, and his visits gave him the basis for making authoritative
comparisons. "I can remember flying over the Mekong Delta
just after the Tet offensive," he wrote, "and seeing not a single
truck, other than military convoys, moving on the roads nor
boats on any of the canals. In 1969 this changed completely as
roads, bridges and canals were repaired and opened." More land
was under cultivation, the rice harvest had increased, and the
herds of livestock were increasing.[13] Thompson judged this to
be the result of the allies' having taken advantage of the opportunities in the countryside in the wake of Tet 1968. Both sides
had pulled forces from rural areas to concentrate on urban fighting during Tet, leaving a vacuum in the hamlets and villages.
"The side which recovered first would gain a rich reward," said
Thompson, and that race was won by South Vietnam's Accelerated Pacification Campaign.[14]

When, in the autumn of 1969, President Nixon asked
Thompson to visit Vietnam and give him an independent assessment of the situation there, Abrams welcomed the visit. "He
should be supported," Abrams told the staff, "and *anything* he
wants to see, and any*one* he wants to see, talk with, however
much time, that sort of thing. Don't bulldoze him around. Let
him at least leave here with a feeling that he's had a free hand

in talking and seeing and looking, just everywhere he wants to go." Abrams had no plans to brief Thompson at MACV Headquarters. "I *hope* that what he decides to do is really get out and go and see for himself," he concluded.

IN OCTOBER, Ambassador Bunker met twice with President Nixon in Washington. "I must say, it's a bit depressing at home," he observed at the next Commanders WIEU. "When I came back, I was glad to be back where some *constructive* work was going on." General Bruce Palmer, reassigned from Vietnam to be Army Vice Chief of Staff, also was shocked at what he found when he got home. "We had no clue over there just how bad it was," he admitted. "Then I came back to Washington and suddenly discovered, my God, they've had a war in Detroit, and Baltimore, and Washington."[15]

Eventually General Walter Kerwin, who had gone out to Vietnam with Abrams two years earlier, was due to rotate home. Before departing, he was invited to lunch with President Thieu. As they ate, Thieu asked Kerwin, "General, what are you going to do when you go back to the United States?" Kerwin replied that he was headed for the Pentagon to be chief of a fairly new staff element for Civil Disturbance Planning and Operations. Thieu was silent for a moment, then observed, "General, that is most unusual. We don't even have one of those in Vietnam."

"VIETNAMIZATION," while an awkward term—and one resented by many South Vietnamese, who took the reasonable position that they had been there fighting the war all along—was an amalgam of several complementary initiatives. After an October 1969 visit to Vietnam, General Wheeler cabled the field to confirm that Secretary Laird's definition of Vietnamization coincided with what Wheeler and Abrams had discussed during his visit, "not merely a program to replace U.S. combat troops with

Vietnamese troops, but . . . that facet plus modernization and improvement of the RVNAF [the Republic of Vietnam Armed Forces], the pacification program in all of its ramifications, social and economic development of RVN, etc."[16]

RVNAF Improvement & Modernization—I&M for short— got most of the publicity, and of course it was centrally important to the program's primary objective, that the South Vietnamese assume more and more of the burden of the war as American forces were withdrawn.[17] Economic development and reform, more effective government among the rural populace, and running a reasonably competent and trustworthy operation overall were also important parts of Vietnamization.

A larger military establishment was essential if the South Vietnamese were to assume the full range of responsibilities from departing American and other allied forces, but expansion was not confined to the traditional RVNAF. Instead, it took place proportionally more, and probably more importantly, in the Regional Forces and Popular Forces providing territorial security.

During the earlier years of the war, the South Vietnamese had been given relatively little in terms of combat support and modern equipment, neglect that affected both their capabilities and their outlook. During the fighting at Tet 1968, remembered Lieutenant General Dong Van Khuyen, RVNAF's chief logistician, "the crisp, rattling sounds of AK-47s echoing in Saigon and some other cities seemed to make a mockery of the weaker, single shots of Garands and carbines fired by stupefied friendly troops."[18]

"I think in the very beginning," observed Ambassador Bunker, "one of the problems and one of the difficulties we had was that we really didn't quite understand the nature of the war, that it was a war new to the American's experience, and I think we had the feeling in the very beginning, before General Abrams got there, that it wasn't going to be as serious a war as it turned out to be, that we could probably finish it up more quickly than we were able to accomplish and, therefore, we really didn't begin to train the Vietnamese with the objective of [their] taking over from us until General Abrams got there."[19]

Only a month into his assignment as deputy commander, Abrams had cabled Army Chief of Staff General Harold K. Johnson. "It is quite clear to me," Abrams told him, "that the US Army here and at home have thought largely in terms of US operations and support of US forces. . . . ARVN and RF/PF are left to the advisors. I fully appreciate that I have been as guilty as anyone. The result has been that shortages of essential equipment or supplies in an already austere authorization have not been handled with the urgency and vigor that characterize what we do for US needs. Yet the responsibility we bear to ARVN is clear. . . . The ground work must begin here. I am working at it."[20]

Briefed on the fact that American forces had a "kill ratio"— the number of enemy killed, proportional to U.S. losses, that exceeded that of ARVN—Abrams was quick to point out the reason why. "The ARVN doesn't have the firepower," he stressed, "it doesn't have the mobility, it doesn't have the communications." When someone suggested that the ARVN also did not get the allocation of air support, Abrams agreed: "That's right!" For Robert Komer this was apparently a new idea. "I was just wondering if this might have some implications when it comes to the modernization of the South Vietnamese forces," he ventured. "*Well*, of course," exploded Abrams. "That's what it's all *about!* It's *aimed* at that *very* thing!" "You've got to face it," he added, "the Vietnamese have been given the lowest priority of anybody that's fighting in this country! And that's what we're trying to correct."

South Vietnam's armed forces needed not only more troops and training, and equipment for those augmentations, but also more modern weaponry, equipment, and supporting forces— B-52 bomber strikes, close air support, artillery and naval gunfire, helicopter gunships and lift ships, the M-16 rifle, the M-60 machine gun, M-79 grenade launchers, and upgraded tactical radios. "Look," said Abrams at a staff conference, "I'm not emotional about ARVN, but if we're ever going to get out of here, we've got to do more to get them ready to take over."

In early November 1969, Secretary of Defense Laird asked MACV to prepare a plan for Phase III RVNAF Improvement & Modernization, which he called the "Consolidation Phase." His instructions included a significant and troubling new condition—no provision for a continuing U.S. support force. "In effect," concluded MACV, "it calls for an RVNAF capable by 1 July 1973 of handling the total threat, both internal and external." The bar was going up sharply on the hurdles the South Vietnamese were going to have to clear.

Laird passed to Abrams the text of a statement he had made before the Senate Foreign Relations Committee on 19 November 1969, and Abrams had it read at a commanders conference. "When the present administration took office," Laird stated, "a program of upgrading the training and equipment of South Vietnamese forces had begun. The goal of this program, however, was limited to increasing the combat capability of the forces of the Republic of Vietnam to the level needed to defeat the Viet Cong once all North Vietnamese forces had been withdrawn from the South. The Nixon administration early this year worked out a new objective with the government of South Vietnam for the training and equipping of the armed forces of South Vietnam. The objective we set was attainment by the South Vietnamese of a level of combat capability which would be adequate to defeat not only the Viet Cong, but the invading North Vietnamese forces as well."[21]

Something about that didn't ring true. "Just a minute," Abrams interrupted. "We, we—I *don't* think—have discussed that with South Vietnam. I have not been authorized to do that. Remember that I raised—?" Ambassador Bunker: "Yes." "Read that part over again," Abrams told the briefer. He did. Apparently Laird had misinformed the Congress concerning prior consultation and agreement with the South Vietnamese. Any such coordination would have been carried out by Bunker and Abrams, who stated before the entire staff and the senior field commanders that they knew nothing about it—and this on the absolutely crucial issue of what threat the South Vietnamese must be prepared to counter.[22]

BY THE END OF OCTOBER 1969 the pacification goals for the whole year—accelerated to the end of the third quarter by President Thieu—had been reached and exceeded. Sixty-three percent of the people outside Saigon were now living in category A or B hamlets, and 92 percent were considered to be in the A, B, or C categories that, taken together, constituted "relatively secure." Thus by late 1969 almost the entire population was thought to be living under substantially secure conditions. More persuasive than the statistics were the obvious improvements in both security and prosperity reflected in daily village life.

INTELLIGENCE MADE further contributions to the progress. In the autumn of 1969 a cryptographic officer who defected to the government side "brought in what we think is going to be the most significant break in the collection effort during this war," said Potts, a total of some 3,500 pieces of information. The professionalism with which intelligence matters were handled at troop level also had been upgraded significantly. "PWs and documents—that hasn't dramatically improved," said Davidson when he was still MACV J-2, "but it's sure gotten a hell of a lot better than it was a year ago. We're *getting* more of them, they're getting translated faster, they're *not* falling between the cracks like they used to. And that's why all this emphasis we put on the *system* in PW's and documents has begun to pay off."

Periodic policy pronouncements issued by COSVN—key documents specifying enemy intentions, outlooks, and plans—provided invaluable information. Over the years virtually every significant COSVN resolution and directive was acquired, and in the few cases where the document itself was not in hand, the contents were deduced from captured lesson plans and the like. At one point, recalled former CIA officer Orrin DeForest, agents known as "The Reaper" and "The Mad Bomber" "reported a startling new COSVN directive, Resolution 20. The fallout from this resolution would soon be providing us with the highest-level informants we had yet had, and insight into the heart of the Central Office of South Vietnam itself."[23]

The issue of enemy use of Sihanoukville continued to rankle. Even when, after literally years of effort, MACV's view finally prevailed, resentment remained. "What was the name of that CIA chap that came out here?" Abrams asked in a mid-December 1969 WIEU. It was Graham, Abrams was told, and Graham had now capitulated. "Yeah," recalled Abrams, "but he's the one that said out here—remember he told Davidson that 'there are political reasons why you should not arrive at the conclusion'? Remember? Davidson told us that here one morning, right here at this table."

MACV had argued that there was no other viable channel than Sihanoukville for delivery of the huge quantities of munitions the enemy was expending and that allied forces were discovering in seized caches. Sea infiltration was effectively blocked, while over the preceding twelve months an estimated average of only eight tons per day had been moved overland through Laos and on southward. "Thus the contention by some intelligence analysts at the Washington level that enemy forces in II, III, and IV Corps are receiving the majority of their ordnance via the Laotian overland route fails to be substantiated by the facts," held MACV. Indeed, the flow was going just the other way.

As the years went on, and the cast of characters changed again and again, Abrams became not only MACV's leader but also its institutional memory. This he frequently demonstrated in analyzing enemy actions and capabilities, comparing the enemy's current operations with what he had done, or tried to do, in an earlier such season or circumstance, then pointing out the

differences as well as the similarities. Pervading this type of analysis was genuine respect and even admiration for the enemy's
resourcefulness, tenacity, and single-mindedness. Thus, coaxing
an analyst to look more deeply into some topic, Abrams urged
him not to rely on the teachings of his alma mater, Fort Leavenworth, "but to be a better *Asian.*"

ON 3 NOVEMBER 1969 President Nixon went on television to
make a major address on progress in dealing with the war in
Vietnam, his famous "silent majority" speech. The effect of the
President's remarks was dramatic; those approving of the way he
was handling the situation in Vietnam spurted up sharply from
58 percent just before the speech to 77 percent immediately
afterward. The figures on those who disapproved also shifted
markedly, dropping from 32 percent to 6 percent.[24] Three weeks
later, additional polling gave strong evidence of how divergent
from public opinion were the antiwar elements in Congress.
"Some United States senators are saying that we should withdraw all our troops from Vietnam immediately," said Gallup.
"Would you favor or oppose this?" Seventy-four percent were
opposed.[25]

As 1969 neared an end, Abrams continued to emphasize to
his field commanders and the staff what the key objectives were.
"Now I know the fighting's important," he began. "I know
they've got to, if the 324 Bravo comes charging down [Route]
547 into Hue, you've got to get out there and really *lick* them.
But all of these things in the pacification, where the machinery
of government and the philosophy that President Thieu is—
building the village and the hamlet, and really building a base
there and so on. I really think that, of *all* the things, *that's* the
most important. That's where the battle ultimately is won."

John Vann, too, had a year-end assessment, one he mailed
to a number of friends back home. "For the first time in my
involvement here," he wrote, "I am not interested in visiting
either Washington or Paris, because all of my previous visits have

been with the intention of attempting to influence or change the policies for Vietnam. Now I am satisfied with the policies. In spite of ourselves, I believe we are accomplishing our objectives, that we will practically eliminate the tragedy of additional US deaths in Vietnam beyond 1972 and that the cost of the war (a war which I think will continue indefinitely) will be drastically reduced and will eventually be manageable by the Vietnamese with our logistical and financial assistance."[26]

A predictably different year-end assessment was provided by Richard Moose and James Lowenstein, staffers sent out to Vietnam by Senator J. W. Fulbright's Foreign Relations Committee. The pair reported that "some senior American military officers in Vietnam continue to talk of victory," a stance the investigators apparently found inappropriate, "and seem to believe that they are held back from achieving it only by public opinion at home." That was not, however, the outlook of the staff members, who reported that "dilemmas . . . seem to lie ahead in Vietnam, as they have throughout our involvement in this war that appears to be not only far from won but far from over." In that, of course, they were quite correct.[27]

11

Leaders

THE YEAR 1970 OPENED with intensified concern about the threat posed to allied aircraft by enemy surface-to-air missiles. Reconnaissance photographs showed occupied SAM sites in the vicinity of two of the key entry points on the Ho Chi Minh Trail, the Ban Karai and Mu Gia passes, the first time such weapons had been sighted there. "We think this is probably the most significant thing that's happened here recently," J-2 Potts told General Abrams. A MACV briefer, citing a recent report that Binh Tram 34 had received 400 tons of 122mm rockets, noted that "increased deployment of antiaircraft artillery and SAM missiles reflects the enemy's determination to protect his improved lines of communication against allied air strikes."[1]

The problem was one example among many of the difficulties derived from the restrictive, complex, and fluctuating "rules of engagement." Especially with respect to the air war, those rules changed continually. In the month of February 1970, two changes were made in operating authorities and rules of engagement, then some of those authorities just provided were temporarily rescinded. Next, reinstatement of the rescissions was requested, and that request was denied. Finally inputs on a

case-by-case basis were requested to support resubmission of requests for certain authorities.[2]

IN THE VILLAGES and hamlets the People's Self-Defense Force
had mushroomed during 1969. At year's end, now organized
into a combat arm and a support arm, the PSDF had more than
1,300,000 men and women in the combat arm, backed up by
about 1,750,000 women, children, and elderly men in the support arm. Four-day PSDF training sessions were conducted nationwide during the last month of the year. Abrams never passed
up a chance to emphasize how important he thought the PSDF,
along with the RF and PF, were to achieving success. "You can
brag about how you've got almost double the artillery in
ARVN, you've got four Huey squadrons flying around in
VNAF, you've got all these boats turned over and the crews are
functioning well and they're aggressive and so on, almost
400,000 M-16s distributed and so on," he began, but that was
not the whole game. The Territorial Forces and the PSDF were
expanding rapidly, they were indispensable to the overall war
effort, and there was a lot of hard work to be done to ensure
that, when the year ended, they were an effective force. "But
when [meaning *if*] you come to the end of 1970 and you've
still got half of the PF that are really unsatisfactory, and three-
fourths of the PSDF couldn't find their way to the outhouse—
I'll tell you, all that other stuff, the boats and the helicopters and
the M-16s and the artillery, is for *nothing*."

EARLY IN 1970 Senator Jacob Javits visited the war zone, where
he received a straightforward assessment of how things stood.
"If you add up your balance on both sides," Colby told him,
"I think you come to a conclusion that a successful outcome
is possible, but not inevitable." A Special National Intelligence
Estimate issued on 5 February concluded, said the JCS history,
"that the enemy was 'in trouble' in South Vietnam, irrespective
of the option selected. His casualties exceeded both infiltration

and local recruitment rates, and the quality of his forces was declining." That meant that the elusive "crossover point"— long sought, sometimes claimed, but never achieved by General Westmoreland—had now been reached. In addition, held the estimate, "there were also troublesome supply problems now that large areas of the South Vietnamese countryside were denied the enemy, limiting access to manpower and resources."[3]

In the United States it was not such a hopeful picture. The stew of people involving themselves in the war continued to roil unabated, fueled by internecine warfare within the government. Nixon, Kissinger (and Haig), Laird, Rogers, and Wheeler each had his own agenda, often radically at variance with the others. These derived from differing perceptions of their own roles and interests, readings of and responses to domestic political pressures, and outlooks on the state of the war and its possibilities. Admiral Elmo Zumwalt, who in early 1970 returned from Vietnam to Washington to become Chief of Naval Operations, called this maneuvering "a species of immorality." He cited "deliberate, systematic and, unfortunately, extremely successful efforts of the President, Henry Kissinger, and a few subordinate members of their inner circle to conceal, sometimes by simple silence, more often by articulate deceit, their real policies about the most critical matters of national security." And, asserted Zumwalt, that "concealment and deceit was practiced against the public, the press, the Congress, the allies, and even most of the officials within the executive branch who had a statutory responsibility to provide advice about matters of national security. The result, which I am sure was the one intended, was to foreclose outside and inside discussion of major policy issues."[4]

In this climate the directions, orders, "guidance," and suggestions dispatched to the field command by various officials often differed in emphasis, timing, and authoritativeness. Some were even in direct conflict with one another. "We had a message in here this morning on Thieu and his ideas on military reorganization—from *State!*" Abrams told his field commanders one day. "We're in a time period where it's the goddamnedest ball game—outfielders are running around in the infield, infielders are out, and people are shoving the pitcher and trying to get a chance at it." And, someone else suggested, "the sportswriters are down on the field, too."

"That's right," Abrams agreed. "Not only that, but some of the *fans* and so on. It's really—it's a *mess. Jesus, everybody's* in the act, and they've completely abandoned the territory that they're supposed to be covering and they're just *roaming.* One other thing—the *officials* have abandoned the field. The umpires are in the locker room."

The pace of the war in the communications channels between Washington and Saigon was consequently hectic. "That war was run on back channels," said Tom Dolvin, who served during this period as MACV chief of staff. "In one day we had 216 messages come into that headquarters. The only way you knew it was Sunday was when red came up on your Seiko watch. Then you knew to go to work one hour later than usual."

STRANGE CONTRASTS now marked the war in different places but at almost the same time. In late July, U.S. paratroopers were driven out of Fire Support Base Ripcord near the A Shau Valley after three weeks of NVA attacks, evidence that heavy fighting could still erupt. When the enemy managed to lob three rockets into the capital, the object of so much intense attention by Abrams during its earlier period under siege, he issued some stiff guidance to Lieutenant General Mike Davison, then commanding II Field Force. "Recent rocket attacks on the Saigon area represent a backward step in security that is not acceptable militarily, psychologically or politically," he stressed.[5] Another night, Abrams was listening to an Armed Forces Radio newscast in which the total report on the war consisted of an action in which two sampans had been sunk. "My God," Abrams asked

William Colby, Creighton Abrams, and Ellsworth Bunker formed a triumvirate of like-minded leaders who conceived and prosecuted a better war.

Abrams with Gen. Earle Wheeler, for six years Chairman of the Joint Chiefs of Staff, and Adm. John S. McCain, Jr., Commander in Chief, Pacific. Wheeler lamented the difficulty of getting President Nixon and other top officials to realize that they were "dealing from a position of military strength."

Ambassador Ellsworth Bunker with Gen. Creighton Abrams. South Vietnamese Ambassador Bui Diem remarked on the shared confidence of the two men, "walking together."

U.S. ARMY CENTER OF MILITARY HISTORY

Earlier in the war U.S. forces hogged most of the available helicopter and artillery support, modern weapons, and communications. Abrams changed that, giving priority particularly to the forces providing close-in security to the people in rural hamlets and villages. NATIONAL ARCHIVES

An ARVN tank commander points out enemy troops in Gia Dinh near Saigon during "mini-Tet." Former NVA Col. Bui Tin concluded that this offensive and another in the autumn were "mistakes," saying "our forces in the South were nearly wiped out by all the fighting in 1968."

INDOCHINA ARCHIVE, UNIVERSITY OF CALIFORNIA AT BERKELEY

These soldiers of the Rhode Island National Guard, here preparing to depart Fort Devens in October 1968, were among the relatively few reserve forces called up during the war. Official reluctance to use such forces deprived the services of valuable experience and maturity. NATIONAL ARCHIVES

Bunker and Abrams with Secretary of Defense Melvin Laird. On his first visit to Vietnam, Laird emphasized withdrawal of U.S. troops, prompting Abrams to observe that Laird "certainly had not come to Saigon to help us win the war."

ABRAMS FAMILY COLLECTION

As pacification advanced, Abrams scaled back the use of tactical air near populated areas and reallocated it to interdiction of enemy logistics traffic.

PATTON MUSEUM LIBRARY

B-52 bombers like these at U Tapao Air Base in Thailand were considered all-important by Abrams, who called them "the theater commander's reserve, his artillery, his interdiction tool, his means for influencing the battle, and in some instances his only means for meeting the enemy immediately upon discovery."

U.S. ARMY CENTER OF MILITARY HISTORY

A scout dog and his handler share breakfast somewhere north of Danang. With Abrams's emphasis on cutting off the enemy's "logistics nose," such teams were invaluable in finding concealed caches of weapons and supplies.

NATIONAL ARCHIVES

Buddhist funeral flags flank coffins of some of the 3,000 people bound and executed by Communist forces during the temporary occupation of Hue during the 1968 Tet Offensive. Terrorist acts by the enemy—assassination, kidnapping, forced labor, shelling of population centers and refugees—against the people they sought to "liberate" constituted a record of unremitting viciousness.

NATIONAL ARCHIVES

Abrams, briefing a visiting Time-Life *group, emphasized his concept of "one war" of military operations, pacification, and improvement of South Vietnam's forces. Body count, he told them, "is really a long way from what is involved in this war."* William E. Colby Collection

William Colby, here talking with a group of villagers, was the architect of the Accelerated Pacification Campaign. That, said Abrams, was the turning point at which the government "took the initiative in South Vietnam in the larger sense of the total war." William E. Colby Collection

This Regional Forces outpost in the Mekong Delta was typical of the expansion of local security by Territorial Forces, upgunned and expanded to 550,000. Lt. Gen. Julian Ewell called them "the cutting edge of the war."

U.S. ARMY CENTER OF MILITARY HISTORY

A 76-year-old member of the People's Self-Defense Forces just after receiving the U.S. Bronze Star Medal. Four million people, with 600,000 weapons, made up the PSDF, evidence of both the loyalty of the population and President Thieu's confidence in their support.

INDOCHINA ARCHIVE,
UNIVERSITY OF CALIFORNIA
AT BERKELEY

President Richard Nixon visited the troops in July 1969. At that time, said Nixon, he changed Gen. Abrams's orders to a primary mission of enabling the South Vietnamese to "assume the full responsibility for the security of South Vietnam." That, of course, was what Abrams had been doing all along.

Maj. Gen. Ngo Quang Truong, then commanding 1st ARVN Division, is decorated by Gen. Cao Van Vien at Hue. Abrams considered Truong South Vietnam's best field commander, telling his officers that Truong's division "does better in the jungle than we do."

These soldiers of the U.S. 25th Infantry Division took part in the 1970 incursion into enemy base areas in Cambodia. While the 60-day operation by U.S. and South Vietnamese forces seized large quantities of matériel, Abrams realistically judged that it caused the enemy "some temporary inconvenience."

himself, "is this what this war has come to—sinking two sampans?"[6]

When Vice President Spiro Agnew passed through, Abrams treated him to one of his favorite analogies. "The kind of war that we have here can be compared to an orchestra. It is sometimes appropriate to emphasize the drums or the trumpets or the bassoon, or even the flute. The Vietnamese, to a degree, realize this and do it. The Koreans, on the other hand, play one instrument—the bass drum."[7]

John Gunther Dean, later U.S. ambassador to Cambodia, was assigned to Military Region 1 as the deputy for pacification support. One day, finding himself faced with a decision about releasing some barracks for refugee support while both the corps commander and his deputy were away, Dean put in a call to Abrams and described the situation. "John, you're in charge, aren't you?" Abrams asked. "Yes, sir," responded Dean. Abrams hung up.

Another morning, Abrams opened the *Saigon Post* to find a photo of a U.S. Army brigadier general, then assigned as assistant commander of a U.S. division, presenting a trophy to the winner of a tennis tournament at the Cercle Sportif in Saigon. That officer was out of Vietnam within twenty-four hours and retired within a week.

Sometimes there was even some comic relief. En route to Southeast Asia, Vice President Agnew stopped in Australia. There, Abrams later mentioned, "in some idle conversation [he] agreed to buy fifteen million bucks' worth of mutton. And got back and said the Army would use it. And the interesting thing about that is, there's a continuing program of surveying the troops to see what it is they like to eat. And *mutton* is down there somewhere close to brussels' sprouts! It's damn near in the *basement!*"

BUDGET PRESSURES, already severe, intensified during 1970. "The Pentagon has got one problem right now," said someone at a commanders conference, "and that's dollars. And the big accounts are out here." Abrams was not sympathetic to the Pentagon's plight. "There's no better place to spend it," he responded.

That was not, however, the Washington outlook. In early February, Abrams became aware of projected cuts so severe that he cabled Admiral McCain, saying, "It appears that the FY 71 budget has become the pivotal factor in determining the course of action to be pursued in Vietnam. This tends to substitute an unstated but clearly deducible timetable for US redeployments in lieu of the cut and try approach and adherence to the President's three criteria relating to Vietnamization." It looked to him like they were also chiseling on what the South Vietnamese were supposed to be provided. If future U.S. actions in Vietnam were to be budget driven, Abrams stressed, and if "what is intended in all this is a South Vietnamese force less than they currently believe they will get, and support from us less than we had visualized but often communicated, then some politically sensitive modifications of South Vietnamese goals as they see them will have to be made. In summary, I must report that this is not the direction or the program I had believed we were on."[8]

Then, having directed preparation of a plan for the South Vietnamese armed forces to go it entirely alone, Laird said he couldn't pay for it. Visiting Saigon in February 1970, he revealed that of the $575 million required for the recommended Phase III RVNAF Improvement & Modernization Program during the coming year, "we've got available in the 1971 budget a total of $300" million. Asking Congress for a supplemental appropriation stood little chance of succeeding in the current climate, Laird judged, so the only other alternative was to accelerate U.S. force reduction—not because the South Vietnamese were ready to take on more of the load, but simply to save money—or complete only part of the I&M program. "We've got a problem here, don't we, Bus?" said Laird to the accompanying General Wheeler.[9]

COMBAT OPERATIONS concentrated on finding and seizing the military wherewithal the enemy had so painstakingly moved into South Vietnam in anticipation of future offensives. Wrote one young officer at the time, "We are as busy as a one-legged man at an ass-kicking contest." The results were sometimes spectacular. In early February 1970, Mobile Strike Force elements northeast of Saigon captured three enemy munitions caches totaling more than fifty tons, and still more was discovered in an extensively booby-trapped area covering several acres. This came to be known as "the Rang Rang cache," and by the time it was all counted up the take amounted to more than 150 tons of rockets, small arms ammunition, rocket launchers from Romania, shovels from India, tires from Cambodia, rifle grenades from North Vietnam, telephones from Czechoslovakia. Ninety-five percent of the haul, though, had come from the People's Republic of China, and—it was calculated—had been in place for not longer than nine months. Typically, Abrams saw it from the soldier's perspective: "How would you feel if you broke your back carrying it that far, and now somebody's picked it up?"

EARLY IN 1970 MACV undertook a comparative analysis of the 1968 and 1969 dry season campaigns in an effort to assess the impact of Commando Hunt, as the air interdiction effort in the Laotian panhandle was known. Taking the last quarter of each year into consideration, the analysis showed that both B-52 strikes and tactical air sorties were down substantially in 1969, primarily due to budget cuts. George Brown estimated that the enemy had put about 25 percent more effort into that campaign than he had the year before, while "*we* put in about 25 percent *less* in airpower. It's not *here*. It's gone *home*." Even so, truck kills had risen significantly, a result attributed to refined target acquisition techniques and operational expertise, introduction of the extremely effective fixed-wing gunships,[10] and—not necessarily a plus—the fact that there were simply more enemy trucks on the road. Someone called it "a target-rich environment," and it was indeed.

Nevertheless, decided MACV, since more trucks kept coming, "It must be assumed that truck replacement was adequate to maintain the enemy's truck inventory in Laos." The practical troop leader in Abrams could see an advantage to the enemy in that: "It may help him with his maintenance—none of the trucks are getting old!"

During 1969, 40 percent more input was noted moving into the panhandle, while the allied air effort damaged or destroyed 50 percent more trucks and reduced throughput by about 50 percent. "Thus," concluded this analysis, "although the enemy increased his effort significantly in 1969, he was less successful in achieving his objectives." Even so, a MACV briefer told Sir Robert Thompson early in 1970, "The enemy is continuing to meet his goals for supplies despite our interdiction effort."

One reason was the flood of matériel into North Vietnam from its Russian and Chinese patrons, estimated during 1969 to total almost 1,900,000 tons by sea and another 200,000 tons by rail. This included about 500 trucks a month—fresh fodder for the gunships—to back up the more than 4,000 trucks that reconnaissance photos showed in truck parks in the North. This was supplemented by the estimated 4,000 tons of arms and munitions delivered through Cambodia. The enemy's "crash logistical program" during the winter of 1969–1970, concluded MACV, "has been successful."

DURING 1969, 65,500 Americans were withdrawn from Vietnam in two increments, exceeding substantially the 50,000 ceiling that Bunker and Abrams had argued for. They discussed the prospects for 1970 with President Thieu, and Abrams then advised General Wheeler that Thieu "felt that 100,000 withdrawal in 1970 was workable and 150,000 was the maximum."[11] As things turned out, the 1970 three-increment total reached 140,000, near the upper limit of Thieu's tolerance. When he visited Vietnam in November 1969, Deputy Secretary of Defense David Packard discussed the withdrawal program with Abrams. "I told the Secretary," Abrams reported to Wheeler and McCain, "that what I had always tried to do was give our most honest and sound judgment on what could be done under the circumstances in the environment prevailing here, and having done that that I had never had any difficulty in complying with the decision and direction of the President."[12]

Abrams also told Packard that he preferred more frequent announcements of smaller increments rather than announcement of a larger number to be taken out over a longer time, feeling that this permitted more realistic consideration of the established criteria on which withdrawals were theoretically based. Abrams's opinion apparently counted for little with the decision makers in Washington, for in April 1970 the President announced that 150,000 men would be withdrawn over the next year. In the same breath he abandoned the approach that Abrams and Bunker, backed by Wheeler and McCain, had strongly advocated. "We have now reached a point," said Nixon, "where we can confidently move from a period of 'cut and try' to a longer-range program for the replacement of Americans by South Vietnamese troops."[13]

"Now, I really don't like the idea of taking 50,000 out of here under the circumstances in January, February, and March [of 1970]," Abrams told his field commanders, looking to the next redeployment increment and the period—including Tet—during which the enemy had always mounted a winter–spring campaign. "I just don't *like* that. Snaking the 1st Division out in January and February—it *lacks* that real *appeal*." Nevertheless, 50,000 U.S. troops were withdrawn during February–April 1970.

As units that had fought in Vietnam, some for years, stood down and prepared to redeploy, Abrams went to tell them goodbye and to thank them for what they had done. To the 1st Infantry Division he said this: "In a changing world, changing times and changing attitudes, going back to 1916, and up to the present—the various fads and interests, the various political motivations that have thrust themselves upon our country—in all that time, and to this moment, the 1st Infantry Division, more than any other division in our Army, represents a constancy of those essential virtues of mankind—humility, courage, devotion, and sacrifice. The world is changed a lot, but this division continues to serve, as it had in the beginning. I choose to feel that this is part of the cement, and the rock, and the steel that holds our great country together." And then he closed by quoting to them their division's own great motto: "No Mission Too Difficult, No Sacrifice Too Great—Duty First."

THE RVNAF COMMAND structure was, to outward appearances, pretty straightforward. The whole of South Vietnam was divided into four corps tactical zones (redesignated in mid-1970 as military regions), each headed by a corps commander. Under him he had the regular military forces assigned to the region, as well as the civil administration—the network of province chiefs who in turn supervised district chiefs and the like. Saigon was in the separate Capital Military District with its own military commander and civil administration. At the national level there was the Joint General Staff, somewhat like the Joint Chiefs of Staff in the United States, with responsibility for planning and support of military operations. Throughout the latter years of the war the JGS was headed by General Cao Van Vien, an intelligent, professional, and serious officer who had the respect of Abrams and the other Americans who worked with him.

What undercut this logical arrangement was the network of long-standing alliances and relationships between President Nguyen Van Thieu and some of his key subordinate leaders.

The Americans were well aware of this, and of its negative effects, but for the most part had little ability to influence it.
Abrams explained to the staff at one point, for example, that
Lieutenant General Hoang Xuan Lam, then I Corps commander, "deals directly with the President on a great many
things." Likewise the III Corps commander, Lieutenant General
Do Cao Tri. "Tri has dinner with the President once or twice
a week. He gets operational approval, that sort of thing, and
Vien's not in on that. In my opinion," said Abrams, "Vien's
trying to do the best job he can administratively and seeing that
the ducks are lined up on things that have got to be done. But
direction of the campaign, that sort of thing, is just not coming
from him. And his hands are tied on it."

As a consequence, said Abrams, "I have a great deal of sympathy for General Vien's position." But he also understood what
Thieu was facing. "I have to give the President credit for—God
knows, *nothing* would move here if he didn't put his shoulder
to it. He just does a little more of it, in some places sometimes,
than he should."

This problem would have devastating consequences later on,
especially during Lam Son 719 and then the final campaign in
1975. Interestingly, it was mirrored almost exactly in the United
States, where the Chairmen of the Joint Chiefs of Staff, Wheeler
and later Admiral Thomas H. Moorer, had virtually no influence
on conduct of the war.

Those Americans in closest contact with South Vietnamese
at the working level were usually the advisors, often a whole
string of them, as successive "counterparts" of a long-serving
Vietnamese. The more thoughtful Americans could only have
sympathy for a Vietnamese battalion commander or province
chief who had been fighting for perhaps a decade, only to look
up and find his fifth or eighth or tenth American arriving to
"advise" him on how to go about it. Lieutenant General Truong
calculated that, "on an average, each tactical commander had
experienced some relationship with from twenty to thirty

different advisors over the war years."[14] Kevin Buckley heard of one Vietnamese who had had forty-seven different American advisors.

Lieutenant General Dong Van Khuyen, author of a perceptive monograph providing the Vietnamese perspective on the advisory effort, wrote that "until 1967 . . . the US advisory relationship seemed to be rigid and formal. But from 1968 on"— from the time Abrams took command of American forces— "this relationship tended to be more relaxed, more open and more sincerely devoted to genuine cooperation."[15]

Abrams himself set the tone as chief advisor to the South Vietnamese leadership. Just how seriously was illustrated by his report to General Wheeler of a meeting he had with President Thieu in early December 1968. Abrams had prepared two loose-leaf notebooks displaying certain data, and at the meeting they spent an hour and a half going through them together, page by page. Abrams showed Thieu how the ARVN 5th, 18th, and 25th Divisions were performing in comparison with other ARVN forces, documenting in great detail how poorly they were doing. Then Abrams laid out for Thieu the facts and implications of the rising desertion rate, a problem that was undermining efforts to expand and improve the overall force. At the end, Thieu asked whether he could keep his copy of the notebook. Abrams assented.[16]

By 1969–1970 there were about 14,300 advisors of all types in Vietnam, the majority—about 8,000—involved with CORDS. Relatively few, 3,000 or so, were combat advisors. These advisors, mostly company-grade officers and noncommissioned officers, had had to be stripped out of U.S. units worldwide, seriously degrading the experience and maturity of the leadership of those elements. Even so, there were simply not enough to go around and still adhere to the desired policy of a minimum of twelve months between tours of duty in Vietnam. Thus some of those eligible were looking at third tours. That put enormous stress on the force, motivating many—usually under intense family pressure—to resign rather than face the prospect of further Vietnam assignments.[17]

Given his strong views about the importance of the advisors to success of the overall enterprise, Abrams was convinced that improvements needed to be made in at least some of them. He told Bill Colby that he wanted to do what he could to improve the kind of advisors they were getting. That meant changing the criteria for their selection. "I think we're kind of hung up on what's quality," he observed. "We have a tendency to look and see if he's been to the Command & General Staff College, to the War College, whether he's been promoted out of zone. And what we *need* are guys that can *lead* in *this* kind of a *thing*. It's *human* relations. It's a *respect* for the Vietnamese. It's a sensitivity, a sensitivity to humans. These are the qualities that are important."

Abrams talked the matter over with his senior field commanders and then, as he told Secretary Laird and General Wheeler early in 1970, went into "*actively* shifting talent from U.S. units into the advisory thing. We've got to dig in there and get some blue chips out of the one bag and stick them in the other."

American advisors in the earlier years had coached South Vietnamese leaders and units in their way of fighting the war. Later, when the Americans changed their approach to the war, it wasn't always easy to bring the South Vietnamese along. "The ARVN have been doing real good now for several months," Abrams said early in 1969. "But they were doing the tactics that we taught them two years ago, and doing them real *well*. In the meantime, we'd found out that those were not the most effective. So we'd *changed* and we had this problem of informing them that it was *now* time to change. And you run into a little bit of a block there. They say, 'Well, Christ, this is what you—. After all, we're doing what you *said!*' and so on."

Still, said Abrams, they were making the adjustment, getting out in smaller units to make contact, then moving other unengaged units in to pile on. But it was difficult. "The idea of going out in *company* strength, or *platoon* strength—*whoo!*—only *battalions!* That was the only way they wanted to go. Well, a *battalion*—it's like trying to sneak up on the enemy with a tank, it's just too damn noisy. If you want to *get* him, if you want to *find* him, you've got to do it with these small outfits. And *then*, once you get him, then everybody jump in! Well, they've been working on it."

HIS ROLE AS SENIOR advisor to the Vietnamese brought Abrams into immediate confrontation with one of the most difficult and intractable problems of the entire war—what to do about inept or dishonest leadership in the South Vietnamese armed forces. It was widely recognized, and long before Abrams came on the scene, that leadership shortcomings were damaging the effectiveness of those forces. The problem was to find people who were better qualified to replace those judged inept. The more the force expanded, and the faster it did so, the more difficult that became.

It is true that at the company and battalion levels some competent and honest junior leaders who could have moved up were for political reasons denied the chance to do so. But at higher levels this was far less often the case. President Thieu himself recognized this reality, at one point admitting to Ambassador Bunker that unfortunately the South Vietnamese did not have "many real generals who know how to command more than a division," and he included himself.[18]

The more insightful of the senior Americans, especially men like Bunker and Abrams, were sympathetic to the precarious state of the South Vietnamese leadership in a society in which the armed forces provided much of the stability and a large part of their constituency. Thieu himself was realistic, admitting that it would take time to remove the armed forces from politics. "The military establishment," he told Major General George Forsythe soon after taking office as president, "had been and still was his major political supporter and the only cohesive force holding the country together." As a consequence, "his American advisers would have to be patient."[19]

During his long years of service in Vietnam, Ambassador Bunker saw a great deal of Nguyen Van Thieu and formed some settled judgments of the man and his performance. "He has handled problems with a very considerable astuteness and skill," Bunker told Secretary Laird. "He is an individual of very considerable intellectual capacity. He made the decision in the beginning to follow the constitutional road, not to rule with a clique of generals, which many of them expected he would do. He has been acting more and more like a politician, getting out into the country, following up on the pacification, talking to people, seeing what they want."[20]

While Thieu may have committed himself to constitutional government, that was not necessarily the case with all of his associates, a reality that the South Vietnamese president bore constantly in mind. In particular the volatile Nguyen Cao Ky represented a potential challenge to Thieu's leadership. Chafing under the ignominy of his secondary role as vice president, Ky was mercurial, restless, conspiratorial, of short attention span, and a willing armature for coalitions in opposition to Thieu. Given that most of the administrative ability resided in the military establishment, and most of the political power as well, Thieu was agonizingly constrained in replacing the corrupt and the incompetent in high places, and likewise felt himself obliged to retain some who were loyal, if not all that able. Later on, his problem became even more intractable. "As U.S. troops are withdrawn," Henry Kissinger pointed out to President Nixon, "Thieu becomes more dependent on the political support of the South Vietnamese military."[21]

Bunker and Abrams understood this, and they were both patient and sympathetic, but they also made very pointed recommendations about senior officers who were not measuring up. Often their advice was accepted, even if some time elapsed while the political groundwork was laid. Over time, then, some major changes took place in South Vietnamese leadership, both civil and military, sometimes forced by battlefield crises. But there was never a wholesale housecleaning, nor could there have been. Not only would political chaos have resulted, but the requisite numbers of more viable replacements simply were not available. Producing them in the necessary abundance would have taken more time than there turned out to be.

What also seems apparent is that comparisons with American leadership, seldom if ever ventured by those most critical of the South Vietnamese, would yield interesting results. Nguyen Van Thieu, for example, was arguably a more honest and decent man than Lyndon Johnson, and—given the differences in their respective circumstances—quite likely a more effective president of his country. General Vien was at least as professional and dedicated as General Earle G. Wheeler, and probably somewhat less irrelevant. And so on.

Even so, there were characteristics of the South Vietnamese, especially among their senior leadership, that were devastating. "The political maneuvering, the political fragmentation, the political jockeying that just goes on *incessantly* among these Vietnamese" was something Abrams could only wonder at.

"I think the biggest problem the President has on the military side is he has to change the commanders of the 5th and 18th Divisions," observed Abrams in January 1969, "and he *just* can't bring himself to *do* it. I've told him that it's the principal strategic deficiency that he's got."

Abrams was not speaking from just theoretical knowledge. He had recently had a discussion with Major General Ellis Williamson, commanding the U.S. 25th Infantry Division, who had scheduled an operation with the ARVN 5th Division. Up in his helicopter at daylight, Williamson could see no evidence of ARVN troops in their assigned positions. He radioed the division advisor, who reported that "the 5th Division is asleep. The division commander consulted with his astrologer, who told him this was not the right day to go on an operation." Subsequently Williamson was called by Abrams, who had a question. "Butch," he asked, "did you call General Lee a son of a bitch?" "Well," responded Williamson, "certainly not to his face, because I have not seen him for several days."[22]

Abrams pointed out to President Thieu how this kind of inept leadership in two of the three ARVN divisions in III Corps was affecting his own freedom of action. "I had to bring the 1st Cavalry Division down here in a hurry so that *I* would feel comfortable that Saigon was in no risk. And it's because the two divisions are not earning their rations." When Secretary of the Army Stanley Resor came out for a visit, Abrams said, "Let's be frank about it—the 5th Division could *not* go backwards. It was as far back as it could go except for just *disbanding*."

Abrams knew, as did Bunker, that there was only so much persuading they could do. "It seems to me you can press it to the point—you can never break off communication, and you can't go to a point where you just become a *nuisance,*" said Abrams. "Otherwise you've just failed. After that, *you're* not ever going to be effective again."

The senior leadership of South Vietnam had pretty much gotten their schooling on the battlefield. Many had literally been fighting all their adult lives, from perhaps midteens on, leaving little time or opportunity for formal education. While there was a rising next generation that had at least mostly completed high school, those at the top during these years of struggle were undereducated for their tasks and handicapped by that to a greater or lesser degree. That developing cohort of younger officers would bring with them other desirable attributes, suggested Lieutenant General Nguyen Duc Thang. "If you can hang in here a few more years," he said to his counterpart, "there's a different generation coming on. Serving the people—that concept's not understood now [by the current generation of leaders]."[23]

Even so, President Thieu—for it was Thieu who made all the important personnel decisions, down at least through province chief—made a large number of courageous reliefs and reassignments, changes that substantially improved leadership as a whole. In the post–Tet 1968 period twenty-two province chiefs—half the total—were removed for corruption and incompetence. "We know it," said Colby, "because we helped comment on them." Of some 170 district chiefs changed, 90 were ones advisors had commented on. "So," Colby told Secretary Laird, "the government *has* a rather intense desire to try to upgrade, and they will accept American advice on the performance of these people." Abrams and Bunker often talked about Thieu's difficult situation of trying to respond to two constituencies, one in the United States and one in his own country, and neither of them unified.

Over the course of years Bunker, Abrams, and Colby had a great deal to do with the senior Vietnamese, both military and civilian. Of these there was one, Tran Van Huong, with whom Abrams formed a special relationship. Huong, who later became vice president, was prime minister when Abrams took command in 1968. Following dinner one evening, after the two men had gotten to know one another, Abrams said to Huong, "If you will allow me, I would like to consider you as my father." To that Huong gracefully replied, "Oh, it's too great an honor for me, but if you should like it, I will consider you as my younger brother." The two men agreed, and that special relationship continued through the rest of Abrams's service in Vietnam and even beyond.[24]

PERHAPS IT WAS NOT surprising, given the multitude of problems, that some of the senior South Vietnamese were doubtful of their country's long-term capabilities. The Saigon CIA station and the U.S. embassy both sent out teams of field observers to talk privately with various Vietnamese leaders and solicit their views as to how Vietnamization was progressing. Some of the reports, including one from a division commander Abrams thought was doing an excellent job, showed that "in some cases they out and out don't believe they can hack it." That struck Abrams as centrally important. "As we go down the road," he told his field commanders, "the development of attitudes and so on is really part of the job. Instilling confidence, independence, that sort of thing is part of what we have to keep working on. The Vietnamese, really, can do anything that they make up their minds to do. I think the sky's the limit. It's not so much a question of what they can do as what they *believe* they can do. And we just have to keep after it, and it's *part* of the *problem*. There are a good many other problems. This is just another one of them."

Colonel Harry Summers recalled how Abrams used to try to explain to young officers the "subtle dimensions of military power." His illustration was the porters used by North Vietnam to carry rice down the Ho Chi Minh Trail. Somewhere back in the jungle they would pass a T-54 tank spotted near their route, and they would be able to pat it as they went by. Then, when they entered the more dangerous territory farther south, they would know in their minds that that tank was back there, and it would affect the way they thought.[25]

Abrams described this aspect of the war to Secretary Laird the next time he came to visit. "When you get into the priority system, or how much of this are you going to be able to do, how much are you going to continue to be able to do [with U.S. forces], you're not playing it against a whole bunch of real *tigers*. Some of these hothouse plants which we hope, with careful work, we'll get into fairly rugged trees—you know, can stand out here in the monsoon and all that—. You can say, 'Well, that's a hell of a state of affairs,' and I agree, but that's what it *is*. And that's what we must build *up,* and build *on,* and so on. The *psychological* part of this is important." Even so, Abrams understood how the thing had to go. "Sooner or later the Vietnamese themselves have got to settle this thing," he observed. "We can only help, and we can only help so much."[26]

12

Cambodia

ON 12 MARCH 1970, while Prince Sihanouk was out of the country, General Lon Nol of Cambodia sent an official message to the North Vietnamese demanding that their forces be withdrawn from his country within three days. Six days later the Cambodian National Assembly passed a resolution deposing Sihanouk. Lon Nol as Prime Minister took charge of Cambodia's affairs, and the stage was set for yet more dramatic changes in the war in Southeast Asia.

A couple of years earlier, Abrams had looked at the Cambodian military capability realistically. "Sihanouk might be able to take on a wounded squad of Italian motorcyclists," he told Admiral McCain, "but that's about—." This situation gave enemy forces almost free rein in that country, and of course Cambodia and Laos had been used for years as sanctuaries for enemy forces, routes for the infiltration of men and matériel, and base camps providing a full range of support, including medical, logistical, and training facilities.

FACED WITH A TURNOVER even among his senior associates about every year or so, Abrams was by this point educating his third set of commanders on the nature of the war and how it had to be fought. Sometimes it was hard going. "I was out in the 4th

Division," Abrams reported one day, "and they were briefing me and they got into the *tactics*. They feel some frustration at not being able to *locate* the enemy and get into these big—well, you know, tackle a battalion or two and really chop them up. They went on to say they'd been quite impressed with the Korean operations. And, I must say, somewhat to my *horror,* they found these multibattalion things quite impressive." Having run one such operation themselves, scarfing up in the course of the five-battalion affair "one or two enemy," the 4th Division attributed the lack of success to inadequate intelligence. That was enough for Abrams. "I don't like to get into directing the tactics some division has conjured up," he said. "But I did undertake to explain to them that I *really* hadn't found these—in fact, had been *trying* to nudge the Koreans *out* of that sort of thing." And he had gone on to explain—again—his concept of the enemy system and how that was the thing to work against.

The Abrams tutorial on the war, aimed at both his staff and field commanders in Vietnam and the leadership in Washington, continued with publication of a study he had commissioned, "The Changing Nature of the War." Presented at a commanders conference in mid-April, it began with this observation: "The nature of the military conflict in South Vietnam has been under change since Tet of 1968. Although shifts in the level of violence, type of military operations, and size and location of forces involved are characteristics of this change, the allied realization that the war was basically a political contest has, thus far, been decisive."

From that realization stemmed primary emphasis on pacification, and from that in turn "the enemy's increasing loss of control over the population. The Accelerated Pacification Campaign, the allied clear and hold strategy, and programs such as Phoenix and Chieu Hoi have contributed to the progress achieved to date." Acknowledging that the enemy nevertheless retained "a viable military and political apparatus throughout the Republic," the assessment cited as current enemy objectives

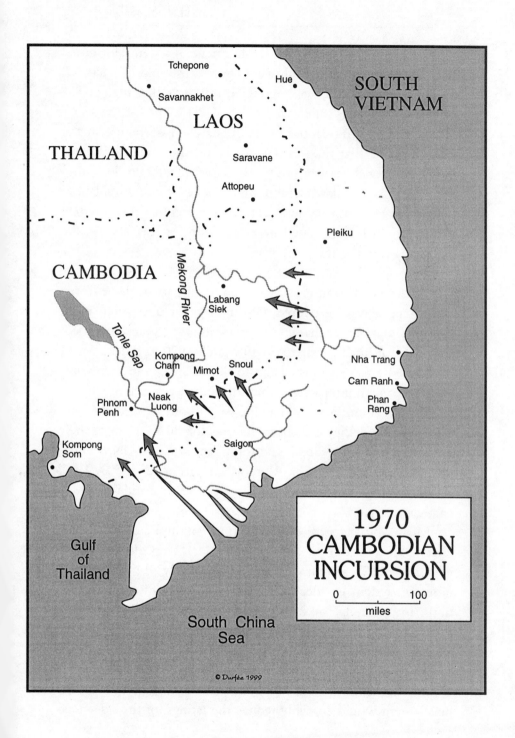

Tchepone

Savannakhet

LAOS

Hue

SOUTH
VIETNAM

THAILAND

Saravane

Attopeu

Pleiku

CAMBODIA

Mekong River

Labang
Siek

Tonle Sap

Kompong
Cham

Mimot

Snoul

Nha Trang

Cam Ranh

Phnom
Penh

Neak
Luong

Phan
Rang

Kompong
Som

Saigon

Gulf
of
Thailand

1970
CAMBODIAN
INCURSION

0   100

miles

South China
Sea

© Durfée 1999

"withdrawal of U.S. troops, establishment of a neutralist coalition government, and an ultimate communist political victory," all now to be achieved by protracted warfare rather than an all-out general military offensive.[1]

Then came the central point of the changed nature of the war. "For the first time in the war," said the briefer, "the enemy's traditional bases of power are being directly challenged—his political organization and his control of the population. While this task has only just begun, it appears that the outcome of the war will be decided here. Presently, at least, both sides are finally fighting the same war."

LAND REFORM WAS an extremely important part of the government's appeal to the people. During 1969 it distributed more land to the peasantry than in the previous seven years combined, and that was just the start of it. In March 1970 President Thieu introduced a far-reaching "Land to the Tiller" program involving some one million acres, a third of all the land currently under cultivation. About 500,000 families were about to become owners of the land they had been renting for 50 percent of their crops. "In one fell swoop," said John Vann, that program "eliminated tenancy in Vietnam. All rents were suspended."[2] By 1972 almost 400,000 farmers would receive title to a million and a half acres of land.

Measuring the state of pacification continued to be a necessary preoccupation. MACV had been running old and modified new HES systems in parallel since July 1969, testing a proposed system less dependent on subjective answers to questions. Interestingly, the new system yielded scores that were on average about 5 percent lower than the old method. District advisors supported the changes, feeling that they would provide a more objective and thus more accurate rating. That they would take this position, knowing that implementation of the new system would probably reduce the ratings for their districts, can only be taken as evidence of unusual professional seriousness and purpose. Pending acceptance by the South Vietnamese, it was planned to switch to the new system—called HES 70—the following year.

After the real progress of the Accelerated Pacification Campaign and the follow-on program in 1969, by April 1970 there was concern on the American side that some of the steam had gone out of the program. "I've just got a gut feeling that pacification has lost its momentum," cautioned George Jacobson, "and if it's not moving *forward*, it *will* move backward." John Vann suggested that the change in the HES rating system had had "a certain depressing effect upon the morale of province and district chiefs. You know, it went down an average of about 6 percent."

That provoked one of the famous Abrams eruptions. "Yeah," he began, "and that comes out of another sickness, and that is the worship of *charts*. It finally gets to the point where that's really the whole war—fucking *charts*, and where they're supposed to go up if you can make them rise, and where they're supposed to go down if you can push them down, and by just about any means whatsoever, instead of really thinking about what the whole thing's about, and what really has to be done. Yeah, all these guidelines and objectives and so on—you can't fault them, and that ought to be *part* of it. But then we get wrapped around the axle watching these charts, and it becomes—somehow the chart *itself* becomes the whole damn war, instead of the *people* and the *real* things!"

INCREASINGLY threatening North Vietnamese air defenses now brought the complex of "rules of engagement" into even greater prominence. These prescriptions, or more often restrictions, governed where and under what circumstances aircraft could retaliate, what forces could be employed in the DMZ and for what purposes, and a range of other situations. One bitter but insightful joke of the day was that the reason the Air Force used two-seater aircraft was so one man could fly and the other could read him the rules of engagement.

During these later years a common practice was for MACV to request, often in advance of an anticipated enemy offensive, certain "authorities," which were often temporary relaxations of existing rules of engagement. "It may be necessary to hammer at Washington again about our authority in the southern half of the DMZ," where they were allowed to operate only with very small elements, Abrams observed in May 1969. He also foresaw the need to request authority to use B-52s in the DMZ. "If that goddamn artillery outfit is going to have a wingding on Ho Chi Minh's birthday, maybe the day before we'll have Teddy Roosevelt Day or something and run B-52s through there to help the 84th or whatever it is get *ready*."[3]

General George Brown, noting that the rules of engagement permitted his air crews to strike enemy installations from which they had taken fire, said, "We're trolling all the time." What the Seventh Air Force commander meant was that they were running aircraft in with the expectation that they would be shot at, thereby permitting them to unload on the enemy missile and gun emplacements. "We can always entice them into shooting at us," Brown affirmed. Sometimes, though, that proved too dangerous a tactic. In March 1970, MACV reported, F-105s targeted against an interdiction point on Route 7, east of Ban Ban in the Lao panhandle, were fired on by four surface-to-air missiles. The aircraft took evasive action and thus suffered no damage, but as a result of the incident instructions were issued prohibiting operations within the SAM envelope. Unfortunately that action also ruled out strikes against the best interdiction point on Route 7.

When this was briefed to General Abrams, he reacted heatedly. "The Air Force does not have the authority to attack that site, even when it's fired at, right?" he asked General George Brown. "No, sir, we can't attack that," Brown confirmed. "Under those circumstances," said Abrams, "I just don't see how you can call on people to go up there to work. That's the whole *point* in this thing, the lack of authority to attack that damn site, or any other site up there in that area that opens up on you. Of course, we've tried to get the authority, and I'll be goddamned if I understand why we can't, because the photo recon guys that go in North Vietnam—they can attack anybody that shoots at *them* from North Vietnam."

Referring acidly to comments by the Pentagon press secretary on the matter, Abrams said, "All this crap about we can take whatever action's required to protect our own forces, protective reaction—all kind of great patriotic speeches have been made about *that!* And if the principle doesn't apply here, I'll be damned—. Of course, I suppose there are policy questions that I don't know about. Anyway, I *must* say, from a rigid parochial position, this is *very* difficult to understand."

Controversy over the rules of engagement, and the application of those rules, would continue throughout the remaining years of the war. Resumption of bombing in North Vietnam on two occasions and expansion of offensive action there to mining of the key ports were among the most momentous decisions of the war, and among the most efficacious. Meanwhile, North Vietnam for a number of years enjoyed a rear base spared the ravages of war.

MUCH OF THE ALLIED air activity that occasioned these concerns had to do with interdiction of the enemy's logistical offensives. At MACV there was respect and even compassion for the enemy's tireless efforts to move the goods. When an intercept revealed that two transportation battalions supporting a way station on the trail had only 58 operable trucks out of the 133 assigned, a deadline rate of about 56 percent, General Frank Mildren, deputy commander of U.S. Army, Vietnam, sized that up. "Well, you know," he observed, "we have a hell of a time maintaining better than 70 percent in hard surfaced motor pools, lighted conditions, sheds to work under—goddamn, all the support they get. And these poor guys are out in the woods getting bombed, driving over lousy roads in the dark. I'm surprised if they *keep* 50 or 60 percent running. That would be pretty *good* under those conditions."

What interested Abrams most about all this was what the enemy intended. "You've got a story going around that he's opted for a protracted war," he reminded Potts at a June 1970 WIEU. "You don't need all this tonnage for a protracted war. We've got a lot of things here that just don't add *up!* Either we've been kidding ourselves *before,* or *something.* How 'bout this protracted war, and then here's all this damn tonnage?" Potts suggested it had been necessitated by the operations in Cambodia, but of course those were very recent, whereas this logistics offensive had been under way since late autumn and would have had to be planned and ordered much earlier than that.

Before that question could be resolved, it was time to anticipate the enemy's *next* dry season campaign and the logistics offensive preparatory to it. Countering that would be more difficult, in part because the complex of roads in use by the enemy had expanded dramatically, from 750 kilometers as recently as 1966 to 3,700 kilometers in 1970, and work continued on further expansion. MACV was thus faced with countering a stronger enemy effort with a reduced force. The solution was to allocate a planned 70 percent of fighter sorties to interdiction, a higher percentage of a smaller total than in earlier years. That meant fewer sorties would be available for South Vietnam, but it would be worth it if interdiction could really make a difference.

Bui Tin maintains that, despite all the allied effort, North Vietnamese "operations were never compromised by attacks on the trail." Even though B-52 attacks sometimes caused major damage, he admitted, "we put so much in at the top of the trail that enough men and weapons to prolong the war always came out at the bottom."[4]

But there is evidence of periodic substantial success in the interdiction campaign in a history of PAVN published in Hanoi. "Because of the expansion of the battlefield [into Cambodia and Laos], our requirement for combined arms combat operations demanded the transportation of an ever-increasing quantity of supplies and technical equipment," said this account. "At the same time, however, the enemy's AC-130E aircraft established control over and successfully suppressed, to a certain extent, our night-time supply operations. The number of trucks destroyed by enemy aircraft during the 1970–1971 dry season rose to 4,000, of which the AC-130E by itself destroyed 2,432, trucks (60.8 percent of the total number of trucks destroyed by the enemy). Our supply effort, conducted during a single season of the year and using a 'single supply route' could not respond adequately to our requirements."[5]

And while getting the goods into South Vietnam was one thing, holding on to them until they could be put to use was something else again. During 1969 nearly 3,000 enemy caches were seized by allied forces, almost half again what had been taken in 1968. These included 1,855 tons of ammunition, twice the previous year's haul, and more than 12,000 weapons.[6] That was cutting off the enemy's "logistical nose" in a big way.

It seems clear that there were points in the war when the enemy had to pull back due to lack of resources—and also that merely prolonging the war was not the enemy's objective, at least as stated in his numerous policy pronouncements over the years. But as a generality Tin's point appears to be valid. Given the constraints on allied forces, especially limitations on cross-border ground force operations, they were never quite able with any finality to choke off that vital enemy lifeline.

It would be difficult to overestimate the importance of the Ho Chi Minh Trail to the enemy, especially after Sihanoukville and the southern supply route through Cambodia were closed in 1970. "It was the only way to bring sufficient power to bear on the fighting in the South," confirmed Bui Tin, and thus an

absolute necessity. Of course MACV understood that reality full
well, expending over the years of the war an immense effort in
analysis, tactics, aircraft, sensors, ordnance, and manpower in
an effort to constrict the enemy logistical flow. In the end the
results seemed to mirror a famous comment, supposedly CIA's
take on the whole war: "Everything worked, but nothing
worked enough."

DURING THE SPRING OF 1969 Abrams and his staff had discussed
the possibility of a ground thrust into Cambodia to disrupt enemy base areas and seize quantities of supplies. Given that the
enemy was then in the process of wholesale violation of whatever "understandings" had been reached in Paris, Davidson
thought a cross-border operation might be attractive to Washington. "They must be suffering some chagrin that we didn't
retaliate, that we took this, just like we took the *Pueblo*," he
speculated.[7] "There's a little national pride involved. We *said* we
would *not* stop the bombing unless we got these guarantees, and
they're violating *both* of them! I'd be embarrassed. I think we
all should be a little ashamed of this. So I think maybe we're
offering them something that they might find attractive."

Colby also favored such an operation, emphasizing the importance of the enemy's base areas and lines of communication
across South Vietnam's borders. "That's the interminable part of
this war," he observed. "Unless you can solve that, you *are* here
forever." Abrams agreed. "No amount of bombing in North
Vietnam is going to cause him to rethink his problem. But if
we go in those base areas, he's got to rethink the *whole* damn
problem! That's the way *I* feel about it."

Later in 1969 Abrams was asked by the Joint Chiefs of Staff
about possible cross-border operations into Cambodia or Laos
by the South Vietnamese acting alone. Under those circumstances, Abrams was cautious. Such attacks would, he said, constitute a major undertaking even with well-trained U.S. forces.
Hard or fortified objectives would have to be avoided, as would

areas in which civilians were living. His response was not a gung ho endorsement of the prospect.[8]

Not until the spring of 1970 was authority granted for an "incursion" of limited duration and depth into Cambodia. Intelligence had indicated, said Nixon, that the enemy was building up large concentrations of men and equipment in the border sanctuaries of Laos and Cambodia. This led him to contemplate actions that "we could undertake to show the enemy that we were still serious about our commitment in Vietnam."[9] Of course the unexpected overthrow of Sihanouk also presented a changed and potentially favorable situation.

In late April, after capture of a number of enemy codebooks enabled MACV analysts to read some earlier intercepted traffic, it was learned that on 27 March COSVN had sent its subordinate elements a directive concerning the current situation in Cambodia. "The analysis," reported MACV, "determined that the U.S. was behind the overthrow of Sihanouk and that the U.S. would not send troops into Cambodia, but would provide finances, advisors, weapons, and war matériel." That was a pretty good analysis, except for two key points—Lon Nol had done it on his own, and U.S. and RVNAF forces were at that moment on the verge of a thrust into the Cambodian base areas.

In the aftermath of Sihanouk's ouster there had been a good bit of dithering in the White House about whether to mount such an operation and, if one were launched, what its dimensions ought to be, especially whether U.S. troops should cross the border. MACV was asked for ideas and submitted them. General Wheeler cabled back that "Higher Authority"—he meant "Highest Authority," the transparent euphemism for the President—"has noted that each option involves considerable US participation." Wheeler then called for a detailed alternate plan for attacks into the Cambodian sanctuaries conducted entirely by South Vietnamese forces. Wheeler's cable, dispatched at 2:49 P.M. Washington time, closed by saying that "a preliminary outline plan submitted here tomorrow would be invaluable."[10] After further consideration in Washington it was decided that U.S. forces would participate, but only after the South Vietnamese had led off by themselves on the first day of the operation.

In Washington, some fairly novel command arrangements surfaced. A presidential blue ribbon commission later reported that, "as was widely noted by the press at the time, . . . Defense Secretary Laird had been bypassed by the Joint Chiefs in advising the White House on preparations to intervene in Cambodia in April and May 1970."[11] Clearly that had been done on orders from the White House. There were other problems, including conflicting guidance from Washington, that led Abrams to state some ground rules. "I should add," he said in a message to Wheeler and McCain, "that in these delicate times I respond only to the direction of the Chairman, CINCPAC, and the Ambassador. My staff will not respond to direction from staffs in Washington or Hawaii."[12]

There were then fourteen enemy sanctuaries along the borders of South Vietnam, ten of them contiguous to III and IV Corps Tactical Zones in the South. The raid was going after those facilities, informed by the belief that "no guerrilla war has ever been able to reach a 'victorious' end without sanctuary." Allied columns—ARVN forces on 29 April and then a combined U.S./ARVN force on 1 May—pushed into the Parrot's Beak and Fishhook areas of Cambodia, thus targeting two of the enemy's most important border sanctuaries. Within a few days numerous other base areas were entered, ten distinct operations in all by both U.S. and South Vietnamese forces.[13]

Even given the restrictions imposed, the operation was for the South Vietnamese a very significant undertaking. At its peak 50,000 men were committed, the first time in history that such numbers of their troops had operated as a single force. It was a challenging new departure, radically different from the role of pacification support to which most ARVN forces had until recently been relegated.[14]

At MACV, President Nixon's speech announcing the incursion to the nation was played on tape at a 1 May update for General Abrams, who must have cringed when he heard the President say that "tonight, American and South Vietnamese units will attack the headquarters for the *entire* Communist military operation in South Vietnam." Everyone at MACV knew that COSVN was a shadowy, mobile, and widely dispersed complex that would be very difficult to locate and even more difficult to put out of action. In fact, queried before the fact about prospects for capturing it, MACV had replied that "major COSVN elements are dispersed over approximately 110 square kilometers of jungle" and "the feasibility of capturing major elements appears remote at this time."[15] Nixon's characterization of the incursion's purposes shifted attention from the far more important goals of disrupting the enemy's lines of communication and cleaning out his base areas, achievements that could set back his timetable for further aggression to the advantage of both RVNAF improvement and U.S. withdrawals.

To a surprising degree the incursion was unopposed. "When facing enemy forces," read a typewritten directive issued by the B-3 Front Headquarters on 17 March 1970 and captured a week into the incursion, Communist forces in Cambodia "should attempt to break away and avoid shooting back. Our purpose is to conserve forces as much as we can."[16] General Brown exulted that the enemy had "a hell of a problem." Abrams agreed, but only to a point. "Well, that's right, George," he responded. "But, you see, he's *used* to a hell of a problem. He *lives* in an environment where he's got a hell of a problem. I get a certain amount of enjoyment, I must say, out of seeing the problem get *complicated*. But it isn't *worth* much. He's a pretty determined chap, when you get right down to it."

Given that respect for the enemy, and his understanding that an incomparable opportunity was at hand, the constraints on the operation in terms of time and depth were agonizing to Abrams as a soldier. "What we need right now is another division—go in deep," he said in the wake of the initial penetrations. "We need to go west from where we are, we need to go north and east from where we are. And we need to do it now. It's *moving*, and—*goddamn, goddamn*." This last was said wistfully, with great sorrow and regret. Someone: "Time to exploit." Abrams: "*Christ*—it's so clear. Don't let them pick up the *pieces*. Don't let them," said very softly, "pick up the pieces. Just like the Germans—you give them thirty-six hours and, goddamn it, you've got to start the war all over again."[17]

AT THE HIGH-WATER MARK the South Vietnamese had more than 29,000 troops in Cambodia and the United States about 19,300. Rumors abounded on what else the allies might have in mind, one suggesting the enemy feared the 101st Airborne Division and 200 tanks were headed north. That took Abrams's fancy. "Well," he speculated, "if some way we could get Peter Arnett to write this stuff, that'd put them in an absolute *frenzy*."

What was actually done was impressive enough. Among the significant cache sites uncovered was one so extensive that it came to be known as "The City." It yielded nearly 1,300 in-dividual- and more than 200 crew-served weapons, along with a million and a half rounds of AK-47 ammunition and much else. Another site, dubbed "Rock Island East" in reference to a famous Army arsenal, contained 329 tons of munitions. To make these numbers more understandable, the commanding general of the 1st Cavalry Division told his men they had seized enough weapons to equip two NVA divisions, more ammunition than the enemy had fired in their corps area during the preceding twelve months, and enough rice to feed all the enemy's maneu-ver battalions in their area of operations for a year.[18]

Major General Nguyen Duy Hinh, author of a postwar monograph, summed up results of the incursion overall, tabu-lating 9,300 *tons* of weapons, ammunition, and supplies seized, plus 7,000 tons of rice, altogether constituting enemy requirements for at least six months of operations in the COSVN area.[19]

THREE WEEKS INTO the operation, Brigadier General Alexander Haig—sent by the White House to look into what was happening in the war zone—arrived in Vietnam. Haig's discussions with Abrams and others were prickly, his perspective relentlessly political. "I'd hate like hell to think that the President was justifying his actions on faulty information, or lagging information," said Haig, voicing an implied criticism. That apparently related to Nixon's announcement that the operation targeted COSVN headquarters. "He maintains, and frankly this is what he was *getting* from his cabinet and from the briefings we were getting, that it was ambiguous." Well, yes, agreed the MACV briefer, "it *was* ambiguous at the time."[20] Obviously there was unhappiness in the White House over some procedural matter, perhaps an assessment of the North Vietnamese outlook on negotiations, even as the operation itself was proceeding admirably.

Those at MACV had their own concerns about ambiguity, and they weren't shy about bringing them up with Haig. "We have two of your messages," he was told. "One of them says 'go get 'em' and the other one says 'hurry up and get out.' What is it you people really want?" "Well," Haig responded, "it's 'go get 'em' until the end of the period."[21]

Virtually on the eve of the Cambodian incursion President Nixon had announced another huge decrement of U.S. forces in Vietnam, 150,000 over the next year, and Haig sought some sympathy for Nixon's predicament from those at MACV. "What the President really wrestled with was, we were pressuring 'for God's sake don't announce another troop withdrawal in the midst of this mess *here*.' And he said, 'Well, it's still ambiguous. I'll go all out with 150,000, and if Hanoi really means they want to settle, there's *some* signal in that announcement.' "[22]

That approach was familiar to MACV, where it was the subject of frequent denunciations for wrongheadedness and futility.
"They're always looking for 'signals' back there in Washington,"
Abrams had observed earlier, "but they have a tendency to put
on *blinders* and they're *selective* about the signals." When on some
occasion the enemy fired a SAM missile at a U.S. aircraft and
then was clobbered in return by a violent protective reaction,
Abrams drew a contrast. "That's the kind of thing—you know,
giving 'signals' and 'sending messages' and all that, that's the kind
they *r-e-a-l-l-y* understand. Some things they understand, and
some things they don't."

About two weeks into the incursion, President Nixon had
asked Abrams for his personal assessment of the operation's effect
on the morale of U.S. and South Vietnamese troops. The South
Vietnamese, Abrams responded, had derived "a sense of accomplishment and confidence" from what they had achieved so far,
and would undoubtedly "become more independent of US influence and support," a development described by Abrams as
"an asset in the Vietnamization program."[23]

As for U.S. forces, Abrams stated candidly that "it has taken
some doing to get the American troops in an offensive mood."
(There he was probably reflecting the inevitable effects of having
passed more and more of the offensive combat mission to the
South Vietnamese.) That achieved, however, "they have reacted
well to attacking the enemy in his secure sanctuaries. American
troops always feel better when they are on the offensive. Not
only the soldiers, but also the leaders at all levels, have taken the
initiative in getting the job done."[24] Said Lieutenant General
Mike Davison, commanding II Field Force, the troops going
into Cambodia asked just two questions: "Why didn't we do
this years ago? Why don't the American people understand why
we're doing this?"

Besides the Haig visit there descended upon MACV in the
middle of this operation what Abrams described as "that whole
goddamn *flood* of messages" from Washington. One suggested

expansion of South Vietnamese armed forces above the 1.1 million level that was already proving extraordinarily difficult to achieve in both manpower and budget. Another asked for a plan to *reduce* South Vietnamese forces 100,000 to save money. Yet another message stressed ensuring that Colonel Cavanaugh's work was utilized in targeting the air effort. Steve Cavanaugh ran the Studies and Observation Group conducting clandestine reconnaissance and the like. "What the *shit* do they think we've been *doing?!*" Abrams exploded. "I mean, what *were* we doing it for? Just to give Cavanaugh a *job?*"

Then there was another message requesting a plan for attack of enemy base areas inside South Vietnam. "And Jesus, it's been an integral part of AB/143–144–145"—Abrams thumping the table as he enunciated the annual campaign plans—"it's been going on for *three* goddamn years! It's *recorded* in every quarterly review. I mean—*why?!*"

The previous day Admiral Thomas Moorer, then acting JCS chairman, had called Abrams at his quarters at 10 P.M., wanting to know *immediately* the situation in Kompong Speu, a town in Cambodia. Fortunately, Abrams was up on that and filled him in. Then Abrams asked what had occasioned the frantic inquiry. "Newspaper reports," admitted Moorer. "*Goddamn!*" commented Abrams. A staffer worried that answering such calls would only encourage more of them. "Well," Abrams reassured him, "let's leave it that I haven't given you the *entire* conversation!"

"I've contemplated sort of trying to take them on," said Abrams, referring to the sources of all this gratuitous input. "See, this has—it's really gotten quite bad. I would say it's really very *unprofessional*. And, in a way, they really ought to be *told* so. But I don't know whether that really winds up *getting* you anywhere. Maybe if we just keep hold—ah—patience, and keep sending back what we *believe* is the right thing to do, and *why* we think it's the right thing to do—."

There was much laughing and kibitzing all through this

exposition. At the end Abrams had an admission to make. "I must say, a little earlier in the day I was *depressed* by all this, but now I'm beginning to—." Clearly Abrams had been buoyed by sharing all this with the staff.

AFTER THE INCURSION the recently deposed Prince Sihanouk told Agence France Presse that "it is true that there are Vietnamese in Cambodia," meaning North Vietnamese. "Why should anyone be astonished that the Indochinese people unite? The Americans have erased the line of demarcation and have turned the Vietnam War into an Indochina War." That drew a positive reaction from MACV, where the briefer observed that "Hanoi will certainly be disconcerted with this statement by Sihanouk, for North Vietnam continues to claim that it has no troops in Cambodia and that the Cambodian Liberation Army is doing the fighting there." During the incursion Lon Nol, Cambodia's new leader, had written to President Nixon to thank him for American aid received and to say candidly that "the problem of the occupation of our territory by Viet Cong and North Vietnamese invaders worries us greatly."[25]

THE CROSS-BORDER operations in Cambodia yielded huge treasure troves of intelligence, more than a million pages of documents and thirty-two cases of cryptographic material in just the first three weeks. "What's coming out of that *really* gives us a much better handle on the enemy's intentions, and what he's done in the past, and what he thinks he can do in the future," Potts reported. The take also provided collateral confirmation of more than 93 percent of the infiltration groups that had—based on intercepts—been projected for arrival during January–May 1970, up from 45 percent confirmation before the cross-border operation.[26]

The reliability of MACV intelligence on infiltration was thus validated conclusively during the incursion. A few days after the operation began Potts, employing one of his favorite techniques, introduced a special little sidebar presentation at the WIEU. "Sir," he stated, "we've had a very significant development here in the past few days. Getting into the documents that were captured out in the Fishhook by the 1st Cav, we have found a seventy-eight-page notebook that reveals the plan for infiltration for 1970. We checked very quickly to see if it compared favorably with the estimate we have here, and it does, almost to a group." The special source of infiltration intelligence was once again on firm ground. The accuracy was not surprising, however, for by this time MACV was reading the traffic of three more *binh trams*—14, 32, and 33—in addition to Binh Tram 18, the original breakthrough.

After the Cambodian incursion there was also no longer any doubt as to the importance of Sihanoukville to the enemy. The forces conducting that operation captured large quantities of confirmatory documents, including ships' bills of lading and trucking company records that laid out all the incriminating detail. At the same time, the advent of the Lon Nol government resulted in closing Sihanoukville—renamed Kompong Som— to the enemy, throwing him back on the Ho Chi Minh Trail as his sole line of communication for all forces in the South. That in turn both concentrated the interdiction target and made the enemy more determined to protect his remaining line of communication.

The flawed CIA assessment may also have had lasting adverse effects on how intelligence was regarded and used by the Nixon administration for the remainder of the war. In November 1970 a CIA report found that "the low estimate on Sihanoukville port, coupled with the valid capability estimate on the overland route, resulted in a mind-set that led CIA astray in its judgments as to what North Vietnam was actually doing." And, wrote General Bruce Palmer, Jr., in a study of intelligence during the war, "the incident badly hurt the Agency in the eyes of the administration and more or less permanently soured relations between CIA and the Nixon White House."[27]

THE THRUST INTO Cambodia was bounded in both time and duration. President Nixon limited U.S. forces to a depth of thirty kilometers across the border, then confounded his commanders by announcing that restriction publicly. He also set 30 June as the date by which all U.S. forces had to be out of Cambodia and back in South Vietnam. Despite the limitations, the results in Cambodia were impressive, even to critics of the operation. The casualties inflicted on the enemy—11,349 killed in action and 2,328 captured or rallied—were almost incidental to the logistical accomplishment.[28]

John Vann called the incursion "the most favorable development, other than Tet, that has occurred in this war." Potts focused on the longer-term significance of the operation, especially in view of the continuation of U.S. troop withdrawals, and concluded that the operation was "going to have a major effect on the future of III and IV Corps. The ARVN can almost handle it by themselves when you take all this away from the enemy."

"I would like to say that the performance of the South Vietnamese forces has really been quite extraordinary," Abrams told a group of Korean generals during the operation. "After all, they had not engaged in this kind of operation, in this magnitude, with this much movement, and the requirement of this much coordination, in the whole history of their armed forces. And they have done an *excellent* job."

When Admiral McCain came out for an update, Abrams praised General Nguyen Viet Thanh for his part in the operation. "The handling of the forces and the tactics by all the forces in IV Corps can only be described as brilliant," Abrams said. "General Thanh, the corps commander—his plan for the assault in the Parrot's Beak was really brilliantly conceived. In fact, he made a lot of the rest of them look like elephants." Given South Vietnam's urgent need for such men to lead the forces, Thanh's death when his helicopter and another collided in flight and crashed in flames during the operation was a severe loss. General Do Cao Tri, commanding ARVN III Corps, also performed well in Cambodia. Tri, said General Bill Rosson, "was a damn fine field commander. His idea was to get up where the action was." His flamboyance and bravery led one newsman to the extreme of calling Tri "the Patton of the Parrot's Beak."

Abrams knew where the real business of the war lay, however, and it was back in South Vietnam. "It seems to me that the other thing we have to do is really get going on the pacification program—the territorial forces and the PSDF—and really get this thing cranked up before he can marshal his efforts again," he said at a MACV commanders conference late in the operation. "It may be difficult for the corps commanders to see that. This is pretty heady wine that they've been drinking here." But "if they can come back into South Vietnam and apply all this enthusiasm and vigor and initiative and aggressiveness and high spirits and so on to the *drudgery* of pacification, the drudgery of the jungle and the base areas, then we've got something. *But* that isn't going to automatically happen."

MIDWAY THROUGH the Cambodian operation a very significant thing took place on the negotiating front. On 31 May Kissinger offered a new proposition, one that included unilateral withdrawal of U.S. forces by a date certain without requiring the North Vietnamese to withdraw reciprocally. While this was in one sense a startling departure from a stubbornly held position, in another it was only, as a perceptive later commentary had it, "an offer that brought the American negotiating position into line with American actions, since American forces were already withdrawing irrespective of North Vietnamese deployments."[29] North Vietnam continued to insist that the United States scuttle

Nguyen Van Thieu as part of any agreement, a provision Kissinger refused to accept, and thus the new initiative lay dormant.

IN THE UNITED STATES, a reenergized antiwar movement reacted furiously to the campaign in Cambodia, spurred on even further when a confrontation between a crowd and the National Guard at Kent State University left four protesters dead. There were also allegations from some quarters that the cross-border operations were *causing* VC and NVA penetrations of Cambodia. At MACV that was known to be false. "There was obviously a movement in the area to reestablish the strategic position in Cambodia prior to any U.S. or ARVN cross-border operations," held the MACV analysis, "and that can be documented." Besides, Abrams added, "we've always accepted that when they wanted to march into Vientiane they could do it. And I think we'd also say if they want to march into Phnom Penh they could probably do it."

Ambassador Bunker had been in the United States for a brief time. "Well, I'm glad to get back to a place where one has a sense of some purpose and commitment, I may say," he remarked at a commanders conference. "Sometimes at home you get the sense that the commitment is against the orderly processes of government and the institutions on which it's based. I must say, too, that the increased polarization that I sensed there, and observed there, is rather disturbing." Bunker also mentioned as a disturbing feature "the dissent within the government and the disclosure of classified documents that's gone on. I don't mean to say," he concluded, "that the country's going to hell in a hat. When you go up to West Point, as I did, and see 4,000 of those young fellows there, you have hope for the young generation."

Meanwhile the Senate bracketed the impending conclusion of U.S. operations in Cambodia by repealing the Tonkin Gulf Resolution—enacted in August 1964 and the basis for initial U.S. introduction of combat forces into Vietnam—a week before U.S. troops pulled back into South Vietnam, then for good measure repealed it again ten days after the withdrawal.[30]

WHEN SIR ROBERT Thompson visited South Vietnam in the autumn of 1970, he found that "progress was most visible in the expanding secure rural road networks and in the increased traffic on both roads and canals." Besides progress in pacification and the capabilities of South Vietnam's armed forces, Thompson saw the effects of the Cambodian incursion at work. Destruction of the enemy base areas, seizure of his supplies, the manpower losses inflicted on him, and the loss of Sihanoukville as a port of entry for military goods had all had their effect, weakening the enemy and forcing him to concentrate on expansion of his lines of communication from the North. The proximate result, especially in Military Regions 3 and 4, was to greatly reduce the enemy threat for a period Thompson calculated to be at least a year, time during which pacification, consolidation, and force improvement by the South Vietnamese could continue to progress, even as U.S. forces continued withdrawing.[31]

At the end of the day, however, the raid into Cambodia probably had—at this late date in the war, and given the limitations placed on it—only ephemeral effect. Brigadier General Tran Dinh Tho was realistic in his appraisal, concluding that "despite its spectacular results, and the great contribution it made to the war effort, it must be recognized that the Cambodian Incursion proved, in the long run, to pose little more than a temporary disruption of North Vietnam's march toward domination of all of Laos, Cambodia, and South Vietnam."[32]

That outcome was, of course, a function of later policies and actions, not inherent in the Cambodian operation itself. The temporary disruption cited by Tho was probably more valuable to the United States, which was trying to extricate its forces from Vietnam, than it was to its South Vietnamese ally, which had to stay and fight on as the enemy rebuilt what had been dislocated. Abrams was in any case realistic about what was being

accomplished, saying in a 23 May cable to Wheeler and McCain that "we feel we must report the facts as we know them. For myself, I would say at this time we may have caused him [the enemy] some temporary inconvenience."[33]

SECRETARY OF THE ARMY Stanley Resor visited Vietnam in June 1970, while the operation in Cambodia was still under way, but his concerns were almost entirely budgetary. There was about $11 billion available to fund the war in 1971, Resor said. That amount, while substantial, was a long way from the $30 billion a year being pumped in at the height of the American effort.[34] Abrams declined to take Washington off the hook by fighting a price-tagged war.

"As you know, Mr. Secretary, we don't approach the problem this way out here," Abrams responded. "We're still using this 'cut and try' approach wherein we have to look at the enemy, we have to look at the progress of improvement and modernization on the RVNAF side, our own posture, and keep an eye out on the state of the economy and pacification, all of these factors, and come in with what we consider our best professional judgment on the military pros and cons, and then we come down on a solution."

But any lingering notion that decisions on withdrawal increments would be based on the situation in Vietnam was by this point clearly fanciful. Like the enemy's supposed "understandings" about restraint following a bombing halt, those criteria—if they ever had any weight or force—were now of no further consequence. "How long we can continue here, how many man-years we can put in from here on out, is a function, in large measure, of two things," said Resor. "One, our casualty rates. And secondly, our costs."

In June 1970 Washington approved the Consolidated RVNAF Improvement & Modernization Program, known as CRIMP for short. The completed force structure would give the South Vietnamese 12 ground combat divisions—10 infantry,

1 airborne, 1 marine—50 air squadrons, more than 1,200 naval craft, and large numbers of RF companies and PF platoons. All this would be complemented by the appropriate logistical structure and specialized units of many kinds, and significant artillery was added, including long-range 175mm howitzers, antiaircraft artillery, and more 105mm howitzers. Other than those augmentations, the major ground units planned were now in existence. The still expanding territorial forces—the Regional Forces and Popular Forces—were integrated into the army, where they comprised more than 50 percent of its strength. Completion of the planned structure for all the services—including long-lead-time pilot training and the like—was scheduled for July 1973. "The ultimate goal," reported MACV, "is to provide a force of sufficient size and capability to be self-sufficient and permit the total withdrawal of US combat forces."

Thus in approximately four years—from 1968 to 1972—South Vietnam's aggregate military forces would have increased from about 700,000 to 1,100,000, a heavy burden in both money and manpower.[35] "They can't support indefinitely the kind of military structure that they've got," Abrams concluded. "In the long pull they've got to get a more modest structure." But in the meantime, faced with the necessity of taking over from withdrawing allied forces, the South Vietnamese saw no alternative to this costly expansion of their military establishment.

"At least we're making progress," said General Wheeler when he was briefed on these augmentations of RVNAF. "This plus pacification, it seems to me, are really our only way out." Then Wheeler revealed something of the depths of his frustration during more than five years in the job of Chairman of the Joint Chiefs of Staff in the midst of an unpopular and, for the first years, unavailing war. "Of course the Congress holds the purse strings. They meter out the money in such a way that you're just *forced* to choose the least of a series of unattractive alternatives—or else compromise, which is what we usually end up doing. We end up sort of allocating deficiencies while trying to preserve to the degree we can a viable military posture to meet our multitudinous commitments, *none* of which the military's ever made. In fact, the goddamn commitments have been *made* by successive administrations and *validated* by successive Congresses. If I sound *bitter*, why—I *am!*"[36]

Abrams was clear about how the South Vietnamese were being asked to vault higher and higher hurdles, and to do so faster and faster. "In this CRIMP thing," he remarked to the staff, "we started out in 1968. We were going to get these people by 1974 where they could whip hell out of the VC—the *VC*. Then they changed the goal to lick the VC and the NVA—in South Vietnam. Then they compressed it. They've compressed it about three times, or four times—acceleration. So what we started out with to be over this kind of time"—indicating with his hands a long time—"is now going to be over this kind of time"—much shorter. "And if it's VC, NVA, interdiction, helping Cambodians, and so on—that's what we're working with. And you have to be careful on a thing like this, or you'll get the impression you're being screwed. You mustn't *do* that, 'cause it'll get you mad."

General Earle Wheeler retired in early July 1970, passing chairmanship of the Joint Chiefs of Staff to Admiral Tom Moorer. In Vietnam, General Fred Weyand reported for duty as deputy to Abrams. "What's the mission?" he asked. "Who the hell knows?" Abrams retorted. "You know what has to be done. I know what has to be done. Let's get on with it."

13

Victory

THERE CAME A TIME when the war was won. The fighting wasn't over, but the war was won. This achievement can probably best be dated in late 1970, after the Cambodian incursion in the spring of the year. By then the South Vietnamese countryside had been widely pacified, so much so that the term "pacification" was no longer even used. Four million members of the People's Self-Defense Force, armed with some 600,000 weapons, represented no threat to the government that had armed them; instead they constituted an overt commitment to that government in opposition to the enemy.

South Vietnam's armed forces, greatly expanded and impressively equipped, were substantially more capable than even a couple of years earlier. Their most impressive gains were in the ranks of the territorial forces—the Regional Forces and Popular Forces—providing close-in security for the people in the countryside. The successful pacification program, one repeatedly cited in enemy communications as a threat that had to be countered, was extending not only security but also elected government, trained hamlet and village officials, and economic gains to most of the population.

In Military Region 3, the critical complex of provinces surrounding Saigon, recalled General Michael Davison, "it is fair to say that by the winter of 1970–1971 the VC had virtually been exterminated and the NVA, which had endeavored to go big time with divisional size units, had been driven across the border into Cambodia."[1] "And by 1971," recalled Colby, "I could go down the canals in the Delta in the middle of the night." And he could—and did—drive out in the countryside around Hue, just two unarmed jeeps in convoy, to show the British ambassador around. They saw people standing guard where three years before divisions had been fighting. "I mean," said Colby, "the hell with the numbers. I don't know about the numbers either, but by God I did it."[2]

"As we go down the road here," Abrams said at a commanders conference near the end of September 1970, "I think *all* of us need to keep thinking and keep trying to see for ourselves what's important, what's critical, where *are* we in the thing? And—I don't want to roll out the champagne here, but you know, if we could be *fairly* successful on this dry season thing, and if we could really get this VCI and the guerrilla mobile forces tamped down to a *relative*—they're *always* going to be here, some number, but get them down to where they really aren't effective, where by God they wouldn't have a *chance* in an election, *then* we—if all *that* happens, we'd say, 'Christ, we can all go home and give lectures on how you fight the people's war, write books, theorize about it—it would be a wonderful thing.' But, anyway, there's a lot of *hard* and *sensitive* kind of *thinking* and *work* that needs to be done."

Not only was the internal war against subversion and the guerrilla threat won, so was that against the external conventional threat—in the terms specified by the United States. Those terms were that South Vietnam should, without help from U.S. ground forces, be capable of resisting aggression so long as America continued to provide logistical and financial support, and—of crucial importance later, once a cease-fire agreement had been negotiated—renewed application of U.S. air and naval power should North Vietnam violate the terms of that agreement.

The viability of such arrangements would be demonstrated in 1972, when the enemy's Easter Offensive was met and turned back after heavy fighting by just that combination of South Vietnamese and American forces and resources. So severely were the invading forces punished that it was three years before they could mount another major offensive, and that despite the complete withdrawal of all U.S. troops in the meantime. At that later fateful juncture, as will be seen, the United States defaulted on all three elements of its promised support and, unsurprisingly, the war was no longer won.

Later, after the war had been lost, Stephen Young observed in a conversation with his former boss, Ambassador Bunker, that "in effect the population was seized away from the enemy, that about 90 percent of the population came under GVN control during 1969, and that in 1970 and 1971 the figure stayed about that level." Young asked Bunker whether General Abrams's strategy had made "it possible to in effect win the war by seizing the population during 1969." Without a pause Bunker answered simply, "I think so, yes."[3]

FROM HIS FIRST DAYS as commander, Abrams had clamped down on excessive use of force, especially in populated areas, reserving to himself authority to permit the use of heavy weapons in cities. Likewise he cut back sharply on unobserved artillery fire. In late August 1970, Abrams again discussed this aspect of the war with his senior field commanders. "I think that there're areas around here in Vietnam right now where the question should be asked whether artillery, gunships, tac air, and all that kind of stuff, whether it ought to be used *at all*. Out here to try to get four guerrillas—three air strikes, and 155s and 105s, and two helicopter gunship runs—."

General Brown suggested it was necessary to do such things

to keep the system viable. "This has got to be *examined,*" Abrams insisted. "I don't want to be just out here banging up the god-damn country in order to keep the *system* going. I don't think it's too *soon* to start thinking of some places around here where you just don't *do* any of that stuff. Now I didn't bring this up on the basis of saving ammunition," he added. "I'm thinking about the Vietnamese people, the whole atmosphere of political and economic and a healthy attitude toward the government and all that kind of stuff!"

These concerns led to a study titled "Where Do We Let Peace Come to Vietnam?" It began with consideration of the application of tactical airpower within South Vietnam, then ex-panded to consider artillery as well. Seventh Air Force was tasked to conduct the study, which was to look at "conditions under which the application of air power produces undesirable consequences, and where that application may be unproduc-tive." Barry Horton, a brilliant Air Force captain who was also a skilled systems analyst, headed it up. General Lucius Clay, who by this time had taken command of Seventh Air Force, told the young officer, "General Abrams is really uncomfortable that we are doing more harm than good."

Horton's study was designed to identify conditions under which application of air power produced undesirable conse-quences for the people supposedly being defended, especially those living in rural areas. Even before the study was fairly under way, however, Abrams's expressed concern began having an ef-fect. For one thing Lieutenant General Michael Davison, com-manding U.S. forces in Military Region 3, had his staff analyze the use of tac air strikes in his area of responsibility.

Since Cambodia, he found, they had been running twenty-five to thirty-five preplanned air strikes a day and ten to twenty immediates, these latter strikes called in on targets of opportunity developed during an operation. Davison's staff analyzed the tar-gets being struck and the bomb damage assessment they were getting from forward air controllers. "And then we just sort of came to some gross conclusions that we had too many pre-planned strikes," said Davison, so they cut back to twelve a day and were doing fine, along with maybe ten immediates. The next step was to influence the South Vietnamese along the same lines.

When, a few months later, the results of Seventh Air Force's study were ready to be briefed, it was anticlimactic. By then, influenced by Abrams's concern, field commanders had already modified their operations to cut back on the use of air and artillery in populated areas, and the analysts had seen that reflected in the data. "We were running out of examples to analyze," said Horton. "We'd had the results without actually having to publish the study."

BY 1970, CONCLUDED George Jacobson, a fundamental change had taken place, one that had a great deal to do with the success of pacification. In the early 1960s "people had regard for the VC, and I believe that—had free elections been possible—they would have won by a very considerable percentage. I *now* believe that, in those areas where they do not have control, the Viet Cong exert their influence by sheer naked terror, and by little else." Thus, "I think if a free election could be held now, the VC would lose. You can't get popular throwing grenades into marketplaces and blowing up school buses." Despite this apparently obvious conclusion, the enemy's devotion to terrorism continued unabated. In the first week of April 1970, Jacobson reported, "the total number of victims was 1,427, which was the highest we've ever had since Tet of 1968, when they were so high we couldn't even keep *track* of them."

When Secretary Laird and General Wheeler made their next visit, Colby discussed pacification statistics. "We have our questions as to the absolute veracity of the HES figures," he said candidly, "but I think the key thing is the change. Approximately three million people, and 2,600 hamlets, last year moved from the something less than 'C' category up to the C or above.

What the absolute level of security is, is another question, but the fact they moved is really not in much doubt. Security *did* expand during 1969." And Colby cited President Thieu's strong emphasis on the People's Self-Defense Force as a base point on which to build the rest of the security structure, calling it "both a paramilitary and a political force for the future." The thrust during 1970 would be on consolidation of security gains, because expansion had gone about as far as it was going in most places.

President Thieu set pacification goals for 1970 at very ambitious levels—100 percent at 'C' or better by the end of the year, and of that 90 percent at 'A' or 'B,' then saw them very nearly achieved. "If 1968 was a year of military contest, and if 1969 was a year of expansion of security," observed Colby, "1970 is going to be a process of economic and political and security consolidation. It's beginning to really solidify." One reason was agreement on the mission at hand. In late September 1969 Abrams had convened his field commanders and their senior pacification advisors for extensive discussions. "And when we got all through," he recalled, "I think it was the unanimous opinion of everyone who was here that the place to put your money now, in terms of energy, effort, imagination, and all the rest of it is into this pacification program—enhancing the security, enhancing the effectiveness of government out among the people. This is not the B-52 league, and it's not the tac air league. It's really not the maneuver battalion league so much. It's all of the little things that you can do in there to push this along."

The key to the whole thing was the people, said Abrams, "that's what both sides are struggling for." That meant that "instead of talking about offensives, we've got to get into that RF/PF, PSDF, NP/NPFF,[4] all that stuff, and we've got to put a lot of effort up there so that pacification continues to march and continues to consolidate. That's the *nature* of the *beast!* Instead of toying around about whether you ought to move another brigade of the 4th Division, something like that. That's *not* the *real* answer!"

Progress in pacification was now being reflected in very practical ways—reduction in VC extortion of "taxes," a decrease in enemy food supplies taken from the villagers, and less in-country recruiting by enemy forces. "If you ever needed any proof that it's just one war after all—pacification, combat operations, Vietnamization—that it's all one thing," observed Abrams, "it's the effect it has on the infrastructure. It makes it tougher for them. The more that advances, the more——."[5] During a visit to Long An Province, Abrams had been shown a very interesting chart, a tabulation by year of kilometers of road open and in use, bridges functioning and serviceable, and so on. "You could kind of trace the war," he said. "You start at the 1963 level, which is when things were in pretty good shape, bustling and all that. Then as you go 1964, 1965, 1966, 1967, 1968 the kilometers of road and the number of bridges just keep going down and down and down. *Then* it starts back up, and in September of 1970 they passed the 1963 level, and are considerably above it now."

Colby visited various places in the countryside twice a week or more, usually staying overnight, a routine that gave him a current and authentic feel for the situation. Frequently he invited one or another of the Saigon press corps to go along. Flying back to Saigon after one such visit, Colby asked the newsman of the day what he thought about the situation. "Nothing much going on," the fellow replied. Colby pondered that for a moment. "Well," he ventured, "you're right. We weren't mortared, nobody attacked us while we slept. People were farming, the school was in operation, some refugees had returned to their homes. Nothing very dramatic, except the *contrast* with how things were there three years ago."[6]

General George Brown, an airman par excellence, understood not only his craft but also pacification and its importance to the outcome in Vietnam. "There's no question in my mind

but what we'll make work the thing that most people understand Vietnamization to be—that is, we'll form the units, equip
them, train them," he affirmed early in 1970. "But, in the time
remaining, we're not going to create a force that will take the
place of the force that's here now. So what you've got to do is
trim the security problem to a dimension that that force you
create can handle. That's pacification, and that means continuing
our presence over here until that pacification reaches the point."
It was a race, and everybody working in Vietnam knew it, a
desperate race to shape what was left to manageable proportions
before all the Americans were pulled out.

Pacification in its broadest meaning thus had another crucially important purpose, freeing ARVN divisions from static
security missions so they could undertake mobile operations
against enemy main forces. Colby described the situation very
graphically for the visiting Richard Helms: "Of your total force
here of roughly 500,000 PSDF weapons, 500,000 RF and PF,
500,000 ARVN, and 500,000 Americans, you're going to drop
out the last one. You're going to *cut* your force by a quarter,
and it's the strongest quarter and the quarter that's been contributing most. ARVN's got to be freed of everything else so it
can replace *that*. *That's* your real *gap*."

IF IT WAS DIFFICULT for Abrams to convince some of his senior
officers that population security and pacification were the essence of the war, so much more so was it—in his view, at
least—to get the press to understand this, let alone report it.
Looking at the situation in Cambodia, where the enemy was
mimicking his earlier actions in South Vietnam by building up
a political structure, establishing an infrastructure, and undermining the mechanisms of government, Abrams saw that as sail-
ing right over the heads of reporters. "You see, the cosmetics of
the thing—you've got the press reporting a raging battle, preparations for the assault on Phnom Penh. Christ, even these
young chaps, they've got to get it into sort of a World War II

context. Otherwise, you can't report it. And that's *not* what's going on over there. It just *isn't*." But that seemed to be the only way the press knew how to explain it. "Christ," Abrams complained, "talk about the *traditionalists*. They're not among *us,* it's these young chaps *reporting*. And this movie on *Patton*, you see—it comes at the wrong time. It just *reinforces* all that. You've got a war on, that's about the only way you can run it."

Abrams was on to something here, and it wasn't confined to Cambodia or any other single aspect of what was happening in Southeast Asia. In these later years the press simply missed the war. Maybe it wasn't exciting enough, maybe it wasn't graphic enough for television, maybe it was too difficult to comprehend or to explain, maybe it ran counter to preconceived expectations or even wishes. Probably some part of this was also due simply to war weariness in the United States, meaning that developments in Vietnam were not news in the same way they had been earlier. Admittedly much of what now constituted the most important aspects of the war was difficult to dramatize or portray. Hamlets in which the population remained secure, refugees who were able to return to their villages, distribution of land to the peasantry, miracle rice harvests, roads kept open for farm-to-market traffic, and the election and training of village governments were less dramatic than whatever fighting still went on, but they were also infinitely more important in terms of how the war was going. The war was, of course, still in the news, but the emphasis continued to be on combat operations.

Some of what the press *did* see in Vietnam never got to the public back home, probably for the same variety of reasons. Abrams recalled one reporter who "grabs this Speedy Four with a peace medal on him, over in Cambodia, and wants to know, 'What do you think about the United States inv–'—tape recorder going, camera—'invading Cambodia?' And the soldier says, 'Shit, it should have been done two *years* ago!' Then the reporter says, 'Well, how can you say things like that and there you are wearing a peace medal?' And this guy says, 'I'm for

peace, but you've got to *fight* for it!' Well, there went that,"
Abrams concluded. The segment never made it on the air.[7]

That prompted Mike Davison to recall a conversation he
had with an NBC newsman who had been in Vietnam for only
a few weeks on his first assignment there. "What was the biggest
surprise you've found since you've been here?" Davison asked
him. "General," the man replied, "all those beads and peace
symbols those soldiers are wearing don't mean a damn thing!"

WHILE AT MACV they were working to understand the war as
well as they could, a parallel task was to enlighten many of the
official visitors coming out from the United States. When Congressman John Marsh was there in January, he came across a
rather distressing organizational shortcoming. "He has discovered to his—it's been rather a *shocking* discovery to him," re-
counted Abrams, "and he's wondering how soon it could be
corrected—he found that the Vietnamese Marines are *not* a part
of the Vietnamese Department of the Navy. He discovered this.
In the first place it's amazed him that they've apparently gotten
on quite well—*despite* the rather tragic error." Abrams decided
to give the matter further thought before trying to get any action
going on it.

In September, George Shultz, at that time in a very significant post as director of the Office of Management and Budget,
arrived in Saigon. Early in his first briefing on the enemy situation Shultz interrupted. "I thought these people didn't have
any administration," he objected. "Low overhead—like Robert
Hall."[8] Abrams almost groaned. "*O-o-o-h,* no. *O-o-o-h,* dear,"
he said. "This is a very sophisticated organizational setup." Step
by step they took Shultz through the enemy's intelligence, logistics, personnel, medical arrangements, the whole system.
With that cleared up, the briefer had barely returned to his task
when Shultz again brought things to a sudden halt, this time
asking whether the enemy was self-sufficient. Abrams patiently
explained that all the enemy's weapons, ammunition, and fuel,

as well as much of his food and other necessities, came from the Soviet Union or China. "They have no capability to support *themselves* in carrying on the war," he emphasized. Then it was back to the planned briefing.

"I'll tell you one thing," Abrams later commented to his field commanders, "they've reduced our strength in many ways out here, but by God, the onslaught of visitors and advice from Washington continues unabated." Fred Weyand had experienced the same thing, including a surprising arrival. "Yeah, Bob Komer showed you how your friends are really helpful," he observed. "Actually," Abrams responded, "my aide just took my pistol away. Otherwise—." That brought a worried question from George Jacobson: "Komer's not coming *back*, is he?" Abrams was reassuring: "I'd say it would be a very unhealthy thing for him to do."

14

Toward Laos

EVEN AS THE CUMULATIVE effect of the "one war" approach was reaching a peak, influences were at work that would eventually undermine much of what had been accomplished. In the United States, these included further erosion of political support for the war, growing budgetary pressures on support for the U.S. forces still in Vietnam and for the South Vietnamese alike, and the influence of both on the pace of withdrawal. Clearly the time would come, and sooner rather than later, when American ground forces could no longer play any significant part in prosecution of the war.

At year's end, the use of those forces still in Vietnam was further curtailed by what was known as the Cooper-Church amendment to the defense appropriations bill, a measure denying funds for U.S. ground force operations in Laos and Cambodia. This left the enemy's sanctuaries and lines of communication once again safe from American interference, this time by Congressional action. Meanwhile, the enemy was contemplating his next round of dry season operations.

Suddenly American forces launched a surprising raid on a prisoner of war camp in North Vietnam, an operation planned and controlled in Washington. It was known that the camp, Son Tay, had held American prisoners. By the time the raid was launched in November 1970, however, those people had been moved elsewhere, apparently as a result of flooding that made Son Tay untenable. Later it was revealed that last-minute intelligence had revealed that fact, but the decision was made to let the raid go anyway. The operation was successful in its own terms, although of course no prisoners were rescued because none were there. Clearly another objective was to let the North Vietnamese know their rear area—the camp was only twenty-three miles from Hanoi—was not as secure as they might have thought. Much later it was learned that the raid benefited the Americans still held captive, since the North Vietnamese subsequently consolidated them in better facilities and their treatment improved significantly.[1]

That was one thing. But there was something else, much more extensive and perhaps more risky, on the minds of Washington planners—a thrust into Laos to interrupt the enemy's buildup of supplies and perhaps preempt his planned offensive. Much earlier in the war, when he still had an abundance of American troops and firepower, Abrams had looked hungrily at the enemy's cross-border base camps. "You know," he told the staff, "we'd really have this thing by the neck if it wound up all being conducted in Laos, fighting over the goddamn caches. That'd be the *climax* of the interdiction. A lot of it smashed up en route and all that, and then finally when they get down there at the end of the line we move in and *scarf it up!* It could have quite a—a-a-a-h."[2] That was in the spring of 1969, two years earlier, and a lot had changed since then. Now Cooper-Church leashed his ground forces, American troops had in any case been drawn down by more than 200,000, and all the emphasis was on passing the burden of the war to the South Vietnamese.

Now there was contemplated a corps-level cross-border operation conducted without accompanying American ground forces or advisors, along a single, poorly maintained route dominated by virtually impassable high ground on one flank and a river on the other, into long-established enemy base areas and without tactical surprise. It looked from the outset like a high-risk operation, not the kind of thing a soldier with the experience, tactical acumen, and terrain sense of Abrams would advocate. Thus a question arises as to the origins of the plan for the raid into Laos.

On the basis of circumstantial evidence, the small group of young officers working under General Alexander Haig in the White House, part of Kissinger's National Security Council staff, seems the likely source. Perhaps Haig himself was the principal author, a prospect congruent with his later involvement in and reaction to the operation.

At some point in all this, orders from Washington, maybe even including specific tactical instructions, apparently reached MACV. In the WIEU on 28 November General Weyand, noting that Abrams (who was not present) would soon be in a position to talk to General Vien, added, "We're going to have to talk to him anyhow about this *strategy* which, I guess, Washington has given to us, and was to be discussed with the GVN."[3] Possibly that was an early reference to the operation that was subsequently named Lam Son 719.

In December 1970, according to General Bruce Palmer, Haig made a trip to Vietnam "to discuss the White House proposals for the second allied cross-border operations with Ambassador Bunker, General Abrams, and President Thieu. By that time, Haig had the confidence of both the president and Kissinger, and, incredibly, his military assessments of the situation in Vietnam were given more weight than the judgments of General Abrams, other responsible commanders in the field, and the Joint Chiefs of Staff."[4] Haig later asserted that, "prodded remorselessly by Nixon and Kissinger, the Pentagon finally devised a plan" for the operation into Laos.[5]

A year earlier, asked about possible operations in Laos or Cambodia, Abrams had cautioned against "the ever present danger of RVNAF indigestion from too much too soon."[6] Since then South Vietnamese corps-level operations had been conducted in Cambodia, but in cooperation with accompanying U.S. forces, U.S. advisors, and of course U.S. artillery and airpower in support. That operation and simultaneous political developments in Cambodia resulted in closing the port of Sihanoukville to the enemy. With Market Time naval operations very effectively cutting off coastal deliveries as a method of resupply, all enemy forces in the South were now dependent on what came down the Ho Chi Minh Trail from the North. The enemy could no longer afford to abandon his base areas without a fight, lest his deployed forces be starved out as a result.

The evidence suggests that by the autumn of 1970 Communist forces had begun preparations for a spring offensive in Military Region 1, the northern provinces of South Vietnam, once the dry season arrived. One indication was formation of a new corps-level headquarters, known as the 70B Front, sometime in October. Also at that time, Abrams was told, "a highly placed VC penetration agent reported on enemy plans to launch an offensive with up to four divisions to take and hold major portions of Quang Tri and Thua Thien Provinces, including Hue and Quang Tri cities."[7] Significantly, formation of the enemy's new headquarters occurred well before any specific allied planning for a thrust into Laos had begun, a situation that discounted the possibility that the new organization was intended primarily to conduct a defense against allied operations.[8]

Several U.S. headquarters had, however, begun discussing the possibility of an allied cross-border operation at least as early as August 1970, when CINCPAC sent the JCS several concepts for operations in Laos and Cambodia that might be conducted by South Vietnamese, Cambodian, Lao, or Thai forces. The following month CINCPAC proposed that during the next dry season an ARVN division interdict enemy lines of communication near Stung Treng in Cambodia.[9] Abrams responded that there were insufficient forces available to conduct such an operation without incurring unacceptable risks to current programs.

Abrams went further in rejecting McCain's suggestions, stating flatly his conviction that such an operation was "infeasible." And, he added, while no recommendations had been requested, he had serious reservations about how such operations would affect Vietnamization programs. "When a new endeavor is launched," he pointed out, "something has to give." With U.S. withdrawals continuing, and U.S. support capability diminishing accordingly, there were not enough resources to go around. Abrams suggested that McCain's concepts be used for broad planning purposes only, and that none be implemented without a revised assessment at the time.[10]

McCain, undeterred, cabled Abrams in October that "the enemy's dependence on the logistics corridor through the Laos panhandle presents us with an unprecedented challenge. There is little doubt," he added, "as to the damage which could be dealt to North Vietnam's aspirations by effectively blocking or even significantly hindering the southward movement of men and matériel." McCain included a "straw man" concept for such an operation, to be conducted by ARVN, that would interdict Base Area 611 and nearby routes in Laos.[11]

In mid-November, Abrams submitted an assessment of Hanoi's current strategy that must have whetted Washington appetites for a move into Laos. There were under way at the time, MACV concluded, seven interrelated conflicts: the war in northern Laos, the logistics war in southern Laos and northeastern Cambodia, the war in Cambodia itself, the war in the COSVN area of South Vietnam, the war with the Viet Cong in the southern provinces of Military Region 1, the war along the DMZ and in the two northernmost provinces of South Vietnam, and the war in the Central Highlands.

All were important, but "the logistics war of southern Laos and northeastern Cambodia," concluded MACV's analysts, "now stands as the critical conflict for the VC/NVA." Every other supply route had been cut off, and the pacification program was reducing enemy ability to obtain supplies in South Vietnam. Thus the enemy must perforce expand and extend the Ho Chi Minh Trail if he were to support and sustain operations in southern Indochina.[12] The target for allied operations was clear.

On 6 December 1970 McCain sent Abrams a cable marked, with classic overkill, "Top Secret Sensitive Hold Extremely Close Absolutely Eyes Only," to say "I am passing within this message a message from Admiral Moorer which is extremely sensitive and must be held extremely close to absolutely prevent any possibility of inadvertent disclosure." Moorer described three operations that were being considered, including "major ARVN ground operations into the Laos panhandle, with maximum U.S. air support." As a rationale, Moorer said "the initial concept for a major ARVN thrust into Laos is predicated on the need to disrupt the enemy time-table and to destroy his stockpile to the maximum extent feasible. Multi-division ARVN strength is envisioned." He added that Haig would be in Saigon in about a week, when "he will be in a position to give you a sense of the urgency with which this concept is being examined."[13] Moorer also acknowledged that "instrumental to the success of such an undertaking of course would be Thieu's attitude, particularly with regard to a move into the panhandle. If the concept and timing is considered feasible, we would hope to obtain Thieu's commitment and full support of GVN participation and firm time-table."[14]

McCain then told Abrams that at CINCPAC "we do not have active planning now underway to satisfy the requirement" for major ARVN ground operations in Laos. "I recognize that this operation may present many problems to you and the RVNAF," he added, "and request that you immediately initiate necessary action for the preparation of this plan."[15]

A day later, Abrams told McCain that he and Bunker had met with Thieu for an hour and twenty minutes. At Bunker's request, Abrams had presented the overall offensive strategy contained in Moorer's message, quoting the planned options verbatim. "President Thieu's reaction to the combined three elements"—a thrust into Laos, ground operations in Cambodia, and covert raids into North Vietnam—"was favorable and he felt they should be done."[16] With respect to the operation in Laos, said Abrams, Thieu "felt that the general area identified by the town of Tchepone should be the objective. Route 9 would be the supporting LOC [line of communication]. Forces should be comprised basically of two divisions and some armored cav units. The timing should follow Tet and last about two or three months, and the[n] linger on using stay-behinds and guerrillas."[17]

There it was, the whole scheme, stimulated by Washington, transmitted by McCain and Abrams, and sketched out by Thieu. Given Thieu's response, McCain authorized Abrams "to contact General Vien and effect such planning and coordination as you deem appropriate in preparation of the Laos plan." McCain added that he wanted to receive a completed plan within the next five days.[18]

On 10 December, Moorer cabled Abrams, forwarding on behalf of the Secretary of Defense a message from the President. "I believe that Cambodian determination, the improved state of VNAF combat effectiveness, and remaining US combat capabilities represent sufficient assets to permit the adoption of bold and aggressive allied counteractions which could seriously disrupt the enemy's dry season strategy," said Nixon. "For this reason, I expect you to undertake, in coordination with the armed forces of South Vietnam and Cambodia, an intensive planning effort that, within the political limitations imposed on US forces, is designed to carry the battle to the enemy to the greatest extent possible. Therefore, I have asked Dr. Kissinger's deputy, General Haig, to visit Phnom Penh and Saigon, arriving in theater on Sunday, 13 December, to further underline the importance I place on this effort and to amplify for you and other responsible

US officials my personal thinking on the nature and scope of allied offensive operations over the coming weeks."[19]

"The more immediate origins of the March 1971 incursion into Laos, namely the White House," later wrote Bruce Palmer, "illustrate how completely President Nixon and his NSC staff dominated the overall control and conduct of both the war and the closely interrelated negotiations to end the war." While acknowledging that as a proper role for the President, who was after all the Commander in Chief, Palmer observed that Henry Kissinger "became for all intents and purposes the de facto chairman of the JCS."[20]

The impending operation in Laos was destined to be something less than a full-fledged success. Critics of the operation have suggested a number of reasons, including an assertion by some that allied planners did not expect the enemy to stand and fight. On 11 December 1970, however, Abrams reported to McCain that the bulk of the enemy's combat units in the region were located in the vicinity of Tchepone, that *binh tram* personnel had received infantry training that made them a potentially significant fighting force, and that the enemy "can be expected to defend his base areas and logistics centers against any allied operation."

Another criticism later raised was that the enemy had anticipated Lam Son 719, yet allied planners were unaware of that and therefore failed to take it into account. But at a 17 December 1970 coordination meeting of regional U.S. ambassadors, Ted Shackley, the CIA's Saigon station chief, reported that there was evidence from the recent COSVN Directive 28 that "the enemy thinks that we're going to make a major move in the tri-border area of Laos, Cambodia, and South Vietnam during this particular dry season, and that's having an impact on *his* planning over the near term."[21]

On 12 December, Abrams submitted a detailed plan, emphasizing that "no US conventional ground combat forces will be employed in Laos." The heart of the plan was a coordinated air-ground attack to sever the enemy line of communications at Tchepone, destroy enemy stockpiles and facilities, and block major north–south routes, a four-phase operation lasting about three months. In the summary, Abrams made two other particularly important points: "Speed of execution is essential to the success of this operation. An operation dependent solely on air mobility would be subject to the vagaries of the weather and the considerable enemy AAA [antiaircraft artillery] threat in the objective area."[22] After an unexplained three-day delay, McCain forwarded the proposal to Moorer, stating, "I wholeheartedly concur with the concept of this plan."[23]

On 14 December 1970 CIA published a study, coordinated with DIA, NSA, and State's Bureau of Intelligence and Research, indicating that "strong NVA infantry, armor, and artillery formations were in southern Laos, and that the largest concentration of these newly arrived forces was in the vicinity of Tchepone. It was also known that formidable air defenses were deployed along the Ho Chi Minh Trail and were particularly dense in the Tchepone area. Moreover, the mountainous, jungle-covered terrain was an added liability. Natural clearings for helicopter landing zones were scarce and likely to be heavily defended."[24] Thus at the Washington level, at least, it was clearly established before the fact that the South Vietnamese, and the U.S. air elements supporting them, were being sent into a very difficult situation.

Meanwhile Haig, having returned to Washington, reported in a 23 December cable to the field that the President had been briefed on a "post-Tet military campaign. During meeting this morning among President, Dr. Kissinger, Secretary Laird, Admiral Moorer and myself, the President outlined his general approval of the concept."[25]

IN EARLY JANUARY 1971, Secretary Laird visited Saigon. Preparing for his visit, Abrams had some instructions for the briefers. "We've got North Vietnam, and the Laos thing, and then the

Cambodian thing," he said, "and we come to Vietnam and it's a different war. It's these things like getting the *last* of the 'B' hamlets, and getting the last of the base areas down there in the Delta, putting a cap on it. The development of the RF/PF and the PSDF and all of that. That's the—those are the *key* things in South Vietnam."

Not only was the war in South Vietnam different than it used to be, Abrams told his associates, but so were the South Vietnamese. "When you get through with all the pluses and minuses, probably the most encouraging thing in the whole business is how in recent months they've been willing to take on this stuff and just go ahead. That's why I've said a number of times that we're dealing with *different* men now. They're the *same* men—the names and all that—but they've changed."

Nevertheless, Abrams felt that Washington was pushing too hard to accelerate the process of Vietnamization. "My position on that is that *nothing* can be accelerated any more," he emphasized. "We've *hurt* ourselves, really, by the amount that we've done. And hurt them. We've bought in on some things I feel kinda bad about. We're pushing them too hard. We're just trying too hard—going too far too fast." Abrams lamented how he had felt, marching over two days in a row to the Vietnamese with things he himself didn't believe in but had been ordered to push. "But then I see some of the things that Ambassador Bunker—the sack of crap that he's been directed to carry over to the Palace!"

IN 1970 ENEMY forces had, by and large, withdrawn farther west during the allied incursion into Cambodia rather than stay and fight for their base areas and supplies. That was not going to be the case the following year in Laos, and Abrams understood this very well. Describing the air interdiction effort during the 1970–1971 dry season to General Vien, he emphasized that U.S. forces were "trying to make the most powerful effort that we can possibly make. Because we feel that although Laos has always been very important to him, that *this* year he doesn't have any other choice. He's *got* to make that work." Cambodia, he added, was "not as tough as it is up in Laos."

A North Vietnamese history published in 1994 also empha- sized the importance of the Laotian corridor. "By January 1971," read this account, "the supplies stored by the various troop supply stations [the *binh trams*] of Group 559 in the cam- paign's area of operations had risen to 6,000 tons, which together with the High Command's supply reserves was sufficient to sup- port between 50,000 and 60,000 troops in combat for four or five months. In addition, more than 30,000 tons of supplies were stored in Group 559's warehouses along the strategic transpor- tation corridor."[26]

Abrams had not lost track of the importance of that lifeline. When Director of Central Intelligence Richard Helms visited Vietnam, Seventh Air Force commander General Lucius Clay described his job of the moment as carrying out instructions given him by General Abrams: "He wants that Ho Chi Minh Trail in such a shape that a crow has to carry his rations to fly over it."

That task was now more difficult due to the drawdown of U.S. forces and budget constraints. Two years earlier, Clay re- called, some 30,000 sorties a month were available for use throughout Southeast Asia. Now that was down to 14,000. Meanwhile, the enemy had expanded his road and trail network, which gave him many more options in movement of supplies to the South, and increased antiaircraft defenses along the routes. Thus it was planned that 70 percent of the air effort would be applied against enemy lines of communication during the dry season offensive and, for the first time, all available B-52s would be used almost exclusively in the Laos interdiction campaign. The successes achieved in pacification and security within South Vietnam made this approach viable.

Given the scattering of the enemy's logistical traffic, the interdiction tactics of the past no longer seemed sufficient. "The dispersal factor has been accomplished *beautifully*," said Clay. "They move at night, they move to one place, stay and hide, unload, pick up another truck and move on down, hiding in the canopy, so it's just an extremely difficult problem." To overcome those tactics, the Seventh Air Force decided to create choke points—areas that could not be avoided and through which they would make it almost impossible to move—and forget the rest. All this was a part of the aerial interdiction campaign aimed at the enemy's logistics offensive, even before Lam Son 719 began.

Four target boxes were chosen, each a rectangle measuring one by two kilometers and sited at one of the prime input areas used by the enemy—the Mu Gia Pass, the Ban Karai Pass, the Ban Raving Pass, and an area just west of the DMZ. A series of new sensor fields using improved technology was installed, and upgraded drones with higher altitude capability were going to be used to monitor the sensors.

The target boxes were scheduled to get 27 B-52 sorties a day and 125–150 tac air sorties, sufficient to ensure ordnance arriving every twenty minutes, twenty-four hours a day, for the next sixty days. The risk, said Clay, was that "we're putting the B-52s right up in the SAM envelope," the area the enemy had covered with surface-to-air missiles. The bombing would be impressively supplemented by gunships, including this year B-57Gs, old airplanes given a new life and a new mission with the addition of multiple sensor capabilities.

Infiltration of enemy troops was being tracked closely. For most of 1970 it had been running at about 60 percent of the previous year's numbers, then in late October that changed dramatically. Potts briefed on nineteen infiltration groups headed for COSVN and due to arrive in February, along with seventeen gap groups. "When we fill in the gap groups," he told General Abrams, "that comes up to 14,450 moving into the COSVN

area in one month. This is an all-time high since back in 1968."
It appeared that the manpower to match the enemy's vigorous
logistical offensive was now on the move.

The infiltration briefer also cited evidence that the 320th
NVA Division was deploying southward, with forward elements
near Tchepone in Laos, then mentioned reports that enemy
forces in the Lao panhandle were plagued by high rates of disease. That triggered an Abrams eruption. "We hear about that
every year," he recalled. "But goddamn it—either they've got
enough that are well or something. But they seem to be able to
work on the roads, keep the trucks going, still fire the antiaircraft, still move the supplies, and unload and load it, backpack
it, and all that. So I'd say they're right on schedule. I don't think
it means that somehow they're going to screw it up."

By early November the primary interdiction effort was
going in just south of the Ban Karai Pass. A combination
of heavy rains and the bombing had rendered the four target
box areas impassable, so much so that no enemy movement had
been observed over four weeks in October. This was having a
decided effect on what enemy capabilities for the coming dry
season might be. By late November, McCain cabled Moorer his
view that "the North Vietnamese will not possess the capability
to conduct an all-out, country-wide, offensive in the Republic
of Vietnam during the Tet period."[27] MACV saw Military Region 1 as the most likely place for the enemy's main effort to
erupt.

Pretty soon the roads began to dry out and the enemy logistics offensive moved into high gear. By mid-January 1971,
Seventh Air Force was devoting 89 percent of B-52 strikes to
the anti-infiltration boxes and achieving record truck kills, but
substantial numbers still got through. "We have done everything
we can, General Abrams, to try to interdict that Route 922,"
said a senior air officer. "It's flat as a pancake. There are multiple
routes to go around. We have seeded, we have CBU-ed, we

have bombed, we've done every *damn* thing we can do. But they *sure* want to come through there."[28]

Ironically, Lam Son 719—which sought to interdict enemy lines of communication through ground action—was going to ease the air attack on the trail. When fierce fighting erupted in the Lam Son area of operations, virtually all B-52 sorties were diverted from interdiction to close air support of the troops in contact. Thanks to the fixed-wing gunships, though, that same week a new record high in truck kills was achieved.

IN JANUARY 1971, before Lam Son 719 commenced, Kissinger asked CIA to prepare a close hold estimate of probable enemy reaction to a large-scale South Vietnamese raid into the Tchepone area of Laos that would be backed by U.S. air support but no U.S. ground force involvement. The assessment, wrote Bruce Palmer, "was remarkably accurate with respect to the nature, pattern, and all-out intensity of the NVA reactions to LAMSON 719."[29]

As the raid into Laos loomed, in Paris on 21 January the hundredth session of the sterile peace negotiations was held, a meeting described as "devoted largely to reviews of known positions."[30]

Meanwhile the drawdown of American troops continued unabated, 60,000 more departing during January–April 1971. "All Americans have got to be pulling in the same direction, and all together," Abrams counseled. "And that's always a neat trick to do under the most ideal circumstances. Americans are all different. They're individualists and enthusiasts, optimists and pessimists, then a slight sprinkling of just screwups."

On 26 January the text of an intercepted enemy message was forwarded to McCain and Abrams. "It has been determined that the enemy [South Vietnam and her allies] may strike into our cargo carrier system in order to cut it off," the document read. "Prepare to mobilize and strike the enemy hard. Be vigilant."[31]

On 29 January Abrams alerted Moorer to further developments in the enemy situation. "The NVA has detected indications of an imminent major operation in northern MR-1,"
he noted. "They recognize the possibility of a cross-border
operation into Tchepone and the decisive effects such an attack
could have on their 1970–1971 crash logistics program, as well
as on their objectives in South Vietnam and Cambodia."[32]

But there was also a substantial element of enemy uncer-
tainty as to just what the allies were going to do. Abrams noted
concerns about an invasion by sea, invasion by air from the
carriers offshore, and so on. "*He* hasn't figured out what's going
on," Abrams concluded on 30 January. Subsequent intercepts
indicated "a high state of alert in the southern provinces of
North Vietnam," with one provincial unit reporting that "extensive preparations were being made against anticipated allied
attacks in North Vietnam."

15

Lam Son 719

On 1 February 1971, as U.S. armor and mechanized forces were moving to open Route 9 west to the Laotian border in a preparatory stage of the Laotian incursion, Abrams cabled McCain to advise that "the bulk of the enemy's combat units in the region are located in the vicinity of Tchepone," the operation's ultimate objective.[1] Whatever else might happen, it was clear that the disposition and strength of enemy forces in and near the area of operations were not going to come as any surprise to the attackers.

By early February, stated a later North Vietnamese history, "our combat forces in the Route 9–south Laos Front had reached 60,000 troops, consisting of five divisions (308th, 304th, 320th, 324th, 2nd), two separate infantry regiments (27th and 278th), eight regiments of artillery, three engineer regiments, three tank battalions, six anti-aircraft regiments, eight sapper battalions, plus rear service and transportation units. This campaign was our army's greatest concentration of combined arms forces in its history up to that point."[2] On the defensive in Laos, the enemy was going to be able to amass and sustain a much larger force than he could have projected into South Vietnam.

Lieutenant General Hoang Xuan Lam, I Corps, was in command of the thrust into Laos. The U.S. counterpart in Military Region 1 was Lieutenant General James W. "Jock" Sutherland, an armor officer who commanded the XXIV Corps. MACV depended heavily on Sutherland and his headquarters to advise, support, and encourage Lam and the Vietnamese during the operation. Lam had under his command for the operation the 1st Infantry Division, the Airborne Division, the Marine Division, the 1st Armored Brigade Task Force, and a Ranger group, the best troops South Vietnam possessed.

On 8 February 1971 these forces began crossing the border into Laos and Lam Son 719 was under way. Alongside the route, a hundred yards before the border, was posted a sign that read: "WARNING, NO U.S. PERSONNEL BEYOND THIS POINT."

The mission was to disrupt the enemy's lines of communication and destroy stocks of war matériel—especially in Base

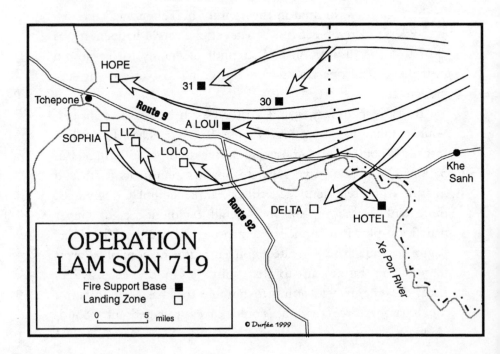

OPERATION
LAM SON 719

Fire Support Base ■
Landing Zone ☐

0 ———— 5 miles

© Durfee 1999

Area 604, centered on Tchepone—thereby setting back the enemy's timetable for aggression, protecting American forces during their withdrawal, and providing more time for South Vietnamese forces to develop. This ground thrust was an integral part of the larger effort to thwart enemy aggression by denying him the wherewithal to carry it out, a complement to the intensive air interdiction campaign along the entire line of communication in the Laotian panhandle and against the target box system that sought to block the entry points into the trail system.

The plan called for an armor task force to drive west along Route 9 toward Tchepone while—by occupying a string of fire support bases to be established paralleling the axis of advance— the Airborne and Rangers protected the northern flank, the 1st Infantry Division protected the southern flank, and the Marine Division constituted the reserve. Later the armor would link up with airborne elements to be helilifted to Tchepone. Leading the way into Laos was the ARVN 1st Armored Brigade Task Force, reinforced by two airborne battalions. Next an ARVN airborne brigade headquarters and one of its battalions moved into position, followed by another airborne brigade and then a ranger battalion. Other units followed.

In the wake of a broadcast by President Thieu announcing the operation, Laotian Prime Minister Souvanna Phouma issued a formal statement of protest. The language of the statement, said a MACV analyst, suggested that it was merely pro forma, couched in the mildest terms that would permit him to claim neutrality. Phouma also stated that "certainly the primary re-sponsibility rests with the Democratic Republic of Vietnam which, scornful of international law . . . , began and continues to violate the neutrality and territorial integrity of the Kingdom of Laos."[3]

North Vietnam's Madame Binh meanwhile cabled an urgent message to sympathizers in the United States: "EARNESTLY CALL

YOU MOBILIZE PEACE FORCES YOUR COUNTRY. CHECK U.S. DAN-
GEROUS VENTURES INDOCHINA."[4]

FROM THE OUTSET it was hard going. Route 9 was at best a
narrow, twisting, nearly unimproved surface, or so it looked
from the air. The reality was much worse. "Jock told me yesterday that on that Route 9 some of those weather cuts that
were in that road were twenty feet deep," Abrams said a few
days after the operation commenced. "They missed that in the
readout of the aerial photography."

Given the restricting Cooper-Church amendment, no advisors accompanied South Vietnamese units into Laos, and of
course no American units participated. Air support of all kinds
was allowed, however, as was artillery and logistical support
from the South Vietnamese side of the border. This generated
a massive operation in support of the incursion. Early on,
Abrams visited the primary base for all this activity, a reopened
Khe Sanh. "It's *hard* to believe," he marveled, "the helicopters,
the trucks, the artillery, the amount of equipment that is in that
whole thing up there. I'll tell you, I've never seen anything like
it in the time I've been here. It's quite remarkable—fifty-three
Chinooks, really something."[5]

U.S. heavy artillery lined up along the border to provide fire
support included eighteen 155mm howitzers, sixteen 175mm
guns, and eight 8-inch howitzers. But the huge amounts of aviation support were the real story of U.S. support for Lam
Son 719.

Seventh Air Force kept up its interdiction campaign against
the Ho Chi Minh Trail, during the first week of Lam Son 719
destroying a new second high number of trucks for the dry
season, but that was now only part of its massive efforts. "I'm
flying roughly 12,000 support sorties a month in addition to
this," said Clay, referring to the number of individual aircraft
missions being launched for various purposes. "I'm flying 21,000
sorties a month in airlift. I'm flying roughly 850–900 sorties a

month in recce. That's all maintenance capability, whether you expend ordnance or not," meaning that every one of these flights generated a maintenance requirement. "There's a limit to what you can do in generating sorties."

ON 10 FEBRUARY advance elements of the armor column linked up with an airborne battalion at A Luoi, some twenty kilometers into Laos, despite truly miserable weather that had set in the previous day. On the same day ARVN I Corps Headquarters, already struggling with the complex tasks of coordinating a multidivision attack under difficult terrain and weather conditions, suffered a serious setback when a helicopter crash resulted in the deaths of two of its most important staff officers, the chief planner and the chief logistician.[6]

From about 12 February on, ARVN forces more or less held in place and hunkered down, not a wise tactic in an operation of this kind. Later it was asserted, by Davidson among others, that President Thieu had issued secret orders to his commanders to halt the advance when 3,000 casualties had been sustained.[7] Nguyen Tien Hung, a former special assistant to Thieu, later cast doubt on that claim, writing that "Thieu insists he never gave such an order."[8]

The next day Vien invited Abrams to meet with him. Vien described President Thieu's visit and briefings in I Corps on 12 February, and "said that after a thorough discussion of intelligence and dispositions, President Thieu directed that the ARVN forces not advance further at this time beyond the western positions they now hold." Vien thought this would be a hold of three to five days and affirmed that they still intended to go to Tchepone. Abrams in turn pointed out the disadvantages of remaining in static positions, "giving the enemy both time and opportunity to organize his reaction in a more effective way."

Subsequently General Sutherland provided some further insight, cabling Abrams that the South Vietnamese had modified the original plan primarily because of heavy enemy contact by the Rangers and the airborne forces on the northern flank of the penetration, and the demonstrated inability of the armor brigade to move rapidly along Route 9.[9]

For quite some time enemy forces had remained cautious and were, in fact, somewhat slow to reinforce. Their first serious counterattack came on the night of 18 February, when two NVA battalions struck the ARVN 39th Ranger Battalion northeast of Ban Dong. Subsequently the major battles of the operation took place on that northern flank of the penetration, especially at Fire Support Bases 30 and 31. On 19 February, eleven days into the attack, MACV J-2 was carrying just six enemy regiments committed against ARVN forces in the Lam Son area of operations. Clearly that wasn't going to last much longer. J-2 concluded that these could be reinforced immediately by three additional regiments from the south and within two days by three more regiments from the west and north.

"The real significance of that Lam Son operation," said Potts, "is the enemy has everything committed, or en route, that he has, with the exception of the 325th Division and the 9th Regiment out of the 304th. So if they're hurt, he's really going to be beat for a long time." And, agreed Abrams, "of course we're trying to welcome them all, best we can." Meanwhile a rallier confirmed earlier intelligence by revealing the identity and location of a new headquarters—designated the 70B Front—controlling the NVA divisions in the Lam Son area of operations, the 304th, 308th, and 320th.[10]

On 20 February, MACV analysts counted eighteen battalion-size ARVN task forces in Laos, mostly involved in search-and-clear operations, with the westernmost elements still about where they had been a week earlier, roughly halfway to Tchepone. Enemy forces were massing to attack, thereby becoming rich targets for reprisals by allied air attacks. When NVA assaults drove ARVN's 39th Rangers off their position, tactical air fell upon the massed enemy forces, killing more than 600 in the one battle. At one point, seven fixed-wing gunships and six flareships were supporting the Rangers.[11] Tac air had a field day with enemy armor, too, destroying seventy-four tanks and damaging twenty-four more to practically wipe out an armored regiment.[12]

On 23 February, farther south, a VNAF helicopter carrying III Corps commander Lieutenant General Do Cao Tri—then directing the operations of some 17,000 ARVN troops in Cambodia—crashed and burned, killing him and a staff officer. Tri was considered a fine field commander, scarce enough in the upper reaches of ARVN leadership, which made this a very serious loss. It turned out to be even more of one when it was learned that he had been slated to move almost immediately to I Corps to replace General Lam, who was proving inadequate to his heavy new responsibilities in command of Lam Son 719.[13]

As late as 27 February, three weeks into the operation, MACV J-2 was carrying only seven enemy regiments in the Lam Son area of operations, up from six with the arrival of the 324B Division's 29th Regiment. Of the twenty-one enemy battalions then committed, five were assessed as having been rendered combat ineffective due to casualties. Nevertheless, fierce fighting was in progress all along Route 9 and at the positions ARVN had staked out north and south of it, especially at Fire Support Base 31 to the north. There an enemy attack that included tanks overran a brigade headquarters of the 1st Division and captured the brigade commander. The 39th Ranger Battalion was also pressured into abandoning its position, joining the nearby 21st Ranger Battalion, after which both were evacuated from Laos.

"What we're in up here," Abrams observed at the end of February, "in both Laos and Cambodia, is a real tough fight. We're just going to have to stick with it and *win* it. We've got the tickets to do it, and that's what's going to be done. We've been in them before. And we've been inundated by the prophets of doom before, as we are now. The one thing that's better about this than any of the rest of them is that some of the units they're fighting with up there in Laos—we used to fight them in Hue.

And this is a better place to fight them. And some of those units that they're fighting over there in Cambodia, we used to fight them in the precincts at one time, down there in Saigon. This is just a better place to do that. I mean, as long as you're going to have to fight, I think this is a better ring than the one we had."

As March began, said General Fred Weyand, Sutherland was reporting by secure phone that "the enemy is all over that goddamn area and seems to be getting stronger, if anything. And so there's a real fight going on up there. Particularly that indirect fire thing is worrying." Just how worrying was demonstrated at Fire Support Base 30, where more than a thousand incoming rounds more than from such indirect fire weapons as mortars and artillery—reportedly including 152mm howitzers— knocked out all the friendly artillery and forced ARVN forces to withdraw. Meanwhile the enemy was paying a heavy price. MACV estimated that "B-52s alone were inflicting losses that were the equivalent of about one combat-effective NVA regiment per week."[14]

THE POOR CONDITION of Route 9, and the inability of ARVN forces to keep it secure, meant that virtually all resupply and medical evacuation for ARVN forces had to be done by air, the bulk of it by U.S. air. Calculating that in any given twenty-four-hour period a helicopter could fly for between five and eight hours, Abrams noted that in Laos the South Vietnamese had "eighteen battalions over there, and ten batteries of artillery—and all the resupply and everything that's got to be done for those eighteen battalions and ten batteries in the five to eight hours every twenty-four. Well, there isn't a lot of sightseeing going on."

A couple of weeks into the thing there wasn't a lot of flying going on, either, at least not compared with the huge requirements the operation was generating. By about 23 February it became apparent that U.S. Army aviation support for Lam Son

719 was having some problems. Not only was the intense and
well-sited enemy antiaircraft weaponry making operations extremely difficult—every mission, even dustoff medical evacua-
tions, had to be planned and executed like a full-scale combat
assault—but maintenance problems were causing many
helicopters to be out of service just when they were needed
most.

Sutherland had apparently been slow to recognize and report
these problems, much less act aggressively to deal with them.
Another senior officer present on the ground judged him to be
"very passive," really "a negative factor" in the operation. Until
23 February, a MACV staff officer told Abrams, "I think it's fair
to say we had no feel that his helicopter situation was quite as
acute."

This news precipitated intense reaction at MACV. "The way
this thing is supposed to work," erupted Abrams, "is that, once
I said *what* the priorities were and *what* was going to be done
around here, *goddamn it,* then these—USARV's responsible to
have maintenance people up there, keeping track of this, *goddamn it!* And they should *know* what's happening! That's their
job! That's McCaffrey's responsibility! And that's what hasn't
been done."

Abrams asked his deputy, Fred Weyand, how it looked to
him. "Well," he began, focusing on Sutherland, "I guess I'm not
too forgiving on Jock. I recognize the truth of what you're
saying, but goddamn it, you've got a corps commander up there
who's supposed to be keeping track of every fucking bird in the
place every hour of the day. There's something wrong there.
You've got an organizational problem of *some* kind. He just
doesn't know what the hell's going on." Weyand recalled that
there had been a battalion on Route 914 for two days before
Sutherland was aware of it, even though they knew it at MACV.
"That tells me that the coordination and tie-in between his
headquarters and Lam's is not fully effective."

There followed a *long* pause, several minutes. Then Abrams

said, "I guess I'd better go up and talk with General McCaffrey now. I just feel we've got to get some people up there today who can be feeding the facts back. Move the goddamn men and the tools and the stuff and get with it."[15]

Colonel Sam Cockerham was acting commander of the 1st Aviation Brigade when he got orders to fly north immediately in an aircraft provided by General Abrams. When Cockerham arrived, Abrams was already there, slumped down on a leather sofa in Sutherland's office. "Worst fucking OR [operational readiness] rate I've seen in U.S. Army aviation history!" he exploded by way of conversational openers. "The entire concept, the entire national strategic concept, is at stake here!" he thundered at Sutherland. Abrams said he was going to give Cockerham all the theater resources in Vietnam to get the operationally ready rate up to USARV standards. That was 80 percent, 5 percent higher than worldwide Army standards.

Abrams asked Cockerham how long that would take. It was then Monday at about 1:00 P.M. "By Wednesday night I'll have it up to standard," Cockerham replied, perhaps not realizing how bad things were. The UH–1C gunship OR rate, for example, then stood at 25 percent. "I want a back channel from you to me every twenty-four hours," Abrams told Cockerham as he left. The meeting made a deep impression on Cockerham, and not just because of the massive task that had been dumped in his lap. "General Sutherland was like a dog with his tail tucked under," he recalled. "I thought the job was beyond him. He wasn't prepared. Abrams worked around him."[16]

Brigadier General Sid Berry, then assistant division commander of the 101st Airborne, also played a pivotal role in restoring order to the realm of Army air support. Taking over responsibility for coordinating all Army aviation in the operation, he went in harm's way over and over again to make things happen. Said an advisor who was there at the time, "General Berry flew to the most critical areas and got things done that lesser men would not touch."[17] Pretty soon things were back in sync. When Lieutenant General Julian Ewell, visiting Vietnam from his assignment with the U.S. negotiating team in Paris, went up to Khe Sanh to have a look around, he was impressed. "Their OR rate when I was up there Sunday was 79 percent," he said, "which I considered astronomical."[18]

EFFORTS TO PUSH through to Tchepone with helilifted infantry, rather than continuing efforts to advance along the inadequate road, began 3 March when a battalion of the 1st Division was inserted to establish a landing zone (LZ) called Lolo, the first in a planned chain of positions extending west toward Tchepone. The assault was met with intense enemy fire—seven helicopters were destroyed and many others damaged—but the troops got into position. The next day two more battalions were brought in, along with artillery and supplies, building up strength on Lolo. Also on 4 March a battalion was airlifted to establish LZ Liz, farther west and closer to Tchepone; again it attacked into the teeth of intense enemy fire. On 5 March two fresh battalions were inserted west of Liz to set up LZ Sophia. Next was LZ Hope.

On 6 March two battalions of the 1st Division were airlifted to the vicinity of Tchepone, in the heart of enemy Base Area 604, the primary objective of the operation. A daisy chain of 276 UH-1 helicopters picked up ARVN troops at Khe Sanh and deposited them at LZ Hope near Tchepone; most ships made three round trips. "No aircraft were lost to ground fire during this operation," recalled Cockerham. "We were using armor tactics as the basis for our operations, designating an objective, intermediate objectives, and so on. We would secure them, then build an air tunnel so as to deny the enemy direct fire and indirect fire observation. We had one aircraft disabled in the final LZ due to engine failure."[19]

That same day General Abrams met with General Vien to review the enemy situation. "I said the operation has shaped up into two things," Abrams told Sutherland. "The flow of logistics must be stopped, including Route 914, and a major battle, which might even be the decisive battle of the war, must be won. I urged the employment of the 2d ARVN Division in Lam Son 719 now. Politically, psychologically and militarily, President Thieu can accept nothing less. We have the resources to do it. It means another month of hard fighting. General Vien agrees with all this; I truthfully think it is the way he feels anyway. He said he would take it to the President."[20]

By this time, XXIV Corps reported to Abrams, General Lam, having gotten some elements to Tchepone, "apparently feels that he has accomplished the mandate given him by President Thieu and is now turning to a more cautious approach as he awaits further instructions from Saigon." Among ARVN commanders "the general feeling is that their mission has been accomplished and it is now time to withdraw. They do not concede that there is still much to be done in inflicting maximum damage or that there is now the opportunity to exploit initial successes with even more telling results."[21]

Assessing the ARVN assault into the Tchepone area, a MACV analyst concluded that "the enemy was slow to react to this, both due to his severe losses and to the rapidity with which ARVN forces moved out after they had remained in the Route 9 area for so long." Later, when Sir Robert Thompson arrived for one of his periodic visits, MACV briefed that "for approximately ten days the enemy was unable to regain the initiative and mount any major counterattacks against ARVN as they were moving rapidly into the Tchepone area." But then, when ARVN forces moved south of Route 9 toward Route 914, the 2nd NVA Division moved to counter that and major battles erupted there.[22]

On 9 March, Generals Vien and Lam recommended to President Thieu that the overall operation be terminated, far ahead of schedule. Major General Nguyen Duy Hinh wrote that "a careful military estimate was made, based upon all the pertinent information available at the time, and the conclusion was inescapable: it was time to get out." And, added Hinh, "it was apparent that President Thieu had decided, at the outset, that once Tchepone had been entered by RVNAF the withdrawal should begin without delay."[23]

Abrams wanted to push the thing, recommending to Thieu that instead of withdrawing he reinforce with the 2nd ARVN Division. Thieu declined, reportedly saying he would do so only if a U.S. division were also committed. Of course both Thieu and Abrams knew that was prohibited, so the response effectively ended discussion of reinforcing the operation. Thieu's unwillingness to commit more forces, said General Vien, "reflected his concern that ARVN divisions were unprepared for a strategic task."[24]

During a visit to Vietnam, Haig had strewn a certain amount of chaos in his wake. At XXIV Corps (Forward) on 18 March he told Sutherland that "Washington would like to see ARVN stay in Laos through April."[25] The following day he visited II Field Force and told Davison "his tentative conclusion is that the time has come for an orderly close-out of the ground operations in Laos."[26] Both field commanders dutifully reported these Haig observations to Abrams, who must have been somewhat bemused.

Pulling out wasn't the way Abrams would have played it. "I'm just more and more convinced that what you've got here is maybe the only decisive battle of the war," he concluded. "And they've got a chance to—it'll be *hard*—a chance to *really* do it." The enemy was committing everything he had, just asking for it, really, given the history of the war. "When we've focused firepower on him, he hasn't been able to hack it." Already, said Potts, "he's lost *half* of his tanks, *half* of his AAA, and *ten* of his thirty battalions."

Friendly losses were heavy, too, though proportionally not as severe. U.S. Army helicopters were being hit hard, with twenty-three lost in combat and six more operational losses during the second week of March alone. ARVN forces counted up

1,118 killed in action, more than 4,000 wounded, and 209 missing, along with much equipment that was destroyed or had to
be abandoned during the withdrawal phase.[27]

Weyand pointed out that air cavalry had been in the
Tchepone area for ten days or more before ARVN got there
on the ground, and that this had been useful in acquiring targeting data later used by B-52s, including strikes on stores that
ground forces had not been able to extract or destroy in place.
This intelligence was supplemented by what long-range reconnaissance patrols acquired, and by reports from ARVN unit
commanders. As a result, concluded Weyand, "there's been
massive destruction far beyond, I would guess, what was done
in Cambodia."

By 18 March the enemy had detected the withdrawal of
ARVN units from the Route 9 area and directed his forces to
surround, annihilate, and destroy those isolated units where they
could. The enemy also told his people that some ARVN forces
were rebelling against their leaders, that some were running
away into the interior, and that the ARVN had been defeated.
"It looks like to me a back-stiffening effort," said Potts. "My
interpretation of these message intercepts is that this whole thing
is one hell of a bloody battle," Abrams replied. And bloody it
was. In one firefight after another the ARVN, while taking substantial casualties, inflicted disproportionately heavier ones on
the enemy—37 versus 245, 85 versus 600, on and on.

Many of these enemy losses were caused by U.S. airpower,
which delivered huge amounts of munitions on massed enemy
forces. During the forty-two days the South Vietnamese operated cross-border, 1,280 B-52 sorties were flown in support,
about 30 a day, every day, for the whole period. Later General
Vien would write that the operation was "hampered by bad
weather and insufficient air support, including helicopters."[28] If
that judgment is correct, it is difficult to imagine what level of
air support would have been sufficient. Some 600 U.S. helicopters were committed to the battle on a daily basis. And there

was so much bombing, recalled General Sid Berry, "that by afternoon the setting sun would be shining through so much smoke and dust that you couldn't see it." Through 24 March, U.S. tactical air flew more than 8,000 attack sorties, an average of nearly 150 sorties a day every day—the equivalent of one every ten minutes around the clock. And every night, all night, three forward air controllers, three flareships, and three gunships were on station, one each for the Rangers, the Airborne Division, and the 1st Infantry Division. Even the tactical airlift support was such that, at peak periods, there was a C-130 arriving at Khe Sanh on the average of one every eight minutes.[29]

Throughout the operation deficiencies at high command levels continued to undermine the abilities and performance of South Vietnam's troops. Colonel Ray Battreall, a very experienced officer who watched most of this firsthand from I Corps Forward at Khe Sanh, later provided some useful insight into the challenges confronting General Lam. Because during normal operations the two division sectors of his I Corps were separated by the Hai Van Pass, observed Battreall, the corps headquarters had never before conducted a multidivision tactical operation. Rather, "Lam followed the example of his predecessors in attending to administrative and logistic matters and exerting little, if any, influence over division tactical operations."

Now, said Battreall, Lam Son 719 presented General Lam with a "nearly insuperable array of new challenges." For the first time he and his staff were working from a field command post distant from their usual fixed headquarters at Danang. They were trying to execute an operations order much of which they did not understand. Neither the corps headquarters nor subordinate units, Battreall concluded, "truly grasped the responsibilities inherent in attachment, the differences between a zone of action and an axis of advance, or the full meaning of the word 'secure.'"

The Airborne and Marine divisions, though highly competent when operating at brigade level, had little experience in

being employed as full divisions, meaning that "the division
commanders and their staffs were totally unprepared for their
tasks." Since both of these division commanders were senior in
rank to Lieutenant General Lam, they were "severely miffed" at
being subordinated to him. "The Marine commander did not
accompany his division from Saigon," recalled Battreall, "and
the Airborne commander refused to attend LTG Lam's command briefings." And finally Lam wasted the armor brigade by
attaching it to the Airborne Division, "which had no idea what
to do with it."[30]

Whatever his inadequacies, Lam got very little cooperation
and even less obedience to orders from several of his senior
supposed subordinates in the operation. Weyand called this "really the hairiest problem we have out there. We've got a whole
bunch of units that, when they want to, they operate indepen-
dently, and it doesn't make any difference whether it's Lam or
who it is." President Thieu's very costly tolerance of such chaos
seemed to demonstrate essential insecurity.

Even so, thought Weyand, there were positive indications
for the future. He saw "a significant difference between the style
of leadership, and the real effective leadership, of guys like
Truong and Minh," who during an earlier period "were regimental commanders and division commanders, as opposed to—
take the other extreme—your Vinh Locs and Lu Lans. And
now even getting down to a man like General Lam, who's
somewhere in between. But you're finding these corps commanders are like the corps commanders we'd like to think we
had, who understood development of a fire plan, coordination
of fires, precision and all that, techniques that are so important."[31]

Colonel Battreall gave Lam high marks for accomplishing as
much as he did under the circumstances. "All initial objectives
were seized," he noted, "and the ferocious NVA counterattack,
while it overran Ranger positions in the North and the Airborne
at Hill 30, never progressed further. Apparently unshaken by the

counterattack, LTG Lam calmly committed the 1st Infantry Division to the east—west ridge south of Highway 9 with the mission of seizing Tchepone."

Several days later, Battreall recalled, he saw a badly shaken U.S. air cavalry squadron commander describe the horrendous antiaircraft defenses surrounding Tchepone and recommend against the planned airmobile assault there. "LTG Lam pondered for a moment and then replied, 'No, we have B-52s. We will use them, and then we will go.' And so it happened," said Battreall. "The antiaircraft was obliterated and several meters of dirt blown off the tops of the ridges, exposing what had been underground warehouses. The 1st Infantry Division assaulted almost unopposed and methodically destroyed everything of military value before commencing what turned out to be a bloody and hard-fought withdrawal. It took real guts for Lam to make that decision, and he made it quite alone with no U.S. advisor twisting his arm. Whatever he did before or after cannot detract from that moment."

By 25 March, recorded General Hinh, "most ARVN forces had already left lower Laos." Unfortunately, "the intended and desired goal to sustain combat until the onset of the rainy season in order to strangle the enemy's supply route could not be accomplished."[32] That was true, but it by no means conveyed an accurate impression of what had been achieved.

Some troop elements had done conspicuously better than others. The ARVN armored units had been especially disappointing. Early in the operation the 1st Squadron, 11th Armored Cavalry had encountered NVA armored elements in a fight at Fire Base 31 and performed brilliantly, destroying six enemy T-54 tanks and sixteen PT-76s without any friendly losses in the first major tank-to-tank engagement of the war.[33] After that, though, the armor floundered. Not only did they contribute little to offensive operations, they came out of Laos with only a fraction of the equipment they took in. Of 62 tanks only 25 were brought back, and of 162 armored personnel carriers only

64 were salvaged. The reason MACV knew these sorry statistics was that a U.S. advisor met them at the border and made a personal count. Had the losses been due to heavy combat, that would have been one thing, but in the main they were just vehicles that had broken down or run out of gas and been abandoned.

The Airborne Division's 3rd Brigade headquarters was captured and its 3rd Battalion essentially annihilated.[34] En route to Tchepone five of the division's nine battalion commanders were killed or wounded.[35] During the withdrawal phase some units panicked, with able-bodied men rushing medical evacuation helicopters, seeking a place on board or, as documented in some widely circulated photos, clinging to the skids of the ships. Not only did the once proud airborne, defending Fire Support Base 30, commandeer medevac flights, but the airborne infantry battalion commander was one of those who forced his way aboard.[36]

Later Abrams reflected on what the American staff had been doing while South Vietnam's armored forces were in a desperate struggle. "And the battle was still *raging*," he recalled. "We were getting on, and doing things, and—everybody was—doing pretty good. They'd got over some of the shocks. But what was the *staff* doing? *Goddamn it,* they were in there gathering *photos* and *making charts* and so on, all about the goddamn armor equipment that had been *lost* over there in *Laos* on Route 9! *That was the* thrust *of the* working *and the* thinking *of the damn* staff! Now—there wasn't *any* way to get that *back*. The *bill* had already been paid! There was a fucking *disaster!!* But there's no point in that being the whole damn subject of conversation, the whole subject of thought, from there on!! Now there's got to be some pos—. That's* what will lick you. That's what will lick you. The guy that doesn't get licked is the guy that never even thinks he *can* be! The thought never comes to his *mind!* He has the patience to accept disaster and disappointment—and *outrage*—but he keeps after it."

16

Aftermath

THE NORTH VIETNAMESE suffered terribly in Lam Son 719. "We believe that during the operation the enemy lost the equivalent of 16 of the 33 maneuver battalions they had committed in the area of operations," said a MACV analyst. "In addition, we believe that he's lost at least 3,500 of the 10,000 to 12,000 rear service personnel that were operating in the area prior to the operation." Added Potts, "that's not just ineffective battalions, that's a complete loss of those battalions." And at least 75 of some 110 enemy tanks were assessed as destroyed. The U.S. intelligence community concluded that the NVA lost more than 13,000 killed in action defending their supply lines, along with large quantities of tanks, ordnance, and supplies.[1] In his monograph on the campaign, Major General Nguyen Duy Hinh put enemy losses at 19,360 killed in action, along with more than 5,000 individual weapons, nearly 2,000 crew-served weapons, more than a hundred tanks, and large quantities of ammunition and rice.[2]

Later, MACV J-2 reported, it was learned from a Polish military advisor to the International Control Commission that "the North Vietnamese were both surprised and hurt by the Lam Son operation. He said that discussions with NVN officials showed that they had lost heavily in personnel, particularly good reserve units which were chewed up. He further believed that they had lost heavily in weapons and supplies. He also pointed out that they suffered a political loss at home because they could not hide their significant military losses." Also, it was reported, North Vietnamese officials had revealed to a source an exact number of 16,224 casualties as a result of Lam Son 719.

Subsequently a surprising source, the French military mission in Hanoi, concluded that "Lam Son 719 had a devastating effect upon the morale of the NVA and of the civilian population of North Vietnam. According to the French analysis," said MACV J-2, "the destruction of nearly two North Vietnamese divisions, and increased defections during the same period, caused the morale of all but the NVA officer corps to disintegrate."[3]

In March CIA's Office of Economic Research submitted a special report to Laird and Kissinger stating that "large-scale enemy military operations in South Vietnam for the remainder of 1971 were probably impossible and that Hanoi would have to undertake a major resupply campaign before any offensive could be launched in 1972."[4]

U.S. forces, even though they had not been on the ground in Laos, also paid a price, including a total of 107 helicopters lost and at least 544 more damaged. "Everybody's got a bullet hole in his aircraft," said one officer. Even so, that represented a loss rate of only around 21 per 100,000 sorties—one combat loss for every 963 flying hours[5]—an indication of both how battleworthy the choppers had proved to be and what a huge air operation had been mounted.[6]

General Weyand summed up his view of the incursion as a whole by saying, "I don't see how we could say anything other than that that operation was worth it. I think it's going to prove to have been terribly decisive."

Subsequently Haig published an extremely negative account of how U.S. forces had performed in supporting the South Vietnamese during Lam Son 719, charging that artillery was malpositioned out of range, that aviation support was inadequate, and that Abrams "had never left his headquarters to assess the battle zone in person."[7] Abrams in fact visited XXIV Corps on 15 January, during the preparatory stages of the operation, and again on 12 February and 11 March, and also made visits to Danang on 16 and 24 February and 11 March. In Saigon, he met with President Thieu just before the operation and again on 22 February. Also, his calendar shows twenty-seven meetings with General Vien, Chief of the Joint General Staff, during Lam Son 719 itself and in the final preparatory stages. In addition he spoke daily by secure telephone with Sutherland at XXIV Corps.

Haig later added that "President Nixon and those of us in the White House involved in the planning were appalled by the Defense Department's handling of the operation which resulted in the serious mauling of an ARVN which had been recently rejuvenated under Vietnamization and at great expense to the American people."[8] But Haig also conceded, concerning the origins of the operation, "I would say that the pressure came from here, from the White House."[9]

James Schlesinger, who in 1973 succeeded Laird as Secretary of Defense, commented that "the military in Vietnam were pushed into the invasion of Laos by civilian officials who thought it would be a good idea. And when it failed, General Abrams was beaten up and there were calls for his removal. It was quite unjust, but not untypical."[10]

Haig has written that on the third day of the operation, "the President called me to his office. The President was in a cold rage. Without preamble, he told me that he was relieving General Abrams of command in Vietnam immediately. 'Go home and pack a bag,' he said. 'Then get on the first available plane and fly to Saigon. You're taking command.'" Haig took the prospect in stride. "I had no doubt that I could do the job; I knew the ground, I knew the enemy, and I knew what the

President wanted," he recalled. But, fortuitously, he advised the President to wait a day before acting. After that brief cooling-off period, Nixon changed the orders rather substantially, instructing Haig merely to visit Vietnam, assess the situation there, and report his findings.[11]

While Haig, relegated to observer status rather than assumption of command, continued to insist in later years that Abrams had mishandled the whole operation, Nixon very quickly came to quite a different conclusion. "The P [President] got into a review of Laos," wrote H. R. Haldeman in his diary for 13 May 1971, "and the fact that casualties were way down now since Laos, just as they were after Cambodia; that there's been no spring offensive, despite the largest materiel input ever in Vietnam, including at Tet; and that it's really remarkable proof of the effectiveness of the operation, but doesn't give us any credit."[12]

DURING LAM SON 719 a public opinion survey of the rural populace, conducted late in the operation and based on sampling in thirty-six provinces, was taken in South Vietnam. The results were astounding: 92 percent favored the operation, 3 percent opposed it, and the remainder had no opinion. Those in favor represented the highest percentage ever recorded on any question on any of these periodic surveys. It was an informed opinion, thought Abrams, because the results of the operation were on the radio every hour and on television every night. "So the people are aware that it's a big price."

Later evaluations of Lam Son 719 were mostly negative, fueled in part, perhaps, by the persistent outlook of those who opposed the war, but also as a function of the price the ARVN had paid and the residual deficiencies it had exhibited. Counterbalancing this were the extremely heavy casualties inflicted on the enemy and the disruptive effects of what had been essentially a preemptive attack. These diverse results were reflected in some very conflicted assessments. Shelby Stanton provided a case in point. "Operation Lam Son 719 was a dismal failure," he concluded, then on the very next page noted that throughout 1971 there was little combat action in South Vietnam because "the NVA units were still suffering from the combined Cambodian-Laotian shocks."[13]

Interestingly, Henry Kissinger was similarly ambivalent in his judgments, observing that "the operation, conceived in doubt and assailed by skepticism, proceeded in confusion." But then, only seven pages later, Kissinger offered the view that "the major enemy thrust in 1972 came across the Demilitarized Zone, where Hanoi's supply lines were shortest and least affected by the operations in Cambodia and Laos. The farther south the North Vietnamese attempted to attack in 1972, the weaker was their impact, because their sanctuaries and supply system had been disrupted by our operations in the previous two years." Thus "the campaigns of 1970 and 1971, in my view, saved us in 1972."[14]

The enemy was jubilant about the operation's outcome, at least from the vantage point of a later history of PAVN. "From the beginning of the war against the Americans," read this account, "this was the first time our army had been victorious in a large-scale counter-offensive campaign and had been able to annihilate enemy forces."[15]

Ambassador Bunker saw it realistically. "The enemy understood that we were after his jugular," he said in a 30 March 1971 reporting cable to the President. "The network represents his lifeline to the south. Without it he is finished. He was bound to react. He threw in almost all his readily available reserves, heavy artillery and tanks. In what proved to be a bloody battle involving some of the hardest fighting of the war, ARVN inflicted far heavier casualties on the enemy than they themselves sustained."[16]

AT ONE POINT during these Laotian and Cambodian cross-border operations, President Thieu called General Abrams in to talk about them. "And then," recalled Abrams, "he wanted to go over leadership. He started with the corps commanders. He said, 'Start at the DMZ and go down to Ca Mau and tell me about the commanders,' which I did. 'Well,' he said, 'if I have to remove some corps commanders, who do I add?' So I told him then that the one I can recommend, without any reservations at all, and with all the humility of an American who doesn't really know Vietnamese, is General Truong. I think he's proved, over and over and in *all* the facets—pacification, military operations, whatever it is." Soon Truong was commanding IV Corps.

When Lam Son 719 was all over, Ambassador Bunker had some comments to make at a commanders conference. "Well," he began, "I think we've got the same problem we've had for the four years *I've* been here. That's the kind of reporting you get in the press. Sometimes they seem to have a vested interest in failure." Nevertheless, Bunker continued, the results had been positive. "I think it's been extremely helpful, this whole operation. It's good to see the President's [Thieu's] attitude toward it, apparently the attitude of the Vietnamese. It's given them, I think, pride in what they've been able to do. I do want to say also that I think what we've done, our forces, on the ground and in the air—not only here, not only in Laos and Cambodia—has been magnificent, the decisive factor, really, in the whole thing. It's been a great performance. And I think the facts will speak for themselves when we get through with this, despite the press."

Abrams saw it the same way. "I certainly join you on that," he said. "It's a struggle. It was a hard *fight,* but its effects for the rest of this year, I think, are going to be substantial. He [the enemy] committed a *lot* to that Lam Son operation, and it's getting pretty badly hurt." In a subsequent conversation with Sir Robert Thompson, Abrams put the thing in a wider perspective. "I think the way we feel is that we've sort of arrived at a crossover point," he said. "The Vietnamese have developed in a whole lot of things, across the spectrum—internal security, they're seriously at work on economic problems, and they face it as a reality, and they're meeting it with reality—not always with perfection, none of us are, but all those things, and their armed forces. And it's gone over the point where I think the North Vietnamese can be successful against them. The *war* won't stop, but North Vietnam has now got a much tougher problem than they *ever* had before."

There came a point, not long after the raid into Laos, when Abrams thought the South Vietnamese were approaching self-sufficiency. "Coalition government is capitulation," he concluded. "And the South Vietnamese *don't* have to do that. As a matter of fact, if the South Vietnamese had a way of getting ammunition, and POL, they're almost in a position where they could tell everybody else to blow it out their ass. I'm saying that on the basis—look at the damned depots that we've just about finished here—tools, power—and the logistical setup they've got in the Air Force—overhaul. We're talking now about surviving. No more Santa Claus stuff—now we're talking survive. I mean, I'm not advocating any of this, I'm just saying that—."

DURING THE SAVAGE battles along the Ho Chi Minh Trail in southern Laos, other significant fighting had for several years been surging back and forth in northern Laos. General George Brown, then commanding Seventh Air Force, once told the visiting General Wheeler of the intense air support that Laotian commander Vang Pao had received, "more than any commander in the history of the warfare there." Then Brown went up to Vientiane, where he talked to Vang Pao about results achieved in the air campaign. "Well, you know, Americans *like* BDA [bomb damage assessment]," Vang Pao told him, "and we like *Americans,* and they come back when they get good BDA." They played it differently with the Thais, Brown found. Vang Pao "said his forward air guys, they don't give BDA to the Thai pilots, because Thai Buddhists don't like to kill people. So that's the way the whole thing works. But at least he admits it."

Cache seizures in the Plaine des Jarres had confirmed that the enemy planned a substantial campaign. The take included twelve tanks, which prompted Abrams to observe that "this is not the stuff you take to a family homecoming. This is *real*. Shows you what those bastards have in mind." On the positive side, though, he thought "that typewriter captured there is probably going to screw things up more than anything else."

Abrams admired Vang Pao as the most capable of the Lao commanders, a "spiritual, religious, military leader all wrapped up in one. If there's a guy in *all* of Laos to support," he observed, "he's the guy. To hell with all the rest of them. *That* fellow's got spirit. We could use *him here*." And Abrams viewed the fighting in northern Laos as an important component of the overall campaign. "We don't want that thing to get out of hand in the Plaine des Jarres," he told the staff. "It's in our interests that it not. If *that* gets out of hand, you run the risk of having *all* the goddamn bombing stopped in Laos. At least, that's the way I see it—as a possibility. We're approaching doing it with mirrors here."

The previous spring things had heated up again in northern Laos, and in the relations between MACV and Embassy Vientiane. "Godley wired me yesterday asking for all kinds of air support," the J-3 told Abrams. "I wired him back asking for target recommendations." That triggered a discussion of the budget crunch in Washington, how the B-52 sortie rate was already under enormous pressure, and how just bombing jungle up in the Plaine des Jarres, with nothing to show for it—the inevitable result of bombing without solid targeting intelligence—would just fuel those who argued that the B-52s weren't accomplishing anything anyhow, so they could safely be cut back even further. "The fact that there's no goddamn intelligence that's worth a shit" coming out of Vientiane, "the fact that the thing has never been tactically run on a sound basis up there, just by a bunch of guys playing soldier—none of that's taken into account," Abrams complained.

They also thought Ambassador Godley was talking out of

both sides of his mouth. "I talked with Shaplen, the *New Yorker* guy, yesterday," Abrams observed at one point. "He said he'd been up in Vientiane, and it is really too bad that Vang Pao couldn't get the air support. And of course he gets that from those *bastards* up there in Vientiane." General John Lavelle, who had taken command of Seventh Air Force, observed that, meanwhile, "I have a wire from Ambassador Godley, saying that they've had more air support than *ever,* accomplished more—thanked me personally." Abrams was not surprised. "Historically, historically, you'll get it from him that way. This other stuff comes out at the same time. That's the way the game's played, and it's just *awful.*"

Inside South Vietnam, with the large number of ARVN forces operating cross-border, the Territorial Forces were carrying the load. In Military Region 4, operations in the U Minh Forest, long an enemy stronghold, had generated the highest weekly total of ralliers in nearly two years. Outposts were being built there, noted MACV, and the people "realize there's a permanent presence going in." Ambassador Bunker recalled visiting a 33rd Regiment base in the Delta, where he asked General Truong if he planned to stay there. "Yes, forever," Truong replied.

OTHER BATTLES WERE being fought in Cambodia where, during Lam Son 719, the South Vietnamese had an equal number of troops deployed in cross-border operations in that country. Before the dual operations began, Abrams coached his field commanders. "Now what we're headed into here, the way he's gathering in Chup and the way they're gathering up there in Laos, is one hell of a battle. Now both of those have got to be won, and they *are* going to be won," he emphasized. He then predicted that the battles were going to last about two months. "We'll give these two things anything it takes that we've got! And I *want* it done!" The battles, he said, were "of critical importance to the rest of 1971 and 1972. It's an opportunity to deal the enemy a blow which probably hasn't existed before as clearly cut in the war. Those *are* military operations, and I'm not pushing this now as sort of a parochial love of a great battle. It's not that at all. I think it's critical. The risks in getting it done were all known and understood in the beginning, and it was felt that it was time to take the risks."

Ambassador Bunker, just returned from consultations in Washington, was able to comment on the decision-making calculus as he had observed it there. "One of the things I think was of great concern," he stated, "is the point that General Abrams has just made—the risk involved if this didn't succeed. And what we'd do, through our policy here—how it would affect the elections, Thieu's position, and the whole situation in Vietnam. There were a good many other things that were taken into consideration—what the effect would be in the northern part of Laos, what the effect would be on the Chinese, and on Souvanna's position. The principal thing was the risk involved in getting into Laos and the South Vietnamese getting chewed up. But these were all weighed very carefully. And the President, of course, made the decision. Obviously I'm glad the way it turned out."

General Abrams described Lam Son 719 as "the largest battle of the war to date."[17] As the results of the operation began to be reflected in the enemy's reduced level of tactical activity, diminished logistical throughput into South Vietnam, reduced rate of personnel infiltration, and concentration on restoration of his lines of communication, Abrams reached a dramatic conclusion. "I'm beginning to have a conviction about Lam Son 719 that that was really a death blow," he said during discussion of a new assessment of the enemy's situation in mid-August 1971.

A GI in Vietnam, Private First Class Clyde Baker, felt so strongly about the thrust into Laos that he wrote to President Nixon on the matter. "In my opinion the Cambodian operation and this operation are the 2 most intelligent moves we have made since we have been in S. Vietnam," he stated. "This operation may end the war and may save hundreds of lives in the long run, and everyone here is putting out 100%." Baker closed with a small apology: "I'm sorry for the lousy handwriting, but I'm writing this letter down inside a tank."[18]

After the 1970–1971 dry season campaign, MACV concluded that, based on all available intelligence, the enemy had succeeded in moving only 9,000 short tons of supplies through the Laotian panhandle into South Vietnam and Cambodia, just 14 percent of the 67,000 short tons he had input into the system and only 40 percent as much as the previous year's throughput. "This forced him to continue a protracted war strategy in the Republic of Vietnam," said MACV, "and it limited his capabilities in Cambodia." That was, perhaps, at least a partial answer to Abrams's earlier question as to the real state of the war.

DURING A LATE APRIL 1971 visit to Vietnam, Secretary of the Army Stanley Resor provided some telling insights into where things could go from there. "It might be fair to say he's in fact achieved the objective of getting us to withdraw ground troops at a fairly steady and significant rate," Resor observed. "He's done that, of course, by the effect he's had in the United States, and that's what's caused it here." Resor suggested the possibility that the enemy's next objective might be to get the U.S. air effort similarly reduced, and to block having a residual U.S. force in South Vietnam.

After that, Resor continued, the goal might be to get military assistance and economic aid to South Vietnam cut off. "And again, working the same way that he's had success before, in other words to try to get Congress to stop appropriating that kind of funds so that the South Vietnamese would essentially be out of ammunition."[19] That was, as things turned out downstream, pretty much the way it was going to evolve.

17

Elections

IN THE AFTERMATH of Lam Son 719, Abrams counseled his senior subordinates on the improvements needed in South Vietnamese forces. "In the past year I have used every opportunity to highlight the changing nature of the war and the challenge of continuing progress towards total Vietnamization in a climate of declining U.S. resources, competing demands on RVNAF, and limited time," he began. "The completion of Phase I Vietnamization will mark an end to U.S. ground force participation in major combat operations. In preparation, U.S. forces will concentrate on dynamic defense"—here he meant aggressive patrolling as opposed to hunkering down and waiting to get hit— "and providing combat support and combat service support to the RVNAF and in assisting the RVNAF to develop and refine operational skills and techniques."

During the past year, Abrams noted, the in-country task had evolved into maintaining stability, with Territorial Forces providing the bulk of the security. The ARVN and VNAF still lacked a real operational interface, staffs were not yet able to perform adequately under combat stress, and expertise was still lacking in coordination of operational support. Solving these problems was essential, Abrams stressed, and would require "nurturing, in the truest professional sense, at various advisory levels."[1]

Meanwhile, suggested John Vann, "the war is gradually shifting to the northern two corps, and moving toward a more conventional confrontation between North and South Vietnam."[2] As so often over the years, Vann had it right, and well in advance of events.

COMPASSION FOR THE Vietnamese was something Abrams felt strongly and could express eloquently. One day he attended a commemorative ceremony at the National Cemetery in Saigon. It was an impressive event, all the diplomatic corps in attendance, the attachés and so on. After it was over, the crowd evaporated quickly and Abrams, whose helicopter had not yet arrived, found himself standing near the entrance with only a couple of MPs. "And here came walking an ARVN soldier," Abrams later recalled. "He was a sergeant. And he had his wife with him. She was pregnant. And they had three little kids. He was carrying one of them. It was so small, you know. *Well*, it was a long walk. And then there was a little boy. I guess he was probably nine. He was carrying a big bag, plastic bag, a handbag. And it had a big wad of those joss sticks sticking up the top of it, and I suppose a little lunch or something in there. They were on their way—they came in the entrance there, and they were on their way to the graveyard. I suppose, I imagine, some relative or something. All this stuff about 'the Asians don't care about life,' or 'don't value life,' and all that—I think it's a real myth. I think they feel about these things a lot like our people do. Here are people trudging out there to pay their respects and so on, not a very easy thing for them to do, and they're doing it."

TET, THE TRADITIONAL celebration of the lunar new year, had also become a traditional time for enemy offensives. Thus it was more than symbolic when Colby and Vann celebrated Tet 1971 by driving across the Delta, from Can Tho to Cau Doc, unescorted, just the two of them on a couple of motorcycles.[3] Vann was by that point, recalled Colby, very satisfied about the success achieved in the pacification program, "even to the extent of keeping his mouth shut once in a while, which was an extreme sacrifice for John."

Vann had admitted as much, telling Colby, "I feel so strongly about the way this thing is working and the way we're running it that I'm even not going to criticize."[4] Meanwhile in the capital, for so long a place of rocket attacks and terrorist atrocities, by this point Sir Robert Thompson could express the "conviction that Saigon was a safer place in which to live and walk around both by day and night than most American cities."[5] The progress achieved led Ambassador Bunker to observe in a reporting cable to the President that "pacification, like golf, becomes more difficult to improve the better it gets."[6]

When, in the autumn of 1971, Tom Barnes returned to Vietnam in the pacification program after an absence of three years, he told General Weyand he was struck by three principal improvements. One was rural prosperity, another the way the Territorial Forces had taken hold, and the third the growing political and economic autonomy of the villages. "One of our greatest contributions to pacification," he said, "has been the reestablishment of the village in its historic Vietnamese role of relative independence and self-sufficiency."

Some insight into how the enemy regarded these developments was provided by a COSVN Directive of October 1971. "During the past two years," it read, "the U.S. and puppet focussed their efforts on pacifying and encroaching upon rural areas, using the most barbarous schemes. They strengthened puppet forces, consolidated the puppet government, and established an outpost network and espionage and People's Self-Defense Force organizations in many hamlets and villages. They provided more technical equipment for, and increased the mobility of, puppet forces, established blocking lines, and created a new defensive and oppressive system in densely populated rural areas. As a result, they caused many difficulties to and inflicted losses on friendly forces."[7] That was a pretty good report card.

THE MALEVOLENT influence of the earlier unproductive years continued to make the regenerative tasks of the later period more difficult in a number of ways. One manifestation was the publication, beginning in mid-June 1971, of the *Pentagon Papers,* the multivolume study of the war ordered in his final months as defense secretary by Robert McNamara. Colby remarked how unfortunate it was that this material had been leaked and published, not because of what was revealed, with which he had no real problem, but because the coverage of these documents ended in May 1968, "just when CORDS had begun its work." The result was—at this later point in the war—to obscure what had been accomplished in the interim, turning attention to "the confused and ineffective conduct of the war prior to the period of success that followed 1968," and reinforcing a feeling of futility about the prospects for success in Vietnam.[8]

Many visitors coming out from Washington during this period, noted Abrams, questioned the utility of continuing to bomb the enemy's lines of communication along the Ho Chi Minh Trail, suggesting that the United States paid a high political price for doing so. Abrams was not persuaded. "That interdiction program over there in Laos is doing a lot to restrict the level of activity that he's able to sustain here in South Vietnam and Cambodia and so on," he believed. "And I don't think there's any *question* about it."

Sometimes Abrams would offer a personal insight or reaction. "I just want to tell you all," he said by way of preliminaries to a commanders conference one day, "I'm not trying to put in for a Silver Star or anything, but after a few years of coming over to this building in the morning, I want to tell you it's about the same as when the battalion commander calls you in and says,

'Men, we're going to take that hill. They've got a regiment up
there, and we've only got two understrength companies. But
we're going to take it. And we're going to take it this morning.'
And that's what it takes to come out of those damn quarters
over there and prepare to receive those messages!" Here Abrams
was referring to the daily avalanche of cable traffic from Washington. "It's unbelievable! I have considered, recently, if I
shouldn't put together a new B-52 targeting outfit. Hell, we've
been using these things out here in Southeast Asia. I've at least
got in my mind some excellent targets."

There was at this point little question about what was left
for the Vietnamese to accomplish. Bunker and Abrams had gone
for a rewarding talk with President Thieu, and Abrams and some
key staffers had what he called a good, frank discussion with
General Vien and his staff. "I think we've given them a good,
honest appraisal," Abrams said in mid-June 1971. "Basically, the
thing that's needed now is a matter of *quality*. They've got to
correct their manpower situation, which is *bad*. And they've got
to correct the leadership deficiencies. Those are the two main
things. Those things cannot be solved by equipment. No way
to solve them with equipment! In fact, you just make the problem *worse* by shoving equipment in."

As one American unit after another formed up and departed
for home, the task of covering all the bases with what was left
behind became progressively more difficult. Wrestling with the
content of the increment scheduled to depart during September–November 1971, Abrams looked back on the experience
to that point. "The redeployment started out with various
goals," he recalled. "We were going to be able to do them at a
certain rate. And then, hell, almost before you get started, they
wanted to accelerate it. Well, not only wanted to—*did*. That
has a *hell* of an impact on logistics and personnel. Well, in the
past we were *big* enough, and had enough people, so that you

could wrench the thing in that way without causing a major disaster. Oh, yes, it caused some problems, but it was not catastrophic, because the whole was big enough to get it done."

Those days were gone. "I might say here we've had to look down into—I call it the chasm—for several months. I'm convinced now that we haven't got that flexibility any more. So we've got to plan quite a ways ahead, in detail, and everybody's got to be in on it. That's the only way we can do anything on personnel that's satisfactory. And on logistics, if we don't do it, I think we'll fail. It's that critical." In planning the thing they were pulled two ways—getting out what had to be gotten out, both people and equipment, and supporting what was left. "There's an awful lot to be done, and if we're going to do it without *scandal,* and without the charges of abandonment, we've got to get in it. And it won't get any better by arguing another week. It just won't. It'll get worse."

The challenges for the South Vietnamese were severe as well, including accepting facilities from departing American units and then maintaining and operating them—750 sites in all, from a five-man team house to a division base camp. When someone suggested that the drawdown had to continue to satisfy domestic political imperatives, Abrams responded, "I don't know if I'll rise to that." Then he did. "We had to do this"—meaning withdraw—he began. "There's very clear evidence, at least to me in some things, that we helped too much. And we *retarded* the Vietnamese by doing it. *We* can't run this thing. I'm absolutely convinced of that. *They've* got to run it. The nearer we can get to that, the better off *they* are and the better off *we* are. It has nothing to do with despair about the disarray at home."

NOWHERE WERE THE horrendous costs of the war to North Vietnam more apparent than in the infiltration numbers. By mid-1970, concluded MACV, "in order to replace the tremendous losses to its forces in the Republic of Vietnam, it is estimated that North Vietnam has infiltrated over 700,000 persons since 1960." For most it had been a one-way trip.

Then things got more difficult, much more difficult, for enemy soldiers coming down the Ho Chi Minh Trail. They were about to experience "Island Tree." Begun in August 1971, this was a program to specifically target infiltration groups as they made their way south. Until then, allied interdiction campaigns had concentrated primarily on logistical traffic, with any personnel casualties inflicted being incidental to attacks on the trucks. Now, thanks to some new concepts and some new technology, that free ride for troops was about to end—and abruptly.

Improved sensor technology was at the heart of the new capability. Sensors were sowed by air at probable enemy bivouac sites—normally located about thirty minutes' walking distance from the main north–south routes—and coordinated with estimated arrival schedules of infiltration groups. The program had been conceived in Washington and more or less force-issued to MACV, and initially Abrams was not optimistic. "We're not sparing any effort to get at it," he told a visiting Ambassador Godley, "but I'm not optimistic at this time that we're going to be able to attrit it by 50 percent."

By the end of 1971, though, some test runs of the new system had produced gratifying results, complete with audio effects returned by the acoustic sensors—secondary explosions, cluster bombs going off, horns blowing, screams. One B-52 could carry 44,000 CBUs (cluster bomb units), and apparently the results achieved had been devastating. That was good news, because special emphasis had been given to targeting stations where the 320th NVA Division, on the move southward and believed destined for the B-3 Front, might be struck. "It sounds like it could be useful," Abrams now admitted. Two weeks later he was a real convert: "Island Tree is producing more than anything. We've really got to stay with it." This newfound capability would take on even more importance as, in early 1972, the enemy's Easter Offensive loomed.

ON 3 OCTOBER 1971 South Vietnam conducted a presidential election that turned out to be—with a single candidate, Nguyen Van Thieu, on the ballot—more of a referendum. Earlier in the year, during Lam Son 719, Ambassador Bunker had looked ahead to this period. "With the elections coming up," he told commanders at MACV, "it is clearly in our interest, I think, to see that this administration continues."

As the date for the election drew near, the slate of candidates—never robust to begin with—dwindled alarmingly. When General Duong Van Minh withdrew, Abrams viewed it as an ominous development. "It's hard to see any good coming from that," he observed. "You can get kind of sad about that, saying, 'Why in the hell, when we're where we're at, why do we have to have that?' It's not a good time for it."

Fred Weyand agreed. "As far as the support back home for this government, it couldn't get much worse." Then, after a pause for reflection, "Well, I guess it could." Weyand also understood the significance of the election, even given the greatly reduced American objectives and expectations. "We finally, under these pressures—political, diplomatic, and all that—have gotten ourselves to the point where the reason we're here is for self-determination, so these people will have a free choice. So that makes the election of great importance. But still, underneath all this, are the real reasons that we came in here, and that is because we want a non-Communist government."

"What'll be interesting to watch," suggested George Jacobson, "is whether the Communists back a candidate, and don't try to screw up the elections, but try to get votes out, or whether they really try to disrupt the election." One piece of evidence was COSVN Directive 38 which, said MACV's analyst, "favors participation in the electoral process, but calls for paramilitary activity to discredit the GVN." A J-2 analyst said they had reports on both sides. "Some of them say, 'Vote for Big Minh,' and the rest of them say, 'Don't go vote at all.'" In the event it turned out to be the latter, but with a conspicuous lack of success.

What was also interesting to watch, if a little sad, was the effect of imposing this democratic ritual on traditional Vietnamese culture. "This is a traumatic experience these days, not only for the enemy, but by god for the Vietnamese people themselves," Jacobson observed, "because for the first time in their whole history they're going to have to back somebody before they know who's going to win. And this is just killing them, just *killing* them! Very un-Vietnamese."

Nguyen Cao Ky had been his usual self-interested and threatening presence through the preelection period. In July, Lieutenant General Ngo Dzu returned from a visit to Saigon and told John Vann the latest political news. Describing a "secret rendezvous" with some representative of Ky that Vann said sounded like a meeting with Ky himself, Dzu mentioned Ky's belief that U.S. support might well shift from Thieu to either neutrality or support of the opposition. "VP Ky wanted Dzu to remain neutral and not place pressure on subordinates to support President Thieu," Vann reported. "VP Ky does not aspire to the Presidency. He wants Gen. Duong Van Minh to win and appoint him Prime Minister." Vann's advice to Dzu was to forget all such maneuverings and get on with the war.[9]

Even with only a single candidate on the ballot, 87.7 percent of registered voters—the largest voter turnout in recent Vietnamese history—cast ballots. Thieu received 91.5 percent of them. Another 5.5 percent deposited invalid ballots in apparent protest of the lack of choice. Tran Van Huong was elected Vice President. Later North Vietnam's representative in Paris, Vo Van Sung, was asked if his country had lost confidence in the Provisional Revolutionary Government, to which he replied, "There has been some evidence of PRG loss of influence in certain sectors." He cited as one example the unsuccessful PRG effort to control voting in the presidential election in areas claimed to be under Viet Cong control.[10] Abrams cited a dramatic contrast: "I notice in the Bangkok municipal elections they had a turnout of 7 percent of the registered voters—*seven!*"

Thieu's solo race, said Abrams, "kind of reminds you of old Dick Russell [a long-serving Democratic senator from Georgia] running for reelection." Then there was "Big" Minh, the noncandidate. "You know, Minh's sitting over in his house, doing nothin'. Just about the same as he'd be doing had he been elected," Abrams told a Mission Council meeting.

In the aftermath Ambassador Sam Berger contrasted the situation with the bad old days in Vietnam. "I think the lessons of 1963–1966 have been fairly well learned here," he said. "They do not want to create a situation which will produce another period of anarchy, and that's one of the most stabilizing factors in the country now. Talk of coup is just talk. It's just nonsense. There's nobody here of any seriousness or of any capability for a coup. Ky's talk of a coup was really talk and did him no good at all. It threw him right up against the grain of the feelings of most people that the country can't stand anything like that. So out of the elections has emerged this quite favorable aspect, a strengthening of constitutional processes in the country."

Abroad, however, the one-candidate election provoked very adverse reaction. "At the time," said Berger, "before and since, we thought that the way President Thieu went at this was very unfortunate. He had the election in the bag and could have won it easily against Ky or Minh or both, and he went out of his way to maneuver them out of running. A price is going to be paid for this in the United States in terms of the increased problems we have with the Congress and in terms of general attitude towards this country."

SECRETARY LAIRD MADE one of his periodic visits to Vietnam in November 1971. Continued redeployment of U.S. forces was, as usual, a high priority topic. Abrams also described his current outlook on how the Vietnamese were doing. "I think actually we may have hoped they would step up to the plate the way they have," he told Laird, "but there certainly wasn't anybody that could *guarantee* it. But I think the *truth* of the matter is the Vietnamese have stepped up to the plate."[11]

Earlier in the year Thomas Polgar, preparing to go out as CIA's Chief of Station in Saigon, had paid a call on Secretary Laird. "As a father of three children," Polgar said, "I really have to consider the advisability of accepting permanent assignment in Vietnam." Laird reassured him. "Oh, don't worry. We are going to have a residual force in Vietnam for thirty years, just like in Germany," he promised.[12]

But Nguyen Tien Hung, returning to his own country on a visit, had a different perspective when he met with President Thieu in Saigon. "You are a professor in America," observed Thieu. "What are they up to?" "Well, Mr. President," Hung replied, "I think they are giving up on us."[13]

BY THE END OF 1971 most American ground forces were out of Vietnam—only 139,000 remained—and the war was already fading from public consciousness. When, in mid-December, the Gallup Poll sampled what people in the United States thought was the most important problem then facing the country, 41 percent responded that it was the state of the economy, nearly three times the 15 percent who said it was Vietnam. An aggregate of 30 percent selected one or another of the same problems that were by then afflicting the forces in Vietnam, including drug abuse, racial hatred, and crime.[14] In an interesting parallel in Vietnam, during the previous year monthly surveys of the population had found almost all their concern was with security, while by 1971 economic issues dominated.

In Vietnam, much attention centered on what the departing Americans were going to leave behind. In Military Region 3, reported Richard Funkhauser, those things most desired were money, B-52s, and Rome plows. The latter were powerful machines capable of clearing jungle in great swaths. "It is commonly believed," said Funkhauser, "that the Rome plow transforms death to life by turning VC/NVA cover into arable land." In his opinion, he added, the Rome plow was "worth its weight in advisors."[15]

William Colby left Vietnam at the end of June 1971 in order to deal with a family crisis; he was succeeded in the pacification job by his deputy, George Jacobson. Back in Washington, Colby soon became Director of Central Intelligence in one of the most difficult and contentious periods of the CIA's existence. Deciding that the Agency's future viability depended on reestablishing its credibility with the Congress, he shared with its oversight and investigating committees the most damaging evidence of past misdeeds from institutional files. That earned him the enmity of some old hands—including, of course, those involved in the wrongdoing—but the admiration and approval of others.

IN 1972 THE ENEMY was going to mount an all-out offensive on three fronts, one of them through the supposedly sacrosanct Demilitarized Zone. Critics would claim that this had caught the allies unaware, that they had naively depended on the enemy's respecting the DMZ. But by June 1971 military developments provided not only forewarning of that possibility but also further actual evidence of enemy disregard for the DMZ.

In the wake of Lam Son 719, with the logistical deficiencies that operation had imposed on him, the enemy was reduced for that year's dry season offensive essentially to operations in the northernmost provinces of South Vietnam. There, with proximity to the DMZ, he could get supplies and troops through without traversing the Ho Chi Minh Trail, and without the long lead time that preparations for operations farther south necessarily entailed. Thus, reported Lieutenant General Welborn Dolvin to Abrams in late June, "he has prudently decided to conduct an intense, though geographically limited, campaign with North Vietnam as his base, the DMZ as his haven and infiltration zone, and roads and trails through the DMZ as direct LOC [lines of communication] to his fighting units."[16]

This battle became quite intense in Quang Tri Province, with successive attacks by fire of 500 and then 800 rounds on Fire Support Base Fuller, and more than 5,400 rounds during the thirty-day period before the position had to be evacuated. Abrams cabled McCain to tell him that "a preemptive campaign against enemy targets throughout the DMZ is considered necessary" and to request the authorities for that.[17] Most such requests for additional authorities were ignored or turned down.

By the end of 1971, Abrams was spending considerable effort analyzing the motives and stratagems of his own government. He looked at the India-Pakistan conflict and concluded that the United States had hoped to attain some measure of peace by fairly sophisticated negotiation, even though that effort failed. And in the Middle East he thought he saw the same thing at work. "That must be the policy thrust," he concluded. "It looks like they're trying to have enough balance on the military side so that nobody, on either side, will think that they can solve it by military action. In terms of *policy* thrust, it seems to me that that's what this government stands for. Now I turn around and apply it to this thing, the problem here—in a way I think they're trying to get some kind of equilibrium here, where military actions just won't solve it, for either side. Now whether that's a successful track to follow, I don't know."

"That would be consistent with our requests for easing of rules and authorities," someone commented. "They've never added an inch. It's almost as though they don't *want* a military advantage. It would *upset* something." Abrams pondered the suggestion. "Yeah, that's right," he concluded.

AT YEAR'S END Ambassador Berger summed up the South Vietnamese outlook as he perceived it. They had, he said, been subjected to "some very serious jolts which have shaken them up," including announcement of President Nixon's trip to Peking. Even more worrisome was "defeat of the U.S. resolution in the U.N., the ejection of Taiwan, and the admission of Red China," demonstrating how sharply limited U.S. powers were in such matters. There followed the imposition of emergency economic and financial measures in the United States, and then Senate rejection of the foreign aid bill. Thus in South Vietnam "there is very, very great concern as to what may happen in 1973 and beyond. There's been no panic here, but there is no question about it—there is a growing uneasiness, not yet anxiety, but worry. That there has been nothing more serious than this, we think, is due in large measure to the feeling that the President, the administration, and the American people will not abandon them after all the support and sacrifices that we have made, and all that they have made here. Up to now, they've always taken the view that it'll be all right, the Americans will be there. And now they're beginning to wonder more and more." Thus, concluded Berger, "we think 1972 will be a fairly painful year."[18]

It was certainly shaping up that way on the battlefield, and by late December 1971—having evaluated all the intelligence on infiltration and the enemy's logistical offensive—it was clear to Abrams what lay ahead. "He's getting ready to do the most that it's possible for him to do," he concluded. "He hasn't *got* anything more he could, you know—He's rolling out everything." It was pretty clear where the heaviest blows were coming, too, as General Fred Kroesen confirmed for Military Region 1. "I think General Lam, and everybody up there, expects the 3rd Division to be tested by the enemy," he stated.

Later General Vien concluded that "the years 1969, 1970, and 1971 were the best years for South Vietnam during President Thieu's administration. The country was not only militarily secure, it was well on its way toward full-scale development as a result of spectacular achievements in pacification. This was the main reason why the GVN embarked on an ambitious four-year plan beginning in 1972, setting high goals for community defense and local development."[19]

When Abrams met with Vien on the last day of the year, and together they listened to an update of the current intelligence assessment, Abrams referred to the enemy's capability of moving into South Vietnam with the divisions he had positioned above the DMZ. "If he moves the 304th, the 308th, and the 324 Bravo into Quang Tri and Thua Thien, that ain't protracted war," he told Vien. "That's main force. That's a big battle."

With that in prospect, it was good that there was, from time to time, some measure of encouragement. Ambassador Bunker provided a memorable ration when he returned from a short visit to the United States, where he had attended a reunion at his alma mater. "I can give you one good piece of news," he said at the next staff meeting. "The Class of 1916 at Yale is solidly behind our Vietnam policy."

18

Soldiers

THE LATTER YEARS of the war in Vietnam coincided with unprecedented turmoil and upheaval in American society generally, indeed in much of the world: spheres within spheres of challenge to established authority, to received wisdom, to long-standing customs, to concepts of individual freedoms and responsibilities, to whatever consensus had previously existed on proper public and personal conduct. There flourished a widely imitated popular culture that included its own music, recreational drug use, and renunciation of any notions of obligation to the larger society. In the United States a decade of protests of various kinds, especially having to do with civil rights and then with the war, shook the establishment to its foundations.

The military establishment was of course not immune to these influences. On the faculty at West Point in 1969 a duly constituted Junior Officer Council solemnly recommended to the Department of the Army that the rank of second lieutenant be eliminated because it was "discriminatory."[1] Throughout the Army, levels of maturity and experience were dropping, a consequence in part of failure to call up reserve forces. When General Harold K. Johnson, then the Army's Chief of Staff, had first learned from Secretary of Defense McNamara in July 1965 that Lyndon Johnson was going to send ground forces to Vietnam in substantial numbers, and do that without calling up reserve forces, he had issued a warning. "I can assure you of one thing," he told McNamara, "and that is that without a call-up of the reserves that the quality of the Army is going to erode and we're going to suffer very badly. I don't know at what point this will occur, but it will be relatively soon. I don't know how wide-spread it will be, but it will be relatively widespread."[2] That proved to be right on the mark.

Without access to the experienced small unit leadership in the reserve forces, the Army was forced to create thousands of new units from scratch while at the same time greatly expanding the force. The increases, Creighton Abrams once observed suc-cinctly, "were entirely in privates and second lieutenants." The result was a long-term trend of diminishing experience and ma-turity of leadership at the crucial troop unit levels, with pre-dictably less capacity to deal with the societal and disciplinary problems that spread throughout the force as the war dragged on.

Soon much of the Army was made up of soldiers with under two years' service, and in overseas assignments of limited du-ration, such as Vietnam, the turnover was so great—at one point reaching 120 percent a year—that it further eroded the expe-rience level. When Captain Joseph Anderson returned to Viet-nam as a company commander in 1970, for example, he found that in his entire unit of 200 men, only he, one of his platoon sergeants, and one of his squad leaders had more than two years of service.[3]

By virtue of a one-year-tour policy the whole of the armed forces in Vietnam was replaced every year or less, guaranteeing a constant influx of soldiers freshly imbued with the influences of domestic America. Many of those influences, it turned out, were incompatible with the good order and discipline on which effective military organizations depend. If American society had some kind of difficulty, so did the armed forces in Vietnam. If there was a problem of racial disharmony in America, there was one in Vietnam. If dissent and indiscipline were rife in America, they were exported to Vietnam in equal measure. If drug use flourished among America's youth, those sent to Vietnam were initiates of that experience. In some respects the problems at home were even more severe than they were in Vietnam. "Actually," Abrams once observed wryly, "I think President Thieu is freer to move around in *his* country than President Nixon is in *his*."

Dealing with these problems in the context of a war, difficult enough in itself, was further complicated by the declining levels of experience and maturity among small-unit leaders, lack of public support at home, the psychology induced by progressive withdrawal of American forces, and the continued rapid turnover within units. "The real thing we've got going for us over here," said Abrams, "has been the attitude of the Americans. Good god, it's been magnificent. I sometimes say if a fellow's really interested in being discouraged, this is probably one of the easiest places in the world to take it aboard in large quantities. But the attitude has been *great*. It's the strongest thing, I think, we've got going for us. It's more important than divisions. If you contemplate what it would be if you didn't have it, *god,* it would—well, it would be unmanageable."

Ultimately the major impact of the drawdown of American forces was not the loss of combat power or support capability, serious though they were, but rather its effect on the morale and discipline of the remaining troops. Once it became clear that the United States no longer sought to win the war, but only to disengage, Abrams performed an impressive feat of leadership in simply holding the diminishing force together long enough to get it redeployed. At one point, understanding the prevailing realities, Abrams told a trusted aide: "I need to get this Army home to save it."

Commanders in the field did what they could to maintain good order and discipline, as exemplified by one famous case involving the 1st Cavalry Division at its base at An Khe in the Central Highlands. Nearby, a Vietnamese-operated establishment known as "The Million Magic Fingers Massage Parlor, Laundry and Tank Wash" sprang up to serve the needs of the troops. When the division commander complained that it was corrupting the health and morals of his soldiers, and threatened to close it down, the proprietor put up a new sign that described the changed situation: "No More Whorehouse, Only Laundry." In time, though, the problems to be dealt with grew much more serious.

The full impact of multiple dysfunctional influences came into play only during the last years of American involvement in Vietnam. While he was in de facto command in April 1968, General Abrams had sent a message to his senior commanders alerting them to racial problems. At that juncture he could observe that "racial problems among our men in South Vietnam are for all practical purposes insignificant," but he saw the tidal wave approaching. Citing his belief that "the racial unrest now exhibiting itself in our country could in some way infect our own men," he directed all commanders to be alert for signs of racial unrest or disturbance and to deal with it promptly should it occur.[4]

When the wave broke, it was going to be all they could do for commanders at all levels to hold things together. Abrams understood this full well. Cautioning his field commanders to take seriously what he viewed as "some modest upswing in incidents among our own troops, either based on racial problems or some other kind of friction," he emphasized that "the most powerful thing we've got here is the attitude of the Americans who are assigned here, military and civilian. And I tell you, if that ever deteriorates substantially, that'll be worse than *any* goddamn thing that Giap or any of the rest of them can think of. This is *important*. It's *critical*." Offering his perspective on how to deal with the problem, Abrams added, "I don't believe you can do it with *poopsheets*. The commander's got to be sensitive to it. He's got to be intelligent about it. They've got to *talk* to their men."

Rapid turnover within units was compounded by shifting men from one unit to another as the drawdown of American forces continued. Abrams returned again and again to issues of human relations and leadership. "We've got some human chemistry going on here which old attitudes are *just not* going to be *adequate* to," he said early in 1970. "There's a sense of pride, an awful lot of it justified by what's been done here," he began. Disrespect for others, whether the Vietnamese or fellow soldiers of another race, could not be tolerated. Where that happened, he felt, the cause was very basic: "not being a satisfactory leader—not communicating with the men, not communicating with your subordinates. You know, it's never changed, it's always been that way. It's different times, but it's *still* necessary, and there isn't any substitute for it."

When racial problems were reported involving soldiers on R&R in Hong Kong, Abrams told his subordinates that this was "commanders' business. This thing with the Negroes is *symptomatic*—it's symptomatic of our lack of success thus far in South Vietnam of dealing effectively with the friction and the problem between the races. It's not only between the blacks and the whites, it's the whites and the Vietnamese, and the older whites and the younger whites, and the older blacks and the younger blacks—I mean, there's all kinds of things involved. And these are the times we're living in, and it does no good to sit around and piss about the good old days, because they aren't here—if they ever were."

When Vice President Agnew visited in August 1970, Abrams told him that the soldier drug problem was "a big and serious problem, and is, in fact, the biggest among all those we have, including black marketeering and currency manipulation." Abrams added that many commanders believed that in forward areas of real danger there was significant self-policing by the men, but that in rear areas the problem was more difficult. Nevertheless, Abrams said, his outlook at that time was that, "while we regard drugs to be a serious problem, and that our major effort here is to solve it, I did not feel the drug problem, in any significant way, interfered with the performance of the tasks of the men in South Vietnam."[5]

Statistical evidence of the size of the drug abuse problem, and of its rapid increase, was only just beginning to become available. Deaths from drug overdoses defined the trend—16 in 1969, 14 in the next seven months, 26 the next month alone, 18 the next, then 35 in a span of just eighteen days at the beginning of October 1970—these last at a rate of 700 a year.[6]

Evidence of extreme indiscipline in the form of "fragging," efforts—many of them successful—to kill or maim leaders by the use of grenades, went up along with the overdose deaths. This connection was explicit, as established by a study of the perpetrators of fraggings incarcerated in the U.S. Disciplinary Barracks at Fort Leavenworth. Dr. Thomas Bond, Chief of Psychiatry at the facility, studied the causes of almost 800 incidents of fragging in Vietnam. "All of the men in the sample," said Dr. Bond, "reported using a wide variety of drugs with no discernible pattern, and 87.5 percent reported being acutely intoxicated at the time of the incident."[7] In 1969 there were 96 such episodes, rising to 209 in 1970; 39 men were killed the first year and 34 the next.[8] Said one young officer who returned to Vietnam for a second tour in 1971—remembering it nearly a quarter of a century later—"it was worse than you can imagine if you were not a part of it at the troop level."[9]

West Point's Class of 1965, entering the Army just as U.S. ground forces were first committed to Vietnam in large numbers, became a barometer of stormy weather. Graduating a total of 596, the class saw 148—a quarter of its entire membership—resign during 1970 alone.[10]

In November 1970 Lieutenant General William McCaffrey, Abrams's deputy commander for Army forces in Vietnam, reported that a recently conducted survey of incoming replacements revealed that more than half had used marijuana or other drugs before coming to Vietnam. "The drug situation," observed

McCaffrey, "like the race area, is again a mirror of the problems we share with the rest of U.S. society."[11] In a report to the Army staff in Washington, McCaffrey posed and answered some tough questions. "Are the officers out here up to the task of holding the Army together during this period of turmoil? Is the erosion of command control at a crisis stage? General Abrams feels strongly that the senior officers in the chain of command are doing a first-rate job under the unprecedented difficulties inherent in the current stage of national attitude toward the war. In addition to the drug abuse problem, we live with race tension, corruption, high malaria rates, excessive vehicle accident rates, about 70 GAO investigations, and a numerous and hostile press." Even so, McCaffrey concluded gamely, "I feel that with a little luck, we'll accomplish the tasks assigned, to the great and lasting benefit of our society. It is a privilege to be here."[12]

LATE IN 1970 General Abrams had a long and thoughtful conversation about these matters with George McArthur, a veteran correspondent. "Why can't you kick ass and get some discipline?" he was asked. "The only way to get anywhere with kicking ass is with an outfit that is already good," Abrams replied. "Then they take it. They know they are good. They say 'the old man is pissed off and maybe we are slipping and maybe we had better humor him and string along' and everything is alright." But, said Abrams, "you can't do that out here." The honesty of the answer was apparent, an acknowledgment that under current circumstances this was not one of those good outfits.

But then Abrams told McArthur about a reconnaissance outfit he had recently visited. It was, he said, "a real fine outfit, everybody up." And they were talking about their problems, talking about drugs. They knew who the people were that were taking them, and they didn't think it was a good thing. They had an amnesty program, and a good psychologist. And, from the commander on down, they were talking about the problem, trying to straighten out those people who were involved. "I thought it was a healthy outfit," Abrams said. "I think that you have to punish the men who are selling the stuff. With the others you just have to work in there and talk it over."

Then, said Abrams, "remember there are still men here who are performing incredible feats. So much of what is being done now is being done by small units. I think this is an advantage. When you have big operations, battalions and all that, with five hundred and many more men, it is hard for non-coms to sense any real responsibility for the outcome. But you get small units out there, five to thirty men, and it is all different."[13]

Abrams had formed that view on the basis of frequent travel to combat units and interactions with soldiers at all levels. In the field one day he visited an ARVN unit and talked to the members of their advisory team, a couple of officers, a sergeant, and a young black soldier who was their radio operator. Abrams went up to the young man and asked him how he was getting along. "I'm doing fine, sir!" he replied. "These people need our help, and they deserve it, and I'm going to do everything I can to help them out." Abrams looked at him for a moment, then said admiringly, "Goddamn—that's a great answer!"

Dwight Birdwell, who served in a cavalry troop in Vietnam and later wrote an honest and affecting account of his experiences, concluded that as early as 1968 "the professional NCO corps had been mostly used up" and identified that as "a primary factor in the decline in morale and performance."[14] But Birdwell's account also raises a puzzling question that has never been fully resolved. His unit, he testifies, experienced increasing racial tensions, widespread drug abuse, and growing indiscipline. Yet, like many other units infected by those cancers, his continued to accomplish the tactical missions assigned it. Somehow the anticipated connection between degraded individual capabilities and diminished organizational effectiveness seems not to have had full effect.

An exception is instructive. Late in the war there occurred,

at a place called Fire Support Base Mary Ann, a shocking incident involving an outfit that *was* riddled by drugs and incompetence. It involved an element of the Americal Division, the
same division that perpetrated the My Lai massacre, the same
division that disobediently continued to employ Agent Orange
herbicide after its use was forbidden.

On 28 March 1971 elements of the 1st Battalion, 46th Infantry at Mary Ann received an attack by fire, followed by a
sapper attack that penetrated the perimeter. At a cost of twelve
attackers killed, the enemy inflicted thirty-three KIA and sev-
enty-eight wounded on the American unit, destroyed one
155mm howitzer and banged up another, and heavily damaged
the battalion's tactical operations center. The disaster was compounded by a cover-up that extended all the way up to the
division commander, who was later relieved from a prestigious
assignment and demoted when the facts belatedly came out.

At Mary Ann the chain of command had clearly failed to
do its job, but it was the soldiers who paid the price, many with
their lives. Not many generalizations can be grounded on what
happened there, however. The enemy was neither stupid nor
inattentive. Had there been other units as careless and undiscip-
lined as the one at Mary Ann, surely the enemy would have
discovered and exploited their weaknesses just as ruthlessly. Yet
that did not happen. Perhaps, even in the midst of the undeniably widespread problems of drugs, race, and indiscipline,
there were enough good soldiers left to do what had to be done
and thus carry a unit that still had a mission to perform.

While Mary Ann clearly was not the norm, the potential for
further disaster was there, and Abrams went at it with a vengeance. "Now this business of winding down the war and so
on, and less fighting—the thing you've got to remember is that
anybody can still get killed anywhere in this country!" he told his
senior field commanders. "What's happening out there in some
places is people aren't paying attention to it. What everybody's
got to understand is that the conditions in this country *just make*

that criminal neglect! You can't have it! And the commanders that *permit* it are doing a very bad thing for their men. They're not accepting their responsibility as a commander, and they're not accepting their responsibility for the security and well-being of their men. And I just don't know of anything worse a commander can do."

And Abrams put it squarely to the top leaders under his command—Weyand, Clay, McCaffrey, Salzer, Dolvin, Wagstaff, Vann, Cushman, and the rest. "And all of us, we've got to see that it is done right. That's what we stand for, and that's the way it's going to *be*. There's no point in sobbing about the problems—'the press is bad,' or 'the people back home are bad'— I mean, to *hell* with *that!* That's not your job! You're *here!* And you're getting *paid,* and your government *expects* you, to face the *heat* and get it done *right!* And that's what we've got to do. *Well,* that's what we're *going* to do."

THE WIDESPREAD problems of racial disharmony, drug abuse, and indiscipline undeniably afflicted the troops in Vietnam, as they did those in the armed services all over the world—and particularly in America itself—but they reached greatest proportions only in the very late stages, when much of the force had been withdrawn and when the combat role of those remaining was much diminished.

When Army Chief of Chaplains Francis Sampson visited Vietnam in early 1971, expecting the worst, he was surprised by what he found. General Bruce Palmer cabled Abrams with a report on Father Sampson's impressions. "He said that prior to his visit he had gained the impression from outside of Vietnam that there had been considerable deterioration of morale, discipline and combat effectiveness of US troops," related Palmer. "He stated that he was pleasantly surprised to learn from his own observations that this was not true; rather, his overall impressions were good with respect to leadership, morale, discipline, attitude, and outlook among US troops and their

noncommissioned and commissioned leaders." But, in a seem-
ingly incompatible observation, "he also said that the hard drug
problem was severe."[15]

In April and May 1971 a three-man team sent out by the
Army conducted informal interviews—guaranteeing anonymity
to the participants—with small combat units throughout U.S.
Army, Vietnam. Two captains and a first sergeant did the interviewing. Their general finding was that "the American soldier
serving in combat arms units in Vietnam is still a responsible,
disciplined individual who is proud of having successfully carried
out his hazardous combat mission."

The interviewers also looked into the matter of "combat
refusals," soldiers who disobeyed orders to go on a mission.
They estimated that most companies had experienced one or
two such incidents over the past six months, but cited the response from a particular interview as most representative of their
findings on the combat soldier. Some infantrymen were poised
to reinforce another company that was engaged with the enemy
in a nearby firefight. The researchers put a hypothetical question
to one young soldier (who happened, they noted, to have a
master's degree in geology). What would he would do if word
came that a sister company was in heavy contact with an NVA
battalion reinforced by tanks? The query was, of course, aimed
at eliciting any thought of a combat refusal. This young trooper
considered the question for a moment, then responded practically. "Well, sir, I'd take a LAW [light antitank weapon]." That,
concluded his questioners, was the essence of the American soldier as they had found him in Vietnam.

The three survey team members knew what they were talking about, for among them they had served a total of ten combat
tours in Vietnam. One of the officers, somewhat ironically, was
Captain Barry McCaffrey. A quarter-century later—as a retired
four-star general—he would become America's "czar" in the
continuing fight against drug abuse.[16]

Concluded Shelby Stanton in assessing the "rise and fall" of the Army during these years, "The front-line soldiers of the 1970 Army in Vietnam were still tough, young, and lean. The Army did not experience breakdowns in unit cohesion until the final withdrawal period of 1971–1972."[17] Researcher B. G. Burkett, author of a comprehensive study of the Vietnam veteran, reported that "the drug rate until 1970 in Vietnam for the U.S. Army was lower than it was Stateside, in Germany, or any other part of the world. However, in 1970 and 1971, it got much worse." But by then, Burkett calculated, 90 percent of all those who would ever serve in Vietnam had already come and gone.[18]

SPRING 1971 SURVEY results had yielded the surprising finding that a larger percentage of drug abusers had begun drug use in the United States than in Vietnam. And in one unit, the 173rd Airborne Brigade, a study of about 1,000 men showed that 84 percent of drug users began use in the United States. It was apparent that, to some significant extent, the one-year tour and consequent frequent turnover of personnel were serving to import the American drug problem into the command in Vietnam. "I think we have a real problem," Abrams repeated.[19]

But Abrams also thought it was important to recognize that, in a time of widespread troubles, most men were doing their duty. "Now, these men of ours come over here, and already quite a significant percentage of them have either tried, experimented, or are on some kind of drug," he acknowledged. "Also, to some degree, they bring with them the racial tensions that have developed in our country, to include personnel on, I guess, both sides of the black-white thing who have been organizers, militants, activists of one kind or another. To some degree they've been exposed to the antiwar movement in our country."

"Then they get here," Abrams continued. "You have to add to that, on the minus side, the sort of human relations between Americans and Vietnamese. There's a cultural chasm there that is pretty big, and some Americans it's just impossible for them to ever bridge it in any workable way. Then you've got all the living conditions and working conditions, that sort of thing. So there's quite a bit there on the negative side, just to start with."

But there was much that was positive, too, Abrams pointed out to his senior field commanders. Some 20,000 men had gone to the United States on a two-week leave program, and only a few had failed to make their scheduled return flights to Vietnam. "The net loss is really insignificant," said Abrams. "I take a little comfort in that. I'm sure that among those who return there are a good many who would prefer not to be here. There're probably some in there, too, who really don't believe that the United States should have been tangled up in this in the first place. But there also must be present among those men at least a sufficient sense of personal responsibility and pride, just in themselves, so that they will go ahead and complete satisfactorily a task which they have to do."

As further evidence, "the conduct of our men on R&R seems to stay at the same satisfactory standard that it has in the past," Abrams added. "I take some comfort from that because, on the negative side—if it really started to rot internally here, you know, men and spirit and all that—I just think when they get in a place like Bangkok or Hong Kong or those places, gee whiz, crime and—. I think they're pretty good men. As we go along here, their attitude, and their spirit, their welfare—. And you know, it's always kind of key. In the darkest hours I think it's probably been the cement, or glue, that kind of held the thing together. It's got to continue that way."

The essence of that, Abrams reminded his commanders, was supervision, support for the chain of command, and concern for the well-being of the troops, all the classic elements of effective leadership. He wanted to see all that function the way it was supposed to function, and to help him ensure that it did, he was going to be sending Inspector General teams around to inquire into how the chain of command was performing throughout

MACV. "I'm talking about doing what all of us know as professionals ought to be being done, and just insisting that it be
done *everywhere*. Nothing new! It's all old. That's what has always
gotten us through in the tight times, and that's what'll do it
now."

In September 1971 the *Washington Post* published a photograph
of a soldier in Vietnam that provoked a somewhat panicky reaction from General Westmoreland, who had apparently been
asked about it by some congressman. The GI in question was
shown hatless, bearded, beaded, sleeves cut off, generally pretty
thoroughly disheveled. Soon there was a message to Abrams in
which Westmoreland, from his Pentagon perspective, deplored
this soldier with a "hippy" appearance and enjoined Abrams to
compel "compliance with Army policy and directives regarding
personal appearance and wear of the uniform" as necessary "to
regain the traditional image of public confidence in the U.S.
Army and the Army chain of command." As a coda Westmoreland added his view that "with competent and alert professional officers in the chain of command, a communication
such as this should not be necessary."[20]

Not long before this episode Abrams had been out to visit
one of the allied units, coming away with an unfavorable impression of its fighting qualities. That led to an observation to
his senior commanders and staff demonstrating how different his
views were from Westmoreland's on such matters in the combat
zone. "I'm not *talking* about everybody *saluting* and all that kind
of—I don't *care* about that," said Abrams. "But there's a business
about running the business, and *fighting*. And I don't care if
they're out of uniform, haven't had a haircut or don't shave or
any of that stuff if they'll *fight* and *know* how to fight and take
care of the things that are *required* to fight."

Certainly there were problems in plenty, just as there were
in the United States, problems recognized by everyone in the

chain of command from Abrams on down. But some of the evidence from Vietnam seems to indicate that the problems, while severe, were nowhere nearly as severe, nor as widespread, as those who were opposed to the war maintained. Colonel Robert M. Cook served as MACV Inspector General for five years, beginning under Westmoreland in August 1967. "When General Abrams arrived in Vietnam," recalled Lieutenant General Herron N. Maples, "the IG Section consisted of four officers and four enlisted men. A year later it consisted of 96 officers and about 170 enlisted men."[21] With that staff, which eventually grew to 400 people, including thirteen full colonels, Cook was able to conduct 458 major investigations and some 5,000 inspections of all kinds, turning up everything from currency manipulation and theft to fraud and murder. His opinion is that "the drug thing was exaggerated, in a negative sense, in many cases."[22]

The performance of soldiers and their units also gave evidence that there was still much good in the command. Successive increments of soldiers did their duty until stand-down and were redeployed in good order. Their equipment was retrograded or turned over to the South Vietnamese. The leader of a reconnaissance platoon scheduled to be withdrawn went to General Putnam and said the entire platoon volunteered to extend if they could go intact as a unit to one of the battalions that was staying in Vietnam. When Abrams heard that, he responded ironically. "That's another one of those torn apart by racial problems, sick with drugs and rebellion and insubordination and so on," he suggested.

IT WAS OBVIOUSLY in the interest of those who opposed the war, and those who evaded it, to portray those who served in the worst possible light. For three decades after the war their negative characterization of the Vietnam veteran pretty much went unchallenged, even though periodically some credible contrary evidence appeared. As early as 1968 the Gallup Poll asked Vietnam veterans about the effects of their service there. Many responded that they were more ambitious, more determined to make something of their lives, others that it had made them more serious or that they appreciated America more, valued life more. "They have," summarized Gallup, "gained self-confidence, firmed up their goals. They have learned to follow and to lead, to accept responsibility and to be responsible for others." And finally there was one more finding, as surprising as it was defining: "While only 26 percent wanted to go to Vietnam in the first place, 94 percent, having returned, say they are glad for the experience. What kind of citizens will they be? Judging by the cross-section we talked to, the answer is: superior."[23]

Over the years, though, very little of that insight found its way into the work of journalists, sociologists, or even historians of the war. Not until an investment counselor who was also a Vietnam veteran, struck by the negative stereotype of the Vietnam veteran he encountered among his clients, set out to establish the truth was the accepted (and wrong) viewpoint challenged. When B. G. Burkett began looking into the backgrounds of criminals and derelicts claiming to be Vietnam veterans—becoming in the course of his research America's leading user of the Freedom of Information Act—he discovered that most had never served in Vietnam and that many had never even been in the armed forces. Yet their false claims of service and fanciful tales of widespread misconduct were often taken at face value—indeed, exploited—by those who had a vested interest in promoting a negative image of those who really had served. The real Vietnam veteran, found Burkett, drawing on rich but neglected Veterans Administration records for the data, was someone quite different—better educated, more prosperous, and better adjusted than his civilian contemporaries.[24]

Another who helped bring out the true story of the Vietnam veteran was Colonel Harry Summers, Jr., a distinguished soldier-turned-author and columnist. Drawing on research conducted at MIT by Arnold Barnett, Timothy Stanley, and Michael Shore,

Summers established that instead of the burden of the war falling largely on the poor, men from prosperous communities were about 10 percent more likely to have been killed in action in Vietnam, the disparity reflecting their "disproportionate presence in such hazardous roles as pilots or infantry captains and lieutenants."[25]

Citing additional research by William Abbott, who analyzed the backgrounds of the war dead listed on the Vietnam Veterans Memorial in Washington, Summers noted that the casualties were proportioned by race in about the same numbers as the population as a whole, and that almost 70 percent of those who were killed in Vietnam had been volunteers. "Instead of 'black, poor, and conscripted' as we have been led to believe," wrote Colonel Summers, "the evidence is those who died in Vietnam were mostly 'white, middle class and volunteers.' And so were most who served there as well. But that is a 'nonfact,' i.e., a fact not acknowledged because it's not politically correct."[26]

Wrote William Buckley, Jr., reflecting on these findings, "That means that Vietnam was indeed an all-American effort, and one that, some of us contend, will one day take its place in the annals of national nobility: a witness to America's disposition to endure special sacrifices in discharge of its heavy international responsibility; to contain the movement that brought death, oppression and poverty to so many millions for so many years."[27]

Susan Katz Keating reported just how decisively volunteers outnumbered those who were drafted—8,720,000 enlistments versus 2,215,000 drafted, a ratio of nearly four to one, for the period August 1964–March 1973. Of those who served in Vietnam, two-thirds were volunteers. "These volunteers," wrote Keating, "speak proudly of their actions. By the time the dust had settled in the 1980s, 91 percent told Harris pollsters they were glad they served; 74 percent said they enjoyed their time in the military; and two out of three said they would serve again, even knowing the outcome of the war."[28]

Perhaps most meaningful of all the evidence is the large

numbers of veterans who, decades after the war, still attend annual reunions of the outfits in which they served. Such behavior suggests they are far from alienated by the experience, or negative with respect to their role and service in the war. Rather they value the friendships they established under the most difficult of conditions, and respect themselves and one another for their service.

19

Anticipation

"By 1972," observed William Colby, "the pacification program had essentially eliminated the guerrilla problem in most of the country."[1] That represented a lot of ground being saved, he suggested, because "this whole aspect of the war, the unorganized part of the war, was not given a great deal of attention during the early part of the war. Only after 1967 was it given a major part of the attention of the military command as well as of the rest of us . . . we put a great deal of effort and energy into it. Essentially . . . I think we won that part of the war, because in 1972 there weren't any guerrillas in the attacks by the North Vietnamese, and in 1975 there weren't any guerrillas in the attack by the North Vietnamese. The guerrillas were all on the South Vietnamese side."[2]

John Paul Vann saw it the same way. "We are now at the lowest level of fighting the war has ever seen," he said in January 1972. "Today there is an air of prosperity throughout the rural areas of Vietnam, and it cannot be denied. Today the roads are open and the bridges are up, and you run much greater risk traveling any road in Vietnam today from the scurrying, bustling, hustling Hondas and Lambrettas than you do from the VC." Vann was also a pragmatist, and to put the matter in perspective he noted that during 1971 there were 1,221 U.S.

servicemen killed in Vietnam, whereas during the same year
there had been 1,647 people killed violently in New York City
alone. Jann concluded, "This program of Vietnamization has
gone kind of literally beyond my wildest dreams of success."[3]

Now, as intelligence of an impending enemy offensive piled
up, Vann practically salivated. "It's beautiful what the enemy is
planning to do," he exulted, "because it appears in II Corps that
he's going to make the same basic tactical error that he made in
Tet 1968, and that is fragment his forces in so many different
directions that he will not put a real weight of effort on any one
attack."

By the beginning of 1972 most of the planned expansion
and improvement of South Vietnam's armed forces had been
completed, providing a formidable capability based on 11 infantry divisions fielding 120 infantry battalions; there were also 58
artillery battalions, 19 armored battalions of various types, and
the appropriate engineer, signal, and other supporting arms and
services. The Airborne Division and the Marine Division, plus
21 Ranger battalions, were the general reserve, while along the
frontier 37 Ranger border defense battalions were positioned.
The Navy had grown to 1,680 craft of many types, and the Air
Force fielded more than 1,000 aircraft. Most important of
all, perhaps, were the Territorial Forces—the Regional Forces
and Popular Forces—at some 550,000 constituting the bulk of
the forces overall and providing the all-important close-in security by means of 1,679 RF companies and 8,356 PF platoons
stationed throughout the country. Complementing the regular
armed forces were the National Police, another 116,000 men,
and the People's Self-Defense Forces, now numbering more
than 4 million.[4]

Meanwhile, the enemy sought yet another time to regain
the initiative and fashion some means of achieving a victory.
"The result of successful Vietnamization and pacification," stated
Sir Robert Thompson, "was that by early 1971 the North decided that the only thing left was to invade."[5] General Vo

Nguyen Giap, observed Douglas Pike, had "spent the period from 1968 to 1971 devising still another variant of armed *dau tranh* [the armed struggle movement], one that would rectify earlier shortcomings." This modified approach, which Pike characterized as a sort of "high-technology armed *dau tranh* strategy," was unveiled in the Easter Offensive. Outmatching the defenders in tanks and long-range artillery, the North Vietnamese launched a massive invasion that was, concluded Pike's analysis, defeated because "air power prevented massing of forces and because of stubborn, even heroic, South Vietnamese defense." The attackers absorbed devastating losses, especially from airpower when preparing to attack. But most important was that "ARVN troops and even local forces stood and fought as never before."[6]

ALLIED INTELLIGENCE on the coming invasion started building up as early as November 1971, when data on enemy infiltration showed an unusual pattern developing. Over the previous three years infiltration into the area of the Central Highlands had been about 10 percent of total infiltration. Now it was running 27 percent. "Something's in the mill for the B-3 Front," Abrams observed. "There's bound to be some heavy fighting up there."[7]

Then he turned to the potential in the area of the DMZ, the B-5 Front, calling it "a variable." Since the bombing halt the enemy had kept "between eighteen and—right now he's got about twenty-three battalions in the DMZ. When he wants to get something going, he brings regiments out of Quang Binh Province, even division headquarters, across the DMZ or around the end of the DMZ and into western Quang Tri and Thua Thien. That's been his pattern," said Abrams. A MACV briefer further emphasized on 8 December that "the B-3 Front and northern Military Region 1 are the two areas in the Republic of Vietnam where the enemy currently possesses his greatest capability."

Lieutenant General James Hollingsworth, senior advisor in

Military Region 3, also anticipated trouble. "I think [Operation Lam Son] 719 is one of the most devastating blows that they've had," he said, looking at the enemy buildup. "And it just could be that they think you might be going to pull another 719 on them, and they're getting set."

As 1972 began, Abrams—reviewing all the indicators of impending combat that had been amassed—said of the enemy, "I feel *very* strongly that he's going to try to materialize all that we have seen here, in some way, in the course of 1972." However, Abrams felt, "We're in about as good a shape as we've ever been in intelligence, especially this far ahead." All this had also been reported to Washington and covered with the field commanders, and with the Vietnamese Joint General Staff as well. President Nixon reacted by announcing that 70,000 more U.S. troops— the largest single increment of the war—would be withdrawn from Vietnam by 1 May. Abrams was philosophical. "On the one hand," he told his field commanders, "we've got Giap's great campaign coming up. On the other hand, we've got the great redeployment thing coming up. There's a tendency in there for some conflict."[8]

One conflict was that it was now necessary to retain those whose skills were most needed, regardless of how long they had been in Vietnam, a change from earlier practice. "There's no way to meet these reductions," Abrams explained to his field commanders, "and still be able to do our job in an effective way and handle everybody on an equal basis. It cannot be done." Abrams let that sink in, then continued: "But there isn't any equity in the world anyway—never has been. It's a dream. What's the equity between an 11 Bravo in a squad and another fellow the same age running a Xerox machine here in MACV Headquarters?[9] What kind of equity is that? Both being paid the same—same grade, one out there humping around in the damn bamboo and booby traps, and—w-e-l-l, equity is a very elusive thing."

In North Vietnam, General Vo Nguyen Giap had just delivered a speech in which he said, "We must fight with determination to win in order to ensure victory, which is near." Adding that "a costly battle is ahead" and that it would involve "much sacrifice and heartache," Giap closed with his own version of "light at the end of the tunnel": "Victory is in sight."[10]

In Military Region 1 the South Vietnamese were in the process of fielding a new division, designated the 3rd ARVN Division, to help compensate for the withdrawal of so many American troops from that critical area. The unit was formally established 1 October 1971 in Quang Tri Province, beginning with seven battalions transferred from other outfits—including the highly regarded 1st ARVN Division—and two newly formed battalions.[11] In early January it was at about 80 percent strength and scheduled to be fully deployed by April. Another new unit being formed, also in Quang Tri, was the 20th Tank Squadron, South Vietnam's only medium tank unit armed with U.S. M-48 tanks.

In each of the four military regions there was now functioning what was called an operational support coordination group. There, air liaison officers (both U.S. and Vietnamese), Army aviation elements, an Air Force advisory team, fire support coordinators, intelligence and operations staff elements, plus logistics, and an Arc Light targeting team were prepared to pull together and apply most effectively the full range of available fire support, thereby correcting a major deficiency encountered in Lam Son 719. These had all been exercised.

"The Vietnamese," said Abrams, "here again, as there's always been, there are deficiencies, inadequacies, inadequate performances, and so on, but the state of readiness, the alertness and activity on the part of the armed forces here in this country is the highest that I've ever seen it, even though there's some that are still asleep at the switch. You're never going to *eliminate* it."

As for the Americans still in country, Abrams had twenty Inspector General teams out combing the country to check on the state of readiness, supplementing what the chain of command was doing. Given later assertions about the condition of the troops at this late stage of the war, what they found is instructive. "I just have to say I'm quite gratified—yeah, he found some things, and of course you've all found a lot more," Abrams told his field commanders, "but *really* the responsiveness of the chain of command, I think, is really quite excellent. The total is *good*. The word got out, right down to the bottom of the thing. People knew what the hell they were doing, and they were responding. I just think that that *part* of it is really quite healthy."

In February, CBS News correspondent Phil Jones filmed a report based on his visit to the 3rd Brigade of the 1st Air Cavalry Division, one of the few U.S. combat units still in Vietnam. Later MACV got a tape of the program and screened it during a WIEU. On the sound track there is the sound of rotor blades as Jones is helicoptered to the field along with Brigadier General James Hamlet, the brigade commander. "You always hear about the protesters and the potheads who are back in the rear areas," Hamlet is heard saying, "but you ask *these* men how *they* feel about their mission. They have volunteered for the most dangerous job left in Vietnam, going into the bush every day looking for the enemy."[12]

When Jones got out with the troops, he found them pretty outspoken. "In the past ten years we've lost a lot of American lives here in Vietnam," said one, "and to just toss them out the window and say 'to hell with it,' that's pretty low. And these are just a different caliber of people than what's out in the world. What you see on the streets in D.C. is pretty disgraceful. But here, I think, is what America should see. These are the *men,* not those freaks or fakes or whatever you want to call them. These are *men*." A trooper from the division's Ranger company spoke proudly of his unit, emphasizing that "the war's not over. Since we're here, I think we have to be professional. And this company is the most professional company in Vietnam."

The broadcast closed with Hamlet's tribute to his men: "From my point of view, the Vietnam story is the story of the American soldier who fights so well and often gets so little credit for it."[13]

After the screening before an appreciative WIEU audience, the MACV Information Officer added a footnote. "Jones, when he finished the film, he said to General Hamlet, 'You know, I'm not so sure that Cronkite is going to put this on.'" Someone pointed out that Cronkite had been in China when the broadcast aired. "*That's* what happened," said Abrams delightedly. "Like when the U.N. decided to support South Korea, the Soviets were out."[14]

A senior MACV officer, just returned from Washington, reported that "all the Secretary could say, when I was back for the commanders conference, was 'don't let a scandal occur in a PDO yard.' They're not thinking about the security of the troops." Things—the stuff piled up in property disposal offices—rather than people were the priority. "I guess the truth of it is," suggested Fred Weyand, "they don't want a scandal of any kind." "That's right—'just don't make no mistakes,'" someone agreed. "That's what the sergeant told me when I came here in 1968: 'Sir, you'll be all right. Just don't make no mistakes.'"[15]

As far as making mistakes went, Abrams had some advice for his field commanders. "About this coming campaign by the Communists," he said. "You know, when the crunch gets on, and some things go wrong, always there's some fellows around that want to put the old dead cat at your door, and say that you did that. I just ask all of you—when the crunch comes, let's not spend *any* time trying to put the dead cat at anybody's door. Let's just get the damn problems solved."

As early as January 1971 Seventh Air Force had been extremely concerned about the MiG threat and how that was tied in with enemy radar coverage. "It's a damn dismal picture," said one senior airman. "We just don't pick 'em up. We don't have the radar coverage. He's got GCI" meaning ground control intercept radar, "and we don't know he's coming." As a consequence Seventh Air Force feared the loss of a B-52.

By August 1971 the dimensions of the problem were clear,
centered in particular on the domestic political situation in the
United States, which meant scant chance of gaining any new
authorities, even for protective purposes. "Jack's probably seized
with some of these 'try harder' messages from Washington," said
Weyand one morning when General John Lavelle, then commanding Seventh Air Force, was missing from a WIEU. "It's
really gotten kind of ridiculous. We keep asking for authorities
to do things, and they keep sending them back. And they always
end up with 'What more assistance do you need from us? From
your faithful friends.' "

In October Lavelle told Abrams, "I'm coming to you with
a study—it'll probably be ready next week—we've been working and working like hell. Our conclusion is, and I think we're
going to give you a professional job this time, and not motherhood, that when they come down there, you're going to have
to get 'em on the ground or you're going to give up a B-52 or
a C-130, 'cause we *can't* get them in the air. The distance is too
short, the terrain masks our radar with the mountains—they
pop up to shoot and get out of there before we can get 'em."

Within days Admiral McCain at CINCPAC cabled the JCS
Chairman asking for additional authorities to deal with this
problem, specifically permission to engage any MiG, whether
airborne or on the ground, in North Vietnam below 19 degrees
north, and permission to destroy GCI radars south of 20 degrees
north when they were controlling MiG activity against friendly
forces.[16] Abrams soon followed up with a message to McCain
going on record that "the constraints of existing rules of engagement," along with other factors, "add up to a very serious
and unacceptable situation. The odds are heavily stacked against
our ability to continue to prevent a shootdown of one of our
aircraft unless we destroy the enemy aircraft before it attacks."

Abrams asked for immediate authority to conduct a preemptive strike to destroy enemy MiG aircraft at Bai Thuong, Quan Lang, and Vinh.[17] Permission was denied.

"What we're going to have to do, Jack," Abrams told Lavelle, "is see if there're some other ways of working the problem. And this thing you bring out, what's it costing us [in terms of sorties devoted to protecting reconnaissance aircraft]? The Secretary of Defense's solution to this is that—don't send the aircraft where these MiGs can get to. I'm surprised we didn't think of *that* one."

The restrictive rules of engagement caused Abrams to think of a hunting analogy. "The difference between a sportsman and a game poacher—the game poacher will get 'em sitting on the water. And the sportsman, he just won't do that. He takes them on the wing. And that's what we are—we're sportsmen."

During one week in mid-December the enemy fired five SA-2 missiles at allied aircraft operating over North Vietnam or near the Laotian border, downing one F-4, the sixth aircraft loss of the year. When this was briefed, Abrams asked about an F-105 shot down earlier. Lavelle, who had talked to the pilot and learned that they had not had any warning, explained the situation: "Apparently the tactics they're using is to home in and get their azimuth, sir, by tracking the aircraft without turning on their Fan Song equipment." Fan Song was the fire direction radar at the missile site. Instead of that, the North Vietnamese were using another radar, an area-coverage type, to align their missiles without giving the warning that turning on the Fan Song would provide. "As a result of that," said Lavelle, "they have their azimuth problem all worked out. They can go ahead and fire the missile without turning the Fan Song on until the last minute, the last twenty seconds, before engagement. So as a result of that the crews getting the signal don't have time to react."[18]

These developments appeared so threatening that the general running the Strategic Air Command, under whose control the

B-52s operated, sent a message in which he threatened to pull
back all the big bombers on the premise that the threat environment was now too hostile to risk them on missions. "I am
deeply concerned about the potential ramifications," Abrams cabled McCain. "The issuance of an order which materially and
suddenly alters the application of combat power to an ongoing
mission without prior consultation with the field commander is
in itself disturbing. Perhaps even more serious are the implications of force employment which are involved." Abrams described recent air missions in which Seventh Air Force had
accepted high risks without hesitation in order to get the job
done. "The whole psychology of force employment in SEA
[Southeast Asia] is involved in the CINCSAC decision to withdraw his force from the threat area. If too great a reluctance to
risk losses becomes the dominant psychology in SEA, it should
be a matter of the highest concern. Such a psychology is infec-
tious and could have widespread impact."[19] Soon the orders
were changed and the B-52s went back to work.

In mid-January 1972 a briefer again described MiGs being
vectored to targets—friendly aircraft aloft—by GCI radar.
Abrams turned the discussion to consideration of the impending
enemy offensive. "Now, Jack," he said to Lavelle, "say this thing
gets going up here in the northern part of the country in March
or April, something like that. This territory in here is all going
to really be part of the battle. It'll have SAMs, you've got the
Dong Hoi airfield in here, and so on. I think we ought to be
studying now the kind of authorities we want for that period."
Abrams stressed that he meant authorities to attack the range of
threatening enemy installations, "including that airfield, including their GCI, including the SAMs—the whole thing."

Clearly Abrams was looking for authority to do more, not
ways to bend the existing rules. "We'll get those things about
'use all your existing authorities to the fullest' and so on" from
Washington, he speculated, "but that ain't gonna work. It *won't*
work. So we better start studying this now on what we're going

to want and what we're going to need, for that, and start working on it." Turning to Potts, Abrams called for "an assessment
of what's developing and the authorities we require, and when,"
to be provided within the week.

Soon Abrams, after briefing Bunker and Deputy Ambassador
Berger on what he was requesting, cabled urgent representations
to Washington of his need for additional authorities to counter
the coming enemy offensive. The three men had gone over the
message line by line, agreeing that Abrams needed authority for
fighter aircraft to strike enemy MiGs on the ground at Dong
Hoi, Vinh, and Quan Lang, and to strike active ground control
intercept radars in North Vietnam below 20 degrees north.
Abrams also asked authority to have fighters strike any occupied
SAM site within range of the DMZ, to emplace sensors in the
DMZ, and for emergency use of aircraft in support of limited
RVNAF cross-border operations.

"The stakes in this battle will be great," Abrams told the
JCS. "If it is skillfully fought by the Republic of Vietnam, supported by all available U.S. air, the outcome will be a major
defeat for the enemy, leaving him in a weakened condition and
gaining decisive time for the consolidation of the Vietnamization
effort. We are running out of time in which to apply the full
weight of air power against the buildup. The additional authorities requested are urgently needed."[20]

Stressing that he expected the major action to occur in the
area just north and south of the DMZ, Abrams closed with an
observation. "In the final analysis, when this is all over, specific
targets hit in the southern part of North Vietnam will not be a
major issue. The issue will be whether Vietnamization has been
a success or a failure."

"Good," said Ambassador Bunker when the full text of the
message had been read. "If you want to add that I've seen it
and concur, glad to have you do it." Abrams discussed plans to
have the senior field commanders in and to show them the
message. "I will not provide any of them with a copy. I want

them to get the flavor of it. As messages go, this is probably the
most unequivocal message we've ever sent—on the situation.
But I think the evidence is very clear." Bunker agreed: "I think
it's time to be unequivocal, because there's so much at stake."
On 20 January the message was dispatched to the Joint Chiefs
of Staff.

Six days later Abrams got an answer. Some authorities were
granted for immediate execution and some for standby execution later. The most crucial—those having to do with strikes
against MiG airfields, active GCI radars, SAM sites, and logistics
facilities—were all "pending approval." Two requests, to put
sensors in the DMZ and to provide emergency air support to
RVNAF cross-border operations, were approved only until 1
May. To call the JCS response modest would grossly understate
the case. One significant authority granted was for conduct—
again only until 1 May—of tac air strikes against enemy troop
concentrations in the northern portion of the DMZ. A similar
request for tac air, naval gunfire, and artillery strikes against
North Vietnamese artillery and rocket sites within range was also
"pending approval, although approval was given to conduct tac
air strikes against 130mm guns north of the DMZ—but only
during a single forty-eight-hour period of the COMUSMACV's
choice, and not later than 17 February."

Admiral Moorer recalled the frustrations of those times:
"Three times the JCS told the Administration that the tanks
being massed north of the DMZ should be hit, and each time
we were told no, that would be a violation of the political agreement Harriman made in Geneva. Then [after the offensive] Senator Margaret Chase Smith said to me, 'Admiral, the intelligence
people never knew about those tanks.' "[21]

But—a very significant development—augmentation of
U.S. air and naval forces in theater had begun. Eighteen F-4s
arrived from Clark Air Base in the Philippines. Provisions were
made for a minimum of two carriers to be maintained on Yan-
kee Station, with a third on forty-eight-hour alert status and a

fourth en route from the United States. The monthly B-52 sortie rate was increased from 1,000 to 1,200, with additional aircraft positioned on Guam sufficient for a surge effort to 1,500. (And that proved to be only a beginning; by June the rate skyrocketed to 3,150, the peak for the entire war.)[22]

Pacific Fleet had placed a cruiser, two guided missile destroyers, and another destroyer on seventy-two-hour alert, ready to reinforce the naval gunline off the coast of South Vietnam. Additional P-3 aircraft were standing by to augment Market Time coastal patrols if needed, and supplemental C-130 and C-141 cargo aircraft were also on standby. The entire American military establishment was geared up and involved, watching to see how Abrams would conduct his last great battle. "The VC side of it is over," said the visiting Sir Robert Thompson. "The people have rejected the VC." Now it was going to be just plain old hard-nosed conventional warfare in a fight to the death.

20

Easter Offensive

On 5 February—based on intelligence of the enemy's continued buildup and the positioning of his major troop units as reviewed with Admiral McCain—General Abrams made a determination that the enemy offensive had in fact begun, a judgment that triggered some of his standby authorities to retaliate. Thus, with all in readiness for the coming offensive, MACV brought to bear on the enemy buildup everything—within the still restrictive rules of engagement—it had. Tactical air sorties, gunships, and B-52 strikes were brought in practically nonstop. As Abrams met with his senior field commanders, a forty-eight-hour maximum effort was begun that concentrated all available airpower against the B-3 Front in the Central Highlands. Then, after a mandatory twenty-four-hour Tet cease-fire, the same thing was applied in MR-1.

"We've got a twenty-four-hour flow of aircraft now," confirmed General Lavelle, "and we can keep the flow now. It's set up, it's scheduled, so there's something every few minutes. And we just keep it coming and change the target area, so whenever General Abrams makes a decision as to where to put the weight of effort, or where to go next, we've already got the flow of aircraft."

These initiatives and others had, it appeared, some significant effect in delaying the enemy's planned attacks. "I think what will happen over the next four or five months—the enemy will make a military effort against South Vietnam which is the greatest military effort of which he is capable," Abrams said on 10 February. "I don't know when it will begin. It could *now* begin any day. It could be tomorrow."

When, despite allied expectations, the enemy still had not attacked, *that* became an issue. Abrams described a visit from Peter Osnos, "the *Washington Post* fellow," thus: "The wicket he appears to be on is that, for some insidious political reason, we have created the myth of this impending campaign." There was not much meeting of the minds. "I'm sure he probably feels that I feel that he's a scurrilous *shit,*" Abrams told Sir Robert Thompson.

Meanwhile President Thieu, faced with the impending battle, still had to be concerned about being undermined domestically as Nguyen Cao Ky took the preinvasion period as an opportunity for some further plotting. At a private home in Dalat on 10 March, reported Lieutenant General Ngo Dzu, Ky chaired a strategy session that decided to concentrate efforts against General Duong Van Minh and his supporters so that Ky could emerge as the only real rival to Thieu. "It was determined that Thieu enjoyed such strong support by the US that overt opposition to him would be fruitless," said a report. "Further, that it would complicate getting subsequent US support for Nguyen Cao Ky." Among those reportedly present were Lieutenant General Nguyen Duc Thang, former National Police Director Major General Nguyen Ngoc Loan, and Lieutenant General Nguyen Bao Tri.[1]

Allied forces took one significant casualty even before the main battle began. General John D. Lavelle, commanding Seventh Air Force, was found to have ordered a number of preplanned "protective reaction" strikes against targets in North

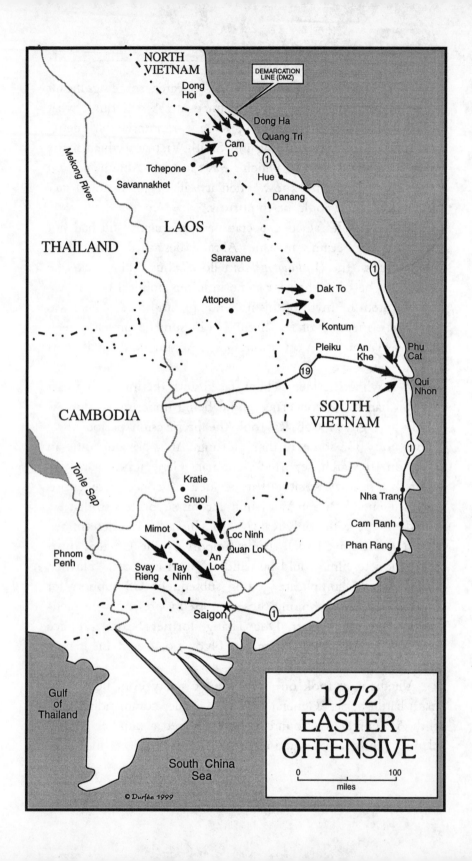

NORTH
VIETNAM

DEMARCATION
LINE (DMZ)

Dong
Hoi

Dong Ha
Quang Tri

Cam
Lo

1

Tchepone

Hue

Savannakhet

Danang

Mekong River

LAOS

THAILAND

Saravane

Attopeu

Dak To

Kontum

Pleiku

An
Khe

Phu
Cat

19

Qui
Nhon

CAMBODIA

SOUTH
VIETNAM

1

Kratie

Snuol

Nha Trang

Mimot

Loc Ninh

Cam Ranh

Quan Loi

Phan Rang

An
Loc

Svay
Rieng

Tay
Ninh

Tonle Sap

Phnom
Penh

Saigon

1

Gulf
of
Thailand

1972
EASTER
OFFENSIVE

0   100

miles

South China
Sea

© Durfée 1999

Vietnam, thereby violating the rules of engagement then in effect. The offense was compounded by the fact that false reports, representing these as genuine protective reactions, were subsequently filed. Summoned home by the Air Force Chief of Staff, Lavelle was relieved of his command and retired in two-star rank. Said Abrams, agreeing that Lavelle had "acted improperly," rules were a way of life in Vietnam. In a purely military sense, he acknowledged, some of those rules looked silly, but "if you are going to hold it together, they must be followed."[2] Lavelle's successor, General John Vogt, arrived just in time for Easter.

AT NOON ON 30 March 1972 the long-anticipated enemy offensive began in Military Region 1 with widespread attacks by fire. By midnight about 4,000 rounds of mortar, 122mm rocket, and 122mm, 130mm, and 152mm artillery fire had inundated friendly fire bases across the front. The next day a heavy ground attack struck Quang Tri combat base and Cam Lo was heavily attacked. Friendly troops were withdrawn from a crescent of fire support bases as enemy tanks were engaged by allied armor south of the Cam Lo River. In an early report to Admiral Moorer, Abrams advised that "the enemy's offensive in Quang Tri Province involves a total of ten infantry and five artillery regiments" from the 304th and 308th NVA Divisions.[3]

This offensive, the enemy told his cadres, was intended to "gain decisive victory in 1972" by means of "wide-spread military attacks coordinated with mass popular uprisings," actions that would "totally change the face of the war in South Vietnam." As the planned offensive neared, recalled North Vietnam's historians, "a seething, excited atmosphere of moving forward to battle existed, similar to that during the early days of 1965 and during the spring of 1968."[4]

Quickly a second prong of the enemy offensive thrust at the Central Highlands and, a day later, yet a third targeted Loc Ninh in Binh Long Province, about 100 kilometers north of Saigon. The defending forces there were quickly overwhelmed and withdrew under heavy pressure toward An Loc to the south.[5] Soon the 325th NVA Division, North Vietnam's last remaining division in the North, was fixed in the Vinh area, 240 kilometers south of its usual location near Hanoi. Six enemy divisions had attacked on three fronts. "It's a *full court press,*" Abrams almost exulted.

After a week President Nixon decided to retaliate for this enemy aggression by launching a strong air offensive in the North. "At 1800 it will be announced that we're striking in North Vietnam," General Weyand said in Saigon. "The wording was given to us from Washington to be put out here, and it's very terse. It simply says it began—commenced."

Two weeks into the offensive John Vann wrote an assessment that he mailed to a number of friends. "There is very little assistance being provided [to the enemy] in I, II, and III Corps by the local forces, and the enemy's infrastructure plays hardly any role at all," he reported. "The explanation for the latter is fairly simple. The existing infrastructure in South Vietnam hardly deserves its name or notoriety. The overwhelming number of the individuals now called members of the infrastructure no longer reside in populated areas, but instead exist in the base areas, carry weapons and are largely indistinguishable from other military personnel."

What was under way, then, was a straightforward conventional invasion on multiple axes. Even at this early stage, and there was much, much hard fighting ahead, Vann forecast the outcome. "It is quite predictable," he wrote, "that their regular forces will both be defeated and will suffer such heavy casualties and losses of equipment as to be ineffective for the next one to two years."[6]

In MR-1 the first five days of heavy assaults on the northern crescent of fire bases resulted in enemy advances as far south as the Dong Hai River, but there ARVN resistance stiffened and the enemy paused to regroup and resupply. A later history of

PAVN acknowledged the effective fight put up by ARVN defenders. "Relying on defensive fortifications already in place and on their reinforced troop strength," it recalled, "the enemy organized a defensive system consisting of three centers—Dong Ha, Ai Tu, and La Vang-Quang Tri. Hundreds of tanks and armored personnel carriers formed a barrier of steel surrounding these bases. Artillery fire bases and tank guns fired scores of thousands of rounds into our positions. All types of tactical aircraft and B-52 strategic bombers dropped hundreds of tons of bombs. Because the enemy had increased his troop strength and his fire support, and because he had changed his defensive plan, the wave of assaults made by our troops on 9 April was not successful."[7]

Sir Robert Thompson noted that the enemy had made only eighteen miles in three weeks, "not exactly an electric advance."[8] When the assault resumed, however, Quang Tri City was captured on 1 May and evacuation of FSB Nancy was forced two days later. The proximate cause of these reverses was withdrawal of the 20th Armored Squadron, ordered by 1st Armored Brigade commander Colonel Nguyen Trong Luat without notifying either higher headquarters or adjacent units. This move spooked other friendly forces into displacing prematurely and opened a convenient hole through which the attacking NVA drove deep into friendly lines.[9]

Merle Pribbenow, who translated the PAVN history, noted a lost opportunity. "The North Vietnamese were so afraid that the U.S. might launch an amphibious assault against North Vietnam itself that for some time they held back their entire strategic reserve—two divisions, six main force regiments, and a provisional division formed using cadet officers from all their military schools—to defend against a possible attack against the 'panhandle' of southern North Vietnam rather than committing this force to the offensive. Those two reserve divisions," Pribbenow concluded, "could have made a real difference in the northern

theater if they had been committed immediately when Quang
Tri fell. The South Vietnamese would have had a very difficult
time defending Hue against a PAVN force including an additional two strong, fresh divisions."

Whether a possible amphibious assault into North Vietnam—
rumors of which Pribbenow heard floating around Saigon at the
time—were deception plans or something seriously being considered, he deduced from the PAVN history that they were in
either case "very effective in tying down significant North Vietnamese forces which could otherwise have been committed to
the offensive."[10]

MACV was dependent on two corporations, Federal Electric
and Pacific Architects & Engineers, for communications and
utilities, and they still had civilians in Quang Tri running those.
"Only one civilian asked out," reported a briefer. "He went to
Can Tho and a volunteer replaced him. And these guys—we're
all just amazed at them. They're sticking in there and pitching.
All the way through, and they're civilians."[11]

George Jacobson said he had lost one man he really couldn't
afford to lose, Norm Fernstall, who had to go back to Washington to appear before the Kennedy committee on refugees.
"Yeah," sympathized Abrams, "I think that's understandable. After all, our Senate has its serious business that it must continue,
an august body, and functioning of government's not going to
stop because of this."

At the end of the third week Abrams brought his field commanders in to review the situation and give it a little perspective.
"There's been some poor performances," he acknowledged.
"But there *always* have been poor performances—in war or anything else. And I think that there always will be. You've got a
few guys do great, few guys who are sort of satisfactory most of
the time, and then you've got a few guys that are just miserable.
But in this thing now, until this is over, there's no point—
you've just got to accept the fact that there're going to be some

poor performances. The trouble is that you're doing it with human beings. If you didn't have them, you wouldn't run into that. Some poor performances are not going to lose it. It's the *good* performances that are going to win it."

"I *doubt* the fabric of this thing could have been held together without U.S. air," Abrams told his commanders. "But the thing that had to happen before that is the Vietnamese, some numbers of them, *had* to stand and fight. If they didn't do that, *ten times* the air we've got wouldn't have stopped them. So—with *all* the screwups that have occurred, *and* with all the bad performances that have occurred—they've been there, but we wouldn't be where we are this morning if some numbers of the Vietnamese hadn't decided to stand and fight."

On 24 April Abrams cabled Laird his personal assessment of the situation. "The North Vietnamese have launched from their sanctuary in NVN an all-out effort against the Republic of Vietnam," he began. "They are holding nothing back. Their last reserve division has been moved south near the DMZ and can enter the battle within two to four days after receiving orders." Four divisions and an independent regiment had already been brought down from North Vietnam, joining the seven divisions, twenty-two independent regiments, and seven artillery regiments already in South Vietnam. "It has been a conventional warfare battle employing the most sophisticated weapons."

"Overall, the South Vietnamese have fought well under extremely difficult circumstances. There has been a mixture of effective and ineffective performance, as in any combat situation, but on the whole the effective far outweighs the ineffective. Thus far the South Vietnamese have prevented the enemy from achieving his major objectives." One major improvement from the battles of Lam Son 719 the previous year was integration of air, armor, artillery, and infantry into a coherent whole. "This has been outstanding," said Abrams. "They have made great progress in this area during the past year in particular."

Perhaps most gratifying of all, given the earlier problems, was that "leadership at the presidential level has been outstanding. President Thieu has provided sound guidance to the Joint General Staff, has made prompt decisions, and has made his personal presence felt by timely visits to combat areas."[12]

WHILE FIERCE GROUND fights were raging along the DMZ, in the Central Highlands, and on the approaches to Saigon, an air and naval campaign of unprecedented ferocity was taking the war to the North Vietnamese. President Nixon ordered available fleet and air elements nearly doubled by rapid reentry into the combat zone of multiple squadrons of combat and supporting aircraft, including a hundred more B-52s—so many that on Guam one whole runway had to be closed for use as a parking lot—and more than fifty naval combatants.[13] Air Force, Navy, and Marine Corps tactical air came streaming into the theater from the continental United States, Hawaii, Korea, Japan, Okinawa, and the Philippines. From 35 tactical air squadrons— USAF, USN, and VNAF—the total increased to 74, including five USMC; they generated more than 55,000 sorties through early June. B-52s contributed another 4,759 devastating sorties, and fixed-wing gunships many more, with the daily average of tac air sorties rising from about 380 to more than 650 and B-52 sorties going from 33 a day to 150. Six aircraft carriers were assigned, putting four on station at all times. On the naval gunline at the high point three cruisers and thirty-eight destroyers provided gunfire support.[14] In a campaign designated "Linebacker," these forces began intensive bombing of targets in North Vietnam, including military facilities in and near the key cities of Hanoi and Haiphong, as well as round-the-clock support for South Vietnam's defending forces.

Soon air strikes brought to a halt all rail traffic south of Hanoi. On 8 May the MACV briefer stated that "pilots reported sixteen bombs out of twenty on the power plant. If there're any lights burning in Hanoi tonight, they'll be candlepower." Ad-

vances in technology since the bombing of North Vietnam earlier in the war were now providing greater accuracy and a
humanitarian dividend as well. Newly introduced laser-guided
bombs made it possible to take out in a single attack such point
targets as key bridges that had withstood hundreds of attempts
to destroy them with conventional munitions.[15] "And with the
smart bombs," reported Seventh Air Force, "we don't have any
problem with the civilian population."

Beginning 9 May all the major North Vietnamese ports were
mined. It took only a minute, literally, for nine Navy aircraft off
the *Coral Sea,* roaring in at 400 knots only 400 feet off the deck,
to put 36 Mark 52 mines—huge magnetic things weighing
1,100 pounds and packing 625 pounds of high explosive—in at
Haiphong, the first target hit and North Vietnam's most important seaport. Over successive days the lesser ports were
sowed, with all mines set to activate at 9 A.M. on 12 May. "It
took us eight years to get permission" to mine Haiphong harbor,
said Admiral Moorer, Chairman of the Joint Chiefs of Staff.
"Afterward not one ship entered or left the harbor until we took
up the mines."[16]

This aerial bombardment campaign, wrote Allan Millett,
"ruined North Vietnam's economy, paralyzed its transportation
system, reduced imports by 80 percent, and exhausted its air
defenses."[17] Commented Lieutenant General Dave Palmer perceptively, "Linebacker was not Rolling Thunder—it was war."[18]

Again the enemy agreed. "This war was different than the
first war of destruction," observed a history of PAVN, contrasting Linebacker with the Rolling Thunder campaign earlier in
the war. "This time the enemy massed larger forces and made
massive attacks right from the first day of operation, using many
types of modernized technical weapons and equipment."[19]

Abrams also paid warm tribute to what the air elements
achieved. "On this question of the B-52s and the tac air," he
told visiting Assistant Secretary of Defense Barry Shillito on 5
May, "it's very clear to me that—as far as my view on this is

concerned—that this government would now have fallen, and this country would now be gone, and we wouldn't be meeting here today, if it hadn't been for the B-52s and the tac air. There's absolutely no question about it." And, Abrams said a few days later, "I had my fifth anniversary the other day," meaning completion of five years in Vietnam, "and this air system is now running the best, and it is the most responsive, that it has *ever* been since I've been over here."

Hollingsworth strongly agreed from his perspective at An Loc, where since retreating from Loc Ninh the South Vietnamese had stubbornly held on. "These people here—the attitude of the commanders, not the soldiers, the attitude of the commanders has been, 'Well, goddamn it, we're in here and somebody's going to take care of us, so we'll just sit here on our goddamned ass and just wait'll they come.' I'm sure, and I feel strongly about this, that the little soldiers have done a magnificent job here, all on their own—for *survival*. It was a matter of either fighting or dying, and they said, 'Well, we might as well *fight*.' And they've fought. And the only reason we're still in here today is because of these little fellows keeping them [the enemy] out so we could kill them with firepower."

At about this same time, said a MACV briefer, Hanoi newspapers were reporting that North Vietnam had "reached a milestone in the air war against the United States. Hanoi claims that, since the war first began, they have downed a total of 3,500 American aircraft over North Vietnam. Included in this exaggerated claim is twelve B-52s." The U.S. count was then 944 fixed-wing aircraft and 10 helicopters lost over North Vietnam since reporting began on 5 August 1964.

IN EARLY MAY the South Vietnamese suffered a series of battlefield reverses so serious that Abrams cabled Laird that "the situation has changed significantly since my assessment of 24 April." In Military Region 1, Dong Ha had fallen, Quang Tri combat base had been evacuated, and Quang Tri City was threatened and would soon fall, overwhelmed by 40,000 attackers and outnumbered three to one. Farther south, Fire Support Bases Bastogne and Checkmate, important positions blocking Route 547 to Hue, also had fallen. In MR-2, the 22nd ARVN Division in the Tan Canh/Dak To area had performed poorly and suffered a costly defeat. In Binh Dinh Province the situation was also very serious, with the only remaining friendly position in the northern half of the province not expected to hold.[20] In MR-3, ARVN troops were hanging on at An Loc in what Douglas Pike called "probably the single most important battle in the war," a terrific struggle in which a heroic and successful defense ended General Giap's hopes for decisive victory in the campaign.[21] Ultimately the enemy would commit to these three attacks his entire combat force—fourteen divisions, twenty-six separate regiments, and a huge array of supporting armor and artillery—save for one division remaining in Laos.[22]

"Enemy staying power is his most effective battlefield characteristic," said Abrams. "It is based first on his complete disregard for the expenditure of resources, both men and matériel, and second on discipline through fear, intimidation, and brutality. An enemy decision to attack carries an inherent acceptance that the forces involved may be expended totally."[23]

Then Abrams set forth the crux of the changed situation. "The RVNAF capability to turn back the enemy offensive is now a function of two intangibles. The first is RVNAF resolve and will to fight. Although the will to fight among senior leaders in MR-1 continues to be strong, there are serious problems in this regard at the lower levels, and command and control is becoming increasingly difficult to maintain." The problems in Quang Tri were serious, said Abrams, "and may be beyond correction." The poor performance of the 22nd ARVN Division in MR-2 put the defense of Kontum City in doubt, but at An Loc and FSB Bastogne surrounded ARVN forces fought well. "Unless the ARVN forces hold on the ground and generate lucrative targets, US and VNAF air power cannot achieve their full effectiveness." The second factor, not yet discernible, was the amount of damage done to the enemy.[24]

Abrams closed with an unvarnished statement of the realities. "In summary of all that has happened here since 30 March 1972, I must report that as the pressure has mounted and the battle has become brutal the senior military leadership has begun to bend and in some cases to break. In adversity it is losing its will and cannot be depended on to take the measures necessary to stand and fight." Abrams cited two known exceptions—General Truong, commanding IV Corps, and the 1st Division's General Phu. "In light of this there is no basis for confidence that Hue or Kontum will be held."[25] Secretary Laird's reply to this evaluation showed that he understood the situation: "It is boiling down, as we have thought, to RVN will and desire."[26]

The next morning Bunker and Abrams met with President Thieu. Abrams showed Thieu the assessment he had sent to Washington the previous evening. Thieu read it carefully, then— said Abrams—described in "big arrow" fashion how the battle should be fought. When he finished, Abrams stated his conviction that the real problem was the effectiveness of South Vietnam's field commanders, then followed that with a detailed by name description of individuals who were not measuring up. "I told President Thieu," reported Abrams to Laird, "that it was my conviction that all that had been accomplished over the last four years was now at stake, and, at this stage, it was the effectiveness of his field commanders that would determine the outcome—either winning all or losing all."

Thieu interrupted the meeting at that point to issue instructions for all corps commanders to report to the Palace later that day. Then Thieu offered the view that if Hue and Kontum could hold for four days, they would have won the battle. Again Abrams expressed a contrary outlook. "I told the President that no one should think in any less terms than six weeks more of heavy, bloody fighting and maybe more. This is a battle to the death, the Communists have planned it that way and will not quit until they have been totally exhausted."[27]

That same day Abrams found it necessary to transmit a grim order to his field commanders: "Effective immediately no Vietnamese commander will be airlifted out of a unit defensive position by U.S. fixed-wing aircraft or helicopter unless such evacuation is directed personally by the RVNAF corps commander. Inform your counterpart."[28]

Meanwhile, recorded H. R. Haldeman in his diary for 1 May, he had learned in a telephone call from Nixon, then at John Connally's house in Texas, that "both he [Nixon] and Henry [Kissinger] agree that regardless of what happens now, we'll be finished with the war by August, because either we will have broken them or they will have broken us, and the fighting will be over. There still seems to be some possibility of negotiation or a cease-fire because it's quite possible, maybe even probable, that the North Vietnamese are hurting even worse than the South Vietnamese, and that both sides may be ready to fold."[29]

Soon thereafter Abrams sketched the nature of the fight and its effects on the enemy for visiting Secretary Shillito. "Every one of these regiments that are in the fight have already been engaged," he said. "It's just an all-out onslaught, and the losses on both sides—I mean, *he's* losing tanks like he didn't care about having any more, *and* people, *and* artillery, *and* equipment. The level of violence, and the level of brutality, in this whole thing right now is on a scale not before achieved in the war in Vietnam. And that's what you're in."

WITH DISASTER IMPENDING in Military Region 1, President Thieu made a dramatic command change, moving Lieutenant General Ngo Quang Truong from MR-4 to take charge in the North. Said General Vien of Lieutenant General Hoang Xuan Lam, who was relieved, "Confronted with conventional warfare . . . he was at a loss." Later Vien was understanding, if not sympathetic, remarking that "the influence of politics on officers of General Lam's generation and their very background perhaps did not contribute to the cultivation of military leadership required by the circumstances."[30]

The effects of the change in command were equally dramatic, and nearly instantaneous. "General Truong is a *symbol* in that part of the country of all that's good in Vietnamese terms," said Abrams. "He went up there day before yesterday to take command. And when he went to Hue, the first thing he did was to get on the radio and television. He told them that they were going to defend Hue. It would not fall. And at the end of it he called on every soldier to report back to his unit—*now.* And those who failed to do it would be shot."

It was not only Truong's personal leadership and charisma that turned things around, but also his professional approach to doing business. "Prior to his arrival we [the South Vietnamese] ran I Corps on the dial exchange telephone by personal calls from the corps commander to division commanders, and then never a staff follow-up to tell everybody else what was said to a particular division," observed General Fred Kroesen, the senior American advisor in MR-1. Things were different under Truong. "He's got the staff functioning for the first time *ever* in I Corps. General Truong has got that staff working, and there's a sense of urgency in the staff that's *never* been there before."

During the battles a new weapon system, the tank-killing TOW missile, was flown in from the United States. Initially, noted Abrams, "I gave twenty to the Marines and the 1st Division because they were the only troops I knew of that had stood and fought. I don't want these things in the hands of the enemy. And on the Airborne, I told General Kroesen [that] when General Truong will give me his personal assurance that they will not be abandoned on the battlefield, then I'll consider it."

In a later account the enemy also paid implicit tribute to Truong's professional competence. After Truong took command in Military Region 1, read a history of PAVN, "the enemy concentrated on consolidating his defensive line along the My Chanh River and utilized this line as a base to strike out to the east and west in order to sabotage our preparations to attack Hue. . . ." Due to intensive B-52 and naval gunfire, "our troops encountered many difficulties in maintaining their supplies." Then, "because we were slow to change our campaign tactics at a time when the enemy had strengthened his forces and solidified his defenses, our assault against the My Chanh defensive line . . . was unsuccessful, and our losses in that attack were twice those suffered during the two previous attacks." Fighting on that front had become "very complicated."[31]

SOMETIME DURING MAY, remembered an officer on the MACV staff, General Abrams arrived for a WIEU and began with an observation. "Every morning, when I walk over to my office from the quarters, I feel just like a company commander on the battlefield, tired and apprehensive. I haven't had enough sleep because the phone from Washington keeps ringing, and I know that there will be another battle waiting, another hill to be taken. And, sure as hell, there won't be enough ammo, the weather will be bad, and replacements not up yet. But all I will hear is, 'Abrams, get moving and take that hill.'" Abrams paused for a moment and with a broad smile looked around at everyone. "But, you know, I like it!"[32]

Colonel William F. Wollenberg was then in charge of preparing daily messages on the "Personal Assessment of the COMUSMACV." After one such message was dispatched, there came a query back: "Can the South Vietnamese hold?" Major General John Carley, the J-3, took it upon himself to draft a six-page reply. Abrams rejected it. Then Wollenberg was given the task. He wrote simply: "It looks to us like the job will get done."

Abrams looked at that, made one change, and the message was dispatched: "It looks to me like the job will get done."

SUBSEQUENTLY, AS the critical point approached on multiple fronts, Abrams determined to mass his most potent weapon, the B-52, for concentrated strikes in sequence on each battlefield in turn. On 10 May he cabled Fred Kroesen in MR-1, John Vann in MR-2, and Jim Hollingsworth in MR-3. "I want to use the three days, 11, 12, and 13 May," he told these commanders, "which we may have before the enemy attack to inflict as much damage as possible on the major enemy troop units and their supporting artillery. Therefore, I have decided to allocate the entire B-52 effort to MR-3 on 11 May, to MR-2 on 12 May, and to MR-1 on 13 May. This means that for two days between 11 and 13 May each of you will have no B-52 support and you must plan your tac air, naval gunfire, and artillery support accordingly. On the day that you have the entire B-52 effort, the targeting will be against enemy troop units posing the greatest threat to An Loc, Kontum, and the Hue area and their supporting artillery and not against the deep logistics areas. You should apply multiple strikes to major enemy troop locations with consecutive TOTs [time on target for each scheduled strike] on each rather than spreading the TOTs over a long period."[33] That concentration of force meant they'd be getting three B-52 sorties every fifty-five minutes, around the clock, for twenty-four hours.

"Frankly," said an Air Force officer of the B-52, "that's no longer an Air Force weapon. We fly the airplane, but the Army puts in the target request; they handle the clearing, etc. The only thing we do is hand out the air strike warning to our own aircraft, so they won't have bombs dumped on them."[34]

The results of this tactic were spectacular. Hollingsworth in particular thought they had been his salvation. When he got the word that Abrams was giving him the total sortie allocation, said Hollingsworth, "if it'd done any good to show my appreciation,

I'd have just jumped out of the damn helicopter. By God, it just saved us, that's all. And I'll say that your intelligence department must be awful damn good—that you knew that that was the time to go. We just couldn't hit her any better on this one."

The enemy saw it the same way. In a subsequent historical analysis the North Vietnamese acknowledged that during April and May "the enemy mobilized a large number of B-52 sorties to viciously attack our campaign rear areas." Thus "three waves of assaults against Binh Long City," apparently the enemy's designation for An Loc, "were all unsuccessful. Our units suffered heavy casualties and over half of the tanks we used in the battle were destroyed. On 15 May, after thirty-two days of ferocious combat, our troops ended the attack on Binh Long City."[35]

In the middle of these fearsome strikes Abrams held a commanders brief at which he spoke very frankly of what he had been telling the South Vietnamese. "For the last several years I've tried to maintain rapport with the Vietnamese that I work with. And I've tried not to do things that they would find insulting—always been kind of careful about that," he began. "But I wanted to tell you, in the last few weeks, in my conversations with General Vien, and with the President, I've said it *straight,* and called it for what it was worth. Just the other day General Vien was telling me about some equipment they wanted, and I told him that we were doing everything we could to get this equipment to them and so on. But I then went on to tell him, I said, '*Equipment* is not what you need. You need men that will *fight.* And you need *officers* that will fight, and will lead the men.' I said, 'No amount of *equipment* will change the situation. It's in the hands of *men,* and if they'll *fight,* and their officers will *lead* them, you've got—even today—you've got all the equipment you need.' I said, 'That's the trouble.' I said, 'I don't think you've lost a *tank* to enemy fire. You lost all the tanks in the 20th because the men abandoned them, led by the officers. You lost most of your artillery because it was *abandoned*

and people wouldn't fight.' Now I don't want you to go back
and tell your counterpart that I told the President off. That's not
why I'm telling you this. I want you to know the way I'm
conducting *my* business with the counterparts I have to deal
with, and I think it has to be straight with them. I'm never
insulting and so on, but it's a *fact*. And that's what we must talk
about are the facts."

While he had them there, Abrams had something he wanted
to say about the American advisors. "I just think that their performance has been magnificent," he said with feeling. "In fact,
it's probably the glue that's held this whole thing together. It's
not only the heroics involved in it, but real toughness and real
ability."

Apparently not everyone agreed. "Different fellows look at
it different ways," Abrams admitted. "And then we have that
great prophet, unfortunately dragged away from here, the former
ambassador to Gabon, who said that there was very little left for
advisors to do. And I want to tell you, if it wasn't for advisors,
none of us would be sitting here in Saigon today. We'd either
be in a PW enclosure, dead, or have managed to escape by
submarine, powerboat, or some other fucking thing! To Hong
Kong. That's what advisors are!"[36]

BY MID-MAY THE friendly situation was looking much more
favorable in the Highlands, in fact all around. "Since the fall of
Quang Tri," said Abrams, the enemy "really hasn't been able to
put anything together. Now you may say, 'Well, that's right. He
didn't plan to. He's just gathering stuff together and he will
eventually.' And maybe that'll happen. But we *do* know that the
divisions in here—the 308th, the 304th, and the 324 Bravo—
have taken really horrible losses." As for retaking Quang Tri,
suggested Abrams, "I think all we've got to do is keep JGS out
of it and let Truong develop a plan. And then it will be a good
one."

The tide of battle was now sweeping back the other way,

the outcome in fact decided; only some more hard fighting was needed to nail it down. Abrams and George McArthur discussed the situation, and McArthur put an interesting question. "You always hesitated to criticize Giap," he observed. "What about now?" Abrams recalled Cornelius Ryan's book about the last hundred days of World War II in Europe. "Those Germans knew the war was over," said Abrams, "they knew that all the decisions had been made, they knew they had lost. They knew they had no hope and they went ahead and just died. In a way I think we might be at that point now. Giap is a very resourceful fellow. But I think"—and here, said McArthur, Abrams was very emotional—"that what is going on now is just a lot of unnecessary killing."[37]

IN MR-1 THE ENEMY was stopped at the My Chanh River, the southern boundary of Quang Tri Province. Late in June the Airborne Division was airlifted south of the river and, attacking with other ARVN and Marine troops, drove the NVA back twenty kilometers to Quang Tri City.[38] "Beginning in late June 1972," observed the North Vietnamese in their later historical analysis, "combat on the Tri Thien Front became very complicated, with fierce back-and-forth fighting between our troops and the enemy."[39] Fielding three divisions against six of the enemy, Truong led a fight that lasted the rest of the summer. With Marines leading the way, he retook Quang Tri City. In late September the reconstituted 3rd ARVN Division began an operation to drive the enemy out of Tien Phuoc and, after a week of bitter fighting, retook the town.

At Kontum City the equivalent of three enemy divisions kept the city under siege for nearly two months. The airfield had to be closed because of enemy fire, and resupply was accomplished by airdrop. But the defenders—now the 23rd ARVN Division, a unit far superior to the routed 22nd Division—held on, inflicting casualties on the enemy estimated to exceed 16,000.[40] The performance of the South Vietnamese Air

Force had counted for a lot. "VNAF came into its own during the 1972 offensive," said a USAF advisor. "In the defense of Kontum the VNAF has been magnificent, absolutely magnificent."[41]

B-52s weighed in at Kontum in a decisive way as well. Late on 14 May the enemy broke through the seam between two defending regiments and began a series of mass assaults. Fortunately two B-52 strikes had been preplanned for that night. "The two B-52 strikes came exactly on time," recalled General Truong, "as planned, like thunderbolts unleashed over the masses of enemy troops. The explosions rocked the small city and seemed to cave in the rib cages of ARVN troops not far away. As the roar subsided, a dreadful silence fell over the scene. At dawn, ARVN search elements discovered several hundred enemy bodies with their weapons scattered all around. Kontum was saved."[42]

The corps commander in MR-2 had also been relieved, Lieutenant General Ngo Dzu giving way to Lieutenant General Nguyen Van Toan. John Vann credited the Territorial Forces, not the army, with much of what went right in MR-2. "The RF and PF, in most places, have performed quite well and were a much more stabilizing force than the ARVN," he reported.

Meanwhile at An Loc the defenders had withstood three months of constant bombardment in what General Hollingsworth called "this desperate, fanatic adventure on the part of Hanoi."[43] Attacks by fire reached a peak on 10 May when more than 7,600 rounds were received, part of more than 47,000 rounds during that month, bombardments punctuated by repeated tank and infantry attacks. General Truong called it "the longest and bloodiest siege of the war."[44] With the B-52 onslaught of 11 May the back of the enemy offensive was broken. Despite one attack after another by three divisions, An Loc could not be taken, and the enemy was left with more than 12,000 casualties to show for his efforts.

In MR-4 things had been much different, the fighting

confined to many attacks against outposts at widely scattered points. While still in command there, General Truong had taken the remarkable step of volunteering to give up forces to more hard-pressed regions, and soon the 21st Division was sent to MR-3 and the 4th Ranger Group to MR-1.

INEVITABLY DURING the offensive Alexander Haig made another of his numerous visits to Vietnam. He returned to tell President Nixon that "ARVN had not been outclassed or outfought as in the past" and later characterized Abrams's warning that the thing could be lost as "an alarmist message."[45]

Also during the Easter Offensive, at a General Conference of the United Methodist Church held in Atlanta, the majority of delegates approved a statement calling American involvement in the Vietnam War "a crime against humanity," then rejected a resolution that would have condemned "the appetite of North Vietnam to wage cruel and inhuman war."[46]

THE SOUTH VIETNAMESE lost more than 8,000 killed in action during the Easter Offensive, about three times that many wounded, and nearly 3,500 missing. During the campaign more than 53,000 men volunteered for military service and nearly 18,000 additional were conscripted, while more than 40,000 of those already serving deserted. Said General William McCaffrey, "The ARVN soldier emerges as a remarkable individual who perseveres in spite of great hardships. He has earned a victory."[47]

North Vietnam claimed, according to an official history published in Hanoi in 1980, that by July 1972 the NVA had "annihilated about 200,000 of the enemy" and "liberated and gained control of more than one million people."[48]

The North Vietnamese Army suffered more than 100,000 casualties in its attacking force of 200,000—perhaps 40,000 killed—and lost more than half its tanks and heavy artillery. It took three years to recover sufficiently from these losses to mount another major offensive, and in the meantime General

Vo Nguyen Giap found himself eased out as NVA commander.[49] A primary reason for Giap's downfall was probably the series of miscalculations ticked off by Lieutenant General Dave Palmer: "The Politburo had surmised that President Johnson would not send American troops to Vietnam in 1965; it had forecast a general uprising of the South Vietnamese people in 1968; it had depended on domestic politics tying Nixon's hands in 1972," he wrote. "It had been wrong each time. Those miscalculations had led to the failure of all three of Hanoi's overt offensives."[50]

On the allied side MACV intelligence officers nailed every significant enemy offensive on their watch, from mini-Tet in May 1968 through the Third Offensive in September, then Tet 1969 and the whole series of subsequent "high points" to the Easter Offensive of 1972. They tracked personnel infiltration down the Ho Chi Minh Trail to an accuracy of 1 percent, fixed the locations of enemy units and followed their movements, advised the Vietnamese, and with them developed highly capable interrogation and document exploitation centers.

As U.S. troops withdrew and other combat resources were cut back more and more, the importance of intelligence grew apace. It was key to making the most effective use of declining assets, and also to influencing the Vietnamese in their planning and deployments. "With this better intelligence," said Secretary of the Army Stan Resor, "General Abrams has been able to make more effective use, first, of the air power and then, secondly, of the forces we have there."[51] Clearly Potts was justified in his conviction that Vietnam was "an intelligence war."[52]

ONE IMPORTANT RESULT of the Easter Offensive was the relief from command of certain ARVN incompetents. Two corps commanders—Lieutenant General Lam and Lieutenant General Ngo Dzu—lost their jobs. Brigadier General Vu Van Giai, who had commanded the newly formed and ill-fated 3rd Infantry Division until its collapse a month into the battle, was not only relieved but also court-martialed and imprisoned. Giai was, it appeared, a victim of General Lam's shortcomings, a radically overextended span of control (at one point two of his own infantry regiments, two Marine brigades, four Ranger groups, an armor brigade, and all the province's Territorial Forces were under his command), and the inevitable fallibilities of a new division. Wrote Major General Hoang Lac sympathetically, "General Giai, a soldier with most of his life sleeping out in the jungle, was sentenced to five years in military confinement and imprisonment. Giai remained there until the NVA took over Saigon and put him in their camp, a fate undeserved for a good and brave soldier."[53]

The Marine Division commander was also relieved, and the commander of the 22nd Division simply disappeared. At the regimental level, the 56th Regiment was surrendered intact by its commander, Lieutenant Colonel Pham Van Dinh, who soon thereafter came on the airwaves urging other ARVN soldiers to come over to the enemy side.[54]

The problem in all such cases was to find replacements more capable, and more willing, than those who were relieved or became casualties. In the case of Truong, this brought South Vietnam's ablest combat leader to the point of decision. And in Brigadier General Nguyen Duy Hinh, who literally re-created the beaten and demoralized 3rd Division, real talent came to the fore.

AFTER THE WAR WAS OVER, General Truong wrote a thoughtful analysis of the Easter Offensive and its aftereffects. "The American response during the enemy offensive was timely, forceful and decisive," he affirmed. "This staunch resolve of the U.S. to stand behind its ally stunned the enemy. Additionally, it brought about a strong feeling of self-assurance among the armed forces and population of South Vietnam."[55]

"When the enemy offensive began," added Truong, "Vietnam's fate was in its own hands. President Thieu, the Joint General Staff and the corps commanders had to decide where, when, and how to fight." Much of that was of course dictated by the dimensions of the enemy offensive, but—as Truong also observed—on the part of the South Vietnamese "there was no change in strategy; the concept of securing all national territory continued to be the order of the day. Every area, every strongpoint, no matter how small or remote, had to be held 'at all cost.' "

Truong recalled President Thieu's strong insistence that "we would not yield even a pebble in Quang Tri or a handful of mud in Ca Mau to the enemy." On other occasions, many other occasions, Thieu had repeated and emphasized what he called his "four nos": "no coalition, no neutralization, no territorial concessions, and never let Communist forces operate openly in South Vietnam." Yet now, despite successful defense against the three major thrusts of the Easter Offensive, some lost territory could not be recovered. "South Vietnam had in effect lost a continuous, wide expanse of territory extending along the border from the DMZ to the northern Delta," wrote General Bruce Palmer, "an area which North Vietnam referred to as the 'Third Vietnam.' "[56]

Said Truong in retrospect of Thieu's rigid stance, "A more pragmatic leader would have recognized that the RVNAF simply did not have the resources to carry out such a policy, at least not without the full support of U.S. and [other allied] combat forces as in years past."[57] The validity of that judgment would become apparent in the next—and last—big offensive of the war.

21

Transition

By June it was known that Abrams, nominated to be next Army Chief of Staff, would soon be leaving Vietnam. The troops he commanded were down to only 69,000, and the requirement was that by 1 July they be reduced another 20,000. Planning and executing that withdrawal was among the last tasks Creighton Abrams undertook as his long service in Vietnam neared an end. The troops retained had to be capable of receiving and issuing a large amount of equipment being provided the South Vietnamese under "Project Enhance," a program to replace the heavy losses of the Easter Offensive. That largesse included M-48 tanks, TOW antitank missiles, and long-range 175mm guns.

A planning session resulted in little agreement on composition of the next redeployment increment. U.S. forces were already so greatly reduced that no one could see how to give up a single additional man. Abrams listened to the agonized discussion for a while, then went to the front of the room and explained the situation. "You know, gentlemen," he began, "this force withdrawal is not optional. We are going down and we will continue to go down till none of us are left. Now, we are going to do that, just as the President ordered, and even a little faster than the schedule calls for. Our job is to simply figure out how best to do it, not to argue about the mission."[1]

Abrams had a last session with the senior Korean officers in Vietnam. Their interpreter began by saying, "Before starting the briefing, sir, General Lee would like to express his feeling of regret at hearing the sad news about Mr. Vann." The night before, the helicopter carrying John Paul Vann from Pleiku to Kontum had crashed and Vann had been killed. When that report reached Creighton Abrams, he wordlessly put the telephone back in its cradle and, head down, just turned away. The next day Radio Hanoi, in a characterization Vann would undoubtedly have enjoyed, reported the death of "one of the most important and most cruel advisors" in South Vietnam.[2] Said a later Air Force history, "The flamboyant, the skilled, the incomparable John Paul Vann was dead. An era had ended."[3]

Two days later Abrams and Ambassador Bunker went to a memorial service for Vann in the chapel at Tan Son Nhut. There Vann was remembered in terms much like those used earlier by Lieutenant General William McCaffrey, so moved by Vann's valor in the battle for the Highlands that he cabled him, "Few soldiers in our history have had to cope with the challenges you face. I have never known anyone so uniquely qualified by courage, energy and ability to do a tough job. From where I sit, John Paul, you are a blooming hero."[4] Now, just as his last great battle was being won, Vann was gone.

At Abrams's final WIEU on 24 June, the agenda included the usual mix of political, military, economic, and logistical concerns. But first, perhaps as sort of a going away present for Abrams, General Potts announced a special presentation. It related to an enemy regiment stationed in North Vietnam. "About twenty minutes ago," he began, "we got a message that had been flashed by this regiment to its subordinates that perhaps is the strongest that I have ever seen concerning the conditions that they're undergoing there. We'd like to read that at this time."

Then a briefer read as follows: "From: The North Vietnamese 290th Reconnaissance Regiment. To: Unidentified regimental elements. Message No. 12. The enemy continues to strike many targets. In past times we have met with the staff of the Lao Dong Party, who are afraid that the violent sacrifices of recent weeks will scare the villagers and their families. Our forces urgently need guidance, but we have pointed out to the soldiers they are serving to hone the people to sharpness before they are completely routed. Even though they are bloody, our strength and health remain. We are still able to accomplish difficult tasks before their very eyes in order to get one last tremendous victory. We have ceaselessly met in the decided areas, and we have seriously reflected upon our losses. It is well we are side by side, even though we have been cut to ribbons. In order to analyze and talk over our problems, we must acknowledge that we cannot yet achieve our goals, and that we are slowly dying for a [word unclear] aim. We are prepared to meet the enemy, but the massive strikes by the B-52s happen outside of our influence. Detachments have risen up to accurse us and concentrate on every [word unclear] affected by the strikes. We try to slip away to the safe areas, but the air strikes also turn it into a wasteland and it continues to ebb away. Signed, Khu Li."[5]

Then, as usual in the WIEU, they covered the war in all its complexities. At the end, Abrams turned to Bunker. "Mr. Ambassador?" he asked. "Yes, I'd like a word, General Abrams," Bunker replied. "When you and I came here, a little more than five years ago, I was hoping we would exit *together*. I just want to say that these five years, I think, have been the most rewarding of a fairly long career that began with the horse artillery in 1916. And they certainly have been fateful years, for the Republic of Vietnam and for our country. I suppose, when the history of this war is written, it will be very clear that *no* country ever put as many restraints on itself as *we* did. And I think it's been probably the most difficult war that we've ever tried to fight. And it's been fateful for our country, because I think the question is whether we *have* the patience and the determination and the will to accept the responsibilities of power. Certainly the armed forces of the United States have shown determination and will and steadiness in a most difficult situation. I think it's clear—it's certainly clear to me—that without *your* leadership, and without what your colleagues have *done* here, there wouldn't *be* any Republic of Vietnam today. And this has been due to your leadership, to not only highest intelligence and *professional* skill, but to sensitivity, effectiveness, *with* what the Yankees call plain common sense. By *that* means you've gained the confidence and trust of the Vietnamese, which has been essential to success here. So we've all learned from *you*. I had a lot to learn, going back to the days of the horse artillery. And now that you're leaving, we all take great satisfaction and pride in the fact that you're taking over as Chief of Staff, the top position in the Army. And I think—you *know*, I don't have to tell you— that you leave with not only the great admiration but the greatest *affection* of all of us."

"*Thank* you, Mr. Ambassador," Abrams responded. "Let's go to lunch, gentlemen."

TRUONG CHARACTERIZED 1968–1972, coinciding with the years General Abrams was in command, as "the period of most intense fighting" in the war.[6] By the time Abrams departed, turning over MACV to his deputy, General Fred Weyand, there were only 49,000 U.S. troops left in Vietnam. At the zenith, early in 1969, there had been 543,400.[7] Thus Abrams had done something that may be unique in the history of warfare—he sent his army home before him.

During the four years of his command, the situation in Vietnam differed in almost every important respect from that of earlier years. Abrams himself, of course, had brought a different conception of the war to bear and had fought the war in a much different way than his predecessor. Beyond those fundamental and crucially important differences, however, were contrasts in a wide range of external factors bearing on the course of the conflict.

Earlier the troops under command had consisted primarily of the cream of the Regular Army, experienced and committed, whereas later the force was largely made up of men drafted or recruited (two-thirds of the total were voluntary enlistees) primarily to fight this war; remarkably, the performance level held up extremely well. A circumstance of almost unlimited funds and people gave way to increasing poverty in both. The forces that had expanded almost continuously were now relentlessly withdrawn. Public, congressional, and even media support of an earlier day gradually eroded as the efforts of that period produced no visible prospect of resolving the conflict, then dropped off precipitously once it was clear that the United States had opted out of the war. Societal problems of drug abuse, racial disharmony, and dissent, moderate in the early years, reached epidemic proportions in the United States and, inevitably, spilled over to the forces in the field. Cumulatively, these differences constituted one of the most difficult challenges to leadership in the military history of the United States, and eventually their effects were felt throughout the forces in every theater.

Said General John Vogt, who had taken command of Seventh Air Force virtually on the eve of the Easter Offensive, "When he left, General Abrams felt the ground situation was good, and secure at that point. The South Vietnamese Army was doing a damn good job by then, exhibiting professionalism. They were in there toe to toe, slugging it out, and winning. The enemy was beat on the ground."[8]

It was in these circumstances that, in the wake of the Easter Offensive, Creighton Abrams went home to become Army

Chief of Staff. "Some of the days are kinda long," he had once remarked of his service in Vietnam, "but the years go by very quickly."

In South Vietnam the war went on. "The basic fact of life," John Vann had said not long before the Easter Offensive, "is that the overwhelming majority of the population—somewhere around 95 percent—prefer the government of Vietnam to a Communist government or the government that's being offered by the other side."[9]

Ambassador Bunker laid out the situation as he saw it, at year's end, citing "Abrams' policy of secure and hold. In other words, secure the areas, the hamlets, the villages, the provinces, and defend them against the enemy's attacks and make, create, secure terrains, secure areas. This is what eventually was demonstrated at the end of the war in 1972. By the end of 1972 one could travel anywhere in South Vietnam without security forces or anything else." American forces were nearly all gone by then, and as Bunker saw it that had been the goal all along. "His objective and mine," he said, speaking of General Abrams, "and all of us, was to put the South Vietnamese in a position to defend themselves. That's why I've always maintained that the war was won in the sense that, by the end of 1972 and the beginning of 1973, we had achieved the objective of enabling the South Vietnamese to defend themselves."[10]

Bunker was asked about the remarkable contrast between the situation in the period 1965–1968, during which, "as the level of American troops increased, while there was some progress, there was always a sense of frustration," and the years 1968–1972, when, "as American troops decreased, there seemed to be the considerable sense of momentum and real progress and even elan." Bunker attributed that to the cumulative effect of a lot of things, the complex of actions and programs they had brought together under the rubric of "one war." He cited improvements in South Vietnamese military capability, a more

effective civil administration and establishment of the constitutional process, land reform, increases in agricultural production.

Over time, then, "one could see noticeable changes in the
countryside, the economic condition of the people, of their ability to buy sophisticated equipment for their farms, tractors, increased modes of transportation, in so many different ways. This
nation-building process was evident."[11] And Bunker acknowledged the beneficial effects of a harmonious team approach on
the American side. "I have never served in a more effective
organization than the embassy and the military in Vietnam," he
concluded.[12]

OVER A PERIOD OF about seven weeks in the autumn, another
glut of military matériel, this increment stimulated by an impending peace agreement, was heaped on the South Vietnamese.
"Enhance Plus" included nine squadrons of various types of
aircraft, nearly three dozen amphibious vehicles, and more than
100,000 tons of other equipment and supplies. Colonel Lung
called it a "last-ditch effort to modernize the RVNAF before
restrictions were imposed by the Paris treaty."[13]

North Vietnam's sponsors were not idle, either. "The quantity of military aid shipped to us by land and by sea from our
fraternal socialist countries," said a history of PAVN, "and the
quantity of supplies shipped from the North to South Vietnam
during 1972 was almost double that shipped during 1971."[14]

IN THE PARIS negotiations each side had long maintained certain
rigid demands that the other would not, or could not, agree to,
thereby guaranteeing a continuing standoff. From the standpoint
of the South Vietnamese, one of the most crucial was the demand that any settlement provide for withdrawal of North Vietnamese forces from the South. In public sessions as late as
December 1970 the United States was holding firm on this essential point. Ambassador David Bruce told Xuan Thuy that
U.S. withdrawals would be discussed only in connection with

similar NVA withdrawals from South Vietnam, Laos, and Cambodia. Of course, as later became known, in the private talks Kissinger had already conceded the point.

There is evidence that from an even earlier time plans had been made based on yielding on this crucially important provision. On 12 August 1969 Melvin Laird approved a proposed RVNAF force structure for Fiscal Year 1970. In doing so, reported the Army Chief of Staff to his general officers, "the Secretary of Defense pointed out that the earlier RVNAF Improvement and Modernization Programs had the objective of developing a balanced, self-sufficient force that would be capable of meeting an insurgency threat upon the withdrawal of U.S., Allied *and* North Vietnamese Army forces. However, the objective of Vietnamization will now be increased to transfer progressively to the RVN increased responsibility for all aspects of the war, assuming that the current levels of NVA and Viet Cong forces remain in-country and that U.S. force redeployments continue."[15] There, more than three years before the Paris agreement, was the fateful provision on which South Vietnam eventually would founder.

During the autumn of 1972 the prolonged discussions in Paris seemed to approach a conclusion. An apparent breakthrough occurred on 8 October when the North Vietnamese dropped their long-standing insistence on overthrow of the Thieu government as a part of any agreement. Coupled with Kissinger's earlier and far more significant action in dropping insistence on mutual withdrawal, this cleared the way for the NVA to hold their positions in South Vietnam.

The United States and North Vietnam then quickly drafted an agreement providing for a cease-fire in place, withdrawal of all U.S. forces, release of prisoners of war, establishment of a Council of National Reconciliation and Concord, cessation of infiltration from the North, internationally supervised elections, and a ban on the introduction into South Vietnam by either side of war matériel other than on a one-for-one replacement basis. The pact was silent on NVA forces in South Vietnam.

Upon returning from Paris, Kissinger told President Nixon— recorded H. R. Haldeman in his diary—that "we got a much better deal by far than we had expected."[16] And, noted Haldeman, "Haig feels that the reason they're doing this is that they've basically given up, they have no more hope and they're now going to try and establish friendship with us."[17] Nixon was so elated that he instructed Manolo the steward to pour the good wine for everyone. "Usually," noted Haldeman, "it's just served to the P and the rest of us have some California Beaulieu Vineyard stuff."[18]

When he took office in 1969, Richard Nixon later wrote, he "was convinced that unless we backed up our diplomatic efforts with strong military pressure, the North Vietnamese would continue their strategy of talking and fighting until we tired of the struggle and caved in to their bottom-line demand: that the United States withdraw unilaterally and acquiesce in the overthrow of the South Vietnamese government in exchange for the return of American prisoners of war. I considered it unthinkable that we would fight a bitter war for four years, lose 30,000 men, and spend tens of billions of dollars for the goal of getting our POWs back."[19] Now, with an additional four years elapsed and the toll approaching 58,000, it had come to just that. The claim that North Vietnam had made a major concession by dropping its demands for overthrow of the Thieu government was at best naive—acquiescence in the continued presence of North Vietnamese troops in the South virtually guaranteed that eventual outcome.

Now Kissinger set about gaining agreement of the South Vietnamese government to their negotiated fate. In late September, dining aboard the presidential yacht *Sequoia,* Nixon had talked over the evolving agreement with Kissinger, Haig, and Haldeman. "Nobody feels that there's much more than about an even chance of Thieu going along with it," wrote Haldeman in his diary, "but if he doesn't, then move to a plan II, which is basically the same thing."[20] The Americans were going to sign an agreement, with or without the South Vietnamese, and Thieu was going to be boxed in.

It is problematical whether under any circumstances North Vietnam would have negotiated a settlement acceptable to the South. Near the end of 1971 MACV decided that "the only possible conclusion" about the intentions of the Vietnamese Communists over the past three and a half years was "that they have never had any intention of conducting serious negotiations which could lead to a peaceful settlement of the war—except under conditions which would be tantamount to the total capitulation of the Republic of Vietnam. Thus the Paris peace talks constitute for the Communists merely a political extension of the confirmed battlefield strategy of protracted warfare."

When, early in 1972, another major enemy offensive had loomed, Abrams—responding to a question from the Koreans—gave his view of its purpose. "The Communists insist on these things: this government here must be overthrown; all troops, all aircraft, all navy belonging to the United States, and all equipment, must be withdrawn from all of Indochina; there must be no military or economic assistance by the United States to South Vietnam. That's what they insist on. *So*—how do you get that? You go to the weakest thing in the whole setup, the will of the American people and the will of the American government. And if they can capture Ben Het, or Kontum City, for a week, and maybe Cam Lo, and threaten Quang Tri, the press and they and all will say Vietnamization has failed. And the last few remaining members of Congress who support continuing economic assistance would have lost their faith. *So,* I think that's what it's aimed at." When that offensive was thrown back with heavy loss to the invading Communists, they had once again shifted their emphasis to the negotiating front, and to that most important front of all—the American political scene.

On 24 October 1972 President Thieu made a nationally televised speech in which he denounced the proposed agreement
as requiring a thinly disguised coalition government and categorically rejected allowing North Vietnamese forces to remain
in the South. Kissinger promptly held a press conference in
which he accused Thieu of sabotaging the Paris agreement, an
accurate enough charge. "In reality," later wrote Major General
Hoang Lac, "a desperate Thieu had only tried to do his best to
obstruct and jeopardize the Paris agreement, but unfortunately
did not have any means to do it."[21]

Kissinger complained, then and later, that earlier Thieu had
acceded to an agreement allowing North Vietnamese troops to
remain in the South, and that in exchange the North Vietnamese had dropped their long-standing insistence on dismissal of
the Thieu government and establishment of a coalition government in its place.[22] The difference now, perhaps, was that Thieu
no longer believed in American assurances of renewed air support if the North Vietnamese violated terms of the agreement
and resumed hostilities. Kissinger reluctantly returned to Paris
with a number of proposed modifications in the tentative agreement—changes designed to placate the South Vietnamese—
whereupon the North Vietnamese backed away from the whole
thing, even repudiating provisions previously agreed upon.

The North Vietnamese viewpoint, as recorded in a 1994
history of PAVN published in Hanoi, was that after a date for
signing the agreement had been set, "the U.S. government demanded another meeting with our representatives and requested
changes in many provisions in the text of the treaty. The U.S.
scheme was to stretch things out and delay the signing of the
agreement in order to buy time to strengthen the puppet army
and puppet government. Then, after the Presidential elections
were over, they planned to win a decisive new military victory
in order to force us to make concessions and agree to treaty
provisions favorable to the U.S."[23]

In a meeting on Sunday, 29 October, Nixon emphasized that

the South Vietnamese had relied on the United States and that we had to back them up. "[George] McGovern wants us to get out," he said disdainfully, "with no agreement on POW's, just hope, and take all our equipment with us, and provide no more economic aid. This would be directly contradictory to all that we have stood for, it would assure the direct collapse of South Vietnam, complete surrender to the enemy."[24] In due course McGovern would get everything—save only lack of an agreement on POWs—he had advocated.

On 30 November President Nixon sat down with the Joint Chiefs of Staff to discuss the draft agreement. The meeting's purpose, Kissinger reminded Nixon in a preparatory memorandum, was "to convey your conviction that [the agreement] is a sound one, and to express your determination to react strongly to any violations by the other side and maintain a strong military presence in the region."[25]

SOON THEREAFTER, faced with a debacle in the collapse of the negotiations, Nixon ordered intensive resumption of bombing in North Vietnam. The campaign, designated Linebacker II, was conducted from Andersen Air Force Base in Guam, 2,900 miles from Hanoi, and from U Tapao Royal Thai Navy Airfield in Thailand. The B-52 flights from Guam, missions that sometimes lasted more than eighteen hours, constituted "the longest sustained strategic bombardment flights ever attempted."

B-52s carried ordnance loads typically consisting of 108 500-pound and 750-pound bombs. With the force on Guam peaking at 155 aircraft, it took five miles of ramp space just to park them all. At a peak rate of sixty-six sorties a day, the operation was consuming two million gallons of JP-4 jet fuel a day.[26]

Linebacker II was conducted under "press-on" tactics, which meant that the aircraft continued to the target regardless of enemy action or mechanical problems. Stringent rules of engagement were also prescribed—most stressfully, instructions allowing no maneuvering from the initial point on the bomb run to the target, a provision intended to ensure the most accurate bombing possible and thus avoidance of civilian casualties. So extensive was the operation that on Guam the last cells—groups of three aircraft—from the first day were landing as the first bombers for the second day were starting their engines. It was in effect an around-the-clock operation, one extending from 18 December until 29 December, suspended for one day over Christmas, 729 sorties in all.

The targets in North Vietnam, including the Hanoi and Haiphong areas, were rail yards and marshaling areas, petroleum storage facilities, missile storage sites, docks, and warehouses. Supporting the bombers was a huge fleet of other aircraft, including escort fighters, those performing suppression of surface-to-air missiles or delivering chaff to fool enemy radars, anti-MiG combat air patrols, electronic countermeasures support, and tankers for refueling. By the end, concluded the Air Force, there were no more "worthwhile" military targets left in the Hanoi and Haiphong complexes.

North Vietnam fired 1,242 SAMs during the bombing raids, and eventually just ran out of missiles.[27] The United States did not run out of B-52s. Altogether fifteen of the big bombers were lost, six on the third day alone, when the enemy fired more than 200 SAMs, but the loss rate dropped sharply as new tactics were introduced and the defenders used up their ordnance. The enemy's slogan "one missile fired, one B-52 killed" was not working out.[28] Conceded the North Vietnamese, in an unconscious tribute Nixon would have savored, "Nixon proved to be extremely obstinate and reckless, and did things Johnson never dared to do."[29]

During the eleven days of Linebacker II, concluded Douglas Pike, "Hanoi officials experienced true, all-out strategic air war for the first time. It had a profound effect, causing them to reverse virtually overnight their bargaining position at the Paris talks."[30] On 28 December Hanoi indicated it would now, once

again, agree to agree, and the following day Nixon called off
the air bombardment.

Historian George Herring concluded that, in what he called
"the ultimate irony," "the U.S. position in South Vietnam was
stronger at the end of 1972 than at any previous point in the
war." But, he added, the commitment required to capitalize on
that position was subsequently undermined by domestic political
factors.[31] Longtime observer of the war Sir Robert Thompson
thought the United States could at this point have dictated the
terms and "the war could have been won, in that a real and
enforceable peace could have been obtained."[32] "In my view,"
he said, "on December 30, 1972, after eleven days of those B-
52 attacks on the Hanoi area, *you had won the war. It was over!*"[33]

22

Cease-Fire

THE KEY ELEMENT in the outcome of the war was the continued presence of North Vietnamese armed forces in South Vietnam. The Paris Agreement was silent on that point, thus allowing the NVA to maintain in place the forces they had always denied were in South Vietnam. This silence constituted a fatal flaw, at least from the South Vietnamese perspective, even if it was also an inevitable acceptance of the battlefield realities. "That cease-fire agreement," wrote Sir Robert Thompson, "restored complete security to the [enemy] rear bases in North Vietnam, in Laos, in Cambodia, and in the parts of South Vietnam that it held. It subjected the South Vietnamese rear base again to being absolutely open to military attack. That is what the cease-fire agreement actually achieved."[1]

As far back as the autumn of 1968, with the possibility of a cease-fire under consideration, General Andrew J. Goodpaster, then MACV deputy commander, suggested that achieving viable security in South Vietnam "might involve substantial continued U.S. presence here. I frankly think that . . . in all likelihood it would *if* the NVA keep any kind of sizable force on the Cambodian border or any kind of sizable force within this country." Later, recalled journalist Kevin Buckley, General Abrams told him that "it would *never* be acceptable for North Vietnamese forces to remain in place in South Vietnam."[2]

The South Vietnamese, and President Nguyen Van Thieu in particular, were desperately afraid of an agreement that left North Vietnamese troops in their country, which would produce what one analyst described as "profound asymmetry."[3] Under increasingly threatening pressure from Nixon and his emissaries, the South Vietnamese still refused to cave in. An observation Ambassador Bunker had made in a reporting cable over four years earlier, in July 1968, could again have been transmitted with full fidelity to the situation: "Profoundly weary of war, nationalist Vietnamese of most political persuasions are also profoundly fearful of the consequences of a peace settlement over which they suspect they may have too little influence. While considerably reassured by our firm posture and our public statements, most Vietnamese still view the Paris talks with more fear and resentment than hope."[4]

The only difference now, and it was immense, was that American assurances were no longer reassuring. President Nixon had transmitted innumerable statements of his firm resolve to punish any North Vietnamese violations of any agreement, repeatedly giving his personal word to Thieu. Henry Kissinger had arrived in Saigon on 18 October 1972 for the purpose of obtaining South Vietnamese acquiescence in the proposed agreement. As an inducement, remembered General Cao Van Vien, Kissinger stressed that the United States "pledged to maintain its air bases in Thailand and to keep the Seventh Fleet off Vietnam to deter any attack by the Communists. Economic and military aid would continue for South Vietnam, while the United States believed that secret understandings with Russia and Communist China would drastically reduce their supply of war materiel to North Vietnam and permit the United States to withdraw its troops and recover its prisoners with honor."[5] Once again naive reliance on "understandings" lent a surreal aspect to the proceedings.

Abrams, newly sworn in as Army Chief of Staff, was taken
to Saigon to help persuade the South Vietnamese. There he said
to them, according to Henry Kissinger's account, "I have always
had great respect and admiration for the South Vietnamese people and military, but I have always believed from the beginning
that the day had to come for you and for your own pride and
your people when the security and the political strength was all
yours, with eventually our air power standing in the wings and
our equipment and supplies coming into your ports."[6] That was
consistent with Abrams's long-held and often-expressed views.
He also had the political insight to see that, if the South Vietnamese did not go along with an agreement, their U.S. assistance
would be abruptly terminated. Given the strong U.S. response
during the recent Easter Offensive, he also had reason to credit
American assurances that they would punish—with force if necessary—any North Vietnamese violations of the agreement's
provisions.

Thieu clearly did not believe he could rely on these words
to overcome what he saw as a fatally flawed agreement. Nor
could he have been encouraged by Kissinger's departing comment: "It is a fact that in the United States all the press, the
media and intellectuals have a vested interest in our defeat."[7] In
all too short a time Thieu would be proved absolutely correct
in his skepticism.

Nevertheless, Kissinger observed, "The United States could
not reject, when Hanoi accepted them, the very peace terms
we had been offering with Thieu's acquiescence for three
years."[8] If the United States thus had no real alternative, neither—despite misgivings about Nixon's assurances—did the
South Vietnamese. If they shunned the Paris Agreement, it was
certain not only that the United States would settle without
them, but also that the U.S. Congress would then move swiftly
to cut off further aid to South Vietnam. If they went along with
the agreement, hoping thereby to continue receiving American
aid, they were forced to accept an untenable outcome in which

North Vietnamese troops remained menacingly within their borders.

With mortal foreboding, they chose the latter course, only to find—dismayingly—they soon had the worst of both: NVA forces in place *and* American support cut off, and for good measure American default on promises to deal with North Vietnamese violations of the peace terms. The flawed arrangement, in the judgment of General Cao Van Vien, was "the turning point that changed it all. The Paris Agreement was served on South Vietnam like a death warrant."[9]

At Key Biscayne on a Sunday in mid-January, Nixon was getting ready for announcement of the renewed Paris Agreement. In discussion with Kissinger, Haig—who was being sent out to put further pressure on the Vietnamese—and Haldeman, Nixon "made the point that Haig must take a very hard line on Thieu," emphasizing that Nixon "will go ahead regardless of what Thieu does. The only diplomacy that Haig should exercise is to trick Thieu, if it looks like he's not going with us." Nixon had some advice for Kissinger, too, saying that in his public explication of the agreement, "Henry must remember that the purpose of his briefing is to stick it to our [political] opponents, not to explain the intricacies of the settlement."[10]

As THE PARIS ACCORDS neared signature, Congressman Gerald Ford—not yet called to higher office—circulated a "Dear Colleague" letter transmitting "an authoritative summary of the deliberate acts of terrorism directed against innocent civilians in Indochina by North Vietnamese and local Communist forces during the past five years." It was a record of unremitting viciousness. "In South Vietnam," read the report, "the Communist attacks have included shelling, rocketing, ground assaults, abductions, forced labor and assassinations. These attacks have been directed at South Vietnam's largest cities as well as its smallest hamlets, at schools, pagodas, medical facilities and refugee

centers. They have involved shooting of refugees attempting to
escape the areas of the fighting near An Loc and Quang Tri and
the large scale Communist trials and executions in Hue and Binh
Dinh Province."[11] Detailed accounts were provided of one
atrocity after another—3,000 people bound and executed at
Hue, hundreds of rockets lobbed indiscriminately into densely
populated areas of Saigon, mortar attacks on refugee centers,
priests and altar boys assassinated in their churches, dynamite in
a pagoda and bombs in a maternity ward, acts of unspeakable
cowardice and brutality. As the voting records of subsequent
months soon made clear, not many of Ford's dear colleagues
much gave a damn.

On 27 January 1973 a four-power "Agreement on Ending
the War and Restoring Peace in Vietnam"—initialed four days
earlier—was signed in Paris, theoretically bringing to an end,
after nearly two decades, the Second Indochina War. It was, said
the North Vietnamese, "the result of the longest negotiations in
this century, negotiations which lasted four years and nine
months and included 202 open sessions and 24 private meetings."[12] Immediately after the cease-fire the NVA issued an Order of the Day citing the "difficult, complex and violent struggle
ahead."[13] Then, recalled a North Vietnamese history trium-
phantly, the United States had to withdraw all its forces and
"acknowledge that in South Vietnam there were two governments, two armies, and two zones of control."[14]

IN A SERIES OF releases a total of 591 American prisoners of war
were given up by Hanoi and flown home;[15] they were among
the very few returning Vietnam veterans to receive a sympathetic welcome in their homeland. The remaining U.S. troops
in South Vietnam—down to about 27,000 by the time of the
accord, the last representatives of some 2,600,000 Americans
who had served in Vietnam and 700,000 more who participated
in the war from stations elsewhere in Southeast Asia—were

also rapidly withdrawn, the last increment departing on 29
March. Only a small Defense Attaché Office continued the U.S.
military presence in Vietnam.

President Thieu sent the last troops off with a poignant message, thanking them for "great sacrifices, not for selfish gains,
but for a noble cause. When the emotions aroused by this long
war have calmed down," concluded Thieu, "the world will acknowledge by consensus that you have played a great role in the
elaboration of peace in freedom, and that you have shaped history for the better. Thank you very much. God bless you."[16]

As part of the agreement the U.S. Navy swept the mines
from Haiphong harbor, thereby releasing a flotilla of ships that
had been bottled up in the port for three hundred days. Not a
single vessel had entered or left since the one decisive minute
in which the blockading mines were laid.[17]

In April 1973 the first Watergate revelations came to light,
beginning a sordid drama that would preoccupy the President
and the nation for the next sixteen months before culminating
in Nixon's resignation and disgrace.

In early May 1973 Ambassador Ellsworth Bunker left for
home, the last of the American triumvirate to depart Vietnam
and—with more than six years at the head of America's largest
embassy—the longest serving. Still starched and tall at nearly
seventy-nine, he had ahead of him yet other challenging tasks,
among them negotiating the Panama Canal treaty for the Carter
administration.

Deputy Ambassador Sam Berger remarked on those who
had worked closely during the years in Saigon—Bunker,
Abrams, Colby, himself: "We were rather a special group together, I think—very close, and all involved in this terribly
tragic business. We knew it was tragic. We would talk very
frankly about our concerns and worries. We were worried about
how things were going to go, but we could also see the progress."[18]

Douglas Pike, who edited the collection of Bunker's Vietnam reporting cables, perceptively described how they were permeated by "the bittersweet sense of what might have been."[19] In his final cable, dated 5 May 1973, Bunker closed with these words: "I feel confident that if we do all we can to deter Hanoi from again seeking a military solution while at the same time encouraging the GVN to negotiate with the other side in a spirit of compromise and reconciliation, peace will finally come to Viet-Nam."[20]

VERY SOON AFTER the Paris Accords were signed the North Vietnamese resumed their attacks. Their task was made easy by the thirteen NVA divisions and 75 regiments—an estimated 160,000 troops in all—still in place in South Vietnam.[21] By 14 March Henry Kissinger was alerting President Nixon that NVA personnel and matériel were pouring into South Vietnam, so brazenly that the enemy was now "operating in daylight and the traffic is so heavy as to be congested"—traffic jams on the Ho Chi Minh Trail. Kissinger recommended planning for a series of air strikes against the trail in southern Laos, to be conducted immediately after release of a third increment of American prisoners two days hence. (He did not mention the possible effect of such strikes on the fate of a final group of prisoners scheduled for release two weeks after that.) Nixon initialed a block labeled "APPROVE," but apparently nothing ever came of it.[22] Thus the latest in a long string of enemy logistics offensives continued unimpeded.

A 1994 history of PAVN boasts of North Vietnam's success in building up forces in the South once the agreement was signed. "From January until September 1973," it states, "the amount of supplies sent from North Vietnam into the South rose to 140,000 tons, four times as much as in 1972. Included in these supplies were 80,000 tons of military supplies (including 27,000 tons of weapons, 6,000 tons of fuel and petroleum products, and 40,000 tons of rice) and 45,000 tons of supplies to be distributed to civilians in the newly liberated zones. In addition there were 10,000 tons of weapons stored in the warehouses along the Annamite Mountain roads. More than 100,000 cadres and soldiers, including two infantry divisions, two artillery regiments, one anti-aircraft artillery division, one armored regiment, one engineer regiment, and units of reinforcement troops marched from North Vietnam to the battlefields in South Vietnam during 1973."[23]

The United States, contrary to all the assurances Nixon had given Nguyen Van Thieu, did not intervene to punish these blatant violations of the peace agreement. "Mr. Nixon thought the North Vietnamese would cheat on the agreement," remembered Colby. "He was prepared to go back and enforce it."[24] When the time came, however, he did not.

Soon it was no longer a matter of volition; the Congress had cut off funding for all further American military activity in the war zone. "Notwithstanding any other provision of law," read the Fulbright-Aiken amendment, "on or after August 15, 1973, no funds herein or heretofore appropriated may be obligated or expended to finance directly or indirectly combat activities by United States military forces in or over or from off the shores of North Vietnam, South Vietnam, Laos or Cambodia."[25] That statute rendered null and void, almost a year before he was driven from office, the assurances Richard Nixon had provided. Congressional distaste for the war, and for those who prosecuted it—at fever pitch long before Watergate reached the crisis stage—doomed South Vietnam's hopes for further U.S. assistance, the later suggestions by Nixon and Kissinger that it was Watergate that undermined their policy notwithstanding.

In July 1973 General Fred Weyand, who had been the last U.S. commander in Vietnam, returned to evaluate the situation. He found enemy forces in a dramatically improved position since the cease-fire, the result of shipping major quantities of supplies in violation of the agreement.[26] Nevertheless, the South Vietnamese were holding their own, coping in a series of bloody battles with many "land and population grab" attempts by the

Communists interspersed with a series of major attacks. Immediately after the cease-fire enemy forces drove the South Vietnamese out of the Cua Viet Naval Base at a cost of a thousand casualties. And the seacoast town of Sa Huynh was seized by the enemy in a division-size attack, then retaken by the 2nd ARVN Division in three weeks of fighting that produced heavy casualties on both sides. In March an attack in division strength against Hong Ngu in Kien Phong Province was countered by the 9th ARVN Division, which drove the attackers back into Cambodia. Also in March enemy forces assaulted Tong Le Chan, a border camp in Military Region 3, where an ARVN Ranger battalion manned the defenses. It took thirteen months, some 10,000 rounds of artillery and mortar fire, and twenty ground attacks before the enemy could finally dislodge the garrison from this isolated outpost. In June another division force seized Trung Nghia, just west of Kontum City in the Central Highlands. In fighting that lasted until September, again with heavy casualties on both sides, ARVN forces retook the position.[27]

At year's end the International Institute for Strategic Studies issued its annual *Strategic Survey*. Assessing the situation in South Vietnam, the Institute noted that North Vietnamese forces there had grown by some 40,000 since the cease-fire, along with a sixfold increase in tanks and a trebling of heavy artillery.[28] Also at the end of 1973 the South Vietnamese government reported that 80,000 people had been killed during the year, the most in any year of the war, leading Olivier Todd to remark, "the most murderous truce this century."[29]

"AFTER VISITING hundreds of villages, training centres, refugee camps and paramilitary units," wrote Sir Robert Thompson in 1974, "I learnt to appreciate the resilience of the Vietnamese, their courage, stoicism and stamina. I soon realized that their qualities and virtues far outweighed their failings and vices and now have the greatest admiration and respect for them. They surmounted national and personal crises which would have crushed most people and, in spite of casualties which would have appalled and probably collapsed the United States, they could still maintain over one million men under arms after more than ten years of war."[30] Now the United States was about to repay such fortitude by bailing out on her sometime ally. The only thing left for South Vietnam to be deprived of was money, and the Congress set about that task with a vengeance.

Major General Ira Hunt served during 1973–1975 as deputy commander of the U.S. Support Activities Group, in effect MACV in exile, at Nakhon Phanom in Thailand. "After we pulled out," he observed, "the South Vietnamese were totally different in their aggressiveness, their ability to do battle, their reporting of intelligence. The Vietnamese had to assume all that burden, and you'd be amazed at how well they did that." After the Paris Accords were signed, said Hunt, it was almost always the NVA that initiated combat actions, "and for about two years the ARVN were cleaning their clocks. The South Vietnamese were giving more than they were getting, there's no question about it. But when we pulled the plug logistically there was no way they could carry on."[31]

Confirmation from the enemy side was provided by General Tran Van Tra, who admitted that by the time of the cease-fire "our cadres and men were exhausted. All our units were in disarray, and we were suffering from a lack of manpower and a shortage of food and ammunition. So it was hard to stand up under enemy attacks. Sometimes we had to withdraw to let the enemy retake control of the population."[32]

In April 1974 President Thieu sent General Cao Van Vien to Washington to make the case for continued U.S. aid to South Vietnam. At the Pentagon, where Vien briefed on the current military situation, complete with photographic evidence of mounting enemy violations and massive movement into South Vietnam, he was assured of full support. On 6 May 1974 a legislative amendment proposed by Senator Edward Kennedy— one of those members of Congress most determined to pull the

Abrams personally assigned commanders of the 11th Armored Cavalry, including Col. George Patton, shown here with Maj. John C. Bahnsen. They took seriously Abrams's message that he was looking for "a conscious, determined effort to seek battle with a will to win."

South Vietnamese Marines with a 240mm rocket and other matériel captured on a sweep north of Saigon. Abrams stressed working inside the enemy's "system" by finding and seizing caches throughout South Vietnam.

Highly mobile 4th Infantry Division artillerymen prepare to load up for rapid displacement to another fire support base in the Central Highlands during the Cambodian incursion. The ability of such units to cover for the large forces deployed cross-border demonstrated how much internal security had improved.

U.S. ARMY CENTER OF MILITARY HISTORY

Adm. Thomas H. Moorer, Joint Chiefs of Staff Chairman during 1970–1974, accompanied Secretary Laird on a visit to Saigon and met with Abrams. "Toward the end," said Moorer, "I got to the point where my sole effort was focused on the POWs."

ABRAMS FAMILY COLLECTION

Ambassador Bunker with President Nguyen Van Thieu after the 1971 election in which Thieu, unopposed, was reelected. Despite disappointment in the lack of an electoral contest, Bunker had said before the balloting, "It is clearly in our interest to see that this administration continues."

INDOCHINA ARCHIVE, UNIVERSITY OF CALIFORNIA AT BERKELEY

Three of the most important Vietnamese military leaders—Lt. Gen. Hoang Xuan Lam, Gen. Cao Van Vien, and Maj. Gen. Ngo Quang Truong—with U.S. Lt. Gen. Richard G. Stilwell at Phu Bai Airport. During the 1972 Easter Offensive Lam was relieved and replaced by Truong, who skillfully took charge and repulsed the enemy in the northern provinces. NATIONAL ARCHIVES

Abrams presented the U.S. Legion of Merit to Gen. Cao Van Vien, Chief of South Vietnam's Joint General Staff. Vien was an intelligent, professional, and serious officer who had the respect of Abrams and other Americans who worked with him.

NATIONAL ARCHIVES

VNA /539, HANOI, APRIL 7.- ... FIGHTERS STORMING DAU MAU BASE ON HIGHWAY 9 QUANG TRI PROVINCE.

HANOI VNA RADIOPHOTO IN ENGLISH TO ADN EAST BERLIN 0928 GMT 7 APR 72 FBIS

A radiophoto dispatched from Hanoi shows an attack on Cau Mau base in Quang Tri Province during the 1972 Easter Offensive. With help from U.S. air and naval forces, the South Vietnamese turned back a massive invasion. Having predicted "decisive victory," the enemy instead suffered such losses that it was three years before another such operation could be launched.

INDOCHINA ARCHIVE, UNIVERSITY OF CALIFORNIA AT BERKELEY

With U.S. troops largely withdrawn, ARVN troops who had taken over conduct of the ground war and successfully withstood the siege of An Loc during the 1972 Easter Offensive celebrate atop a captured T-54 tank.

U.S. ARMY CENTER OF MILITARY HISTORY

When negotiations collapsed in the autumn of 1972 and President Nixon resumed bombing of North Vietnam, these U.S. naval forces deployed in the Gulf of Tonkin contributed to the powerful attack that soon brought an agreement to end the fighting.   U.S. ARMY CENTER OF MILITARY HISTORY

President Thieu presents a land title to a former tenant farmer. By 1972 the "Land to the Tiller" program had given over 400,000 farmers title to 2.5 million acres of land. "In one fell swoop," said John Paul Vann, the program "eliminated tenancy in Vietnam."

NATIONAL ARCHIVES

Former Viet Cong prisoners given amnesty for good behavior swear allegiance to South Vietnam in a ceremony at Danang. Over 47,000 former enemy rallied to the government side during 1969 alone. NATIONAL ARCHIVES

Gen. Fred Weyand, last U.S. commander in Vietnam, is saluted by South Vietnamese Boy Scouts as he makes his way to Saigon's National Military Cemetery. LON HOLMBERG PHOTOGRAPH

Henry Kissinger and Le Duc Tho, with members of their delegations, meet in Paris to negotiate an end to the war. "The Paris Agreement," said Gen. Cao Van Vien, "was served on South Vietnam like a death warrant."

U.S. ARMY CENTER OF MILITARY HISTORY

With South Vietnam in its death throes, President Gerald Ford—who earlier had given amnesty to those who dodged the draft to avoid service in Vietnam— gratuitously announced that, as far as the United States was concerned, the war was finished.

U.S. ARMY CENTER OF MILITARY HISTORY

With their country near final collapse, South Vietnamese refugees crowd the U.S. merchant ship Pioneer Contender in the South China Sea. In the war's final days the U.S. evacuated 130,000 at-risk South Vietnamese.

U.S. ARMY CENTER OF MILITARY HISTORY

On April 30, 1975, this North Vietnamese Army tank crashed through the gates of Independence Palace in Saigon. The war was over. North Vietnam's long quest to subjugate all of Vietnam under its authority was finally crowned with success.   INDOCHINA ARCHIVE, UNIVERSITY OF CALIFORNIA AT BERKELEY plug on South Vietnam—was accepted. It cut $266 million for South Vietnam from a supplementary military aid bill and signified, suggested Thompson, "that perhaps the major lesson of the Vietnam war is: do not rely on the United States as an ally."[33]

Fiscal Year 1975 also brought bad news for South Vietnam. While $1 billion had been authorized (instead of the $1.47 billion requested), that was reduced to $700 million in the appropriation process. After costs of supporting the Defense Attaché Office in Saigon and shipping charges were deducted, the residual amounted in real terms to only about $654 million before adjusting for inflation—then skyrocketing due to a global energy crisis. In a nakedly mean-spirited act, provisions were inserted prohibiting even the purchase of fertilizer for South Vietnam in FY 1975.[34] "The final appropriation," observed General Vien, "came as a shock to the army and people of South Vietnam. It was certain that the huge gap between requirements and resources that had just been created could never be closed no matter how much self-restraint was imposed and how well the budget was managed."[35]

General Harold K. Johnson, when he was Army Chief of Staff, had spoken in New York shortly after returning from an April 1966 trip to Vietnam. "We could withdraw from Southeast Asia," he admitted. "To do so would be to abandon everything we have been fighting and dying for in Vietnam. To do so would be to close for all time the book of our American heritage."[36] That point had now been reached.

As a result, South Vietnam's armed forces adopted some fairly drastic austerity measures, none calculated to increase their military power. The Air Force reduced fire support, tactical airlift, and reconnaissance by half and helilift by 70 percent, inactivated more than 200 aircraft and canceled orders for upgraded fighters, called home 400 men from pilot training in the United States, and converted a thousand airman trainees to infantry. The Navy inactivated more than 600 boats and river craft, cutting river patrols by 72 percent. Vien pointed out that "not a single plane, ship, or boat was replaced after the cease-fire." The ammunition inventory was shrinking, spare parts were getting scarce, and more than 4,000 vehicles were deadlined for parts. According to Vien's calculations, his armed forces would run out of fuel by mid–May 1975 and out of ammunition by June.[37]

Ambassador Bui Diem, who had represented South Vietnam in Washington with dignity and perceptiveness, was both understanding and bitter. "The manner in which the United States took its leave was more than a mistake," he concluded. "It was an act unworthy of a great power, one that I believe will be remembered long after such unfortunate misconceptions as the search and destroy strategy have been consigned to footnotes."

Diem could understand the troop withdrawals, but not the rest. "The United States fought long and hard in Vietnam, and if in the end circumstances required that it withdraw, it may be considered a tragedy but hardly an act of shame. The same cannot be said, however, for the manipulation and callous manner with which the American administration and the American Congress dealt with South Vietnam during the last years of the war."[38]

On 30 June 1974 a milestone had been reached with the final flight of Air America, CIA's regional proprietary airline, out of Udorn, Thailand. The crew as logged consisted of a single member, named Rhyne, and on the flight operations schedule for the day he or someone else—perhaps a man named Vira—wrote: "So ends the last sentence of the final paragraph of a saga that may have an epilogue, but never a sequel. It has been to each participating individual an experience which varied according to his role and perspective. However, there is the common bond of knowledge and satisfaction of having taken part in something worthwhile and with just a slight sense of pity for those lesser souls who could not, or would not, share in it. This last flight is dedicated to those for whom a previous similar schedule represented an appointment with their destiny."

In July 1974 Admiral Thomas Moorer ended four years as

Chairman of the Joint Chiefs of Staff, turning the post over to General George Brown, in an earlier day commander of Seventh Air Force in Vietnam. Said Moorer, "Towards the end I got to the point where my sole effort was focused on the POWs."[39]

On 9 August 1974 Richard Nixon, faced with impeachment and his policies and reputation in tatters, resigned from the presidency. He was succeeded by Gerald R. Ford, who first pardoned Nixon, then gave amnesty to those who had dodged the draft to avoid service in Vietnam.

On 4 September 1974 Creighton Abrams succumbed to cancer, not quite two years into his assignment as Army Chief of Staff. In that post he had set about rebuilding an Army badly battered by its lengthy conduct of an unpopular and ultimately unsuccessful war, one waged without recourse to its reserve forces and at the expense of the health and readiness of other forces worldwide. The shift to an all-volunteer force mandated by civilian leadership early in 1973 made the task of attracting and fielding a professional Army that much more difficult, especially given the low level to which public support for the armed forces had declined during the war.

In his short tenure Abrams set the course for those who followed, beginning the reforms and initiatives that the next generation's leaders would credit with producing the victorious force of the Gulf War. General John Vessey, a former Chairman of the Joint Chiefs of Staff, stated the case very eloquently. "When Americans watched the stunning success of our armed forces in Desert Storm," he observed, "they were watching the Abrams vision in action. The modern equipment, the effective air support, the use of the reserve components and, most important of all, the advanced training which taught our people how to stay alive on the battlefield were all seeds planted by Abe."[40]

"General Abrams was convinced—he said it to me—that if properly supported the South Vietnamese could make it on their own," recalled General Donn Starry.[41] Now an early death spared Abrams the eventual outcome in Vietnam, where he had given all he had to give. In the Army, at least, he was remembered for that, for his moral force and stature, and for some of his favorite "sayings"—especially "soldiers are not *in* the Army, soldiers *are* the Army" and "soldiering is an affair of the heart," and of course the immortal Pig Rule: "Never wrestle with pigs—you get dirty, and they enjoy it!"

BY LATE 1974 the deep slashes in U.S. military and economic assistance to South Vietnam were reflected in the operational tempo the forces could maintain. The ammunition supply rate (daily allowance) for rifles was set at 1.6 rounds per man (compared with 13 rounds authorized for U.S. forces when they were still in the war). Machine guns got 10.6 rounds (versus 165), mortars 1.3 rounds (instead of 16.9), and 105mm howitzer shells authorized per gun were 6.4 (not 36.5).[42] Said Colonel Hoang Ngoc Lung, "Stories of RF and PF units in IV Corps buying grenades out of their pocket money were, though incredible, nevertheless true."[43]

The profligacy with which the enemy continued to expend ammunition pointed up the contrast. At just one location, the Tong Le Chon border camp, the Communists shelled the base 300 times over a period of sixteen weeks, expending more than 10,000 rounds in the process. Meanwhile, primarily for budgetary reasons, the overall strength of the RVNAF had by the end of 1974 dropped from the peak of 1.1 million to 996,000 men.[44]

Major General John Murray, then U.S. Defense Attaché, was at one point asked by a fellow soldier how things were going. "Every morning when I get up," he responded, "I pad to the bathroom, turn on the light, look in the mirror and say, 'Good morning, Alice,' because I damned well know I am in wonderland."[45]

During 1974 the North Vietnamese had completed a POL pipeline as far south as Loc Ninh, only seventy-five miles above

Saigon, improved and extended their road network, and stock-piled huge quantities of ammunition within South Vietnam. "In summary," a contemporary assessment of these more robust ca-pabilities noted ominously, "the Communists have improved their logistics system to the point that logistics no longer rep-resent a major constraint upon their military options."[46]

23

Final Days

DECLINING U.S. SUPPORT for the South Vietnamese had been a fact of life since long before the cease-fire. "This drastic cutback," observed Brigadier General Tran Dinh Tho, "gravely affected not only the RVNAF combat capabilities, but also the morale of their cadres and troops."[1] Meanwhile the enemy buildup proceeded vigorously, evidence of the continuing robust assistance being provided by North Vietnam's patrons.

"The quantity of supplies transported along the strategic transportation corridor from the beginning of 1974 until the end of April 1975," read a history of PAVN, "was 823,146 tons, 1.6 times as much as the total transported during the entire previous thirteen years." Also, "during the years 1973–1974, more than 150,000 North Vietnamese youths entered the army. Many combat units at full strength, 68,000 replacement troops, 8,000 cadre and technical personnel, and scores of thousands of assault youth members marched off to the battlefield." These forces were well provided for. "Compared with 1972, the quantity of supplies was nine times as high, including six times as high in weapons and ammunition, three times the quantity of rice, and twenty-seven times the quantity of fuel and petroleum products."[2]

Following the difficult but ultimately successful repulse of the enemy's 1972 Easter Offensive, General Cao Van Vien had concluded that ARVN forces were "fully capable of confronting the NVA if U.S. support were provided in three vital areas: tactical and strategic air, to include troop transport; sea transport; and the replacement of weapons, materials, and supplies."[3] The United States was now in default on all three. Americans would not have liked hearing it said that two totalitarian states—the Soviet Union and the People's Republic of China—had proved more faithful and more reliable as allies than the American democracy, but that was indeed the fact.

Thus what might have been was not to be. Ambassador Ellsworth Bunker later observed, "I gave Thieu personally three letters from President Nixon committing us, in case of a violation of the Paris agreements by the other side, to come to their assistance. Well, the other side violated the agreements almost from the day they signed them . . . but we never came to their assistance, because Congress refused to appropriate the money. The result was, and as each day went by, the South Vietnamese had fewer guns, fewer planes, fewer tanks, diminishing ammunition with which to fight, while the North was being fully supplied by the Soviets and the Chinese. The result was inevitable."[4]

In Vietnam the now uneven struggle went on, building toward the climactic battle. In early December 1974 rebuilt and augmented Communist forces began their most ambitious attacks since the cease-fire, concentrating in MR-3 and MR-4. Soon the entire province of Phuoc Long, north of Saigon and hard against the Cambodian border, was threatened. In an emergency meeting on 2 January President Thieu considered requests for reinforcements to MR-3 so that Phuoc Long, by then surrounded and cut off from all but aerial resupply, might be relieved. Regretfully the requests had to be denied. The JGS no longer had any forces in reserve, and none could be withdrawn elsewhere without risking other losses. It was close to checkmate.

On 6 January 1975 Phuoc Long Province fell to the enemy in what the Defense Attaché Office called "a defeat of major significance. Phuoc Long was the first province to fall completely under communist control since 1954."[5] The U.S. Department of State marked the occasion by issuing a "strong protest."[6] Bui Tin later recalled that when Richard Nixon resigned, the North Vietnamese knew they would win, that Pham Van Dong said of Gerald Ford, "He's the weakest president in U.S. history." Then, said Tin, "we tested Ford's resolve by attacking Phuoc Long. When Ford kept American B-52's in their hangars, our leadership decided on a big offensive against South Vietnam."[7]

Some critics of the American performance as advisors to South Vietnam later complained that the South Vietnamese had been persuaded to develop armed forces mirroring those of the United States and therefore organized and trained for the wrong war. Such a thesis collapses under even cursory examination. South Vietnam was faced with a multitude of threats, and on several levels, not one type of war but many, those many also changing over time. The forces required had to meet and repulse such diverse challenges. And, as we have seen, how much of the total threat South Vietnam was expected to handle without help kept increasing, in the process changing the tasks facing her armed forces and therefore their necessary size and composition.

The South Vietnamese armed forces as they evolved over these last years of the war differed substantially from American forces. They became, to begin with, a huge establishment proportional to the size of the population base upon which they rested, 1.1 million men in all. Had the United States fielded a comparable force, it would have numbered perhaps 15 million instead of the 2.5 million in the actual forces at that time.[8]

The divisions making up the bulk of the ARVN, South Vietnam's army, were light by comparison with American forces, stripped down in terms of heavy equipment, integral transportation, and helicopters (which in any case, in the Vietnamese scheme of things, were found in the Air Force rather than the Army). As the counterinsurgency war was brought under control and the enemy shifted once again to conventional tactics, these South Vietnamese forces were beefed up with medium tanks, longer-range artillery, and the like, but they remained light by comparison with the U.S. division and consequently packed less punch and were less mobile.

But the more important difference between South Vietnam's forces and those of its U.S. mentor was in the Territorial Forces, the Regional Forces and Popular Forces providing close-in security for the rural hamlets and villages of the country. There was, of course, no American counterpart to these elements. Eventually, at a strength of some 550,000, they constituted the bulk of South Vietnam's regular armed forces. Police Field Forces and the People's Self-Defense Force, though outside the regular military establishment, represented significant South Vietnamese capabilities that differed from the forces fielded by the United States.

Finally there were aspects of the U.S. contribution that could not be duplicated in South Vietnam's forces, whether for reasons of cost or manpower or simply technological complexity. These included much of the more sophisticated intelligence-gathering capability, deep-draft naval vessels and especially aircraft carriers, and in airpower the B-52 bombers in particular.

The armed forces developed with and by South Vietnam were configured—within the limits of budgetary and manpower constraints—to meet the threat as it evolved over the years. As they demonstrated at Tet 1968 and again at Easter 1972, they were appropriate to the challenges they faced so long as the United States provided the continuing airpower, naval forces, logistics, and financial support that had always been factored into calculations of the appropriate South Vietnamese forces.

By Tet of 1975, seeking to reconstitute a strategic reserve and gain more combat power, ARVN had added a fourth brigade

to the Airborne and Marine divisions and created two new
Ranger groups, two composite armor squadrons, and a mixed
artillery battalion.[9] This amounted to eating the seed corn, because the wherewithal for these new units was taken from the
training equipment of the Armor and Artillery schools, but in
view of the coming crisis it was a prudent decision.

THE BEGINNING of the end came in early March 1975 when an
invasion force numbering twenty divisions launched what
turned out to be the final offensive of the war. On 10 March,
at Ban Me Thuot in the Central Highlands, the fateful blow
fell. With three NVA divisions greatly outnumbering the defenders—25,000 men against 1,200 by one account—the garrison was defeated in a matter of days, thus unhinging the
defenses of Pleiku and Kontum farther north.

The loss of Ban Me Thuot precipitated a disastrous attempt
to withdraw forces from the Highlands and reposition them farther south and east. On orders from President Thieu issued 14
March, Kontum and Pleiku provinces were now to be abandoned—in fact, the whole of the Central Highlands. When,
with little planning or supervision and no advance notice, the
first elements left Pleiku, trying to escape along a little-used
secondary route, panic set in among the civilian population and
military forces alike. Soon the road was clogged with intermin-
gled refugees and troop units, a target the enemy harvested en-
thusiastically.

Cabled Tom Polgar from Saigon, "Ultimate outcome hardly
in doubt, because South Vietnam cannot survive without U.S.
military aid as long as North Vietnam's war-making capacity is
unimpaired and supported by Soviet Union and China. Chief
of Station."[10]

As MR-2 was collapsing, things also came unglued in MR-1
to the north. President Thieu had withdrawn crucial elements
of the forces there for use closer to Saigon, and what was left

could not hold their positions. Quang Tri, Quang Ngai, Hue, and Danang fell in quick succession, almost one a day, and four ARVN divisions went with them. As in the Highlands, rivers of terrified civilians clogged every artery. "Wherever it went," observed General Vien, "the refugee flow brought along chaos and disintegration."[11] Soon the major coastal cities of MR-2—Qui Nhon, Tuy Hoa, and Nha Trang—melted away as well. "Militarily," conceded General Vien, "the withdrawal had resulted in a rout of strategic proportions."[12]

Polgar drew a contrast. "In South Vietnam in 1972, their morale was good and they fought like hell and successfully because they knew the Americans were in it. In 1975, when they had the feeling that the Americans are no longer backing them, then their morale gave out and they did not fight."[13]

As first one tent peg and then another pulled out of the sand, former Ambassador Edmund Gullion returned from a trip to Washington to join a conference at the Fletcher School of Law and Diplomacy, where he was the dean. Remarking on the distressing news from Vietnam, he said to the conferees, "I was struck today by the contrast between smiling daffodil-yellow Washington and the winter in Boston, and in my heart." Many in the audience jeered and cheered.

IN EARLY APRIL General Fred Weyand, now Army Chief of Staff as successor to the late Creighton Abrams, was dispatched to Vietnam by Gerald Ford with instructions to size up the situation. Upon his return Weyand met with the National Security Council, telling its members on 9 April that the South Vietnamese still cherished the hope, however vain, "that the U.S. will help them." Weyand found the situation critical, with the ARVN reduced to rationing rifle bullets and grenades. He said that he had—incredibly—advised the leadership to "find enemy divisions and destroy them wherever they are," bizarrely impossible advice to follow for an army already reeling backward under an avalanche of enemy divisions and terrified refugees. But he had the main point right: "I believe the South Vietnam-ese are on the brink of total military defeat."[14]

As Weyand was rendering this gloomy, but wholly accurate, assessment, one of the most gallant performances of the entire war was about to begin at Xuan Loc, forty miles northeast of Saigon, where a determined defense was mounted by the ARVN 18th Infantry Division, Brigadier General Le Minh Dao com-manding. This was a sadly ironic situation, for it was the 18th Division, then under the inept Major General Do Ke Giai, that had once provoked Abrams to denounce its commander as "not only the worst general in the Vietnamese Army, but the worst general in any army."[15] But now, under assault by three and then four divisions of the North Vietnamese Army, with the war irretrievably lost and the country in ruins, the 18th Division virtually destroyed three of the attacking divisions and held out for almost a month before finally going under.

When Nguyen Cao Ky, relentless in his determination to undermine the government, sought even in these waning days to involve Dao in a coup to overthrow President Thieu, Dao responded, "Too busy fighting the communist, cannot partici-pate."[16] Brigadier General Tran Quang Khoi, who commanded III Armor Brigade and fought to the very last day, called the epic battle of Xuan Loc "the war's bloodiest."[17] Said longtime advisor Colonel Ray Battreall, "That magnificent last stand de-serves to live on in military history, if we can overcome the bias, even in our own ranks, that ARVN was never capable of doing anything right."[18]

The Defense Attaché Office's final assessment praised the 22nd ARVN Division, a unit that as recently as the 1972 Easter Offensive had essentially collapsed but had since been rebuilt under the command of Brigadier General Phan Dinh Niem. Now, said DAO, "throughout the desperate days of March and April, the 22nd fought gallantly and skillfully. Out-gunned and out-manned, it gave ground grudgingly. Of all the divisions in

RVNAF, it probably gave the best account of itself. It certainly gave all it had."[19]

In the midst of this President Nguyen Van Thieu resigned, hoping that a successor could negotiate with the enemy and avoid further death and destruction. A few days later, in a speech at Tulane University, President Ford gratuitously announced that, as far as the United States was concerned, the war in Vietnam was finished. By then, it was true, the war was almost over as far as everyone was concerned. Seven NVA divisions had Saigon nearly encircled, and six more were on the way. Only four viable ARVN divisions remained to offer any resistance.

Secretary of Defense James Schlesinger, a man of decency and compassion, dispatched a message to all members of the American armed forces. "For many of you," he acknowledged, "the tragedy of Southeast Asia is more than a distant and abstract event. You have fought there; you have lost comrades there; you have suffered there." Schlesinger reminded those who fought the war that they had been victorious and had left the field with honor, stating also his conviction that America's involvement had not been without purpose. "I salute you for it," he told the forces worldwide. "Beyond any question you are entitled to the nation's respect, admiration and gratitude."[20]

In South Vietnam, Vice President Tran Van Huong succeeded to the presidency, but was immediately rejected by the Communists as merely a surrogate for Thieu. Four days later, Huong resigned in favor of the ubiquitous Lieutenant General Duong Van Minh, rumored to be more acceptable to the enemy. That proved at best a vain hope, and the hapless Minh had no more success in stemming the final assault than had his predecessors.

The final hours saw feverish efforts to evacuate all the Americans still left in Vietnam, along with a large number of at-risk South Vietnamese. Massive airlifts from Tan Son Nhut and then, when enemy shelling closed that airfield, from rooftops around Saigon and eventually the American embassy itself resulted in all the Americans and some 130,000 South Vietnamese being delivered to U.S. ships standing offshore.[21] In Washington the State Department received a message that read in its entirety: "Plan to close mission Saigon approximately 0430 Saigon time, dependent on performance of military evacuation channels. Due to necessity to destroy commo gear, this is the last Saigon message to SecState."[22] At 4:58 A.M. on Wednesday, 30 April 1975, the last helicopter lifted off from the embassy roof, Ambassador Graham Martin among its cargo of evacuees.[23]

At midmorning of that same day, NVA tanks approached the Independence Palace in Saigon and, ramming their way through the wrought iron gates, took up positions in the courtyard. There Colonel Bui Tin accepted unconditional surrender from General Minh—South Vietnam's President for all of about forty hours—bringing to an end nearly two decades of Communist quest for domination of all Vietnam.

General Khoi had heard the radio broadcast in which the new President ordered all Republic of Vietnam armed forces to cease fire and surrender. "It was 1025 hours, 30 April 1975 by my watch," he recalled. "This was the end. I was most sorry for the outcome of the war, but I had done my best." There followed the inevitable. "I was, of course, arrested by the Communists and held captive in various concentration camps for seventeen years."[24]

ABRAMS HAD ALWAYS known, and often said, that the Vietnamese could do anything they *thought* they could do. The converse was painfully demonstrated in the final battles. "The army that had fought so well against such a strong force in 1972," noted Douglas Pike, "didn't fight at all against a lesser force in 1975."[25] They had run out of that conviction, no doubt helped by the realization that their sometime ally the United States had abandoned them, and by the impending depletion of the means to carry on the fight. And, it must be admitted, they ran out of leadership. Concluded South Vietnam's best field general, Ngo

Quang Truong, in the final words of an insightful and scrupulously honest analysis, "Good leadership and motivation were definitely not developed to an adequate extent and . . . this failure had a disastrous effect on the eventual outcome of the war."[26]

As the end neared, one could only feel great sympathy for President Thieu. Years earlier he had admitted to Ambassador Bunker that he had little experience in command above division level, while the military challenges that confronted him during his last years in office were difficult indeed. Faced with agonizing choices between attempting to hold and defend all the people and territory of South Vietnam—a nearly impossible task while the enemy held the initiative, and one that became ever more difficult as support from the United States continued to erode—or pulling back to a more constricted and defensible perimeter, he could not bring himself to give anything up. For years he had advanced the slogan of the multiple nos, including no coalition, no neutralization, and no territory ceded. It proved simply impossible to abandon that position, psychologically or physically, until the point where to do so was in itself to invite disaster.

Then, too, Thieu continued to be constrained in his actions by fear of a coup. Even though the nation had, largely under pressure from the United States, adopted the mechanisms of a democratic republic, the earlier tradition of frequent coups and countercoups was too recent to be far from the president's consciousness. And the malevolent presence of Nguyen Cao Ky, disappointed presidential aspirant, volatile and dangerous egotist, and perennial potential coup leader, was a constant shadow on Thieu's presidency. "I thought that Thieu was a wiser, more solid person," Ambassador Bunker once observed. "Ky was too unpredictable, too emotional, too flamboyant. Thieu was more solid."[27]

The collapse of the South Vietnamese has been attributed to any number of causes, but over time three have stood out as the most prominent. One, a simple matter of fact, had to do with the termination of political support, reduction of matériel support, and eventually even denial of fiscal support to the South Vietnamese by their sometime American ally. This was the work of the Congress, wrought over the strong and eventually ago- nized protests of the administration, military leaders, and of course the South Vietnamese. It stood in stark contrast to the uninterrupted support rendered North Vietnam by her Soviet and Chinese allies. Ambassador Bunker, for one, argued that "we eventually defeated ourselves, but we were not defeated when we signed the Paris peace treaties. We had, I think, then achieved our objective. The fact that it slipped our grasp was our own doing."[28]

A second cause had to do with the task, never adequately accomplished, of providing effective leadership for a military es- tablishment rapidly and hugely expanded over a relatively short time, and for the expanded civilian bureaucracy as well. Bui Tin, speaking from the enemy's perspective, said that a key step for the allies to win the war would have been to "train South Viet- nam's generals. The junior South Vietnamese officers were good, competent and courageous, but the commanding gen- eral officers were inept."[29] Despite some very significant excep- tions, that judgment was hard to argue with, and in fact it was one that responsible South Vietnamese themselves made after the war.

A third key cause was failure to isolate the battlefield, to cut off enemy infiltration and resupply, and to deny the sanctuaries in Cambodia, Laos, and North Vietnam. Again Bui Tin was pointed and succinct, arguing that to succeed the allies needed to "cut the Ho Chi Minh trail inside Laos."[30]

BY THIS POINT Abrams was gone, the only Army Chief of Staff to die in office. Thus mercifully spared witnessing the sad end of the war, he could not give his own final assessment, but his close friend Samuel Berger thought he knew his mind on the

matter. "He thought there was always a chance," Berger recalled, "but he didn't delude himself. He neither deluded himself
nor let anyone else delude him."[31] Said Bruce Palmer, who was
also very close to Abrams, "He died feeling we could have won
that war. He felt we were on top of it in 1971, then lost our
nerve."[32]

The prospects for the South Vietnamese to make it, to preserve their freedom and independence of action in the circumstances after the Paris Accords were signed, were questionable
at best. On one hand, since the advent of Vietnamization much
had been done for them and they had accomplished much. "The
improvements that took place in those four years were fantas-
tic—in the quality and fighting abilities of the Vietnamese, the
arms that they had, and the improvement of the Regional and
Popular Forces," said Berger.[33] But always the long-term prospects for success were conditional. "Had we made good on our
commitments," observed Ambassador Bunker, "it could well
have been a different story."[34]

The price paid by the South Vietnamese in their long struggle to remain free proved grievous indeed. The armed forces
lost 275,000 killed in action. Another 465,000 civilians lost their
lives, many of them assassinated by Viet Cong terrorists or felled
by the enemy's indiscriminate shelling and rocketing of cities.
Of the million who became boat people an unknown number,
feared to be many, lost their lives at sea. Perhaps 65,000 others
were executed by their liberators. As many as 250,000 more
perished in the brutal reeducation camps. Two million, driven
from their homeland, formed a new Vietnamese diaspora.[35]

While the costs to the United States were modest compared
with those suffered by the Vietnamese, they were substantial
nonetheless. There were, to begin with, more than 58,000 lives
lost, more than 47,000 of them due to enemy action.[36] There
was the money expended, perhaps not very significant in the
long run, but still a lot of money—$150 billion by one estimate.
And there was the splintering of the social compact in American

society, already under great stress for other reasons and not easily, if at all, put back together again. Finally there was the unalterable alienation of those who served from those who did not and would not, a permanent schism derived from absolutely incommensurable interests and values.

The enemy's losses had been staggering, horrifying—estimated by Douglas Pike at perhaps 900,000 dead by 1973.[37] Nor had they ended there. The newly unified Communist Vietnam went to war with Cambodia, and then with China, occasioning yet more death and destruction. Later it was revealed that, almost twenty years after the Vietnam War, there were 300,000 Communist soldiers still unaccounted for.[38] Even higher casualty numbers were later cited, one estimate suggesting that overall 3.6 million Vietnamese deaths had occurred.[39]

And for what? Former Viet Cong Colonel Pham Xuan An had an embittered answer: "All that talk about 'liberation' twenty, thirty, forty years ago, all the plotting, and all the bodies, produced this, this impoverished, broken-down country led by a gang of cruel and paternalistic half-educated theorists."[40]

THERE ARE MANY POINTS along the way for pondering the multitude of "what ifs" associated with this long, sad war. Some historians argue against such speculation, denigrating it as "counterfactual analysis." No soldier would be so dismissive, for every military leader is taught early on to make what is called an "estimate of the situation," the heart of which is consideration of what enemy courses of action might be provoked by various friendly courses of action, with similar calculations performed for a range of alternative courses of action. Such calculations are the essence of modern war gaming as well, and often have significant impact on how a commander uses the forces at his disposal. Sometimes seen from the outside as the products of intuitive genius, in reality calculations of "what if" are the essence of the art of war.

Retrospective assessment of missed opportunities in the

Vietnam War is bittersweet at best. While demonstrating that more effective options were available at many stages of the war, such calculations also remind us that time after time those chances were missed, ignored, rejected, or proscribed on the basis of one rationale or another. The signposts along the road of better alternatives are numerous, and include the selection of William C. Westmoreland as U.S. commander in Vietnam, LBJ's failure to call up reserve forces or to effectively mobilize public support for U.S. involvement in the war, failure to take the war to the enemy—and in particular to cut the Ho Chi Minh Trail, neglect of the enemy infrastructure in South Vietnam's villages for too many years, failure to develop South Vietnamese forces during the period of American domination of the war, a year's delay in Abrams's succession to the top command, and in consequence of all these the squandering of literally years of substantial support from the American public, Congress, and even media.

Under new leadership in both Washington and Saigon during the later years, crucially important differences included wisdom and stability in the ambassadorial post; better field generalship; a more adept national leadership involving Nixon, Kissinger, and Laird—even given the vigorous internecine warfare they frequently waged against one another—compared with LBJ and McNamara; a wholly different approach to conduct of the war within South Vietnam, one in which population security, not body count, was the measure of merit; different tactics in South Vietnam, with "clear and hold" rather than "search and destroy" the mode; an attitude of nurturing and improving the South Vietnamese armed forces rather than basically shoving them out of the way, as was done in the earlier period; concentration on "one war" involving pacification, combat operations, and improvement of South Vietnamese armed forces rather than fixation primarily on American combat operations; and of course the radical differences in context and the American domestic scene, resulting in withdrawal of American forces rather than continually building them up, in eroding political support for the war, and ultimately in abandonment of the South Vietnamese.

In December 1975 Donald Rumsfeld, recently installed as Secretary of Defense, made his first visit to American troops in Europe. Workmen took advantage of his absence to refurbish Rumsfeld's Pentagon office, in the process taking down the huge relief map of Southeast Asia that had hung on the wall for probably a decade. Old and unwanted, the displaced artifact reposed in the corridor for half a day, then disappeared forever.

Twenty years to the day after the fall of Saigon and the descent of what had been South Vietnam into its long night of tyranny, a remarkable editorial, almost a redemption, appeared in the *Washington Post*. "There was such a thing as communism on the march," it read. "It was not a 'misunderstanding.' It was a threat to what deserved to be called the free world." And "for a reason—because it faced an armed takeover by an outside Communist regime—South Vietnam inevitably became a place where the confrontation was played out."[41]

General Cao Van Vien, a decent man and a good soldier, in an unflinchingly honest and insightful monograph admitted that, though South Vietnam's senior leadership had done its best, "it still proved inadequate for this most difficult episode of our nation's history." But Vien proved himself a man with eloquence and vision to match his soldierly qualities, concluding with "hope and with prayers for the reemergence of a free South Vietnam in the not too distant future, a South Vietnam led by men of talent and high morals—the truly great leaders of Vietnamese history."[42]

EPILOGUE

IN VIETNAM, Ambassador Ellsworth Bunker, General Creighton Abrams, and Ambassador William Colby fought as hard as they could for as long as they could with everything that was left to them to try to win the war. Maybe others in Washington or elsewhere were interested in stalemate or disengagement or some other palliative solution, but these three men and the forces they led were striving for just one thing: victory—victory defined as a South Vietnam capable of defending itself and determining its own political, economic, and cultural future.

In so doing, they by their actions defined stewardship—doing the best you can with what you have to work with, and doing it with selflessness, dignity, and integrity. Over these later years the vast majority of American men and women who served in Vietnam exhibited the same admirable traits, demonstrating by their actions that the negative stereotypes so widely circulated then and later were neither representative nor fair.

In the wake of the defeat came untold further misery. Two decades after the North Vietnamese conquest, Colonel Bui Tin said sorrowfully, freedom in Vietnam "remains a distant dream."[1] Not many who had opposed American involvement in the war were heard from when this dreadful suffering followed the enemy victory, but one who spoke out with decency and regret was William Shawcross. "It seemed to me then, and still seems to me today," he wrote long years after the end, "that those of us who were opposed to the American effort in Indochina should be humbled by the scale of suffering inflicted by the Communist victors—especially in Cambodia but in Vietnam and Laos as well."[2]

Nearly a quarter-century after the war Nick Sebastian, a West Point graduate then with the Immigration and Naturalization Service, spent three months in what had once been Saigon interviewing candidates for political asylum in the United States, former "boat people" who had been forcibly returned from refugee camps elsewhere in Southeast Asia. It was for Sebastian a moving and humbling experience, for he found both the country of Vietnam and its people beautiful, persevering with admirable spirit under a repressive regime and terrible economic hardship. "The people I met throughout the country," he reported, "accept their loss and in many cases unbelievable subsequent persecution with an equanimity, fortitude, strength of character, and will to survive that is awe-inspiring."[3]

Long after the war was over, after the fighting had ended, after Bunker was dead, and Abrams too, after the boat people and all the other sad detritus of a lost cause, the eldest of General Abrams's three sons, all Army officers, was on the faculty of the Command & General Staff College at Fort Leavenworth. There someone reminded him of what Robert Shaplen had once said, that his father deserved a better war. "He didn't see it that way," young Creighton responded at once. "He thought the Vietnamese were worth it."

ACKNOWLEDGMENTS

FOLLOWING THREE DECADES of public service I began researching and writing about topics in military history, work that has produced two biographies and now this volume. I have in the process, I concede, become something of a dinosaur, spending the past fifteen years primarily in contemplation of another fifteen-year period, Vietnam during 1960–1975.

Over the course of these years my work has been assisted by many people, both those with firsthand knowledge of the events of interest and the indispensable community of archivists, librarians, researchers, and historians upon whom so much depends. Perhaps of greatest significance, in part because of my exclusive access, this volume has benefited importantly from a previously unknown, and therefore unexploited, treasure trove of unique and authentic contemporaneous materials. Given that there exist at the U.S. Army's Military History Institute at Carlisle Barracks, Pennsylvania, open holdings referred to as the "Abrams Papers," I will, to avoid confusion, use the term "Abrams Special Collection" to differentiate the new materials.

When General Creighton W. Abrams returned in 1972 to become Army Chief of Staff, he brought with him certain highly classified materials relating to his service in Vietnam. When, in the autumn of 1974, Abrams died in office, his successor, General Frederick C. Weyand, ordered that these materials be sequestered, with both their existence and their location treated as classified information. Eventually, however, I learned of these materials from sources in the Army hierarchy who were friendly to my work.

A number of years passed and then, with the invaluable help of Brigadier General Harold W. Nelson, the Army's Chief of Military History, my request for access to the "Abrams Special Collection" was forwarded to Army Chief of Staff General Gordon R. Sullivan, coincidentally the only armor officer other than General Abrams to have held the post of Chief of Staff. General Sullivan granted my request and, after concurrence from certain other agencies sharing a security interest in the materials involved, I commenced research in these holdings.

Thus began what turned out to be a yearlong endeavor. The collection was housed in a secure facility at Carlisle Barracks, some two hours from where I resided. Beginning in May 1994, I departed home at 5:30 A.M. each Monday morning, getting to Carlisle Barracks by the time the vault opened for the day's business. There I typically spent a ten-hour day, working with the materials until the vault closed in late afternoon. In the evenings I used the fine library of the U.S. Army War College, also located at Carlisle Barracks. My home away from home for each week was a modest but friendly motel frequented primarily by drivers of eighteen-wheeler trucking rigs. Friday evenings I would, after the day's work, make my way home. This routine continued for an entire year of weekdays, interrupted only by holidays and other occasions on which the vault was not open, and by a one-week respite for our family's annual beach outing.

The heart of the collection turned out to be 455 tape recordings made at Headquarters, U.S. Military Assistance Command, Vietnam, during the four years General Abrams was in command. These tapes, of the old reel-to-reel variety, ran two to six hours in length, and I used up or wore out three ancient machines in the process of screening them all. Frank Cox, chief of audiovisual services for the Army War College and an old friend from my days on the faculty there, performed the invaluable service of keeping these machines limping along or finding successors when they finally collapsed, a hard job with which Bill Robinson also helped. In the final weeks the last machine was kept going only through use of a wooden jig, inserted to hold the worn-out play lever in place, carved for me by Captain Ray Miller, my patient and friendly host and custodian of the vault.

Listening to these tapes and making handwritten single-spaced notes that eventually ran to nearly 3,200 pages was a laborious and time-consuming process, but also fascinating, for one never knew what the next tape would reveal. What emerged was a portrait of a senior commander and his closest associates—something like Napoleon and his marshals—working together to prosecute a complex and challenging military campaign in an equally complex and difficult political context. The interchanges were candid, spirited, often funny, and included not only what were called the Weekly Intelligence Estimate Updates—Saturday morning sessions held at MACV Headquarters—but also many sessions conducted for such visitors as the Secretary of Defense, the Chairman of the Joint Chiefs of Staff, the Commander in Chief, Pacific, and consultant Sir Robert Thompson.

In May 1995, almost exactly a year after I began, my screening of these materials was complete. It took most of another year to get the notes through the mandatory declassification review process by the Army, the National Security Agency, and the Central Intelligence Agency. In this entire process there is no one to whom I owe more than Mr. Randy Rakers, security manager at the U.S. Army Military History Institute, who assisted me in screening the materials, reviewed my notes on the Army's behalf, performed the laborious tasks of duplicating the notes and forwarding them for review by the other agencies concerned, and helped me get those agencies to respond. This is the third book on which I have had his assistance, and my admiration for his energy, goodwill, and ability has continued to grow over the years of our association.

Even so, I needed the absolutely invaluable assistance of three senior officers who are also valued and longtime friends to reach a favorable outcome. Charles A. Briggs, once my supervisor at the Central Intelligence Agency, helped me gain CIA approval for

access to these materials. Lieutenant General Lincoln D. Faurer, a
former Director of the National Security Agency, was instrumental
in getting NSA's agreement. And Lieutenant General James A. Williams, formerly Director of the Defense Intelligence Agency,
stepped in at a critical point to help get NSA to process my reclama
on certain redactions in the notes. I am extremely grateful to all
three for their effective interventions on behalf of my work.

Once the cleared notes had been returned to me, it took over
two months of more or less nonstop work to enter them—nearly
835,000 words in all—in a computer. That was a task worth doing,
however, for then the material was searchable and much easier to
shape and exploit. The results form an important part, but only a
part, of the documentary underpinnings of this book. It is my intention to publish an annotated volume or volumes of the most
interesting and historically significant portions of the notes in the
fairly near future. I am also most grateful for help with this part of
the research to Michael Smith, Linda Huffman, and Pamela Phillips
at NSA, and to Dr. John H. Hedley at CIA.

Many other public records and private recollections yielded valuable research material. Over the past decade and a half I have
interviewed about 500 people, many of them repeatedly, for this
book and the two preceding biographies. Those whose recollections contributed to this particular work are listed in the bibliography, and I am most grateful to them all.

At the U.S. Army Military History Institute at Carlisle Barracks, I have over a number of years been assisted by virtually every
member of the staff in one way or another. Colonel Thomas W.
Sweeney, Colonel Stephen L. Bowman, and Colonel W. Thomas
Vossler served successively as Director during the period of my most
recent research there. Dr. Richard Sommers, Chief Archivist, allowed me to virtually take up residence in his reading room, where
David Keough and Pam Cheney were invariably friendly, helpful, and knowledgeable. John Slonaker and his library staff, including Louise Arnold-Friend and Dennis Vetock, were very supportive. Also at Carlisle Barracks, in the U.S. Army War College

Library, I benefited from the help of Jane Gibish, Lydia Gole, and Pat Knuth.

My work in the Indochina Archive at the University of California, Berkeley, was assisted immeasurably by the interest and assistance of Dr. Douglas Pike, Curator, and Dr. Donald S. Marshall, who was then in residence there and whose own papers formed part of the collection. Some key documents found there may well be the only copies to have survived. This valuable material has subsequently—thanks, I am proud to say, to my having introduced Dr. Pike, when he was seeking a new home for the archives, to Dr. James Reckner, founder of Texas Tech's Vietnam Center— been relocated to the Vietnam Archive at Texas Tech University, as has Dr. Pike himself (not, of course, as an artifact).

During recent years the Army Center of Military History has been led by Brigadier General John W. Mountcastle, Chief of Military History, an officer I first met three decades ago in the Central Highlands of Vietnam where, as a young and able lieutenant, he reported for duty to the tank battalion of which I was the executive officer. He, Chief Historian Dr. Jeffrey J. Clarke, Dr. John M. Carland, Vincent H. Demma, Dr. William M. Hammond, Dr. Richard A. Hunt, Dr. George MacGarrigle, Dr. Joel D. Meyerson, Dr. Robert K. Wright, Jr., Steve Hardyman, and Roger Wright have all been very friendly to my work and helpful with the research.

Dr. Richard P. Hallion, Chief of Air Force History, Yvonne Kinkaid, and particularly Dr. Wayne Thompson have assisted me in important ways. At the Marine Corps Historical Center, I thank my friend Dr. Jack Shulimson, Fred Graboske, and Brigadier General Edwin H. Simmons, USMC, Director Emeritus. General Wallace M. Greene, Jr., former Commandant of the Marine Corps, generously gave me access to his valuable papers there.

At the National Archives my friend Dr. Timothy K. Nenninger was his usual informed and helpful self. Pat Anderson introduced me to the intricacies of the Nixon Presidential Materials Collection, with help also from Dmitri Reavis, and Richard Boylan again pointed me to valuable materials. Thanks also to Eric Freiwald and Mike McGinn. At the Martin Luther King Memorial Library in Washington, Photo Librarian Mary C. Ternes was an enormous help in making available that useful and extensive collection.

General Bruce Palmer, Jr., who knew all the principals and himself played an important role in the events described in this book, has been a friend of long standing and a patient, knowledgeable, invaluable resource, as was the late Ambassador William E. Colby. Merle L. Pribbenow has provided splendid translations of North Vietnamese retrospective analyses of the war. Once again Albert D. McJoynt assisted me by preparing excellent maps. And no scholar working in the period of the Vietnam War can fail to acknowledge the superb volumes prepared by Professor William Conrad Gibbons, valuable for making accessible so much documentation on the war and for insightful commentaries, logical structure, and catholicity of sources.

Ambassador Ellsworth Bunker's son John kindly granted access to his father's oral history at the LBJ Library, and his son Samuel allowed me to screen his father's photograph collection. Stephen B. Young generously gave me access to his extensive and valuable but as yet unpublished oral history of Ambassador Bunker. Dean Vincent Davis provided access to the Vann Papers at the Patterson School of Diplomacy and International Commerce, University of Kentucky. Jo Lavelle granted access to the Air Force oral history of her late husband, General John D. Lavelle. Colonel William E. LeGro lent me valuable period maps.

My friend Major H. R. McMaster generously shared research materials from his own fine work on the Vietnam War. Ambassador Sally Shelton-Colby gave me access to the photographs of her late husband, Ambassador William E. Colby. And George McArthur magnanimously gave me his file of notes on interviews with General Abrams conducted during the years George reported from Vietnam. George Dalley, proprietor of Dalley Book Service, runs a superb source of hard-to-find books on Vietnam with diligence and good cheer. Donna Davidson made available a useful set of videotaped recollections by her late husband, Lieutenant General Phillip B. Davidson, former MACV J-2.

My West Point classmates have been an enormous source of encouragement and often of substantive help as well. I thank them all, and particularly Brigadier General John C. Bahnsen; Colonel Stuart W. Bowen, USAF; Brigadier General Zeb B. Bradford, Jr.; Lieutenant General Frederic J. Brown III; Colonel William F. Cody; Colonel Rude DeFrance; William Robert Devoto; Lieutenant General Thomas N. Griffin, Jr.; Colonel Jerry H. Huff; Colonel John J. McGinn; Brigadier General John W. Nicholson; Lieutenant General Dave R. Palmer; Colonel William K. Schrage, Jr.; General John A. Shaud, USAF; Major General Perry M. Smith, USAF; Colonel William L. Weihl; and Lieutenant General John W. Woodmansee.

Others who helped with advice, photographs, documents, and insights include Major General John R. Alison, USAF; Brigadier General David A. Armstrong; Colonel Raymond R. Battreall; Colonel Paul F. Braim; B. G. Burkett; Major General Neal Creighton; Lieutenant General John H. Cushman; General Michael S. Davison; Joseph DiFranco; Colonel David E. Farnham; Dr. Forrest R. Frank; Dr. William A. Hamilton; Colonel Morris J. Herbert; Seymour Hersh; Stanley Karnow; Charles Krohn; Professor Guenter Lewy; Colonel John J. Madigan III; Larry McKay; Colonel Warren H. Milberg, USAF; Renee Godfrey Mountz; Mark Moyar; Keith William Nolan; Mark Perry; Dr. Walter S. Poole; Dr. John Prados; Major Melvin G. Radley; Carolyn Rogers; William L. Rogers; Dr. Richard W. Schneider; Olivier Todd; Edward C. Tracy; Lieutenant General Richard G. Trefry; Colonel Michael Treinen; Dr. John F. Votaw; Colonel William F. Wollenberg; and Commander Moira Wuertzel. I am especially grateful to Lou Dunham, who cheerfully and efficiently solved computer problems when time was short and it mattered a lot.

Walt Bode, my editor at Harcourt Brace, has been a delight to collaborate with and has made this a better book. Over now quite a number of years my agent, Peter Ginsberg, has also become a valued friend. I am most grateful for his tenacity and belief in the value of the work. This book is dedicated to my sister, Judith Sorley Chalmers, whose loyalty, encouragement, energy, generosity, and sense of fun have enriched my life beyond measure.

Finally, and always, I record my profound gratitude to my wife, Virginia Mezey Sorley, who, in addition to her multitude of other fine attributes, is a superb professional research librarian.

GLOSSARY OF TERMS
AND ABBREVIATIONS

AAA	antiaircraft artillery
APC	Accelerated Pacification Campaign
Arc Light	B-52 bomber strike
ARVN	Army of the Republic of Vietnam
ASC	Abrams Special Collection
BDA	bomb damage assessment
Binh tram	military way station on the Ho Chi Minh Trail
BOQ	Bachelor Officers' Quarters
CBU	cluster bomb unit
Chieu Hoi	program to induce ralliers to the GVN
CIA	Central Intelligence Agency
CICV	Combined Intelligence Center, Vietnam
CINCPAC	Commander in Chief, Pacific
CINCSAC	Commander in Chief, Strategic Air Command
CMH	U.S. Army Center of Military History
COMINT	communications intelligence
COMUSMACV	Commander, U.S. Military Assistance Command, Vietnam
CONARC	Continental Army Command

CORDS	Civil Operations and Revolutionary Development Support (later Civil Operations and Rural Development Support)
COSVN	Central Office for South Vietnam
CRIMP	Consolidated Republic of Vietnam Armed Forces Improvement & Modernization Program
CTZ	Corps Tactical Zone
DAO	Defense Attaché Office
DIA	Defense Intelligence Agency
DMZ	Demilitarized Zone
DOD	Department of Defense
FARK	Forces Armées Royales Khmères (Royal Khmer Armed Forces)
FBIS	Foreign Broadcast Information Service
FFV	Field Force, Vietnam
FMFPAC	Fleet Marine Force, Pacific
FSB	Fire Support Base
FWMAF	Free World Military Assistance Forces
GCI	ground-controlled intercept
GDRS	General Directorate of Rear Services
GVN	Government of Vietnam (South Vietnam)
HES	Hamlet Evaluation System
H&I	harassment and interdiction (artillery fire)
Hoi chanh	rallier under the Chieu Hoi program
HQ	headquarters
ICC	International Control Commission
IISS	International Institute for Strategic Studies
JCS	Joint Chiefs of Staff (U.S.)
JGS	Joint General Staff (RVN)

KIA	killed in action
LAW	light antitank weapon
LOC	line of communication
LZ	landing zone
MAAG	Military Assistance Advisory Group
MACV	Military Assistance Command, Vietnam
MAF	Marine Amphibious Force
MCHC	Marine Corps Historical Center
medevac	medical evacuation
MHI	Military History Institute (U.S. Army)
MIA	missing in action
MiG	Soviet fighter aircraft
mm	millimeter
MOS	Military Occupational Specialty
MR	Military Region
NAVFORV	Naval Force, Vietnam (U.S.)
NIE	National Intelligence Estimate
NP	National Police
NPFF	National Police Field Force
NSA	National Security Agency
NSC	National Security Council
NSIC	National Strategy Information Center
NVA	North Vietnamese Army
NVN	North Vietnam
OR	operational readiness
OSD	Office of the Secretary of Defense
PA&E	Pacific Architects & Engineers
PAVN	People's Army of Vietnam (North Vietnam)
PDO	Property Disposal Office
PF	Popular Forces
Phoenix	program for neutralizing VCI (U.S. term)

Phuong Hoang	program for neutralizing VCI (RVN term)
PLAF	People's Liberation Armed Forces
POL	petroleum, oil, and lubricants
POW	prisoner of war
PROVN	Program for the Pacification and Long-Term Development of Vietnam
PSDF	People's Self-Defense Force (formerly Popular Self-Defense Force)
PW	prisoner of war
Rallier	enemy who comes over to the GVN side in the Chieu Hoi program
RF	Regional Forces
ROE	rules of engagement
ROK	Republic of Korea (South Korea)
Rolling Thunder	air operations over North Vietnam
R&R	rest and recreation
RVN	Republic of Vietnam
RVNAF	Republic of Vietnam Armed Forces
SAC	Strategic Air Command
SAM	surface-to-air missile
SDF	Self-Defense Forces
SEA	Southeast Asia
SNIE	Special National Intelligence Estimate
SOG	Studies & Observation Group
SSDF	Secret Self-Defense Forces
SVN	South Vietnam
Tac air	tactical air
Tet	Vietnamese lunar new year
TOT	time on target/time over target
TOW	tube-launched, optically tracked, wire-guided [antitank missile]
US	United States
USMACV	U.S. Military Assistance Command, Vietnam

VC	Viet Cong
VCI	Viet Cong infrastructure
WIA	wounded in action
WIEU	Weekly Intelligence Estimate Update

NOTES

A NOTE ON THE NOTES

THE DOCUMENTARY RECORD of the later years of the Vietnam War is very rich. This volume draws, for example, on some 455 previously unexploited tape recordings, running in the aggregate to thousands of hours, made at MACV Headquarters during the years 1968–1972. The oral histories of many of the senior American officers involved in prosecution of the war are extensive, as are the papers of some of those officers. Archival materials at the U.S. Army Military History Institute, the U.S. Army Center of Military History, the Air Force History Office, and the Marine Corps Historical Center have also been used, as have files in the National Archives, including the Wheeler Papers.

These materials have been supplemented with some 200 interviews conducted by the author for this book, as well as several hundred interviews conducted by him during the preparation of two previous works of biography.

Given this abundance of material, it would have been possible to footnote virtually every line, but that seemed unnecessarily distracting and pedantic. The author has, however, prepared a fully annotated copy of the manuscript, and will gladly respond to inquiries through the publisher as to the source of any quoted material. All materials drawn from the work of other scholars have of course been credited in the notes.

KEY TO NOTE ABBREVIATIONS

These abbreviations are used throughout the notes to indicate sources. In the selected bibliography a full citation may be found for each item. When items appear only in notes and not in the bibliography, the full citation is given in the note.

ASC:	Abrams Special Collection, USAWC
CMH:	U.S. Army Center of Military History
CWAP:	Creighton W. Abrams Papers, MHI
GRF:	Gerald R. Ford Library
LBJ:	Lyndon Baines Johnson Library
MHI:	U.S. Army Military History Institute
NA:	National Archives and Records Administration
USAC&GSC:	U.S. Army Command & General Staff College
USAWC:	U.S. Army War College

The frontispiece quotation is from Kevin Buckley, "General Abrams Deserves a Better War," *New York Times Magazine* (5 October 1969).

PROLOGUE

1. William E. Colby, "Vietnam After McNamara," *Washington Post* (27 April 1995).

CHAPTER 1

1. Mark Perry wrote in *Four Stars* (p. 136) that "Westmoreland had been hand-picked for the assignment by the martyred Kennedy, who had been impressed by Westmoreland when they first met in June 1962 and had pushed him as Harkins' replacement in the weeks before his assassination." Very probably the influence of General Maxwell Taylor was also a factor in Westmoreland's selection for the top job in Vietnam. Dr. Walter S. Poole, a JCS historian, wrote that "despite his disclaimers, Taylor was responsible for choosing Harkins and Westmoreland, both of whom proved quite unequal to their tasks." Letter to Major H. R. Mc-Master, 30 July 1996, copy provided the author by Brig. Gen.

David Armstrong, JCS Historian. Charles MacDonald, ghost writer for Westmoreland's memoirs, had written into the text the observation that "there are those who say knowing Max Taylor helped my career." Westmoreland deleted the passage, said MacDonald, because "he didn't want to attribute it [his success] to anyone else." Remarks, U.S. Army War College, 17 May 1976, MHI.

2. Samuel Zaffiri, *Westmoreland,* p. 160. Regarding terminology, while PAVN, for People's Army of Vietnam, and PLAF, for People's Liberation Armed Forces, are technically the correct terms for North Vietnam's armed forces and those of the insurgents in the South, the more familiar language of Americans fighting the war—NVA for North Vietnamese Army and VC for Viet Cong—is used throughout this account.

3. During 1968 there was a very limited mobilization for deployment to Vietnam of certain reserve force units, some of which mounted political and legal challenges to being sent to the combat zone. General Ralph Haines, who had just finished a year as Army Vice Chief of Staff, told MACV that "because the reserve components have been a haven from the draft, [they] have very, very, very large numbers of college graduates or college-experienced personnel. So you're talking about—many of these units, 70 to 80 percent of them have some college and maybe, of your enlisted personnel, 20 percent are college graduates. And this is even true in a *truck* company." Abrams: "Should be very high-quality units." Someone else: "More capable of writing their congressmen." All: Laughter. Recording, WIEU, 24 August 1968, ASC.

4. William Conrad Gibbons, *The U.S. Government and the Vietnam War,* pt. IV, *July 1965–1968,* p. 358, citing cable Saigon 5378. Hereafter Gibbons IV.

5. Lt. Gen. Phillip B. Davidson, LBJ Library Oral History Interview, as quoted in Mark Moyar, *Phoenix and the Birds of Prey,* p. 49.

6. *Pentagon Papers,* Gravel edition, IV:387.

7. *Life* (11 November 1966), quoted in Clyde Pettit, *The Experts,* pp. 301–302.

8. Later, recalled General Donn Starry, "General Westmoreland called me and said, 'I never said we were going to win the war in 1967.' 'I'm sorry, general,' I replied, 'I was there and heard

you say it several times.' " Starry interview, 31 May 1995.

9. Message, Wheeler to Westmoreland, JCS 1284, 170000Z FEB 1967, U.S. Army Military History Institute (hereafter MHI), reporting what he had told LBJ.

10. George C. Herring, " 'Cold Blood': LBJ's Conduct of Limited War in Vietnam," in Showalter and Albert, eds., *An American Dilemma*, p. 78.

11. Gibbons IV:541, citing the draft of a Lodge "Vietnam Memoir" in the Lodge Papers at the Massachusetts Historical Society.

12. Keith William Nolan, *Battle for Saigon,* p. 141.

13. Lewis Sorley, *Honorable Warrior,* pp. 231–232.

14. Message, Wheeler to Sharp and Westmoreland, JCS 9298, 312237Z OCT 1967, MHI.

15. Gibbons IV:712.

16. Gibbons IV:894.

17. Alain C. Enthoven and K. Wayne Smith, *How Much Is Enough?,* p. 305.

18. *Pentagon Papers,* IV:464, quoting 1 May 1967 draft of Alain Enthoven, Memorandum for the Secretary of Defense, Subject: Increase of SEA Forces.

19. Norfolk *Virginian-Pilot* (23 April 1967).

20. Douglas Kinnard, *The War Managers,* p. 45.

21. Bunker Reporting Cable #29, 29 November 1967, in *The Bunker Papers,* ed. Douglas Pike. Cited hereafter by number and date.

22. Gen. William E. DePuy, "Our Experience in Vietnam," *Army* (June 1987), p. 32.

23. Gibbons IV:939.

24. George C. Herring, "The Reluctant Warrior: Lyndon Johnson as Commander in Chief," in David L. Anderson, ed., *Shadow on the White House,* p. 100.

25. Gibbons IV:938.

26. Gibbons IV:891.

27. Gen. Bruce Palmer, Jr., Oral History Interview, General Creighton Abrams Story, MHI.

28. Gen. Bruce Palmer, Jr., *The 25-Year War,* p. 64.

29. R. W. Komer, *Organization and Management of the New Model Pacification Program,* p. 106.

30. William Bundy, Deposition, *Vietnam, A Documentary Collection: Westmoreland vs. CBS,* p. 186.

31. Lt. Gen. Ngo Quang Truong, *The Easter Offensive of 1972,* p. 5.

32. John Paul Vann, Remarks, Lexington, Ky., 8 January 1972, Vann Papers, Patterson School of Diplomacy and International Commerce, University of Kentucky. Hereafter cited as Vann Papers.

33. Lt. Gen. Ngo Quang Truong, *Territorial Forces,* pp. 49–50. In certain provinces where recruitments lagged, noted General Truong, the RF and PF were authorized to recruit from the prime age group of eighteen to thirty. "As a last resort," he wrote, "this measure was reluctantly taken because the JGS was fully aware that by doing so it tacitly condoned draft evasion and desertion. In fact, experience revealed that almost all of those recruited in the RF and PF who fell between these draft age limits were either draft evaders, illegal deferments and exemptions, or deserters. As such, they should have all been arrested and prosecuted by military tribunals." That was not done. "After all, convicted or not, they would eventually end up either in the military or in enemy hands. It was much better to accept them in the service and have additional combatants than lose them to the enemy." Ibid., p. 50.

34. See Lewis Sorley, *Thunderbolt,* pp. 194–195, and *Honorable Warrior,* pp. 270–273, for the evidence on this point.

CHAPTER 2

1. Quoted in Charles R. Smith, *U.S. Marines in Vietnam,* p. 10. General Westmoreland had been invited to comment on a draft of this volume in the official Marine Corps history of the war. The published volume includes his observations on this point: "In commenting on the 'one war' concept, promulgated by General Abrams, General Westmoreland stated: 'It was not Abrams that did it, it was the changed situation which he adapted to. The change was the situation, it was not the personality because, General Abrams was my deputy for over a year. He and I consulted about almost every tactical action. I considered his views in great depth because I had admiration for him and I'd known him for many years. And I do not remember a single instance where our

views and the courses of action we thought were proper, differed in any way.' " (p. 10n). There was more. Westmoreland refused to give Abrams any credit for *any* changes he might make. In a Marine Corps oral history interview these Westmoreland comments followed immediately after those quoted above: "Any changes that Abrams made in strategy and tactics that was presumably mine—and it was my watch and I assume full responsibility for them—or any policies as practiced by me, there was [*sic*] any changes made in my view were the function of the changed situation after the defeat of the Tet offensive." Westmoreland, Marine Corps Oral History, MCHC. Presumably General Westmoreland was not pleased with the Army's official history, either, since it titled the chapter dealing with the years 1969–1970 "A New Direction." Jeffrey A. Clarke, *Advice and Support*. In any event, as the enemy's COSVN Resolution 9 made very clear, it was the changes instituted by Abrams that forced the enemy to change, not the other way around.

2. Message, Abrams to McCain, MAC 8819, 09094Z [cite defective] JUL 1969, ASC.
3. Lt. Gen. Julian J. Ewell and Maj. Gen. Ira A. Hunt, Jr., *Sharpening the Combat Edge,* p. 221.
4. Stephen B. Young, "What Really Happened in Vietnam?," p. 17.
5. Lt. Gen. Charles A. Corcoran, Oral History Interview, General Creighton Abrams Story, MHI. This was a radical change from the way things worked under Westmoreland, who let two Marine battalions—the first American ground combat forces introduced into Vietnam—land at Danang without alerting the ambassador that this was about to take place. Since the Joint Chiefs of Staff and the State Department also had not seen fit to let him know, Maxwell Taylor was not pleased. John Taylor, *General Maxwell Taylor,* p. 310.
6. Ambassador Bui Diem, Interview, 9 June 1988.
7. Message, Abrams (Deputy COMUSMACV) to Johnson, MAC 5756, 020111Z APR 1968, CMH.
8. Letter, Abrams to Marshall, 13 May 1968, Marshall Papers, Indochina Archive, University of California at Berkeley. Cited hereafter as Marshall Papers.

9. Phillip B. Davidson, *Vietnam at War,* p. 411.
10. "Indochina: A Cavalryman's Way Out," *Time* (15 February 1971), p. 26. Abrams was in this issue the subject of the cover story. "Weigh-the-rice" referred to Abrams's emphasis on preempting enemy operations by finding and seizing his prepositioned supplies, or logistics "nose," including rice caches.
11. Douglas Kinnard, *The War Managers,* p. 75.
12. Gen. William C. Westmoreland as quoted in Peter Braestrup, *Big Story,* II:163.
13. *MACV Quarterly Evaluation* (October–December 1968), MHI.
14. Message, Abrams to Multiple Addressees, MAC 7236, 020158Z JUN 1968, CMH.
15. Message, Abrams (Deputy COMUSMACV) to Cushman, MAC 04619, 061734Z APR 1968, CMH.
16. Bui Tin, *Following Ho Chi Minh,* p. 63.
17. Col. Hoang Ngoc Lung, *The General Offensives of 1968–69,* p. 105.
18. Westmoreland remarks, departure press conference transcript, Saigon, 10 June 1968, Westmoreland History, CMH. Later Westmoreland criticized Abrams for what he termed "an undue preoccupation with the safety of Saigon" and, demonstrating that he understood nothing whatsoever about what motivated Abrams, attributed this concern to "the high visibility even a minor incident in the capital commanded in the American press." William Westmoreland, *A Soldier Reports,* pp. 502–503.
19. Quoted by AP in *Washington Post* (17 June 1968). According to the same article, "last week, in a valedictory, Westmoreland said it was 'almost an impossibility' to stop the rocket attacks because the launchers could be set up and dismantled too quickly."
20. Bunker Reporting Cable #55, 13 June 1968. While the Viet Cong were rocketing South Vietnam's capital of Saigon, Americans were burning their own capital in Washington.
21. Message, Abrams to Weyand, MAC 7766, 121126Z JUN 1968, CMH. Gia Dinh was the province within which the autonomous capital city of Saigon was located.
22. Debrief, HQ FMFPAC, Camp Smith, Hawaii, May 1968, filed with Lt. Gen. John A. Chaisson, Oral History, MCHC.

23. After the 22 August attack, on only two other days during the remainder of the year did rockets strike Saigon.

24. Bunker Reporting Cable #54, 8 June 1968.

25. Discussion, National Defense College, Saigon, 9 August 1968, Marshall Papers.

26. Bunker Reporting Cable #64, 29 August 1968.

27. Amb. Ellsworth Bunker, Oral History, unpublished transcript of interviews by Stephen Young, p. 45.

28. Daniel Ellsberg et al., "The Situation in Vietnam," Vann Papers.

29. As quoted in the *Washington Post* (unknown date after 25 May 1968), p. A1, "Lull."

30. As quoted by Cecil B. Currey, based on his 12 December 1988 interview of Giap in Hanoi, *Vietnam* magazine (April 1991), p. 22. Giap went on to observe that Abrams "believed he would win and was defeated."

CHAPTER 3

1. Message, Abrams to Wheeler, MAC 10181, 280742Z JUL 1968, CMH, in which Abrams quoted from his message to the field.

2. Harry G. Summers, Jr., *Vietnam Almanac,* pp. 142–143. The maximum number of U.S. troops deployed never reached the authorized ceiling of 549,500, peaking at 543,400 on 30 April 1969.

3. Recording, SecDef Briefing, 6–10 March 1969, ASC.

4. Col. Hoang Ngoc Lung, *The General Offensives of 1968–69,* p. 41. Besides suffering from the same subjectivity as ARVN intelligence, Lung suggested, "U.S. military intelligence also failed to come to any solid conclusion as far as the scope, size, and timing of the enemy offensive were concerned."

5. Lt. Gen. Phillip B. Davidson, Oral History Interview, LBJ Library.

6. Jeffrey J. Clarke, *Advice and Support,* p. 298.

7. Clark Clifford, Telephone Interview, 19 January 1989.

8. Gen. Andrew J. Goodpaster, Oral History Interview, MHI.

9. Ibid.

10. Clark Clifford, *Counsel to the President,* p. 551.

11. Recording, Commanders Conference, 20 September 1968, ASC.

The quotations are from Amb. Komer, reporting what Pike had told him.

12. Quoted in Beverly Deepe, *Christian Science Monitor* (23 October 1968). This and a number of other pertinent press accounts may be found in the Brigadier General Costas Caraganis Collection at the Chilton Library, Norwich University, Northfield, Vt.

13. Ibid. It is clear that Deepe had an excellent source for these and many other quotations from Abrams, because what he reports tracks very well with what is on the tapes of the relevant WIEU sessions.

14. War Experiences Recapitulation Committee of the High-Level Military Institute, *Vietnam: The Anti-U.S. Resistance War for National Salvation 1954–1975,* p. 104.

15. During the earlier period of American involvement in Vietnam, when body count was the primary measure of merit, similar doubts about the accuracy of the reporting on the allied side were common, as reflected, for example, in Douglas Kinnard's later survey of Army officers who commanded in Vietnam. *The War Managers,* p. 75.

16. Beverly Deepe, *Christian Science Monitor* (7 August 1968).

CHAPTER 4

1. Harry G. Summers, Jr., *Vietnam War Almanac,* p. 287. Also numerous first-person accounts by surviving POWs.

2. Dean Rusk, Interview, Duke University Living History Program, Durham, N.C., 26–27 March 1981.

3. Olivier Todd, Remarks, Chapters Bookstore, Washington, D.C., 18 December 1997.

4. Douglas Pike, *PAVN: People's Army of Vietnam,* p. 310, n. 5. Pike suggests that, while North Vietnamese casualties can be less reliably estimated, they were probably about 25,000 killed and 75,000 wounded.

5. Bui Tin, *Following Ho Chi Minh,* p. 47.

6. Recording, Brief for Ambassador Sullivan, 18 March 1969, ASC.

7. Recording, WIEU, 24 May 1969, ASC. Binh Tram 8 was later redesignated Binh Tram 18. As time went on, signal traffic from certain

other *binh trams*, including 34, also was acquired and read. Recording, Blue Ribbon Defense Panel Briefing, 8 January 1970, ASC.

8. Recording, WIEU, 21 September 1968, ASC. The figures indicate that more than 90 percent of the total for the year had been detected in communications intelligence, a very high proportion attesting to the reliability of the source. General Davidson gave the figure for total infiltration in 1967 as 86,842. At the following week's briefing, these numbers were given for earlier years: 1964: 12,000; 1965: 36,000; 1966: 89,000. Recording, WIEU, 28 September 1968, ASC.

9. A. J. Langguth, *New York Times* (5 May 1968).

10. Tuesday Lunch, 15 October 1968, Tom Johnson's Notes of Meetings, Box 3, LBJ Library.

11. Message, Abrams (Deputy COMUSMACV) to Peers, MAC 7601, 091000Z JUN 1968, CMH.

CHAPTER 5

1. Roger Hilsman, Interview, Columbia University Oral History Program. Quoted by permission.

2. National Security Council, Memorandum, "Revised Summary of Responses to NSSM 1: The Situation in Vietnam," 22 March 1969.

3. Amb. Clay McManaway, Telephone Interview, 18 September 1997.

4. Ambassador Komer's News Conference, 24 January 1968, Indochina Archives. Komer had engineered quite a bureaucratic promotion for himself in snagging the pacification account at the White House, where a little earlier he had handled such duties as routing to LBJ for approval the text of a message the State Department had prepared to go in the catalog of a planned Turkish art exhibition. National Security File, Files of Robert Komer, Box 1, LBJ Library.

5. Ibid.

6. Brig. Gen. Zeb B. Bradford, Jr., "With Creighton Abrams in Vietnam," *Assembly* (May/June 1998), p. 31.

7. Ibid., p. 32.

8. Gen. Walter T. Kerwin, Jr., Oral History, LBJ Library. Among

the LBJ Library staff Komer's oral history is widely known as a
paean of self-congratulation.

9. Colby had a radically different outlook on how to deal effectively
with the South Vietnamese. "Alliance relationships are delicate in
all situations," he wrote in a dissenting foreword to a Komer
treatise, "but particularly when one ally is clearly dependent on another. In most such cases, more can be gained by 'persuasion' than 'pressure.'" William E. Colby, "Foreword," in
Robert W. Komer, *Bureaucracy at War*, p. xiii.

10. Maj. Gen. Hoang Lac and Col. Ha Mai Viet, *Blind Design*, p.
301.

11. Brig. Gen. Tran Dinh Tho, *Pacification*, p. 162.

12. As quoted by Thomas W. Scoville in R. W. Komer, *Organization
and Management of the New Model Pacification Program*, p. 92.

13. Komer Deposition, *Westmoreland* v. *CBS* Libel Trial, in *Vietnam,
A Documentary Collection*, p. 89.

14. General Frederick C. Weyand, Interview, 23 June 1989. Even
Hanoi Radio reported that Komer had been "fired," as Komer
himself acknowledged in a farewell Saigon press conference.
Broadcast of 14 October 1968, per 3 November 1968 press conference. According to Douglas Pike, Komer had an interesting
though fleeting career as Ambassador to Turkey, where "he was
an ambassador who never got off the airplane. When they landed
the plane, there were demonstrators out there, so they pulled it
out to the end of the field, where they sat for about six hours.
When the Turkish police finally cleared the field, the plane took
off and went home. He had the shortest tenure of any ambassador
in history—he landed in the country, and that was it." Douglas
Pike, Interview, 16 November 1988.

15. William Colby, *Lost Victory*, pp. 253–254.

16. Message, Abrams to Multiple Addressees, MAC 14143, 200328Z
OCT 1968, CMH. The recipients included Lt. Gen. Cushman,
USMC (III MAF); Lt. Gen. Peers (I FFV); Lt. Gen. Kerwin (II
FFV); Vice Adm. Zumwalt (NAVFORV); and Maj. Gen. Eck-
hardt (SA IV CTZ), with Gen. Brown (Seventh AF) an infor-
mation addressee.

17. Bart Barnes, Jacobson obituary, *Washington Post* (25 May 1989).

Col. Jacobson began his Vietnam experience in 1954 with an assignment to the MAAG, then returned in 1961 for continuous service that ended only when he was lifted out by the last helicopter to leave the U.S. embassy roof on 30 April 1975.

18. For the translation of *Phuong Hoang,* Richard A. Hunt, *Pacification,* p. 116.

19. Remarks, William E. Colby, Military Writers Symposium, Norwich University, 12 April 1996. Videotape.

20. William E. Colby, Oral History Interview, LBJ Library.

21. Gen. Cao Van Vien and Lt. Gen. Dong Van Khuyen, *Reflections on the Vietnam War,* p. 149.

22. These militia elements were usually equipped with grenades and had among their main duties "to stand guard, dig trenches and tunnels, and lay mines and booby traps." Sam Adams, *War of Numbers,* p. 55.

23. Colby, *Lost Victory,* p. 185.

24. Col. Hoang Ngoc Lung, *The General Offensives of 1968–69,* p. 63.

25. George McArthur, Interview Notes of 18 December 1970. Emphasis in original.

26. Vien and Khuyen, *Reflections on the Vietnam War,* p. 60.

27. Lt. Gen. Phillip B. Davidson, Jr., Interview, 27 March 1995. The acronyms stand for Self-Defense Forces and Secret Self-Defense Forces, elements of the Viet Cong infrastructure.

28. Director CICV, Current MACV Strength Briefing, in *Vietnam: A Documentary Collection,* p. 33438.

29. Chief of Staff's *Weekly Summary* (30 April 1968), p. 12.

30. Amb. Ellsworth Bunker, Oral History (unpublished transcript).

31. Tom McCoy, as quoted in Thomas Powers, *The Man Who Kept the Secrets,* p. 182.

32. John Paul Vann, Remarks, University of Denver, 19 February 1969, Vann Papers.

33. BDM Corporation, *A Study of Strategic Lessons Learned in Vietnam,* p. VI-36.

34. Hunt, *Pacification,* p. 204.

35. William E. Colby Deposition, in *Vietnam, A Documentary Collection,* p. 100.

36. Joint Chiefs of Staff, *The History of the Joint Chiefs of Staff: The Joint Chiefs of Staff and the War in Vietnam, 1960–1968*, p. 52–45.

37. "Basic conflict exists between Vung Tau's CIA-supported cadre concept for winning the war and that of the JGS based on RF/PF," Col. Volney Warner had written in a 24 June 1968 trip report to Amb. William Leonhart, successor to Komer as pacification staffer in the White House (Volney F. Warner Papers, MHI). Under the new leadership team the Regional Forces and Popular Forces were greatly expanded and improved and the Revolutionary Development cadre concept phased out.

38. Lt. Gen. Ngo Quang Truong, *Territorial Forces*, pp. 34, 127. Abrams's appreciation for the Regional Forces and Popular Forces was unusual. Truong observed that "their virtues were seldom extolled and their accomplishments usually slighted. This evaluative misconception seemed to derive basically from prejudice coupled with a nearsighted tendency to measure results only by body count and weapons captured. Most Vietnamese citizens, especially the city-dwellers, were unable to realize that such achievements as hamlets pacified, the number of people living under GVN control, or the trafficability on key lines of communication were possible largely due to the unsung feats of the RF and PF." Ibid., pp. 133–134.

39. Thomas C. Thayer, in *The Lessons of Vietnam*, ed. W. Scott Thompson and Donaldson D. Frizzell, p. 262.

40. Colby, *Lost Victory*, p. 259.

41. Letter, Colby to parents, 24 January 1969, Colby Family Papers.

42. Vietnam Military History Institute, *History of the People's Army of Vietnam*, p. 318.

43. John Paul Vann, Remarks, University of Denver, 19 February 1969, Vann Papers.

44. Colby, *Lost Victory*, p. 243.

45. Recording, WIEU, 21 December 1968, ASC. Later Komer tried to take credit for the accelerated campaign, telling an interviewer it "was personally designed by me." Robert Komer, Oral History Interview, LBJ Library. That claim is disputed by others who were

part of the program. For example, Clay McManaway said the APC "was done by Colby, Montague and me." Amb. Clay McManaway, Telephone Interview, 18 September 1997.

46. Message, Abrams to Wheeler and McCain, MAC 17418, 221046Z DEC 1968, ASC.

CHAPTER 6

1. Stephen Young, "How North Vietnam Won the War," interview with Bui Tin, *Wall Street Journal* (3 August 1995).
2. Gen. Earle G. Wheeler, Oral History, LBJ Library. Wheeler also stated, surprisingly, that the first time he had discussed the proposed partial bombing halt face-to-face with the President was at this session with General Abrams.
3. Speech broadcast on Hanoi Domestic Service in Vietnamese on 20 December 1984 and reported by Foreign Broadcast Information Service, *Asia and Pacific Daily Report* (21 December 1984).
4. John Schlight, "Response to Letter to the Editor," *The Journal of Military History* (January 1995), pp. 200–201.
5. George Christian, *The President Steps Down*, p. 118.
6. As quoted in Joint Chiefs of Staff, *History, . . . 1960–1968,* III: 47–4.
7. Ibid., p. 47–48.
8. This account is based on Maj. Gen. Jack A. Albright, Interview, 28 September 1989. Albright added an entertaining footnote: "Later it was said that Lady Bird had persuaded him not to run for reelection," he recalled, "but it was the general consensus of people in the White House that she couldn't convince him to go to the bathroom unless he wanted to do it himself." About a month later, Albright was sitting at a staff table in the White House Mess with some other people when Marvin Watson joined them. After a while, Watson said, "I want to ask you would-be politicians your honest opinion as to why LBJ chose not to run." Most of the answers had to do with spending more time with his family and the like. Watson said he would tell them the real reason. On 10 March 1968 there had been a poll of the Democratic

party leadership in each of the fifty states, asking for their estimate of LBJ's chances of getting the nomination, and of his being elected if he were nominated. Watson said that all fifty states reported the same thing—he could not win. "Only four of us ever saw the report," he said. "We gave him that advice and—for once—he took it." Doris Kearns wrote in *Lyndon Johnson and the American Dream* (p. 351) that "there is little doubt that, as the convention neared, Johnson began to feel that his withdrawal might not be irrevocable, that he might find vindication more real and immediate than the verdict of history—in the vote of the Democratic Party and the American people." Years later Sidney Blumenthal observed that, "in private, Johnson still harbored a fantasy that out of the chaos he might rise phoenixlike to the nomination." *New York Times Book Review* (22 June 1997), p. 7.

9. Message, Abrams to Wheeler and McCain, MAC 12743, 200940Z SEP 1968, CMH.
10. Lyndon Baines Johnson, *The Vantage Point,* p. 520.
11. Christian, *The President Steps Down,* p. 87. But, said General Andrew Goodpaster, then deputy to Abrams in Vietnam, MACV's agreement to the bombing halt "was always on the understanding that suitable terms would be reached under one formula or another." Oral History Interview, LBJ Library.
12. Message, Abrams to Wheeler, MAC 14482, 271142Z OCT 1968, CMH.
13. Letter, President Lyndon B. Johnson to Gen. Creighton W. Abrams, 29 October 1968, Abrams Family Papers. In the letter LBJ had also said "I want you to inspire the ARVN to do the same. If you need anything that we can get you quickly, let me know." General Wheeler, Chairman of the Joint Chiefs of Staff, apparently got wind of that, because a few weeks later he cabled Abrams with a plaintive request. In JCS planning for the improvement of the RVNAF, he said, "it also came out that . . . it appears that you have a directive, presumably from the Highest Authority [a euphemism for the President], to push ahead post haste on improving the RVNAF. While I know that this is a matter of high priority, I am not aware of any specific directive, particularly one

in writing. Do you have such a directive? If so, are you at liberty to communicate it to me?" Message, Wheeler to Abrams, JCS 14412, 092319Z DEC 1968, CMH.

14. Clark Clifford, *Counsel to the President,* p. 522.
15. Townsend Hoopes, *The Limits of Intervention,* p. 228.
16. Message, Abrams to Multiple Addressees, MAC 14710, 010158Z NOV 1968, CMH.
17. Message, Abrams to Wheeler, MAC 15746, 131027Z NOV 1968, ASC.
18. Clifford, *Counsel to the President,* p. 455.
19. Letter, Gen. Andrew J. Goodpaster to author, 17 September 1997.
20. Mark Perry, *Four Stars,* p. 196, citing Perry's interview of Gen. Goodpaster.
21. George M. Seignious II, *A Grandfather Reports,* pp. 18–19.
22. Letter (handwritten), Abrams to Harold K. Johnson, 4 June 1968, Box 112, The Harold K. Johnson Papers, MHI.
23. John S. Bowman, ed., *The Vietnam War Almanac,* p. 211.
24. Young, "How North Vietnam Won the War." Later Fonda claimed that when she spoke with American prisoners in North Vietnam, "without exception, they expressed shame at what they had done." *Washington Post* (26 July 1972). Fonda also asserted that "POWs who reported that they were tortured are hypocrites and liars." Associated Press, 31 March 1973. Both as quoted in Ken W. Clawson, Memorandum for H. R. Haldeman and Ronald L. Zeigler, Subject: POW Compilation, 4 April 1973, Box 178, H. R. Haldeman, Staff Member Office Files, White House Special Files, Nixon Presidential Materials Collection, National Archives.
25. Adm. Elmo R. Zumwalt, Jr., Vietnam War Symposium, Texas Tech University, 18 April 1996.
26. Douglas Pike, *War, Peace and the Viet Cong,* p. 128. In *Cruel April* Olivier Todd wrote of the more limited period of the 1968 Tet Offensive that "by Giap's own admission it cost the National Liberation Front 40,000 men," p. 78.
27. Young, "How North Vietnam Won the War."
28. Letter, John Vann to Sam Yorty, 14 November 1968, Vann Papers.
29. Message, Abrams to Wheeler, MAC 17664, 290427Z DEC 1968,

CMH. Information addressees included Adm. McCain at CINC-PAC, Amb. Bunker, and Lt. Gen. Kerwin at II FFV.

30. Message, Abrams to Bunker and Kerwin, MAC 004, 010242Z JAN 1969, MHI.

CHAPTER 7

1. Message, Abrams to Wheeler, MAC 1765, 090310Z JAN 1969, ASC.

2. Later Richard Nixon wrote that Lyndon Johnson admitted to him that "all the bombing pauses were a mistake and he had accomplished nothing." *RN: The Memoirs of Richard Nixon,* p. 431.

3. Vietnam Military History Institute, *History of the People's Army of Vietnam,* II:359.

4. Ibid., II:335ff.

5. Lt. Gen. Sak Sutsakhan, "Khmer Participation," in Brig. Gen. Tran Dinh Tho, *The Cambodian Incursion,* p. 142.

6. Lt. Gen. Phillip B. Davidson, Jr., Interview, 27 March 1995. Later Amb. Stephen Lyne, who while assigned to the Department of State's Bureau of Intelligence and Research had accompanied Graham to Saigon when the "Graham Report" was being put together, was asked about this comment. "If it had been determined that Cambodia was an important source of enemy supply," said Lyne, "something would have to be done about it. Since the State Department did not want to widen the war, this finding could not be permitted." Comment made during discussion at Cantigny Conference, "Vietnam 1965–1975," Wheaton, Ill., 5–6 March 1997.

7. One company of the division's 27th Infantry, for example, rotated its three platoons through a cycle consisting of a daytime reconnaissance and night ambush, a day of defending the local militia outpost, and a day of training and rest. Shelby L. Stanton, *The Rise and Fall of an American Army,* p. 308.

8. Richard L. Prillaman, "Vietnam Update," *Infantry* (May–June 1969), p. 18. This team was sent out by CONARC, the Continental Army Command.

9. Ibid., p. 19.

10. Ibid.

11. Quoted in the *Philadelphia Bulletin* (13 January 1969), DOD Press Archives.

12. Message, Abrams to Multiple Addressees, MAC 30430, 13 OCT 1968, CMH.

13. Joint Chiefs of Staff, *The History of the Joint Chiefs of Staff: The Joint Chiefs of Staff and the War in Vietnam, 1969–1970,* p. 38.

14. Col. Hoang Ngoc Lung, *The General Offensives of 1968–69,* pp. 116–117.

15. In the 29 March 1969 WIEU the briefer stated that, while enemy killed in the current offensive approximated those for the May 1968 attacks, friendly killed were down more than 11 percent. "This trend predominates with U.S. killed," he added, "despite the fact the enemy is concentrating on U.S. targets in a declared attempt to inflict as many U.S. casualties as possible."

16. Joint Chiefs of Staff, *The Joint Chiefs of Staff and the War in Vietnam, 1969–1970,* pp. 40–41.

17. Richard Nixon, *No More Vietnams,* p. 107.

18. William Safire, *Before the Fall,* p. 368n.

19. Richard Nixon on NBC's *Meet the Press,* 10 April 1988, as quoted in Bruce Oudes, ed., *From: The President,* p. 1.

20. Walt Rostow, Memorandum for the President, 14 February 1968, in Gareth Porter, ed., *Vietnam: The Definitive Documentation of Human Decisions,* II:500.

21. Message, Abrams to Wheeler, MAC 2560, 271118Z FEB 1969, ASC.

22. Message, Abrams to Wheeler, MAC 3441, 170437Z MAR 1969, ASC.

23. Recording, COMUS Update, 14 July 1969, ASC. This outlook on Abrams's part is in refreshing contrast to earlier periods when Westmoreland told his J-2, General Davidson, that reporting higher order of battle figures would create a political bombshell, and when General Wheeler told Westmoreland that he couldn't go to the President with statistics reflecting an increase in enemy-initiated incidents.

CHAPTER 8

1. Joint Chiefs of Staff, *The History of the Joint Chiefs of Staff: The Joint Chiefs of Staff and the War in Vietnam, 1969–1970,* p. 43.
2. Ibid, p. 86, citing *New York Times* (1 June 1969).
3. Recording, SecDef Briefing, 6–10 March 1969, ASC. The nineteen tapes covering this visit are all marked with the span of time rather than individual dates.
4. *1969 MACV Objectives Plan,* Marshall Papers, Indochina Archive, University of California, Berkeley.
5. Message, Abrams to McCain, MAC 5636, 030933Z MAY 1969, CMH.
6. The ARVN divisions were customarily assigned to corps as follows: I Corps, 1st and 2nd Divisions; II Corps, 22nd and 23rd; III Corps, 5th, 18th, and 25th; IV Corps, 7th, 9th, and 21st. The Airborne and Marine divisions were considered theater reserve and were deployed where needed.
7. Davidson offered a fascinating insight on the McNamara encounter. "*That* visit the theme was, 'What are you doing with your own troops?' And this is the thing, Mr. McNamara bad-mouthing General Westmoreland's manpower conservation and use, I'm confident kept poor General Westmoreland over one more year than he was supposed to have been kept over. And, in effect, led him down the Tet path, et cetera, et cetera. I'm absolutely convinced of it."
8. Quoted in Charles R. Smith, *U.S. Marines in Vietnam,* p. 129.
9. Gen. Alexander M. Haig, Jr., Interview, 29 November 1988.
10. Henry Kissinger, *White House Years,* pp. 32–33.
11. William Colby, *Lost Victory,* p. 286. "My outlook," said Colby, "was I've got a race on my hands. I've got to get the country pacified before the soldiers are gone." William E. Colby, Interview, 18 August 1989.
12. Message, Abrams to McCain, MAC 14877, 050237Z NOV 1968, ASC.
13. Richard Nixon, *RN: The Memoirs of Richard Nixon,* p. 382.

14. William J. Duiker, *The Communist Road to Power in Vietnam*, p. 284.

15. Amb. Ellsworth Bunker, Oral History, LBJ Library. On 9 May 1969 the *New York Times* published the first public reports of this bombing.

16. Department of Defense White Paper, "Report on Selected Air and Ground Operations in Cambodia and Laos," 10 September 1973.

17. Nixon, *RN: The Memoirs of Richard Nixon*, p. 380.

18. Melvin R. Laird, Interview, 4 October 1988.

19. Gen. Bruce Palmer, Jr., *The 25-Year War*, p. 97. JCS historians later reported an interesting aspect of this bombing: "Following the revelation of the secret Cambodian bombing, both former Secretary of Defense Melvin R. Laird and the former Chairman of the Joint Chiefs of Staff, General Earle G. Wheeler, initially disavowed knowledge of any falsification of official reports on the attacks, but subsequently recalled otherwise." Joint Chiefs of Staff, *The Joint Chiefs of Staff and the War in Vietnam, 1969–1970*, p. 260.

20. *Washington Post* (9 August 1973), citing Abrams's testimony before the Senate Armed Services Committee.

21. As quoted in Richard Nixon, *No More Vietnams*, p. 111.

22. Recording, COMUS Special Brief, 24 July 1969, ASC.

23. Col. Harry G. Summers, Jr., *Vietnam War Almanac*, p. 50.

24. Project CHECO, *The Air War in Vietnam, 1968–1969*, p. 68, citing an Abrams message of 15 October 1968.

25. Truong Nhu Tang, *A Vietcong Memoir*, pp. xiii, 158, 167.

26. Message, Abrams to Wheeler, MAC 7730, 171003Z JUN 1969, CMH. On his one visit to Saigon, Kahn had taken entirely the wrong approach. "Now, general, you do as I tell you, and I'll make you look good," he told Abrams. "I don't care a damn what you make *me* look like," Abrams roared. "I'm out here to win the war!" George Jacobson, Interview, 5 December 1988.

27. Douglas Kinnard, *The War Managers*, pp. 24–25.

28. Joint Chiefs of Staff, *The Joint Chiefs of Staff and the War in Vietnam, 1969–1970*, pp. 69, 134–139.

29. Message, Abrams to Wheeler and McCain, MAC 4036, 301218Z MAR 1969.

30. Alexander M. Haig, Jr., *Inner Circles,* p. 225.

31. Jeffrey J. Clarke, *Advice and Support,* p. 532. In a surprisingly rapid bureaucratic recognition and response, the retitling took effect 26 March 1969.

32. Amb. Ellsworth Bunker, Oral History Interview, LBJ Library.

33. Clark Clifford, Memorandum for the President, "Trip to South Vietnam, July 13–18, 1968," 18 July 1968, Clifford Papers, Vietnam Files, Box 5, LBJ Library.

34. Nixon, *No More Vietnams,* p. 96.

35. Amb. Samuel Berger, Oral History Interview, General Creighton Abrams Story, MHI.

36. As quoted in Nguyen Tien Hung and Jerrold L. Schecter, *The Palace File,* p. 35. Amb. Bui Diem later wrote that, forever after, President Thieu "rankled at having been compelled to meet with Nixon in this desolate and gooney bird-ridden place. As did we all." *In the Jaws of History,* p. 261.

37. Nixon, *RN: The Memoirs of Richard Nixon,* p. 392. After the Midway announcement, recalled General Bill Rosson, he was at a Vietnamese function at the Presidential Palace in Saigon at which President Thieu "said that Mr. Nixon's announcement regarding his [Thieu's] recommendation was erroneous, that he had made no such recommendation, and in fact that Nixon had told him that he had a mandate to withdraw the forces." Gen. William B. Rosson, Interview, 31 March 1997.

38. Elmo R. Zumwalt, Jr., *On Watch,* p. 376.

39. Gen. Donn A. Starry, "Review of *Thunderbolt,*" *Armor* (September–October 1992), p. 51.

40. Ibid.

41. Gen. Maxwell R. Thurman, Interview, 2 August 1995.

CHAPTER 9

1. Lt. Gen. William E. Potts, Interview, 12 March 1996. The reference to enemy strength is particularly important, an allusion to

the difficulties General Westmoreland had created for himself in estimates of the enemy order of battle, infiltration, strength, and the elusive "crossover point."

2. Letter, Maj. Gen. Thomas M. Tarpley to Mrs. Abrams, 11 September 1974, CWAP.

3. Message, Wheeler to Abrams, JCS 09112, 231308Z JUL 1969, forwarding the text of Wheeler's trip report, CM-4441–69, dated 21 July 1969.

4. Coincidentally these comments were made on Ho Chi Minh's birthday and, up in the A Shau Valley, the battle at Hamburger Hill was nearing an end.

5. Maj. Mark A. Olinger, "Task Force Remagen," *Armor* (March–April 1998), pp. 30–32.

6. Memorandum, Charles B. MacDonald to SJS MACV, 15 April 1969, CMH.

7. Conmy was born while his father was commanding a company in the 3rd Infantry, then located at Fort Snelling, Minn. Before his service in Vietnam, Conmy commanded the 3rd Infantry, then stationed at Fort Myer, Va. That regiment, which knew a real soldier when they saw one, later named their ceremonial building Conmy Hall in his honor. Conmy was one of only 230 men who have earned three awards of the CIB.

8. Lt. Gen. Frank A. Camm, Eulogy for Joseph B. Conmy, 26 April 1994.

9. Col. Joseph B. Conmy, "I Led a Brigade at Hamburger Hill," *Washington Post* (27 May 1989).

10. Memorandum, CJCS Wheeler to Secretary of Defense, CM-4247–69, 21 May 1969. Also Project CHECO, *A Shau Valley Campaign,* p. 22 and passim.

11. Conmy, "I Led a Brigade."

12. Message, Wheeler to Abrams, JCS 06172, 211343Z MAY 1969, CMH.

13. That year the University of New Hampshire's *Granite,* yearbook of Zais's alma mater, included a slanderous attack on him as a heartless killer who got a thousand men killed trying to win personal glory and promotion at Hamburger Hill. But Zais also got a letter from more than nineteen hundred soldiers of his 1st

Brigade, written on scraps of paper by men sitting out on fire
bases or wherever they happened to be, then pasted together and
sent to him, telling Zais they appreciated how he had looked after
them and demonstrated that he cared about them. Gen. Melvin
Zais, Oral History Interview, MHI.

14. As related by Robert Timberg, *The Nightingale's Song,* p. 150.
15. Bunker Reporting Cable #84, 10 February 1970.
16. The allies had fuel pipelines, too, and they were the source of
huge problems due to pilferage. During April 1969 losses on one
line north to Phu Cat reached 600,000 gallons, and overall they
were at that point losing 4,500,000 gallons a month. Burial of the
lines was under way to make them less vulnerable to theft. Meanwhile, Abrams asked for a letter to the Minister of Defense requesting help in dealing with the problem. Gen. Ewell suggested
setting ambushes for the South Vietnamese civilians who were
stealing the fuel. "I'd like to try this other thing [the letter] first,"
said Abrams, "before you go ambushing." Recording, Commanders WIEU, 21 June 1969, ASC.
17. Lt. Gen. Ngo Quang Truong, *Territorial Forces,* p. 63.
18. U.S. Congress, Senate, Committee on Foreign Relations, *Vietnam: December 1969, A Staff Report,* p. 4. Preliminary results for
the following year, through October, indicated "the percentage
killed was almost double that in 1968." Ibid. Through 31 July
1972, Mark Moyar established, a total of 81,740 VCI had been
neutralized (26,369 killed, 33,358 captured, and 22,013 rallied).
See *Phoenix and the Birds of Prey,* p. 236. Meanwhile the enemy,
who were running a real assassination program aimed at innocent
civilians, executed an estimated 36,725 through 1972. Summers,
Vietnam War Almanac, p. 284.
19. Douglas Pike, *PAVN,* p. 211.
20. The categories were A for leaders, B for those in key positions,
and C for rank-and-file members. Summers, *Vietnam War Almanac,* p. 283.
21. War Experiences Recapitulation Committee of the High-Level
Military Institute, *Vietnam: The Anti-U.S. Resistance War for National Salvation 1954–1975,* English-language version, p. 122.
22. Stanley Karnow, *Vietnam: A History,* p. 602. Also Videotape,

Remarks, William E. Colby, Military Writers Symposium, Norwich University, 12 April 1996.

23. Message, Abrams to Wheeler, MAC 13117, 280610Z SEP 1968,
    CMH, in which Abrams quotes the operational guidance he is
    issuing to his field commanders.

24. Maj. Gen. Nguyen Duy Hinh, *Vietnamization and the Cease-Fire,*
    p. 88.

25. Message, Abrams to Wheeler, MAC 7376, 100313Z JUN 1969,
    ASC.

26. Recording, WIEU, 26 July 1969, ASC.

27. Ibid. Brig. Gen. William Potts, the MACV J-2, also mentioned
    Harriman's distortion of the facts in a briefing for Lt. Gen. Fred
    Weyand, who was then serving with the Paris delegation. "He
    [Harriman] said, 'Because of the bombing halt in '68, they pulled
    out all of this,' " said Potts, but "all of that was done *before*
    the bombing halt. *Since* the bombing halt they've put it back
    in." "Yeah," Weyand agreed, laughing. Recording, Lieutenant
    General Weyand Briefing, 26 October 1969, ASC. Ambassador
    Bunker saw it the same way. "That's the one thing I've never
    forgiven Governor Harriman for, when he said that, because I
    really—the information was available to him for a sounder con-
    clusion," said Abrams. "That's right," agreed Bunker. Recording,
    COMUS Brief, 17 May 1972, ASC.

28. Amb. John H. Holdridge, Interview, 12 November 1997. Lt.
    Gen. George M. Seignious II, who succeeded Goodpaster as JCS
    representative on the delegation in Paris, where he served with
    Harriman, confirmed that Harriman had misstated the facts about
    enemy withdrawals in order to make his case. "That was not
    correct what Harriman said about withdrawals," said Seignious.
    "He was trying to do what he could to get Democrats elected."
    Seignious interview, 22 September 1997.

    Others who were exposed to Harriman during this period
    had reason to question not just his grasp of reality but his basic
    integrity. One was Sybil Stockdale, who was obliged to deal with
    Harriman during her efforts to help her husband, Captain (later
    Vice Admiral) James B. Stockdale and others being held prisoner
    in North Vietnam. Regarding "reassurances received during sec-

ond personal visit with Averell Harriman," she recalled, "I knew from my covert communication he was not telling the truth." Sybil Stockdale, Remarks, Cantigny Conference, "Vietnam 1965–1975," Wheaton, Ill., 5–6 March 1997.

In the postwar book that he and his wife coauthored, Admiral Stockdale revealed that "it was Averell Harriman who insisted on keeping the torture evidence under wraps in the interest of furthering his 'delicate' negotiations on the prisoners' behalf, all of which ultimately came to nothing. Even after the Johnson administration left office, Harriman tried to prevail upon the new secretary of defense, Melvin Laird, to continue the 'keep quiet' policy." Stockdale and Stockdale, *In Love and War,* p. 506.

29. Message, Abrams to McCain and Wheeler, MAC 10174, 061117Z AUG 1969, ASC.

CHAPTER 10

1. Message, Abrams to Moorer (Acting CJCS), MAC 13033, 061012Z OCT 1969, ASC, forwarding the text of a briefing presented to General Wheeler the previous day.
2. Col. Hoang Ngoc Lung, *The General Offensives of 1968–69,* p. 154; Recording, WIEU, 18 October 1969, ASC.
3. By the end of 1971, General Potts stated, MACV J-2 had "analyzed over 115 enemy instructions over a four-year period—resolutions, directives and pamphlets put out by the enemy." And, he pointed out, "In every case where a COSVN resolution comes out, some of that is reflected up in MR-TTH and in MR-5 and so forth, even though they're not under COSVN." Recording, Special Assessment Briefing, 10 December 1971, ASC.
4. Recording, Briefing for General Wheeler, 4 October 1969, ASC.
5. Lt. Gen. Charles A. Corcoran, Interview, 20 February 1996.
6. Walter Cronkite, *A Reporter's Life,* pp. 264, 383.
7. Ibid., p. 350.
8. Ernest W. Lefever, *TV and National Defense,* pp. 30–31, 110, 128, 143. Not all journalists subscribed to even the theory of unbiased reporting. "The idea of fairness and objectivity (as in the FCC

doctrine) is specious," Neil Sheehan told an audience at the Army War College, Carlisle Barracks, Pa., on 1 November 1974.

9. Keyes Beech, *Not Without the Americans,* pp. 303–305.

10. Subsequently the term "phase" was replaced by "increment." Fourteen increments were withdrawn from July 1969 through November 1972, bringing the remaining U.S. forces in Vietnam to 27,000, a reduction of 522,500 from the highest authorized figure of 549,500 (and nearly half a million below the highest actual strength reached of 543,400). Jeffrey J. Clarke, *Advice and Support,* p. 524. For the highest actual strength reached, dated at 30 April 1969, Harry G. Summers, Jr., *Vietnam War Almanac,* p. 50.

11. The numbers did not tell the whole story, either. By 15 April 1970, although withdrawals to that point were only 115,500 of the high-water mark total of 543,400, they represented about one-third of U.S. combat strength, both air and ground.

12. Sir Robert Thompson, *Peace Is Not at Hand,* author profile.

13. Ibid., p. 67. In October 1969 Henry Kissinger cabled Amb. Bunker to advise him that "the President has asked Sir Robert Thompson to go to Vietnam on his behalf to provide independent assessment of security situation and general political, economic and military conditions throughout country." Message, Abrams to Wheeler and McCain, MAC 13631, 201023Z OCT 1969, quoting Kissinger's message. Thompson returned to Vietnam frequently during these later years.

14. Thompson, *Peace Is Not at Hand,* p. 62.

15. Gen. Bruce Palmer, Jr., as quoted in Kim Willenson et al., *The Bad War,* p. 155.

16. Message, Wheeler to McCain and Abrams, JCS 13096, 221548Z OCT 1969, CMH.

17. The term "Vietnamization" is usually credited to Secretary of Defense Melvin Laird, but journalist Mark Perry has written that "Laird took credit for the term that corresponded to the doctrine, but in fact 'Vietnamization,' inculcated as official American policy in April 1969 (in NSSM 36), was first used by Creighton Abrams during his talk with Lyndon Johnson's 'wise men' in March 1968." *Four Stars,* p. 223n.

George Ball provides confirmation in his memoir, recalling that Abrams told the "Wise Men" during his March 1968 visit to Washington how he was training the South Vietnamese armed forces with the object of "Vietnamizing" the war. *The Past Has Another Pattern,* p. 408.

The JCS historians also placed the origins of Vietnamization in the earlier administration, writing that "President Johnson began the process in 1968 when he initiated planning to improve and modernize the RVN forces with a view to their shouldering a larger share of the war." *The History of the Joint Chiefs of Staff: The Joint Chiefs of Staff and the War in Vietnam, 1969–1970,* p. 373.

Richard Nixon later credited Abrams with, if not the term, implementation of the concept. "General Creighton Abrams had initiated this shift in strategy when he took command of our forces in Vietnam in 1968," wrote Nixon. "I reemphasized the critical importance of our pacification programs and channeled additional resources toward them." Richard Nixon, *No More Vietnams,* p. 105.

To the South Vietnamese the term, if not actually insulting, was bemusing. "It doesn't mean anything to me because really, see—as a Vietnamese Marine, we have been Vietnamized for a long, long time. Really!" said Lt. Gen. Le Nguyen Khang. Vietnam Interview, Marine Corps Oral History Program, 30 September 1975, MCHC.

18. Lt. Gen. Dong Van Khuyen, *RVNAF Logistics,* p. 57.
19. Amb. Ellsworth Bunker, Oral History Interview, General Creighton Abrams Story, MHI.
20. Message, Abrams to Johnson, MAC 5307, 040950Z JUN 1967, CMH.
21. Recording, Commanders WIEU, 22 November 1969, ASC.
22. Ibid.
23. Orrin DeForest and David Chanoff, *Slow Burn,* p. 184.
24. George H. Gallup, *The Gallup Poll: Public Opinion 1935–1971,* Vol. 3: *1959–1971,* p. 2179.
25. Ibid., p. 2224.

26. Letter, John Paul Vann to Maj. Harry G. Harris, U.S. Air Force Academy, 9 December 1969, Vann Papers.

27. U.S. Congress, Senate Committee on Foreign Relations, *Vietnam: December 1969, A Staff Report,* pp. 10, 18.

CHAPTER 11

1. This awareness of the increasing enemy antiaircraft threat along his lines of communication, a year before the incursion into Laos, is significant.

2. Message, Abrams to McCain, MAC 2716, 281615Z FEB 1970, CMH.

3. Joint Chiefs of Staff, *The History of the Joint Chiefs of Staff: The Joint Chiefs of Staff and the War in Vietnam, 1969–1970,* pp. 174–175.

4. Elmo R. Zumwalt, Jr., *On Watch,* p. xii. Zumwalt thus, from his own observations, foreshadowed exactly the conclusions of William Bundy's careful study published nearly three decades later. See Bundy's *A Tangled Web,* passim.

5. Message, Abrams to Davison, MAC 5011, 160809Z APR 1970, CMH.

6. As reported by George McArthur, *Pacific Stars & Stripes* (20 March 1970).

7. As reported by Abrams in Message, Abrams to McCain, MAC 11711, 281127Z AUG 1970, copy loaned to author by Gen. Weyand.

8. Message, Abrams to McCain, MAC 3081, 081210Z MAR 1970, CMH.

9. Recording, SecDef Laird and CJCS Wheeler Brief, 11 February 1970, ASC.

10. The gunships included AC-119, AC-123, and AC-130 models.

11. Message, Abrams to Wheeler and McCain, MAC 15092, 211219Z NOV 1969, ASC.

12. Ibid.

13. As quoted in Joint Chiefs of Staff, *The Joint Chiefs of Staff and the War in Vietnam, 1969–1970,* p. 385.

14. In Gen. Cao Van Vien and Lt. Gen. Dong Van Khuyen, *The U.S. Adviser,* p. 73.
15. Lt. Gen. Dong Van Khuyen, *RVNAF Logistics,* p. 445.
16. Message, Abrams to Wheeler, MAC 17004, 120729Z DEC 1968, CMH.
17. Jeffrey J. Clarke, *Advice and Support,* pp. 372–373.
18. As quoted in ibid., p. 312.
19. Ibid., p. 307.
20. Lt. Gen. Samuel T. Williams, who served as chief of the U.S. Military Assistance Advisory Group during the period 1955–1960, knew Thieu as a colonel. In Thieu's dossier he wrote, "This is the most efficient Vietnamese officer that I have met in Vietnam, and one that will probably go the highest." In a later interview, Williams added, "I thought he was the smartest and most intelligent man I had ever come in contact with in Vietnam, Diem excepted, of course." Oral History Interview, LBJ Library.
21. Kissinger, Memorandum for the President, 10 September 1969, as quoted in Henry Kissinger, *White House Years,* p. 1481n11.
22. Lee was not the only South Vietnamese leader mocked for trust in astrologers and for consulting them before making important decisions. To Americans this seemed bizarre, but that was in the days before we had a President of the United States who, through his wife, consulted an astrologer as to when to hold a news conference.
23. As quoted by Col. Paul F. Braim, Interview, 26 August 1997. In stark contrast to the earlier period of one coup after another, South Vietnam's leadership in these later years was remarkably stable. During the ten years President Thieu led his country, the United States cycled through three presidents. While General Vien served ten years as Chairman of the JGS, three men—Wheeler, Moorer, and Brown—filled the comparable role in the United States. And in Vietnam itself, the senior military advisor to Thieu and Vien similarly turned over three times during the decade, with Westmoreland, Abrams, and then Weyand filling the role in turn.
24. Letter, Tran Van Huong to Julie Abrams, 6 September 1974,

CWAP. Huong recalled that when he saw Abrams during a 1973 visit to the United States he had a presentiment that it was for the last time. Later, he wrote to Mrs. Abrams, on 4 September 1974 he was receiving the ambassador of Korea and their conversation happened to turn to General Abrams. "I did not know why," wrote Huong, "but my eyes were full of tears. Only the next day did I get the news of the passing away," on that very day, "of Abrams."

25. Col. Harry G. Summers, Jr., U.S. Army War College Reserve Forces Symposium, Rosslyn, Va., 24 October 1992.

26. Quoted by George McArthur, *Los Angeles Times* (26 February 1970).

CHAPTER 12

1. The analysis recognized the changing balance of enemy forces in the South, now about 75 percent NVA and 25 percent VC, a complete reversal of the situation since 1966, and the enemy's fragmentation of forces during 1969, as when headquarters such as that of the 10th NVA Regiment was disbanded and its battalions resubordinated to provincial control.

2. John Paul Vann, Remarks, Lexington, Ky., 8 January 1972, Vann Papers.

3. The next day Abrams cabled JCS Chairman Wheeler, noting that there were twelve NVA maneuver regiments in or near the DMZ and that intercepted messages referred to upcoming rocket attacks. "The present restrictions on maneuver and fires in the southern DMZ continue to handicap the operations of our forces and endanger the security of friendly forces in northern I CTZ," he stated. "The enemy can sit in the DMZ, build up his forces and position weapons to attack our installations with relative immunity from decisive attack." Thus he recommended "that authority be granted to employ friendly forces in the southern DMZ of a size appropriate to the enemy threat, supported by tac air, artillery, and naval gunfire," and that he also be granted authority to conduct B-52 strikes there. Message, Abrams to Wheeler, MAC 6002, 111139Z MAY 1969, ASC.

4. Stephen Young, "How North Vietnam Won the War," interview with Bui Tin, *Wall Street Journal* (3 August 1995).

5. Vietnam Military History Institute, *History of the People's Army of Vietnam,* II:362.

6. Message, Abrams to Wheeler and McCain, MAC 2505, 211059Z FEB 1970, ASC.

7. The *Pueblo* was a U.S. electronic monitoring ship seized in international waters by the North Koreans on 23 January 1968. President Lyndon Johnson decided not to retaliate.

8. Message, Abrams to Wheeler, MAC 15405, 281300Z NOV 1969, ASC.

9. Richard Nixon, *RN: The Memoirs of Richard Nixon,* p. 445.

10. Message, Wheeler to McCain, JCS 05404, 201949Z APR 1970, CMH.

11. Report, Blue Ribbon Commission, 1 July 1970, p. 197.

12. Message, Abrams to Wheeler and McCain, MAC 5760, 291815Z APR 1970, CMH.

13. Before the operation was over, Base Areas 352, 353, 550, 367/706, and 709 had also been scoured. Message, Abrams to Moorer, MAC 6626, 150828Z MAY 1970.

14. Brig. Gen. Tran Dinh Tho, *The Cambodian Incursion,* p. 169.

15. Message, Abrams to McCain and Moorer, MAC 6774, 181631Z MAY 1970.

16. As quoted in Tho, *The Cambodian Incursion,* p. 95. Lt. Gen. Mike Davison, commanding U.S. II Field Force, Vietnam, had a contrasting take on the enemy's reaction. "We saw it in a little different light than that," he said at a commanders conference about three weeks into the operation. "I think there's clear evidence in the Parrot's Beak that FR2 and FR3 and their units attempted to defend in place, for which we were duly thankful, because I think the ARVN cut both of them up pretty badly. The regiment of the 9th Division that was down in that area attempted on at least two occasions to defend against the ARVN and suffered moderately heavy casualties." In the Fishhook area the 165th and 209th Regiments of the 7th NVA Division have "fought very effective delaying actions, and they've really kept us out of what we think is another cache area for about six days. I really wouldn't

characterize it as a withdrawal." Recording, Commanders WIEU, 23 May 1970, ASC.

17. Recording, Intelligence Update, 3 May 1970, ASC.

18. Lt. Gen. John J. Tolson, *Airmobility 1961–1971,* pp. 227–233.

19. Maj. Gen. Nguyen Duy Hinh, *Lam Son 719,* p. 7, in which Hinh described retrospectively what was accomplished in Cambodia as prelude to his discussion of the subsequent thrust into Laos.

20. Recording, Brig. Gen. Haig, 21 May 1970, ASC. Haig later calculated that he had made a total of fourteen trips to Vietnam. "I was sort of Mr. Vietnam, among other things, for Nixon and Kissinger," he said. Gen. Alexander M. Haig, Jr., Interview, 29 November 1988.

21. Recording, Brig. Gen. Haig, 21 May 1970, ASC.

22. Ibid.

23. Message, Abrams to Moorer, MAC 6571, 141029Z MAY 1970.

24. Ibid.

25. Quoted in Message, Wheeler to McCain and Abrams, JCS 08729 JUN 1970, CMH.

26. Message, Abrams to Wheeler, MAC 7844, 101018Z JUN 1970, ASC.

27. Gen. Bruce Palmer, Jr., "US Intelligence and Vietnam," *Studies in Intelligence* (1984 Special Issue), pp. 78–79.

28. Tho, *The Cambodian Incursion,* p. 172. Three weeks into the operation, concluded Brig. Gen. Potts, "we've saved ourselves 9,597 attacks by fire at the 6.7 rounds average."

29. David Fulghum and Terrence Maitland, *The Vietnam Experience,* p. 101. Earlier, in August 1969, Kissinger had held the first of a series of secret meetings with Xuan Thuy.

30. Chester L. Cooper, *The Lost Crusade,* p. 462.

31. Sir Robert Thompson, *Peace Is Not at Hand,* p. 78.

32. Tho, *The Cambodian Incursion,* p. 182.

33. Message, Abrams to Wheeler and McCain, MAC 7015, 231059Z MAY 1970, ASC.

34. Resor charted the decline from the $30 billion level as $22 billion in 1969, $17 billion in 1970, and now $11 billion for 1971.

35. Maj. Gen. Nguyen Duy Hinh, *Vietnamization and the Cease-Fire,* p. 181.

36. Recording, Briefing for General Wheeler, 4 October 1969, ASC.

CHAPTER 13

1. William A. Hamilton, "The Influence of the American Military," unpublished dissertation, citing Gen. Michael S. Davison, 5 January 1978 letter to the author.
2. Quoted in Kim Willenson et al., *The Bad War,* p. 157.
3. Amb. Ellsworth Bunker, Oral History (unpublished transcript).
4. Abrams was referring to the Regional Forces/Popular Forces, People's Self-Defense Force, and National Police/National Police Field Force.
5. The quotation reflects Abrams's familiar technique of, once he could see that his audience had grasped his point, simply leaving off in midsentence and moving on to something else.
6. Videotape, Remarks, William E. Colby, Military Writers Symposium, Norwich University, 12 April 1996. Warren Milberg, who was stationed at a small and remote compound in Quang Tri Province, recalled a visit from Colby. He came alone, solicited Milberg's views, and calmly endured a mortar and rocket attack in a handy bunker. "He was the only guy up from Saigon who ever stayed overnight with us," said Milberg. Col. Warren Milberg, Interview, 20 May 1996.
7. "Speedy Four" was GI slang for Specialist Four, a rank comparable with corporal.
8. Robert Hall was a widely known discount men's clothier of the day, famous for advertising the "plain pipe racks" in its showrooms.

CHAPTER 14

1. See Benjamin F. Schemmer, *The Raid,* pp. 267ff. for a description of how the raid resulted in improved conditions for American prisoners.
2. Recording, WIEU, 1 March 1969, ASC. A few months later,

though, Abrams commented on government forces in Laos that "they're going to run into a *hornet's* nest if they try to get into Tchepone. Christ, that's a—." Recording, Commanders WIEU, 27 September 1969, ASC.

3. In his diary entry for 4 March 1971, H. R. Haldeman wrote about Nixon that "he also is concerned about tempering down the NSC staff, who are going to push for accomplishing more and more in Vietnam, and feels we've got to calm them down." *The Haldeman Diaries.*

4. General Bruce Palmer, Jr., *The 25-Year War,* p. 108.

5. Alexander M. Haig, Jr., *Inner Circles,* p. 273.

6. Message, Abrams to Wheeler, MAC 15405, 291300Z NOV 1969, ASC.

7. Message, Sutherland to Abrams, QTR 0446, 211040Z MAR 1971.

8. Later, however, Abrams recalled October 1970 as "when they had that spate of rumors, started by the Japanese, that we were going into Laos *then,*" so possibly that was a factor in the enemy's decision to establish the front headquarters in Laos at that time. Recording, Commanders WIEU, 21 August 1971, ASC.

9. Message, McCain to Abrams, 110253Z OCT 1970, ASC.

10. Message, Abrams to McCain, MAC 11467, 230420Z AUG 1970, CMH.

11. Message, McCain to Abrams, 110253Z OCT 1970, ASC.

12. Message, Abrams to Moorer, MAC 14841, 180827Z NOV 1970.

13. Message, McCain to Abrams, 062132Z DEC 1970.

14. Ibid.

15. Ibid.

16. Message, Abrams to McCain, MAC 15603, 071130Z DEC 1970.

17. Ibid.

18. Message, McCain to Abrams, 080435Z DEC 1970.

19. Message, Moorer to Abrams, CJCS 16390, 100051Z DEC 1970.

20. Palmer, *The 25-Year War,* p. 106.

21. Recording, SEACORDS Brief, 17 December 1970, ASC.

22. Message, Abrams to McCain, MAC 15808, 120952Z DEC 1970.

23. Message, McCain to Moorer, 150236Z DEC 1970 ASC.

24. Gen. Bruce Palmer, Jr., "US Intelligence and Vietnam," *Studies in Intelligence* (1984 Special Issue), p. 87.
25. Message, Haig to Godley, WH 02234, 232231Z DEC 1970.
26. Vietnam Military History Institute, *History of the People's Army of Vietnam,* II:374ff.
27. Message, McCain to Moorer, 220016Z NOV 1970, ASC.
28. "Seeding" referred to cloud seeding to induce rain, while "CBU-ing" meant sowing the route with cluster bomb units.
29. Palmer, "US Intelligence and Vietnam," p. 87. Palmer included a 3 February CIA follow-up on the enemy's reinforcement capability in reaching this judgment.
30. Henry Kissinger, Memorandum for the President, 22 January 1971, Box 1, NSC Files: POW/MIA, Nixon Presidential Materials Collection, National Archives.
31. Message, Moorer to McCain and Abrams, CJCS 00902, 262124Z JAN 1971, ASC.
32. Message, Abrams to Moorer, MAC 00955, 291012Z JAN 1971, ASC.

CHAPTER 15

1. Message, Abrams to McCain, MAC 01061, 011129Z FEB 1971, ASC.
2. Vietnam Military History Institute, *History of the People's Army of Vietnam,* II:374ff.
3. Recording, WIEU, 13 February 1971, ASC, quoting from Souvanna's statement.
4. As quoted in Todd L. Newmark, "Theoretical Framework," *Vietnam* (December 1997), p. 69.
5. The Chinook, or CH-47, was a heavy lift cargo helicopter.
6. Maj. Gen. Nguyen Duy Hinh, *Lam Son 719,* p. 69. Those lost were the corps G-3, or operations officer, and the G-4, his logistics counterpart.
7. Phillip B. Davidson, *Vietnam at War,* p. 646.
8. Nguyen Tien Hung and Jerrold L. Schecter, *The Palace File,* p. 44.

9. Message, Sutherland to Abrams, DNG 0443, 141220Z FEB 1971.

10. Ultimately the enemy committed his entire combat force save for the 325th Division. Message, McCain to Abrams, 162110Z JUL 1971, ASC.

11. Project CHECO, *Lam Son 719,* pp. 7, 51–52.

12. Ibid., p. 15.

13. Cecil B. Smyth, Jr. in CSM Michael Martin, *Angels in Red Hats,* p. 43n3.

14. Gen. Bruce Palmer, Jr., "US Intelligence and Vietnam," *Studies in Intelligence* (1984 Special Issue), p. 88.

15. Recording, COMUS Update, 24 February 1971, ASC.

16. Brig. Gen. Samuel G. Cockerham, Interview, 12 November 1997. Another instance in which Abrams worked around Sutherland involved the U.S. advisor to the ARVN Airborne Division. The man in the job was relieved, and Abrams sent Col. Jim Vaught to take his place. With Vaught in his office, Abrams called Sutherland and told him Vaught was coming up. "He's going to put the Airborne Division back in the fight. He's going to work directly for me. You got any problem with that?" Sutherland did not. Lt. Gen. James B. Vaught, Telephone Interview, ca. 15 January 1998.

17. Lt. Gen. James B. Vaught, Letter to author, 4 February 1998. Berry later recalled: "Haig and some of his hangers-on came up to where I was working the aviation support for Lam Son 719 at Khe Sanh. I was busy, and the sight of them, pasty-faced, some obviously not even military, in clean, unlaundered fatigues, offended me. I didn't have much time for them. They were there to tell us how to do it, and I really resented that." Lt. Gen. Sidney B. Berry, Telephone Interview, 6 January 1997.

18. Recording, Lieutenant General Ewell Update, 16 March 1971, ASC.

19. Brig. Gen. Samuel G. Cockerham, Interview, 12 November 1997. Cockerham was acting CO of the 1st Aviation Brigade during Lam Son 719. Two days before the helilift to LZ Hope, Abrams had been told that Brig. Gen. Jack Hemingway, an expert on Army aviation, "felt that our aviators, our Army helicopter operators, had been possibly too aggressive in the beginning.

They'd been in-country [meaning in South Vietnam] in a relatively permissive environment. They went over there [into Laos]
with the same kind of an approach, and he said they took some
pretty significant losses. He said they were backing off now and
taking another look at how they should approach this thing."
Recording, COMUS Update, 4 March 1971, ASC.

20. Message, Abrams to Sutherland, MAC 02372, 061014Z MAR
1971.

21. Message, Robertson to Abrams, QTR 0282, 080620Z MAR
1971.

22. Abrams also told Thompson that Admiral McCain had called that
morning to say that "Jack Anderson apparently has an article
which discloses a plot developed by General Wheeler, Admiral
McCain, and General Abrams which finally has been brought out
into the light of public cognizance. And poor old Jack [McCain]
read me his press release. Jesus! I said, 'Jack—the Pig Rule, the
Pig Rule!' " The Pig Rule, often cited by Abrams in a variety of
situations, was "never wrestle with pigs—you get dirty, and they
enjoy it!"

23. Hinh, *Lam Son 719,* pp. 100, 103.

24. Gen. Cao Van Vien and Lt. Gen. Dong Van Khuyen, *Reflections
on the Vietnam War,* p. 103. Abrams described the matter like this:
"Gen. Vien suggested to me that he would commit the 2d ARVN
Division if I would insert 1st Brigade, 5th Mech and two brigades
of the 101st Airborne Division in the east–west valleys on the
north of the present ARVN Airborne Division AO. I reaffirmed
that under no circumstances would U.S. ground forces be inserted
in Laos." Message, Abrams to Sutherland, MAC 02455, 091232Z
MAR 1971.

25. Message, Sutherland to Abrams, DNG 0843, 181425Z MAR
1971.

26. Message, Davison to Abrams, HOA 0552, 190700Z MAR 1971,
CMH.

27. Project CHECO, *Lam Son 719,* p. 77.

28. Gen. Cao Van Vien, *The Final Collapse,* p. 13.

29. Project CHECO, *Lam Son 719,* pp. 13, 39, 48.

30. Col. Raymond R. Battreall, Letter to author, 31 March 1995.

31. Weyand was referring approvingly to Lt. Gen. Ngo Quang Truong, commanding IV Corps, and Lt. Gen. Nguyen Van Minh, commanding III Corps, contrasting them with such inept past leaders as Maj. Gen. Vinh Loc and Maj. Gen. Lu Mong Lan, both former commanders of II Corps.
32. Hinh, *Lam Son 719,* pp. 121, 152.
33. Simon Dunstan, *Vietnam Tracks,* p. 185.
34. Cecil B. Smyth, Jr., in Martin, *Angels in Red Hats,* p. 40.
35. Brig. Gen. John D. Howard, in ibid., p. 19.
36. Message, Sutherland to Abrams, QTR 0197, 021420Z MAR 1971.

CHAPTER 16

1. Gen. Bruce Palmer, Jr., "US Intelligence and Vietnam," *Studies in Intelligence* (1984 Special Issue), p. 89.
2. Maj. Gen. Nguyen Duy Hinh, *Lam Son 719,* p. 132.
3. Recording, Commanders WIEU, 21 August 1971, ASC. The assessment was obtained from the French attaché in Washington, leading Abrams to observe that this was "kind of a little bit out of character, too."
4. Palmer, "U.S. Intelligence and Vietnam," p. 90.
5. Brig. Gen. Samuel G. Cockerham, Interview, 12 November 1997. When he wasn't filling in as acting CO of the 1st Aviation Brigade, Cockerham commanded the 34th General Support Group. In that job he had theater maintenance responsibility for all Army aviation in Vietnam. "Nobody knew more about helicopters in Vietnam than myself," he asserted confidently. Asked whether there was any validity to Air Force charges of concealed Army helicopter losses during Lam Son 719, Cockerham's reply was, "No, none whatsoever."
6. Since the war there has been a continuing controversy over the actual helicopter losses sustained by U.S. Army elements, with some Air Force sources claiming that those losses were much higher, perhaps even double the stated number, and that the real losses were covered up by the Army to hide their vulnerability (in comparison with the more rugged Air Force systems, it is

implied, an argument that has budget implications). When a 103 loss figure was briefed at MACV as a final count for Lam Son 719, General Lucius D. Clay, Jr., Seventh Air Force commander, said, "I've got slightly higher figures." Asked what his numbers were, Clay responded, "I've got 108." Later Lt. Gen. Sidney Berry, who as ADC of the 101st Airborne Division had been in charge of Army aviation support during the operation, stated the facts in a public dialogue. "Herein," he wrote, "I report the correct figures of American helicopters lost to hostile action during that operation. During an average day of Lam Son 719, more than 600 American helicopters supported the Republic of Vietnam ground forces fighting communist forces in Laos and in adjacent areas of the Republic of Vietnam. The U.S. Army's after-action analysis shows that 107 helicopters were lost to hostile action during Lam Son 719. These losses occurred during 353,287 sorties and 134,861 flying hours." Berry concluded that, "operating against the bulk of North Vietnam's regular army divisions supported by a daunting array of antiaircraft weapons, American helicopters proved themselves remarkably tough and difficult to destroy." Lt. Gen. Sidney B. Berry, "Letter to the Editor," *Washington Post* (18 May 1995).

7. Alexander M. Haig, Jr., *Inner Circles,* pp. 275 (for the quoted passage) and 276.
8. Gen. Alexander M. Haig, Jr., Letter to author, 9 March 1993.
9. Gen. Alexander M. Haig, Jr., Interview, 29 November 1988.
10. James R. Schlesinger, Remarks, Society for Military History Annual Meeting, Bethesda, Md., 9 April 1994. H. R. Haldeman stated in his diary entry for 12 February 1971 that at Key Biscayne Nixon had a discussion with Rogers and Kissinger on "the whole Laotian situation." Nixon "discussed the fact that it's important for some civilian input into military planning and cited some of the earlier instances where he pushed the military to go further than they themselves had intended to go, and that it was beneficial and desirable that he had done so. He's doing that again on this one. . . ." *The Haldeman Diaries.*

Ambassador John Holdridge, on the NSC staff at the time, observed that Lam Son 719 "was a Mickey Mouse plan, but it wasn't Abrams's fault. That was forced on him." (Interview, 12 November 1997.) There was one other witness, Monsignor John Benson, Abrams's close friend and the priest who had the year before instructed him for his conversion to Catholicism. Here Benson was reflecting what he could have gotten only from Abrams himself. "About that Laotian operation," he said, "Abe didn't want to do that at all." (Interview, 11 September 1989.)

11. Haig, *Inner Circles*, p. 276. This could not have been, as Haig recalled it, after the third day of the campaign. Haig's trip to Vietnam took place in March, a month or so after the operation commenced on 8 February 1971. Said Henry Kissinger: "There is no truth to the idea that Nixon ever thought of relieving and replacing Abrams, after Lam Son 719 or at any other point, with Haig or anyone else." Interview, 24 January 1989.

12. *The Haldeman Diaries*, 13 May 1971.

13. Shelby L. Stanton, *The Rise and Fall of an American Army*, pp. 337 – 338.

14. Henry Kissinger, *White House Years*, pp. 1002 and 1009.

15. Vietnam Military History Institute, *History of the People's Army of Vietnam*, II:374ff.

16. Bunker Reporting Cable #92.

17. Message, Abrams to Westmoreland, MAC 05720, 100918Z JUN 1971, CMH.

18. PFC Clyde N. Baker, Letter to President Nixon, 17 July 1971, Box 10, President's Office Files, Staff Members Office Files, White House Special Files, Nixon Presidential Materials Collection, National Archives.

19. Recording, Secretary of the Army Brief, 26 April 1971, ASC.

CHAPTER 17

1. Message, Abrams to Multiple Addressees, MAC 06474, 050611Z JUL 1971, MHI.

2. Message, Vann to Potts, MRT 0339, 301045Z MAY 1971, MHI.

3. William E. Colby, Oral History Interview, LBJ Library.

4. Ibid.

5. Sir Robert Thompson, *Peace Is Not at Hand*, p. 65.

6. Reporting Cable #91, 28 January 1971.

7. Directive No. 01/CT 71, as quoted in Gareth Porter, ed., *Vietnam: The Definitive Documentation,* II:551.

8. William E. Colby, *Lost Victory,* p. 329.

9. Message, Vann to Abrams, NHT 0428, 171210Z JUL 1971, MHI.

10. Recording, WIEU, 13 November 1971, ASC.

11. At almost the same time Laird was in Vietnam, President Nixon was, revealingly, sending Henry Kissinger a note saying "I think we ought to find an occasion where we can get Moorer in alone with me without Laird to talk about national defense matters. Try to arrange this at some time in the near future." Quoted in Bruce Oudes, ed., *From: The President,* p. 335. When Nixon rated the Cabinet, wrote John Ehrlichman in his notes, he described Laird as "sneaky but manageable." John Ehrlichman, Papers, Box 2, 16 May 1972, Hoover Institution Archives, Stanford University. Kissinger had his own reservations about Laird, considering him— so wrote William Safire—"a devious man, but when cornered a patriot." *Before the Fall,* p. 396.

12. Thomas Polgar, as quoted in Kim Willenson et al., *The Bad War,* p. 102.

13. Nguyen Tien Hung and Jerrold L. Schecter, *The Palace File,* p. 10.

14. George H. Gallup, *The Gallup Poll,* III:2338.

15. Message, Funkhauser to Abrams, HOA 2204, 160145Z NOV 1971, CMH.

16. Message, Dolvin to Abrams, MAC[?] 06186, 250708Z JUN 1971, ASC.

17. Message, Abrams to McCain, MAC 06205, 260124Z JUN 1971, ASC.

18. Recording, SEACORD Meeting, 11 December 1971, ASC.

19. Gen. Cao Van Vien, *Leadership,* p. 156.

CHAPTER 18

1. Per Memorandum, Captain Barry R. McCaffrey to Superintendent, USMA, 9 October 1973, in Abrams Correspondence File, MHI.

2. Lewis Sorley, *Honorable Warrior,* p. 212.

3. Michael Maclear, *The Ten Thousand Day War,* p. 269.

4. Message, Abrams (Deputy COMUSMACV) to Multiple Addressees, MAC 04599, 060834Z APR 1968, ASC.

5. As reported by Abrams in Message, Abrams to McCain, MAC 11711, 281127Z AUG 1970, copy loaned to author by Gen. Weyand.

6. Message, Abrams to Multiple Addressees, MAC 14089, 280901Z OCT 1970, CMH.

7. Dr. Thomas C. Bond, "Fragging: A Study," *Army* (April 1977), p. 47.

8. Lester A. Sobel, ed., *South Vietnam,* VI:231.

9. Col. K. E. Hamburger, "Fading Away," Friends of the West Point Library *Newsletter* (March 1995), p. 10.

10. U.S. Military Academy Association of Graduates, *1996 Register of Graduates and Former Cadets,* passim.

11. Message, McCaffrey to Kerwin, ARV 3276, 160630Z NOV 1970. In a comprehensive study conducted after the war, the BDM Corporation found that "the pattern and incidence of drug abuse in Vietnam was not markedly different than that encountered by American soldiers worldwide during that same period." *A Study of Strategic Lessons Learned in Vietnam,* p. VII-14.

12. Message, McCaffrey to Kerwin, ARV 3276, 160630Z NOV 1970.

13. George McArthur interview notes of 26 September 1970. Mr. McArthur very generously presented his folder of Abrams interview notes to the author.

14. Dwight W. Birdwell and Keith William Nolan, *A Hundred Miles of Bad Road,* p. 105.

15. Message, Palmer to Abrams, WDC 02173, 061747Z FEB 1971. Dr. Jerome H. Jaffe, a psychiatrist and professor in the College of Physicians and Surgeons at Columbia University, headed a program on drug abuse established by Pres. Nixon. Jaffe went to Vietnam to help deal with the problem there, and later wrote to Abrams, "I have thought often of . . . my visit to Vietnam in 1971, and of the superb job that was done under your direction to implement the program for controlling the heroin problem.

Perhaps when the dust of Watergate settles still further, that unique accomplishment will be given due recognition." Letter, Dr. Jaffe to Abrams, 24 August 1974, CWAP.

16. Department of the Army, *The American Soldier in Vietnam 1971*, n.p.

17. Shelby L. Stanton, *The Rise and Fall of an American Army*, p. 331.

18. B. G. Burkett, "Telling It Like It Is," *Vietnam* (February 1997), p. 30. Burkett is also the coauthor of *Stolen Valor*.

19. Recording, Commanders Conference, 20 May 1971, ASC.

20. Message, Westmoreland to Abrams, WDC 18112, 012044Z OCT 1971, ASC.

21. Lt. Gen. Herron N. Maples, Remarks, U.S. Army War College, Carlisle Barracks, Pa., 2 May 1974. Maples served as Inspector General of the Department of the Army.

22. Col. Robert M. Cook, Oral History Interview, MHI, and Telephone Interview, 25 July 1998.

23. George Gallup, "What Combat Does to Our Men," *Reader's Digest* (June 1968), no pp. in reprint edition.

24. B. G. Burkett and Glenna Whitley, *Stolen Valor*, passim.

25. Harry Summers, "Lingering Fiction about Vietnam," *Washington Times* (5 February 1993).

26. Ibid.

27. William Buckley, Jr., "Rich Man, Poor Man," *Washington Times* (1 November 1992).

28. Susan Katz Keating, "The Draft," *Washington Times* (30 September 1992).

CHAPTER 19

1. William E. Colby, Keynote Address, Vietnam Symposium, Texas Tech University, 18 April 1996.

2. Colby Testimony, 3 December 1975, House Select Committee on Intelligence, *Hearings: U.S. Intelligence Agencies and Activities: Risks and Control of Foreign Intelligence*, Part 5, p. 1718.

3. John Paul Vann, Remarks, Lexington, Ky., 8 January 1972, Vann Papers. In 1969 Joseph Kraft had written that Vann was "the all-

pro pessimist among American officials here and the true source of much journalistic skepticism and not a few Pulitzer Prizes." *Chicago Daily News* (25 August 1969).

4. Brig. Gen. James Lawton Collins, Jr., *The Development and Training of the South Vietnamese Army*, pp. 90–91.

5. Sir Robert Thompson, in W. Scott Thompson and Donaldson D. Frizzell, *The Lessons of Vietnam*, p. 103.

6. Douglas Pike, *PAVN*, pp. 224–225.

7. By early December 1971 General Potts could state: "We see the emphasis still on the B-3 Front. 1970: 5,600 total to the B-3 Front. In 1971: 19,000, of which 6,300 [are scheduled to] come in in December. And now for January: 1,800, and for February: 1,800. And when four gap groups are filled in it will be 5,600 just for January and February, the same as for all of 1970." Recording, WIEU, 4 December 1971, ASC.

8. Nixon made the announcement on 13 January 1972. This increment had to be out by 1 May, leaving the U.S. with 69,000 troops in Vietnam. At that time, Abrams noted, "We will have redeployed 95 percent of the maneuver battalions, 97 percent of the artillery battalions, and 91 percent of the attack aircraft squadrons." Recording, COMUS-ROK Minister of National Defense Brief, 10 February 1972, ASC.

9. 11B, or "11 Bravo" in GI slang, referred to the MOS (Military Occupational Specialty) of a combat infantryman.

10. Printed in the 19 December 1971 issue of *Nhan Dan,* as quoted in Recording, Commanders WIEU, 22 January 1972, ASC.

11. Message, Dolvin to Abrams, DNG 3399, 031200Z DEC 1971.

12. Recording, WIEU, 4 March 1972, ASC.

13. Ibid.

14. Ibid.

15. The "Secretary" referred to is presumably the Secretary of the Army, for it would have been an Army commanders conference the officer attended. At that time Robert F. Froehlke held the office.

16. Message, CINCPAC to CJCS, 120025Z OCT 1971, ASC.

17. Message, Abrams to McCain, MAC 10076, 201126Z OCT 1971, ASC.

18. The area radar was called GCI (ground control intercept). Normally used to vector fighter aircraft to their targets, it remained on all the time and therefore provided no warning of an impending missile launch.

19. Message, Abrams to McCain, MAC 11312, 011028Z DEC 1971.

20. Recording, Special Authorities Brief, 20 January 1972, ASC.

21. Adm. Thomas H. Moorer, NSIC Meeting, Washington, D.C., 7 December 1988.

22. James Pinckney Harrison, *The Endless War,* p. 255.

CHAPTER 20

1. Message, Vann to Abrams, PKU 0434, 201100Z MAR 1972, MHI. Vann learned these details from General Dzu, but Dzu apparently received the report from someone else rather than having attended the meeting himself.

2. Abrams's comments were made in his confirmation hearing as Army Chief of Staff–designate.

3. Message, Abrams to Moorer, MAC 03019, 042335Z APR 1972, ASC.

4. Vietnam Military History Institute, *History of the People's Army of Vietnam,* II:389ff. Once again, as at Tet 1968, the enemy hoped in vain for "mass popular uprisings," apparently a classic case of hope springs eternal.

5. By MACV's calculations the enemy had initiated the offensive on the night of 30 March in MR-1, on 31 March in the B-3 Front, and on 1 April in western MR-3. Recording, Commanders WIEU, 22 April 1972, ASC.

6. John P. Vann, Letter for "My Friends," 12 April 1972, Vann Papers.

7. Vietnam Military History Institute, *History of the People's Army of Vietnam,* II:389ff.

8. As quoted in Michael Charlton and Anthony Moncrieff, *Many Reasons Why,* p. 197.

9. Cecil B. Smyth, Jr., in CSM Michael Martin, *Angels in Red Hats,* p. 43n2. Luat had previously been a problem as commander of the 17th Armored Squadron during Lam Son 719.

10. Merle Pribbenow, Letter to author, 6 April 1998.

11. Said Maj. Gen. John Murray, Defense Attaché in Saigon after U.S. troops were withdrawn, "There's a lot of unsung heroes among our logistics legacies to Vietnam. While it isn't recorded on any Vietnam Wall, RMK–BRJ had 52 civilian employees killed in action and another 248 casualties due to enemy action." "Back to Vietnam: Reflections on a Lost War," *Vietnam* (August 1997), p. 48. The initials refer to the consortium Raymond, Morrison, Knudsen–Brown, Root, Jones.

12. Message, Abrams to Laird, MAC 03757, 241111Z APR 1972, CMH.

13. David Fulghum and Terrence Maitland, *The Vietnam Experience,* p. 142. Also Elmo R. Zumwalt, Jr., *On Watch,* p. 379.

14. Lt. Gen. Ngo Quang Truong, *The Easter Offensive of 1972,* p. 77.

15. MACV Command Briefing, 23 October 1972.

16. Adm. Thomas H. Moorer, Interview, 26 September 1994.

17. Allan R. Millett and Peter Maslowski, *For the Common Defense,* pp. 564–565.

18. Dave Richard Palmer, *Summons of the Trumpet,* p. 321.

19. Vietnam Military History Institute, *History of the People's Army of Vietnam,* II:389ff. "Because the enemy had escalated rapidly," continued the PAVN history, "was bombarding us massively, and was using many types of new weapons and items of technical equipment (laser-guided bombs, guided missiles, various types of jammers, etc.) many units and local areas suffered heavy losses. Almost all the important bridges on the railroad and on the road corridors were knocked down. Ground transportation became difficult. Coastal and river transportation were blocked. The quantity of supplies shipped across the Gianh River forward to the battlefields was only a few thousand tons for one month. Enemy jamming equipment made it difficult to locate targets, especially B-52's. Our low combat efficiency, as revealed by the ineffectiveness of our targets and by the low number of enemy aircraft shot down, became a source of concern."

20. Message, Abrams to Laird, MAC 04021, 011601Z MAY 1972, CMH.

21. Douglas Pike, *PAVN,* p. 225.

22. Truong, *The Easter Offensive of 1972,* p. 13.

23. Message, Abrams to Laird, MAC 04021, 011601Z MAY 1972, CMH.

24. Ibid.

25. Ibid.

26. Message, Laird to Bunker and Abrams, OSD 04321, 031617Z MAY 1972, CMH.

27. Message, Abrams to Laird, MAC 04039, 020443Z MAY 1972, CMH.

28. Message, Abrams to Multiple Addressees, MAC 04040, 020452Z MAY 1972.

29. *The Haldeman Diaries,* 1 May 1972.

30. Gen. Cao Van Vien, *Leadership,* pp. 138–139.

31. Vietnam Military History Institute, *History of the People's Army of Vietnam,* II:389ff.

32. As quoted by Maj. Gen. Stan L. McClellan, Letter to Mrs. Abrams, 8 October 1974, enclosing "Recollections of Maj. Gen. Stan L. McClellan on 4 September 1974."

33. Message, Abrams to Multiple Addressees, MAC 04325, 100730Z MAY 1972, ASC.

34. Project CHECO, *Kontum,* p. 34.

35. Vietnam Military History Institute, *History of the People's Army of Vietnam,* II:389ff.

36. The reference was to Richard Funkhauser, former Ambassador to Gabon subsequently assigned to Vietnam in the pacification program.

37. George McArthur, Notes of 24 May 1972, provided to the author by Mr. McArthur.

38. Smyth, in Martin, *Angels in Red Hats,* p. 40.

39. Vietnam Military History Institute, *History of the People's Army of Vietnam,* II:389ff.

40. MACV Command Briefing, 23 October 1972.

41. Maj. Gordon E. Bloom, as quoted in Project CHECO, *Kontum,* p. 83.

42. Truong, *The Easter Offensive of 1972,* p. 98.

43. Message, Hollingsworth to Vogt and Monger, ARV 0969, 221550Z APR 1972, CMH.

44. Truong, *The Easter Offensive of 1972,* p. 176.
45. Alexander M. Haig, Jr., *Inner Circles,* pp. 283 and 287.
46. Facts on File, *South Vietnam,* 7:64.
47. Lt. Gen. William J. McCaffrey, Senior Officer Debriefing Report, December 1972, MHI.
48. War Experiences Recapitulation Committee of the High-Level Military Institute, *Vietnam: The Anti-U.S. Resistance War,* English-language version, p. 148.
49. Harry G. Summers, Jr., *Historical Atlas of the Vietnam War,* p. 178. Other estimates of the enemy's casualties are much higher. Sir Robert Thompson, for example, writes that "the 'great sacrifices' called for by General Giap had been paid to the extent of an estimated 130,000 men killed and disabled." *Peace Is Not at Hand,* p. 121. Gen. Bruce Palmer, Jr., stated in his study of CIA intelligence on the war that enemy "losses for the March–September 1972 period were conservatively estimated at over 100,000 killed." "US Intelligence and Vietnam," *Studies in Intelligence* (1984 Special Issue), p. 94. Palmer's work also demonstrated that by this point CIA was virtually ignoring the war. A National Intelligence Estimate published in April 1971 was the last NIE or SNIE on Vietnam until October 1973, almost two and a half years later. Ibid., p. 91.
50. Dave Palmer, *Summons of the Trumpet,* p. 327.
51. Stanley R. Resor, Oral History Interview, LBJ Library.
52. Lt. Gen. William E. Potts, AUSA Annual Meeting, Washington, DC, 17 October 1995.
53. Maj. Gen. Hoang Lac and Col. Ha Mai Viet, *Blind Design,* p. 78. General Truong agreed, stating that "to put it briefly, the 3d Division failed because it was overburdened." Truong, *The Easter Offensive of 1972,* p. 166.
54. Col. G. H. Turley, *The Easter Offensive,* p. 274. In commenting on this development, Col. Harry Summers, Jr., recalled how, during the Battle of the Bulge in World War II, the U.S. 106th Infantry Division panicked and two of its regiments surrendered to the Germans. *Vietnam War Almanac,* p. 292.
55. Truong, *The Easter Offensive of 1972,* p. 179.

56. Bruce Palmer, "US Intelligence and Vietnam," p. 94.
57. Truong, *The Easter Offensive of 1972*, pp. 168–169.

CHAPTER 21

1. Maj. Gen. Stan L. McClellan, Letter to Mrs. Abrams, 8 October 1974, enclosing "Recollections of Maj. Gen. Stan L. McClellan on 4 September 1974."
2. Edward W. Knappman, ed., *South Vietnam*, p. 106. Col. George W. Aldridge, Jr., ran the Emergency Operations Center at MACV. Asked whether Vann had been flying the helicopter when it crashed, his answer was succinct: "Sure." Telephone Interview, 6 June 1989.
3. Project CHECO, *Kontum*, p. 70. Said General Bruce Palmer: "Vann was one of my heroes. I never knew anyone with more courage. He was brave as a lion. He went in there and defied them. He wasn't afraid of them. He went out at night looking for them. John Vann was a great patriot, and he loved the Vietnamese people." Telephone Interview, 2 December 1997.
4. Message, McCaffrey to Vann, ARV 1037, 270135Z APR 1972, MHI.
5. Spelling of sender's name notional.
6. Lt. Gen. Ngo Quang Truong, *Territorial Forces*, p. 128.
7. Harry G. Summers, Jr., *Vietnam War Almanac*, p. 50.
8. Gen. John Vogt, Interview, 14 June 1989. Abrams received a different kind of testimonial from Terence Cardinal Cooke, who had been to Southeast Asia during the Christmas season. "Seeing you there [in Bangkok with his family] and then a few days later being with you in your command gave me the balanced picture of a great human being and a great gentleman—a man of peace striving to come successfully to the end of a difficult and awful war and anxious to guarantee a just peace for his own people and for those others to whom he had been sent to help and support. I never have the chance to be with you but that I come away grateful to God for the dedication and for the courage which you

have." Letter, Cardinal Cooke to General Abrams, 14 January 1972, Abrams Papers.

9. John Paul Vann, Remarks, Lexington, Ky., 8 January 1972, Vann Papers.

10. Amb. Ellsworth Bunker, Oral History (unpublished transcript).

11. Ibid. The question was put by interviewer Stephen Young.

12. Ibid.

13. Col. Hoang Ngoc Lung, *Strategy and Tactics,* p. 55.

14. Vietnam Military History Institute, *History of the People's Army of Vietnam,* II:389ff.

15. U.S. Army, Office of the Chief of Staff, *Weekly Summary* (2 September 1969), p. 3.

16. *The Haldeman Diaries,* 12 October 1972.

17. Ibid.

18. Ibid.

19. Richard Nixon, *No More Vietnams,* p. 103.

20. *The Haldeman Diaries,* 28 September 1972.

21. Maj. Gen. Hoang Lac, "How the Superpower U.S. Lost the Vietnam War," unpublished English translation of Vietnamese-language manuscript privately printed in 1990, p. 68.

22. See, for example, Henry Kissinger, *White House Years,* p. 1314.

23. Vietnam Military History Institute, *History of the People's Army of Vietnam,* II:424.

24. *The Haldeman Diaries,* 29 October 1972.

25. Henry A. Kissinger, Memorandum for the President, 29 November 1972, Box 1, Top Secret, Central Files, White House Special Files, Nixon Presidential Materials Collection, National Archives.

26. Brig. Gen. James R. McCarthy and Lt. Col. George B. Allison, *Linebacker II,* passim.

27. Sir Robert Thompson, *Peace Is Not at Hand,* p. 135. Wrote Thompson later, "I was surprised at the lengths to which the United States Air Force had gone to ensure hitting military targets and avoiding civilian areas, at greatly increased risks to both aircraft and crews. Admittedly, there were three bad accidents, including the hitting of Bach Mai hospital adjacent to and just north of Bach Mai airfield. In the prevailing conditions of the air war it is surprising that there were not more. In fact, the greatest

civilian damage was done by one B52 which crashed down a street in the centre of the city, but not even Hanoi claimed that this was intentional. According to Hanoi's own estimates the number of civilians killed was between 1,300 and 1,600 over eleven days. While everyone should regret even a fraction of that figure, the credit for such a low figure goes entirely to the United States." Ibid., p. 135. As late as 1980, although many visitors to Hanoi had seen firsthand that such claims were false, the North Vietnamese stubbornly maintained that during Linebacker II the United States "haphazardly bombed hospitals, housing areas, schools, bus stations, and railroad stations," although still— a remarkably low total if those charges had been true—claiming only 2,368 dead. War Experiences Recapitulation Committee, *Vietnam,* English-language version, p. 151. A 1994 history of the PAVN published in Hanoi continued the false charges, claiming that in Linebacker II the United States "carpet-bombed hospitals, schools, and crowded residential areas, committing extremely barbarous crimes against our people." Vietnam Military History Institute, *History of the People's Army of Vietnam,* II.

28. Cited in ibid.
29. War Experiences Recapitulation Committee, *Vietnam,* English-language version, p. 148.
30. Douglas Pike, "North Vietnamese Air Defenses During the Vietnam War," in William Head and Lawrence E. Grinter, eds., *Looking Back on the Vietnam War,* p. 171.
31. George C. Herring, "The Nixon Strategy in Vietnam," in Peter Braestrup, ed., *Vietnam as History,* p. 57.
32. Thompson, *Peace Is Not at Hand,* p. 135.
33. Sir Robert Thompson, as quoted in W. Scott Thompson and Donaldson D. Frizzell, *The Lessons of Vietnam,* p. 105. Emphasis in the original.

CHAPTER 22

1. Sir Robert Thompson in W. Scott Thompson and Donaldson D. Frizzell, *The Lessons of Vietnam,* p. 105.
2. Kevin Buckley, Telephone Interview, 5 July 1994. Former

Secretary of State Dean Rusk was later quoted as saying that the accords "were in effect a surrender. Any agreement that left North Vietnamese troops in South Vietnam meant the eventual takeover of South Vietnam." Jeffrey Record, "Vietnam in Retrospect," *Parameters* (Winter 1996–1997), p. 54.

3. Anthony James Joes, *Modern Guerrilla Insurgency,* p. 147.
4. Bunker Reporting Cable #59, 11 July 1968.
5. Gen. Cao Van Vien, *The Final Collapse,* p. 19.
6. Henry Kissinger, *White House Years,* p. 1374.
7. Ibid., p. 1390.
8. Henry Kissinger, *Years of Upheaval,* p. 310.
9. Vien, *The Final Collapse,* p. 6.
10. *The Haldeman Diaries,* 14 January 1973.
11. Rep. Gerald R. Ford, Letter, 15 January 1973, Box 178, H. R. Haldeman, Staff Member Office Files, White House Special Files, Nixon Presidential Materials Collection, National Archives.
12. War Experiences Recapitulation Committee of the High-Level Military Institute, *Vietnam,* English-language version, p. 156. Lyndon Johnson, whose presidency had been dominated, and blighted, by the war in Vietnam, died the day before the peace agreement was initialed.
13. As quoted in Sir Robert Thompson, *Peace Is Not at Hand,* p. 137. On the same day the final accord was signed, Secretary of Defense Laird announced the end of the draft for U.S. military forces.
14. Vietnam Military History Institute, *History of the People's Army of Vietnam,* II:389ff.
15. Harry G. Summers, Jr., *Historical Atlas of the Vietnam War,* p. 182. Elsewhere Summers gives 587 as the number of prisoners repatriated. *Vietnam War Almanac,* p. 170.
16. As reprinted in Office of the Chief of Staff, *Weekly Summary* (11 April 1973), CMH. For the numbers who served, *Pacific Stars & Stripes* (29 January 1973).
17. John Prados, *The Hidden History of the Vietnam War,* p. 273.
18. Amb. Samuel Berger, Oral History Interview, General Creighton Abrams Story, MHI.
19. Ellsworth Bunker, *The Bunker Papers,* ed. Douglas Pike, p. xiv.
20. Bunker Reporting Cable #96, 5 May 1973. An interesting insight

into the apparently deteriorating relationship between the President and the U.S. mission in Saigon during these events may be derived from the frequency with which Ambassador Bunker submitted periodic reporting cables, messages that went directly from him to the President. Bunker began his assignment in Saigon in April 1967, and during the remainder of Lyndon Johnson's presidency transmitted reporting cables almost weekly. When Richard Nixon assumed the office, Bunker maintained contact on approximately a monthly basis, at least until the late summer of 1969, when skips of two and even three months began to appear. After June 1971 only two more cables were sent, one thirty weeks later in January 1972, and the last of this long series of ninety-six messages in May 1973, sixty-five weeks after the penultimate one.

21. Summers, *Historical Atlas of the Vietnam War,* p. 182.

22. Henry Kissinger, Memorandum for the President, 14 March 1973, Box 2, NSC Files: POW/MIA, Nixon Presidential Materials Collection, National Archives.

23. Vietnam Military History Institute, *History of the People's Army of Vietnam,* II:458.

24. Remarks, William E. Colby, Videotape of Military Writers Symposium, Norwich University, 12 April 1996.

25. Gareth Porter, ed., *Vietnam: The Definitive Documentation,* p. 639.

26. Minutes, NSC Meeting, 9 April 1975, GRF Library. In reporting on a later trip, Weyand recalled his findings on this earlier visit.

27. Vien, *The Final Collapse,* pp. 31–33.

28. IISS, *Strategic Survey 1973,* p. 70.

29. Olivier Todd, *Cruel April,* pp. 15 and 21.

30. Thompson, *Peace Is Not at Hand,* p. 58.

31. Maj. Gen. Ira A. Hunt, Jr., Interview, 28 April 1997.

32. As quoted in Todd, *Cruel April,* p. 79.

33. Thompson, *Peace Is Not at Hand,* p. 200n66.

34. P. Edward Haley, *Congress and the Fall of South Vietnam,* p. 46.

35. Vien, *The Final Collapse,* p. 47.

36. Gen. Harold K. Johnson, Address, Economic Club of New York, 27 April 1966, Box 58, Harold K. Johnson Papers, MHI.

37. Vien, *The Final Collapse,* pp. 48–53.

38. Bui Diem, *In the Jaws of History,* p. 341. "Search and destroy" was

the discredited Westmoreland approach to conduct of a war of attrition.

39. Adm. Thomas H. Moorer, Interview, 26 September 1994.

40. Gen. John W. Vessey, prepublication comments on Sorley, *Thunderbolt.*

41. Gen. Donn A. Starry, Interview, 31 May 1995.

42. Maj. Gen. Nguyen Duy Hinh, *Vietnamization and the Cease-Fire,* p. 77.

43. Col. Hoang Ngoc Lung, *Strategy and Tactics,* p. 59.

44. Vien, *The Final Collapse,* pp. 33, 44.

45. Quoted in Richard G. Trefry, "Ashes to Ashes?" *Parameters* (Summer 1995), p. 58.

46. Fact Sheet, "Logistics Capabilities," n.d., GRF Library.

CHAPTER 23

1. Brig. Gen. Tran Dinh Tho, *Pacification,* p. 187.

2. Vietnam Military History Institute, *History of the People's Army of Vietnam,* II:473–475.

3. Gen. Cao Van Vien and Lt. Gen. Dong Van Khuyen, *Reflections on the Vietnam War,* p. 110.

4. Amb. Ellsworth Bunker, Oral History Interview, LBJ Library.

5. Defense Attaché Office, Saigon, *RVNAF Final Assessment,* p. 1-3.

6. Gen. Bruce Palmer, Jr., "US Intelligence and Vietnam," *Studies in Intelligence* (1984 Special Issue), p. 108.

7. Stephen Young, "How North Vietnam Won the War," Interview with Bui Tin, *Wall Street Journal* (3 August 1995).

8. Amb. Ellsworth Bunker, Thayer Award Address, West Point, N.Y., as printed in the *Congressional Record* (28 May 1970), p. E4732.

9. Gen. Cao Van Vien, *The Final Collapse,* p. 43.

10. As quoted in Olivier Todd, *Cruel April,* p. 145.

11. Vien, *The Final Collapse,* p. 116.

12. Ibid., p. 95. Vien had long thought withdrawing to a more defensible perimeter was essential, but by this point "it was already too late." Ibid., p. 80.

13. As quoted in Kim Willenson et al., *The Bad War,* p. 119.

14. Minutes, NSC Meeting, 9 April 1975, GRF Library. In the wake

of Weyand's visit the South Vietnamese did receive some additional rifles and machine guns, plus 5 M-113 APCs, 56 105mm howitzers, and 127,050 steel helmets (accompanied by only 67,698 helmet liners). Lt. Gen. Dong Van Khuyen, *RVNAF Logistics,* p. 436.

15. Robert Komer, in W. Scott Thompson and Donaldson D. Frizzell, *The Lessons of Vietnam,* pp. 229–230. The 18th Division had once been the 10th Division. In 1967, recalled General Truong, "upon recommendation of the 10th Division Commander, Brigadier General Do Ke Giai, who believed that number 10 was a bad number, the 10th Division was changed into the 18th, presumably a luckier number." No such luck. Lt. Gen. Ngo Quang Truong, *RVNAF and US Operational Cooperation and Coordination,* p. 45n4.

16. Maj. Gen. Hoang Lac and Col. Ha Mai Viet, *Blind Design,* p. 239.

17. Brig. Gen. Tran Quang Khoi, "Fighting to the Finish," *Armor* (March–April 1996), p. 22.

18. Col. Raymond R. Battreall, Letter to author, 31 March 1995.

19. Defense Attaché Office, Saigon, *RVNAF Final Assessment,* p. 5-17.

20. As quoted in Olivier Todd, *Cruel April,* p. 333.

21. William E. Colby, Keynote Address, Vietnam Symposium, Texas Tech University, 18 April 1996. Colby also pointed out that with 200,000 more South Vietnamese leaving their country under the "orderly departure program," plus the boat people, there were now a million Vietnamese living in the United States. Col. Bui Tin has stated that "after 1975, in the South, some 200,000 were jailed without hearing or trial. More than one million boat people fled, many of whom died on the sea. Overseas there are now more than two million Vietnamese who are refugees from their own country." Cantigny Conference, "Vietnam 1965–1975," Wheaton, Ill., 5–6 March 1997.

22. Department of State Cable, Saigon to Washington, 291215Z APR 1975, Saigon 00000.

23. Maj. Gen. Homer D. Smith, in Defense Attaché Office, Saigon, *RVNAF Final Assessment,* p. 16-A-5.

24. Khoi, "Fighting to the Finish," p. 25. Former ARVN Lt. Gen.

Nguyen Vinh Nghi, who spent nearly thirteen years in reeducation confinement after the war, later said "approximately 400,000 South Vietnamese soldiers, officers, diplomats and professionals went into re-education camps and an estimated 250,000 died there." Edvins Beitiks, "South Vietnamese General Relives Capture," *San Francisco Examiner* (9 August 1989).

25. Douglas Pike, *PAVN,* p. 225.
26. Truong, *RVNAF and US Operational Cooperation and Coordination,* p. 183.
27. Amb. Ellsworth Bunker, Oral History Interview, LBJ Library.
28. Amb. Ellsworth Bunker, Oral History (unpublished transcript).
29. Young, "How North Vietnam Won the War."
30. Ibid.
31. Amb. Samuel Berger, Oral History Interview, General Creighton Abrams Story, MHI.
32. Gen. Bruce Palmer, Jr., Interview, 26 September 1994.
33. Berger Interview, MHI.
34. Amb. Ellsworth Bunker, Oral History (unpublished transcript).
35. For the 465,000 civilian dead, Douglas Pike, *PAVN,* p. 310n5; for the 65,000 executed and the 250,000 who died in camps, Lt. Gen. Nguyen Vinh Nghi, as quoted by Beitiks, *San Francisco Examiner;* for the 275,000 military deaths, Col. Stuart Herrington, *The Fall of Saigon,* The Discovery Channel, 1 May 1995.
36. Harry G. Summers, Jr., *Vietnam War Almanac,* p. 113.
37. Douglas Pike, "The Other Side," in Peter Braestrup, ed., *Vietnam as History,* p. 73.
38. Fred Joyce, "Letter to the Editor," *Army* (January 1995), pp. 4–5. Adm. Zumwalt said that when he talked with Gen. Giap during a 1974 visit to Vietnam, Giap said they had 330,000 missing in action. Adm. Elmo R. Zumwalt, Jr., Vietnam War Symposium, Texas Tech University, 18 April 1996. James H. Webb, Jr., has noted that "Ha Noi officially announced a loss of 1.1 million soldiers." Letter to author, 13 October 1997.

Meanwhile there grew up in the United States what might almost be called an industry dealing with the issue of servicemen declared missing in action. The Vietnam War produced a total of

2,504 in that category. After the war strenuous efforts by the Joint Casualty Resolution Center, a Department of Defense entity established specifically and solely for the purpose of resolving as many missing in action cases as possible, reduced the total of unresolved cases to 2,097 still unaccounted for as of 31 January 1998. Some element of the public remained unconvinced, however, that there were no living persons remaining among those missing.

The probability of that being the case, however, seems low, especially in comparison with the totals of missing in action from earlier wars. About 8,200 remain unaccounted for from the Korean War, for example, while World War II missing in action total almost 79,000. The Vietnam War total of 2,097 compares with the combined total of 94,120 World War I, World War II, Korean War, and Vietnam War servicemen and women missing in action or lost or buried at sea who are commemorated at the facilities maintained by the American Battle Monuments Commission. Given the many years the Vietnam War lasted, the nature of the terrain in Southeast Asia, and the highly destructive munitions and high-performance weapons employed, what seems remarkable is that so few casualties went unrecovered or unidentified.

39. David K. Shipler, "Robert McNamara and the Ghosts of Vietnam," *New York Times Magazine* (10 August 1997), p. 50, citing a September 1995 article by a General Uoc.

40. Col. Pham Xuan An, in *Vietnam* (August 1990), p. 6.

41. "Mr. McNamara's Other War," *Washington Post* (30 April 1995).

42. Gen. Cao Van Vien, *Leadership,* p. 171. Ten years after the war, reported WLTT Radio in Washington on 1 April 1985, "two out of every five people questioned in a recent survey don't even remember whether the United States backed North or South Vietnam in the war."

EPILOGUE

1. Colonel Bui Tin, "Remarks," Cantigny Conference, Wheaton, Ill., 6–7 March 1996.

2. William Shawcross, "Review of David P. Chandler's *Brother Number One*," *New York Review of Books* (12 August 1993), p. 38.
3. Nicholas H. Sebastian, Jr., "Recent Experiences in Vietnam," electronic message posted to the West Point Forum, 29 August 1998.

SELECTED
BIBLIOGRAPHY

BOOKS

Adams, Sam. *War of Numbers: An Intelligence Memoir.* South Royalton, Vt.: Steerforth Press, 1994.

Ambrose, Stephen F. *Nixon: Ruin and Recovery, 1973–1990.* New York: Simon & Schuster, 1991.

————. *Nixon: The Triumph of a Politician, 1962–1972.* New York: Simon & Schuster, 1989.

Andrade, Dale. *Trial by Fire: The 1972 Easter Offensive.* New York: Hippocrene, 1995.

Ball, George, *The Past Has Another Pattern: Memoirs.* New York: W. W. Norton, 1982.

Beech, Keyes. *Not Without the Americans: A Personal History.* Garden City, N.Y.: Doubleday, 1971.

Birdwell, Dwight W., and Keith William Nolan. *A Hundred Miles of Bad Road.* Novato, Calif.: Presidio Press, 1997.

Bowman, John S., ed. *The Vietnam War: An Almanac.* New York: World Almanac, 1985.

Braestrup, Peter. *Big Story: How the American Press and Television Reported and Interpreted the Crisis of Tet 1968 in Vietnam and Washington,* 2 vols. Boulder, Colo.: Westview Press, 1977.

————, ed. *Vietnam as History: Ten Years After the Paris Peace Accords.* Washington, D.C.: University Press of America, 1984.

Bundy, William. *A Tangled Web: The Making of Foreign Policy in the Nixon Presidency.* New York: Hill and Wang, 1998.

Bunker, Ellsworth. *The Bunker Papers: Reports to the President from Vietnam, 1967–1973,* ed. Douglas Pike, 3 vols. Berkeley: Institute of Asian Studies, University of California, 1990.

Burkett, B. G., and Donna Whitley. *Stolen Valor: How the Vietnam Generation Was Robbed of Its Heroes and Its History.* Dallas: Verity Press, 1998.

Butler, David. *The Fall of Saigon.* New York: Dell, 1986.

Chanoff, David, and Doan Van Toai. *Portrait of the Enemy.* New York: Random House, 1987.

Charlton, Michael, and Anthony Moncrieff. *Many Reasons Why: The American Involvement in Vietnam.* London: Scolar Press, 1978.

Christian, George. *The President Steps Down: A Personal Memoir of the Transfer of Power.* New York: Macmillan, 1970.

Clarke, Jeffrey J. *Advice and Support: The Final Years, 1965–1973.* Washington, D.C.: Center of Military History, U.S. Army, 1988.

Clifford, Clark, with Richard Holbrooke. *Counsel to the President: A Memoir.* New York: Random House, 1991.

Clutterbuck, Brigadier Richard L. *The Long, Long War: Counterinsurgency in Malaya and Vietnam.* New York: Praeger, 1966.

Colby, William. *Honorable Men: My Life in the CIA.* New York: Simon & Schuster, 1978.

———. *Lost Victory.* Chicago: Contemporary Books, 1989.

Coleman, J. D. *Incursion: From America's Chokehold on the NVA Lifelines to the Sacking of the Cambodian Sanctuaries.* New York: St. Martin's Press, 1991.

Cooper, Chester L. *The Lost Crusade: America in Vietnam.* New York: Dodd, Mead, 1970.

Cosmas, Graham A., and Terrence P. Murray. *U.S. Marines in Vietnam: Vietnamization and Redeployment, 1970–1971.* Washington, D.C.: History and Museums Division, Headquarters, U.S. Marine Corps, 1986.

Cronkite, Walter. *A Reporter's Life.* New York: Knopf, 1996.

Davidson, Lieutenant General Phillip B. *Secrets of the Vietnam War.* Novato, Calif.: Presidio Press, 1990.

————. *Vietnam at War: The History, 1946–1975*. Novato, Calif.: Presidio Press, 1988.

DeForest, Orrin, and David Chanoff. *Slow Burn: The Rise and Bitter Fall of American Intelligence in Vietnam*. New York: Simon & Schuster, 1990.

Diem, Bui. *In the Jaws of History*. Boston: Houghton Mifflin, 1987.

Duiker, William J. *The Communist Road to Power in Vietnam*. Boulder, Colo.: Westview Press, 1981.

————. *Historical Dictionary of Vietnam*. Metuchen, N.J.: Scarecrow Press, 1989.

Dunstan, Simon. *Vietnam Tracks: Armor in Battle 1945–1975*. Novato, Calif.: Presidio, 1982.

Ellsberg, Daniel. *Papers on the War*. New York: Simon & Schuster, 1972.

Engelmann, Larry. *Tears Before the Rain: An Oral History of the Fall of South Vietnam*. New York: Oxford University Press, 1990.

Enthoven, Alain C. and K. Wayne Smith. *How Much Is Enough? Shaping the Defense Program, 1961–1969*. New York: Harper & Row, 1971.

Fulghum, David, and Terrence Maitland. *South Vietnam on Trial: Mid-1970 to 1972 (The Vietnam Experience)*. Boston: Boston Publishing Company, 1984.

Gallup, George H. *The Gallup Poll: Public Opinion 1935–1971*, Vol. 3, *1959–1971*. New York: Random House, 1972.

Haig, Alexander M., Jr., with Charles McCarry. *Inner Circles: How America Changed the World: A Memoir*. New York: Warner Books, 1992.

Halberstam, David. *The Best and the Brightest*. Greenwich, Conn.: Fawcett, 1969.

Haldeman, H. R. *The Haldeman Diaries: Inside the Nixon White House*. Santa Monica, Calif.: Sony Electronic Publishing Company, 1994. CD-ROM.

Haley, P. Edward. *Congress and the Fall of South Vietnam and Cambodia*. Rutherford, N.J.: Fairleigh Dickinson University Press (Associated University Presses), 1982.

Hammond, William M. *The Military and the Media 1968–1973*. Washington, D.C.: Center of Military History, U.S. Army, 1996.

Harrison, James Pinckney. *The Endless War: Fifty Years of Struggle in Vietnam*. New York: Free Press, 1982.

Head, William, and Lawrence E. Grinter, eds. *Looking Back on the Vietnam War: A 1990s Perspective on the Decisions, Combat, and Legacies*. Westport, Conn.: Praeger, 1993.

Herring, George C. *America's Longest War: The United States and Vietnam 1950–1975*, 2d ed. New York: Knopf, 1986.

———. *"Cold Blood": LBJ's Conduct of Limited War in Vietnam*. Washington: Government Printing Office, 1990.

Herrington, Stuart A. *Silence Was a Weapon: The Vietnam War in the Villages*. Novato, Calif.: Presidio Press, 1982.

Herz, Martin F. *The Prestige Press and the Christmas Bombing, 1972*. Washington, D.C.: Ethics and Public Policy Center, 1980.

Hoopes, Townsend. *The Limits of Intervention*. New York: David McKay, 1969.

Hosmer, Stephen T., Konrad Kellen, and Brian M. Jenkins, eds. *The Fall of South Vietnam: Statements by Vietnamese Military and Civilian Leaders*. New York: Crane, Russak, 1980.

Hung, Nguyen Tien, and Jerrold L. Schecter. *The Palace File*. New York: Harper & Row, 1986.

Hunt, Richard A. *Pacification: The American Struggle for Vietnam's Hearts and Minds*. Boulder, Colo.: Westview Press, 1995.

Joes, Anthony James. *Modern Guerrilla Insurgency*. Westport, Conn.: Praeger, 1992.

———. *The War for South Viet Nam, 1954–1975*. Westport, Conn.: Praeger, 1989.

Johnson, Lyndon Baines. *The Vantage Point: Perspectives of the Presidency, 1963–1969*. New York: Holt, Rinehart and Winston, 1971.

Joint Chiefs of Staff. *The History of the Joint Chiefs of Staff: The Joint Chiefs of Staff and the War in Vietnam, 1960–1968*, 3 parts. Washington, D.C.: Historical Division, Joint Secretariat, Joint Chiefs of Staff, 1970.

———. *The History of the Joint Chiefs of Staff: The Joint Chiefs of Staff and the War in Vietnam, 1969–1970*. Washington, D.C.: Historical Division, Joint Secretariat, Joint Chiefs of Staff, 1976.

Karnow, Stanley. *Vietnam: A History*. New York: Viking Press, 1983.

Kearns, Doris. *Lyndon Johnson and the American Dream.* New York: Harper & Row, 1976.

Kinnard, Douglas. *The War Managers.* Hanover, N.H.: University Press of New England, 1977.

Kissinger, Henry. *White House Years.* Boston: Little, Brown, 1979.

———. *Years of Upheaval.* Boston: Little, Brown, 1982.

Knappman, Edward W., ed. *South Vietnam: U.S.-Communist Confrontation in Southeast Asia,* vol. 7. New York: Facts on File, 1973.

Komer, Robert W. *Bureaucracy at War: U.S. Performance in the Vietnam Conflict.* Boulder, Colo.: Westview Press, 1986.

Lac, Major General Hoang, and Colonel Ha Mai Viet. *Blind Design: Why America Lost the Vietnam War.* Privately printed, 1996.

Lanning, Michael Lee, and Dan Cragg. *Inside the VC and the NVA: The Real Story of North Vietnam's Armed Forces.* New York: Ivy Books, 1992.

Lefever, Ernest W. *TV and National Defense: An Analysis of CBS News, 1972–1973.* Boston, Va.: Institute for American Strategy Press, 1974.

Lewy, Guenter. *America in Vietnam.* New York: Oxford University Press, 1978.

Maclear, Michael. *The Ten Thousand Day War, Vietnam: 1945–1975.* New York: St. Martin's Press, 1981.

Martin, Command Sergeant Major Michael. *Angels in Red Hats: Paratroopers of the Second Indochina War.* Louisville, K.Y.: Harmony House, 1995.

Matthews, Lloyd J., and Dale E. Brown, eds. *Assessing the Vietnam War.* Washington, D.C.: Pergamon-Brassey's, 1987.

Millett, Allan R., and Peter Maslowski. *For the Common Defense: A Military History of the United States of America.* New York: Free Press, 1984.

Moyar, Mark. *Phoenix and the Birds of Prey: The CIA's Secret Campaign to Destroy the Viet Cong.* Annapolis, Md.: Naval Institute Press, 1997.

Nixon, Richard. *No More Vietnams.* New York: Arbor House, 1985.

———. *RN: The Memoirs of Richard Nixon.* New York: Grosset & Dunlap, 1978.

Nolan, Keith William. *Battle for Hue: Tet, 1968*. Novato, Calif.: Presidio Press, 1983.

———. *Battle for Saigon: Tet 1968*. New York: Pocket Books, 1996.

———. *Death Valley: The Summer Offensive, I Corps, August 1969*. Novato, Calif.: Presidio Press, 1987.

———. *Into Cambodia: Spring Campaign, Summer Offensive, 1970*. Novato, Calif.: Presidio Press, 1990.

———. *Into Laos: The Story of Dewey Canyon II/Lam Son 719; Vietnam 1971*. Novato, Calif.: Presidio Press, 1986.

Oudes, Bruce, ed. *From: The President: Richard Nixon's Secret Files*. New York: Harper & Row, 1989.

Palmer, General Bruce, Jr. *The 25-Year War: America's Military Role in Vietnam*. Lexington: University Press of Kentucky, 1984.

Palmer, Dave Richard. *Summons of the Trumpet: A History of the Vietnam War from a Military Man's Viewpoint*. New York: Ballantine Books, 1978.

Perry, Mark. *Four Stars*. Boston: Houghton Mifflin, 1989.

Pettit, Clyde Edwin. *The Experts*. Secaucus, N.J.: Lyle Stuart, 1975.

Pike, Douglas. *PAVN: People's Army of Vietnam*. Novato, Calif.: Presidio Press, 1986.

———. *Viet Cong: The Organization and Techniques of the National Liberation Front of South Vietnam*. Cambridge, Mass.: MIT Press, 1966.

———. *War, Peace and the Viet Cong*. Cambridge, Mass.: MIT Press, 1969.

Powers, Thomas. *The Man Who Kept the Secrets: Richard Helms and the CIA*. New York: Alfred A. Knopf, 1969.

Prados, John. *The Hidden History of the Vietnam War*. Chicago: Ivan R. Dee, 1995.

Safire, William. *Before the Fall: An Inside View of the Pre-Watergate White House*. Garden City, N.Y.: Doubleday, 1975.

Schemmer, Benjamin F. *The Raid*. New York: Harper & Row, 1976.

Schlight, John. *The War in South Vietnam: The Years of the Offensive, 1965–1968*. The United States Air Force in Southeast Asia. Washington, D.C.: Office of Air Force History, U.S. Air Force, 1988.

Seignious, George M. II. *A Grandfather Reports*. Privately printed, 1996.

Shackley, Theodore. *The Third Option: An American View of Counter-insurgency Operations.* New York: Dell, 1981.

Shapley, Deborah. *Promise and Power: The Life and Times of Robert Mc-Namara.* Boston: Little, Brown, 1993.

Shawcross, William. *Sideshow: Kissinger, Nixon and the Destruction of Cambodia.* New York: Simon & Schuster, 1979.

Sheehan, Neil. *A Bright Shining Lie: John Paul Vann and America in Vietnam.* New York: Random House, 1988.

Shulimson, Jack, et al. *U.S. Marines in Vietnam: The Defining Year 1968.* Washington, D.C.: History and Museums Division, U.S. Marine Corps, 1997.

Smith, Charles R. *U.S. Marines in Vietnam: High Mobility and Stand-down 1969.* Washington, D.C.: History and Museums Division, U.S. Marine Corps, 1988.

Sobel, Lester A., ed. *South Vietnam: U.S.-Communist Confrontation in Southeast Asia,* vols. 5 and 6. New York: Facts on File, 1970 and 1971.

Sorley, Lewis. *Honorable Warrior: General Harold K. Johnson and the Ethics of Command.* Lawrence: University Press of Kansas, 1998.

————. *Thunderbolt: General Creighton Abrams and the Army of His Times.* New York: Simon & Schuster, 1992.

Spector, Ronald H. *After Tet: The Bloodiest Year in Vietnam.* New York: Free Press, 1993.

Stanton, Shelby L. *The Rise and Fall of an American Army: U.S. Ground Forces in Vietnam, 1965–1973.* New York: Dell, 1985.

————. *Vietnam Order of Battle.* Washington, D.C.: U.S. News Books, 1981.

Starry, General Donn A. *Armored Combat in Vietnam.* New York: Arno Press, 1980.

Stockdale, Jim, and Sybil Stockdale. *In Love and War,* rev. ed. Annapolis, Md.: Naval Institute Press, 1990.

Summers, Harry G., Jr. *Historical Atlas of the Vietnam War.* Boston: Houghton Mifflin, 1995.

————. *On Strategy: The Vietnam War in Context.* Carlisle Barracks, Pa.: Strategic Studies Institute, U.S. Army War College, 1981.

————. *Vietnam War Almanac.* New York: Facts on File, 1985.

Tang, Truong Nhu, with David Chanoff and Doan Van Toai. *A Vietcong Memoir*. New York: Harcourt Brace Jovanovich, 1985.

Taylor, John M. *General Maxwell Taylor: The Sword and the Pen*. New York: Doubleday, 1989.

Terzani, Tiziano. *Giai Phong! The Fall and Liberation of Saigon*. New York: St. Martin's Press, 1976.

Thompson, Sir Robert. *Peace Is Not at Hand*. London: Chatto & Windus, 1974.

Thompson, W. Scott, and Donaldson D. Frizzell, eds. *The Lessons of Vietnam*. New York: Crane, Russak, 1977.

Timberg, Robert. *The Nightingale's Song*. New York: Simon & Schuster, 1995.

Tin, Bui. *Following Ho Chi Minh: Memoirs of a North Vietnamese Colonel*. Honolulu: University of Hawaii Press, 1995.

Todd, Olivier. *Cruel April: The Fall of Saigon*. New York: Norton, 1987.

Turley, Colonel G. H. *The Easter Offensive*. Novato, Calif.: Presidio Press, 1985.

Turley, William S. *The Second Indochina War*. New York: New American Library, 1986.

Vietnam Military History Institute. *History of the People's Army of Vietnam*, vol. 2. Hanoi: People's Army Publishing House, 1994. Unpublished translation by Merle L. Pribbenow.

Vinh, Pham Kim. *The Vietnamese Culture*. Privately printed, n.d. Solana Beach, Calif.

Westmoreland, General William C. *A Soldier Reports*. Garden City, N.Y.: Doubleday, 1976.

Willenson, Kim, et al. *The Bad War: An Oral History of the Vietnam War*. New York: New American Library, 1987.

Zaffiri, Samuel. *Hamburger Hill: May 11–20, 1969*. Novato, Calif.: Presidio Press, 1988.

———. *Westmoreland: A Biography of General William C. Westmoreland*. New York: William Morrow, 1994.

Zumwalt, Elmo R., Jr. *On Watch: A Memoir*. New York: Quadrangle, 1976.

Zumwalt, Admiral Elmo, Jr., and Lieutenant Elmo Zumwalt III. *My Father, My Son*. New York: Macmillan, 1986.

BOOK CHAPTERS

Birch, Harold. "Vietnam and the Gulf War: Comparing Decision-Making in America's Longest and Shortest Wars." In Marcia Lynn Whicker, James P. Pfiffner, and Raymond A. Moore, eds., *The Presidency and the Persian Gulf War.* Westport, Conn.: Praeger, 1993.

Diem, Bui. "Reflections on the Vietnam War: The Views of a Vietnamese on Vietnamese-American Misconceptions." In William Head and Lawrence E. Grinter, eds., *Looking Back on the Vietnam War.* Westport, Conn.: Praeger, 1993.

Herring, George C. "The Reluctant Warrior: Lyndon Johnson as Commander in Chief." In David L. Anderson, ed., *Shadow on the White House: Presidents and the Vietnam War, 1945–1975.* Lawrence: University Press of Kansas, 1993.

Stuckey, John D., and Joseph H. Pistorius. "Mobilization for the Vietnam War." In Lloyd J. Matthews and Dale E. Brown, eds., *Assessing the Vietnam War: A Collection from the Journal of the U.S. Army War College.* Washington, D.C.: Pergamon-Brassey's, 1987.

ARTICLES

Bradford, Zeb B., Jr. "With Creighton Abrams in Vietnam." *Assembly* (May/June 1998), pp. 27–32.

Braestrup, Peter. "The Abrams Strategy in Vietnam." *The New Leader* (9 June 1969), pp. 3–5.

Buckley, Kevin P. "General Abrams Deserves a Better War." *New York Times Magazine* (5 October 1969), pp. 34ff.

Burkett, B. G. "Telling It Like It Is." *Vietnam* (February 1997), pp. 26–33.

Davis, General Raymond G., USMC. "Politics and War: Twelve Fatal Decisions That Rendered Defeat in Vietnam." *Marine Corps Gazette* (August 1989), pp. 75–78.

Ford, Harold P. "An Honorable Man: William Colby: Retrospect." *Studies in Intelligence* semiannual unclassified edition, no. 1 (1997), pp. 1–5.

Khoi, Brigadier General Tran Quang, ARVN. "Fighting to the Finish." *Armor* (March–April 1996), pp. 19–25.

Kroesen, General Frederick J. "Hiep Duc: Triumph and Tragedy." *Army* (July 1994), pp. 45–46.

Langguth, A. J. "General Abrams Listens to a Different Drum." *New York Times Magazine* (5 May 1968).

Olinger, Major Mark A. "Task Force Remagen: Sustaining a Heavy Task Force via Aerial Resupply." *Armor* (March–April 1998), pp. 30–32.

Palmer, Laura. "The General at Ease: An Interview with Westmoreland." *MHQ: The Quarterly Journal of Military History* (1988), pp. 30–35.

Prillaman, Richard L. "Vietnam Update." *Infantry* (May–June 1969), pp. 18–19.

Whitley, Glenna. "Stolen Valor." *D Magazine* (June 1998), pp. 70–77.

Young, Stephen. "How North Vietnam Won the War," interview with Bui Tin. *Wall Street Journal* (3 August 1995).

Zhang, Xiaoming. "The Vietnam War, 1964–1969: A Chinese Perspective." *Journal of Military History* (October 1996), pp. 731–762.

STUDIES AND REPORTS

BDM Corporation. *A Study of Strategic Lessons Learned in Vietnam: Omnibus Executive Summary.* McLean, Va.: BDM Corporation, 1980.

Buckingham, William A., Jr. *Operation Ranch Hand: The Air Force and Herbicides in Southeast Asia 1961–1972.* Washington, D.C.: Office of Air Force History, U.S. Air Force, 1982.

Collins, Brigadier General James Lawton, Jr. *The Development and Training of the South Vietnamese Army 1950–1972.* Washington, D.C.: Department of the Army, 1975.

Defense Attaché Office, Saigon. *RVNAF Final Assessment: Jan Thru Apr FY 75.* Embassy of the United States of America, Residual Defense Attaché Office, APO San Francisco 96558, 15 June 1975.

Department of the Army. *Area Handbook for Vietnam.* Washington, D.C.: U.S. Government Printing Office, 1962.

————. *Army Activities Report: SE Asia*. U.S. Army Military History Institute (MHI), 26 March 1969 (first issue) and after.

————. *Army Buildup Progress Report*. MHI, 4 January 1967–19 March 1969 (final issue).

————. *A Program for the Long-Term Pacification and Development of Vietnam (PROVN)*. Washington, D.C.: Department of the Army, 1 March 1966.

Eckhardt, Major General George S. *Command and Control, 1950– 1969*. Vietnam Studies. Washington, D.C.: Department of the Army, 1974.

Ewell, Lieutenant General Julian J., and Major General Ira A. Hunt, Jr. *Sharpening the Combat Edge: The Use of Analysis to Reinforce Military Judgment*. Washington, D.C.: Department of the Army, 1974.

Fulton, Major General William B. *Riverine Operations, 1966–1969*. Washington, D.C.: Department of the Army, 1973.

Ginsburg, Gordon A. *The Lavelle Case: Crisis in Integrity*. Maxwell Air Force Base: Air University, 1974.

Heiser, Lieutenant General Joseph M., Jr. *Logistic Support*. Washington, D.C.: Department of the Army, 1974.

Hinh, Major General Nguyen Duy, ARVN. *Lam Son 719*. Washington, D.C.: U.S. Army Center of Military History, 1979.

————. *Vietnamization and the Cease-fire*. Washington, D.C.: U.S. Army Center of Military History, 1980.

————, and Brigadier General Tran Dinh Tho. *The South Vietnamese Society*. Washington, D.C.: U.S. Army Center of Military History, 1980.

International Institute for Strategic Studies, *Strategic Survey 1973*. London: IISS, 1974.

Jenkins, Brian. *The Unchangeable War*. Santa Monica, Calif.: Rand Corporation, November 1970.

Khuyen, Lieutenant General Dong Van, ARVN. *The RVNAF*. Washington, D.C.: U.S. Army Center of Military History, 1980.

————. *RVNAF Logistics*. Washington, D.C.: U.S. Army Center of Military History, 1980.

Komer, R. W. *Bureaucracy Does Its Thing: The Impact of Institutional*

Constraints on US/GVN Performance in the Vietnam War. Santa Monica, Calif.: Rand Corporation, February 1971.

————. *Organization and Management of the New Model Pacification Program, 1966–1969.* Santa Monica, Calif.: Rand Corporation, 7 May 1970.

Larsen, Lieutenant General Stanley R., and Brigadier General James Lawton Collins, Jr. *Allied Participation in Vietnam.* Washington, D.C.: Department of the Army, 1975.

Lavelle, Major A. J. C., ed. *Airpower and the 1972 Spring Invasion.* Washington, D.C.: U.S. Government Printing Office, 1976.

LeGro, Colonel William E. *Vietnam from Cease-fire to Capitulation.* Washington, D.C.: U.S. Army Center of Military History, 1981.

Lung, Colonel Hoang Ngoc, ARVN. *The General Offensives of 1968–69.* Washington, D.C.: U.S. Army Center of Military History, 1981.

————. *Intelligence.* Washington, D.C.: U.S. Army Center of Military History, 1982.

————. *Strategy and Tactics.* Washington, D.C.: U.S. Army Center of Military History, 1980.

McCarthy, Brigadier General James R., and Lieutenant Colonel George B. Allison. *Linebacker II: A View from the Rock.* Maxwell AFB: Airpower Research Institute, 1979.

Ott, David. *Field Artillery, 1954–1973.* Vietnam Studies. Washington, D.C.: Department of the Army, 1975.

Palmer, General Bruce, Jr. "US Intelligence and Vietnam." *Studies in Intelligence* (special issue). Washington, D.C.: Central Intelligence Agency, 1984.

Pearson, Lieutenant General Willard. *The War in the Northern Provinces 1966–1968.* Washington, D.C.: Department of the Army, 1975.

Pike, Douglas. *The Viet-Cong Strategy of Terror.* Saigon: U.S. Mission, February 1970.

Project CHECO, 7th Air Force. *The Air War in Vietnam 1968–1969.* Headquarters, Pacific Air Force, n.d.

————. *A Shau Valley Campaign, December 1968–May 1969.* Headquarters, Pacific Air Force, n.d.

————. *The Bolovens Campaign: 28 July–28 December 1971.* Headquarters, Pacific Air Force, 1974.

―――――. *Kontum: Battle for the Central Highlands, 30 March–10 June 1972*. Headquarters, Pacific Air Force, n.d.

―――――. *Lam Son 719: 30 January–24 March '71, The South Vietnamese Incursion into Laos*. Headquarters, Pacific Air Force, n.d.

Rienzi, Major General Thomas M. *Communications-Electronics 1962–1970*. Washington, D.C.: Department of the Army, 1972.

Robson, Jon R. *Civilian Control in a Limited War: MacArthur and Lavelle*. Maxwell Air Force Base: Air University, 1975.

Schlight, John, ed. *Second Indochina War Symposium*. Washington, D.C.: U.S. Army Center of Military History, 1986.

Scoville, Thomas W. *Reorganizing for Pacification Support*. Washington, D.C.: U.S. Army Center of Military History, 1982.

Sharp, Admiral U. S. G., and General W. C. Westmoreland. *Report on the War in Vietnam*. Washington, D.C.: U.S. Government Printing Office, 1969.

Tho, Brigadier General Tran Dinh, ARVN. *The Cambodian Incursion*. Washington, D.C.: U.S. Army Center of Military History, 1979.

―――――. *Pacification*. Washington, D.C.: U.S. Army Center of Military History, 1980.

Tolson, Lieutenant General John. *Airmobility 1961–1971*. Washington, D.C.: Department of the Army, 1973.

Truong, Lieutenant General Ngo Quang, ARVN. *The Easter Offensive of 1972*. Washington, D.C.: U.S. Army Center of Military History, 1977.

―――――. *RVNAF and US Operational Cooperation and Coordination*. Washington, D.C.: U.S. Army Center of Military History, 1980.

―――――. *Territorial Forces*. Washington, D.C.: U.S. Army Center of Military History, 1978.

U.S. Congress. House. Select Committee on Intelligence. *Hearings: U.S. Intelligence Agencies and Activities: Risks and Control of Foreign Intelligence*, Part 5. Washington: Government Printing Office, 1976.

U.S. Congress. Senate Committee on Foreign Relations. *Vietnam: December 1969, A Staff Report*. Washington: Government Printing Office, 1970.

U.S. Joint Chiefs of Staff. *The History of the Joint Chiefs of Staff: The Joint Chiefs of Staff and the War in Vietnam 1969–1970*. Washington, D.C.: Historical Division, Joint Secretariat, Joint Chiefs of Staff, 26 April 1976.

———. *The History of the Joint Chiefs of Staff: The Joint Chiefs of Staff and the War in Vietnam 1971–1973*. Washington, D.C.: Historical Division, Joint Secretariat, Joint Chiefs of Staff, September 1979.

Veterans Administration. *Myths and Realities: A Study of Attitudes Toward Vietnam Era Veterans*. Washington, D.C.: U.S. Government Printing Office, 1980.

Vien, General Cao Van, ARVN. *The Final Collapse*. Washington, D.C.: U.S. Army Center of Military History, 1983.

———. *Leadership*. Washington, D.C.: U.S. Army Center of Military History, 1981.

Vien, General Cao Van, and Lieutenant General Dong Van Khuyen, ARVN. *Reflections on the Vietnam War*. Washington, D.C.: U.S. Army Center of Military History, 1980.

———. *The U.S. Adviser*. Washington, D.C.: U.S. Army Center of Military History, 1977.

Westmoreland, General William C. *Report of the Chief of Staff of the United States Army, 1 July 1968 to 30 June 1972*. Washington, D.C.: Department of the Army, 1977.

Willbanks, Lieutenant Colonel James H. *Thiet Giap! The Battle of An Loc, April 1972*. Fort Leavenworth, Kan.: U.S. Army Command & General Staff College, 1993.

DOCUMENTS

Abrams, General Creighton. Papers. U.S. Army Military History Institute, Carlisle Barracks, Pa.

———. Special Collection. U.S. Army War College, Carlisle Barracks, Pa.

American Battle Monuments Commission. *American Memorials and Overseas Military Cemeteries*. Washington, D.C.: ABMC, 1994.

Association of Graduates, U.S. Military Academy. *Register of Graduates and Former Cadets*. West Point, N.Y.: AOG, various years.

Bunker, Ambassador Ellsworth. Oral History (unpublished transcript). Interviewed by Stephen Young.

Chaisson, Lieutenant General John R., USMC. Diaries and Letters. Hoover Institution Archives, Stanford University, Stanford, Calif.

Erlichman, John. Papers. Hoover Institution Archives, Stanford University, Stanford, Calif.

Gibbons, William Conrad, ed. *The U.S. Government and the Vietnam War: Executive and Legislative Roles and Relationships*, parts I–IV. Washington, D.C.: U.S. Government Printing Office, 1984–1994.

Goodpaster, General Andrew J. Papers. National Defense University Library, Fort McNair, Washington, D.C.

Gravel, Senator Mike, ed. *The Pentagon Papers: The Defense Department History of United States Decisionmaking on Vietnam*, 5 vols. Boston: Beacon Press, 1971–1972.

Indochina Archive. University of California, Berkeley.

Laird, Secretary of Defense Melvin. *Final Report to the Congress*. Washington, D.C.: Department of Defense, 8 January 1973.

Marshall, Colonel Donald S. Papers. Indochina Archive, University of California, Berkeley.

Montague, Brigadier General Robert M., Jr. Papers. U.S. Army Military History Institute, Carlisle Barracks, Pa.

Office of the Chief of Staff, U.S. Army. *Weekly Summary*. Washington, D.C.: OCSA, various dates.

Pike, Douglas, ed. *The Bunker Papers: Reports to the President from Vietnam, 1967–1973*, 3 vols. Berkeley: Institute of East Asian Studies, University of California, 1990.

Porter, Gareth, ed. *Vietnam: The Definitive Documentation of Human Decisions*, vol. 2. Stanfordville, N.Y.: Coleman Enterprises, 1979.

XXIV Corps. *Lamson 719 After Action Report: 30 January–6 April 1971*. MHI. Microfilm file.

U.S. Congress, Senate, Committee on Armed Services. *Hearing on the Nomination of William E. Colby to Be Director of Central Intelligence*. Washington, D.C.: U.S. Government Printing Office, 1973.

U.S. Congress, Senate, Committee on Veterans Affairs. *Myths and Realities: A Study of Attitudes toward Vietnam Era Veterans*. Washington, D.C.: U.S. Government Printing Office, July 1980.

U.S. Military Assistance Command, Vietnam. *Compendium of COSVN*

Directives (1966– 1971). Headquarters, MACV: Strategic Research & Analysis Division, Directorate of Intelligence Production, MACV J2, 11 October 1971. Copy in MHI.

————. MACV Command Briefing, "The Changing Nature of the War." 1972.

Vann, John Paul. Papers. Patterson School of Diplomacy and International Commerce, University of Kentucky.

Vietnam, A Documentary Collection: Westmoreland vs. CBS. New York: Clearwater Publishing, 1985. Microform.

War Experiences Recapitulation Committee of the High-Level Military Institute. *Vietnam: The Anti-U.S. Resistance War for National Salvation 1954– 1975: Military Events.* Hanoi: People's Army Publishing House, 1980. English-language version, Arlington, Va.: Joint Publications Research Service, Foreign Broadcast Information Service, 3 June 1982.

Warner, General Volney F. Papers. U.S. Army Military History Institute, Carlisle Barracks, Pa.

Wheeler, General Earle G. Papers. National Archives, College Park, Md.

UNPUBLISHED MANUSCRIPTS

Bundy, William. "Memoir." John F. Kennedy Library.

Cushman, Lieutenant General John H. "A Personal Memoir: An Account of the 2d Brigade, 101st Airborne Division, September 1967 Through June 1968." 27 July 1995. Xerographic format.

Hamilton, William Alexander. "The Influence of the American Military upon United States Foreign Policy, 1965–1968." Unpublished Ph.D. dissertation, University of Nebraska, 1978.

Scoville, Thomas W., and Charles B. MacDonald. Interview with Ambassador Robert W. Komer and Colonel Robert M. Montague. Washington, D.C.: Office of the Chief of Military History, Department of the Army, 6–7 November 1969. Typescript.

Young, Stephen B. "What Really Happened in Vietnam? Lessons for Our Time of Troubles." Unpublished essay.

OTHER SOURCES

Interviews Conducted

Brigadier General Creighton W. Abrams III; General John N. Abrams; Julia (Julie) Harvey Abrams; Lieutenant Colonel Robert Bruce Abrams; Stephen Ailes; Major General Jack A. Albright; Major General John R. Alison, USAF; Lieutenant General Elmer H. Almquist, Jr.; Major General Theodore Antonelli; Lieutenant General Robert J. Baer; Colonel Francis R. Baker; Major General Edward Bautz, Jr.; Keyes Beech; Kenneth E. BeLieu; General Donald V. Bennett; Charles Benoit, Jr.; Monsignor John Benson; Major General Robert Bernstein; Robert W. Berry; Lieutenant General Sidney B. Berry; Betty Wheeler Besson; Command Sergeant Major Myron J. Bowser; Brigadier General Zeb B. Bradford, Jr.; Noel Abrams Bradley; Peter Braestrup; Colonel Paul Braim; Lieutenant General Frederic J. Brown; Kevin P. Buckley; Ambassador Carol Laise Bunker; Lieutenant General Frank A. Camm; Brigadier General Lawrence H. Caruthers, Jr.; Dr. George A. Carver, Jr.; Brigadier General Geoffrey Cheadle, USAF; General Ferdinand J. Chesarek; Major General Richard L. Clutterbuck, British Army; Brigadier General Samuel G. Cockerham; Ambassador William E. Colby; Colonel Joseph B. Conmy, Jr.; Colonel Robert M. Cook; Sergeant Major of the Army Silas Copeland; Lieutenant General Charles A. Corcoran; Daniel Cragg; Walter Cronkite; Lieutenant General John H. Cushman; Edwin Dale, Jr.; Dr. Jeanne Abrams Daly; Lieutenant General Phillip B. Davidson, Jr.; General Raymond G. Davis, USMC; Dr. Vincent Davis; General Michael S. Davison; Ambassador John Gunther Dean; General William E. DePuy; Lieutenant General William R. Desobry; Ambassador Bui Diem, RVN; Lieutenant General Welborn G. Dolvin; General Tran Van Don, ARVN; Lieutenant General David K. Doyle; Elizabeth Abrams Doyle; Colonel Trevor N. Dupuy; Robert Eidson; Major General James N. Ellis; Daniel Ellsberg; Lieutenant General Julian J. Ewell; Colonel David E. Farnham; Lieutenant General Edward M. Flanagan, Jr.; Lieutenant General Eugene P. Forrester; Lieutenant General Ralph Foster; Robert Froehlke; Major General Robert N. Ginsburgh, USAF; Major General George A. Godding; General Andrew J. Goodpaster; General Paul F. Gorman; Brigadier General Michael J. L. Greene; General Wallace M. Greene, Jr., USMC; General Alexander J. Haig, Jr.; General Ralph E. Haines, Jr.; David Halberstam; Dr. William M. Hammond; Colonel Thomas J. Hanifen; Major General Ben L. Harrison; Major General Michael D. Healy; Ambassador Richard Helms; Gerald Hickey; Ambassador Richard C. Holbrooke; Ambassador John H. Holdridge; Lieutenant General James F. Hollingsworth; Lieutenant General Harris W. Hollis; Major General Frank B. Horton III, USAF; Major General Ira A. Hunt, Jr.; Lieutenant General Oren E. Hurlbut; Colonel Thomas G. Irwin; George D. Jacobson; Brigadier General John H. Johns; General David Jones, USAF; Lieutenant General James G. Kalergis; Brigadier General Theodore S. Kanamine; Dr. William W. Kaufmann; Colonel John B. Keeley; General Donald Keith; Orr Kelly; General Walter T. Kerwin, Jr.; Lieutenant General Nguyen Khanh, ARVN; Admiral Isaac C. Kidd, Jr., USN; Brigadier General Douglas Kinnard; Major General Robert L. Kirwan; Dr. Henry A. Kissinger; Brigadier General Albion W. Knight, Jr.; General William A. Knowlton; Ambassador Robert W. Komer; Dr. Fritz G. A. Kraemer; Melvin R. Laird; Colonel James H. Leach; Colonel William E. LeGro; Ambassador William Leonhart; General William J. Livsey; Major General Bernard Loeffke; Colonel Hoang Ngoc Lung, ARVN; Major General George L. Mabry, Jr.; Colonel Donald S. Marshall; Brigadier General Theodore C. Mataxis; Dr. John F. Mazzuchi; Lieutenant General Dennis P. McAuliffe; George McArthur; Lieutenant General William J. McCaffrey; Frank McCullough; David E. McGiffert; Ambassador Clay McManaway; Robert S. McNamara; Lieutenant General John B. McPherson, USAF; General Jack N. Merritt; General Edward C. Meyer; Colonel Warren Milberg, USAF; General Frank T. Mildren; Colonel Paul Miles; Brigadier General Robert M. Montague, Jr.; Admiral Thomas H. Moorer, USN; Major General John E. Murray; Brigadier General John W. Nicholson; Thomas E. Noel; General Wallace H. Nutting; Major General Delk M. Oden; Lieutenant General William E. Odom; General Bruce Palmer, Jr.; Lieutenant General Dave R. Palmer; Colonel Rod Paschall; Brigadier General Hal C. Pattison; Major General George S. Patton III; Lieutenant General Willard Pearson; Mark Perry; Brigadier General Paul D. Phillips; John Pickering; Lieutenant

General George Pickett; Dr. Douglas Pike; Brigadier General James Piner, Jr.; General James H. Polk; Lieutenant General William E. Potts; Edward Proctor; Major General George Prugh; Lieutenant General Robert E. Pursley, USAF; Lieutenant General William W. Quinn; Major General Lloyd Ramsey; General Dennis J. Reimer; Stanley R. Resor; Colonel Robert B. Rheault; Elliot Richardson; Major General Walter B. Richardson; Lieutenant General Thomas M. Rienzi; Peter W. Rodman; General Bernard W. Rogers; William P. Rogers; General William B. Rosson; Walt Rostow; Robert L. Sansom; Dr. Herbert Y. Schandler; Benjamin F. Schemmer; Dr. James R. Schlesinger; Colonel Fred B. Schoomaker; Colonel Daniel F. Schungel, Sr.; Lieutenant General Brent Scowcroft, USAF; Lieutenant General George M. Seignious II; General Robert W. Sennewald; Theodore G. Shackley; Dr. Harry J. Shaw; Barry J. Shillito; General Robert M. Shoemaker; Lieutenant General Charles J. Simmons; Major General John K. Singlaub; Major General Albert H. Smith, Jr.; Lieutenant General DeWitt C. Smith, Jr.; Major General Homer D. Smith, Jr.; Major General James C. Smith; Major General Charles E. Spragins; General Donn A. Starry; Colonel William Steinberg; General Richard G. Stilwell; Major General Adrian St. John; Colonel Harry G. Summers, Jr.; Lieutenant General Orwin E. Talbott; Command Sergeant Major Charles Theriac; General Maxwell R. Thurman; B. Hugh Tovar; Lieutenant General Richard G. Trefry; Lieutenant General Ngo Quang Truong, ARVN; Lieutenant General Walter F. Ulmer, Jr.; Colonel Carl C. Ulsaker; Sergeant Major of the Army Leon L. Van Autreve; Cyrus R. Vance; Lieutenant General James B. Vaught; Lieutenant General Dale A. Vesser; General John W. Vessey, Jr.; Colonel Ha Mai Viet, ARVN; General John Vogt, USAF; General Volney F. Warner; Lieutenant General Richard L. West; General William C. Westmoreland; General Frederick C. Weyand; Dr. Gilmore S. Wheeler; Ambassador Charles S. Whitehouse; General John A. Wickham, Jr.; Major General Lawrence H. Williams; Major General Ellis W. Williamson; Charles E. Wilson; Lieutenant General Joseph G. Wilson, USAF; Colonel William F. Wollenberg; Sergeant Major of the Army William O. Wooldridge; General James K. Woolnough; R. James Woolsey; Lieutenant General William P. Yarborough; Stephen B. Young.

U.S. Army Military History Institute Oral History Interviews Consulted

Julia Harvey Abrams; Chaplain John D. Benson; Ambassador Samuel Berger; Major General (Chaplain) Charles E. Brown, Jr.; Ambassador Ellsworth Bunker; Lieutenant General Arthur S. Collins, Jr.; Colonel Robert M. Cook; Lieutenant General Charles A. Corcoran; General Michael S. Davison; General William E. DePuy; Lieutenant General William R. Desobry; Chief Warrant Officer Lyle Engelstad; Lieutenant General Julian J. Ewell; Lieutenant General George I. Forsythe; Lieutenant General Ralph Foster; General Andrew J. Goodpaster; General Harold K. Johnson; General Walter T. Kerwin, Jr.; Lieutenant General Harry W. O. Kinnard; General William A. Knowlton; General Frederick J. Kroesen; Colonel Jonathan F. Ladd; Admiral John McCain, USN; General Frank T. Mildren; Admiral Thomas H. Moorer, USN; Mr. Tom Noel; General Bruce Palmer, Jr.; Major General George S. Patton III; Colonel Robert B. Rheault; General Donn Starry; Lieutenant General James W. Sutherland; General John L. Throckmorton; Major General Elias C. Townsend; Lieutenant General Walter F. Ulmer, Jr.; General William C. Westmoreland (draft); Major General Roderick Wetherill; Lieutenant General John M. Wright, Jr.; General Melvin Zais.

Other Oral History Interviews Consulted

Major General Norman J. Anderson, USMC, Marine Corps Historical Center; Lieutenant General Robert J. Baer, U.S. Army Tank-Automotive Command; William P. Bundy, LBJ Library; Ambassador Ellsworth Bunker, Duke University Living History Project and LBJ Library; Lieutenant General John A. Chaisson, USMC, Marine Corps Historical Center; Ambassador William E. Colby, LBJ Library; General Robert E. Cushman, Jr., USMC, Marine Corps Historical Center; Lieutenant General Phillip B. Davidson, LBJ Library; General Raymond G. Davis, USMC, Marine Corps Historical Center; General Andrew J. Goodpaster, LBJ Library; Lieutenant General Daniel O. Graham, USAF, LBJ Library; W. Averell Harriman, Columbia University Oral History Collection; General Walter T. Kerwin, Jr., LBJ

Library; Lieutenant General Le Nguyen Khang, VNMC, Marine Corps Historical Center; Robert Komer, LBJ Library; Lieutenant General Victor H. Krulak, USMC, Marine Corps Historical Center; General John D. Lavelle, USAF, Air Force History Office; Lieutenant General John N. McLaughlin, USMC, Marine Corps Historical Center; Robert S. McNamara, Duke University Living History Program; Major General Otis Moore, USAF, Air Force History Office; Admiral Thomas H. Moorer, USN, LBJ Library; Lieutenant General Herman Nickerson, Jr., USMC, Marine Corps Historical Center; Stanley R. Resor, LBJ Library; Dean Rusk, Duke University Living History Program; Vice Admiral Robert S. Salzer, USN, U.S. Naval Institute; Dr. James R. Schlesinger, Duke University Living History Project; Major General Rathvon McC. Tompkins, USMC, Marine Corps Historical Center; General William C. Westmoreland, Marine Corps Historical Center; General Earle G. Wheeler, JFK Library and LBJ Library.

INDEX